OMAHA BEACH

A FLAWED VICTORY

Adrian R. Lewis is Associate Professor of History at the
University of North Texas. A retired major in the US Army,
he taught history at the US Military Academy and was Professor
of Military Science at the University of California, Berkeley.
He lives in Texas.

OMAHA BEACH
A FLAWED VICTORY

ADRIAN R. LEWIS

TEMPUS

To my wife
Colleen Michele Lewis
and our daughters
Alexandria Adrienne, Allison Michele, Aubrey Danielle,
Anastasia Kathryn and Angelica Noelle

First published 2001 by North Carolina University Press
This edition first published 2004

Tempus Publishing Limited
The Mill, Brimscombe Port,
Stroud, Gloucestershire, GL5 2QG
www.tempus-publishing.com

British Library Cataloguing in Publication Data.
A catalogue record for this book is available from the British Library.

ISBN 0 7524 2975 2

Typesetting and origination by Tempus Publishing Limited
Printed and bound in Great Britain

Contents

Illustrations

Acknowledgments

Historians bring to the task of research and writing their life's experiences. I have been an infantry soldier most of my life, although I have never served in combat. This book is the product of two careers, academic and military.

I have benefited from the knowledge, advice, encouragement, and friendship of my dissertation supervisors Michael Geyer and Walter Kaegi at the University of Chicago; John Shy at the University of Michigan; and Malcolm Muir at Austin Peay State University. To Professor Geyer I owe much. No-one has done more to influence my thinking and my career. Without his faith and confidence in my ability, his guidance and assistance, I could not have written this book.

Most of the research for this book was conducted at the Eisenhower Library, Abilene, Kansas; First Division Museum, Wheaton, Illinois; Marine Corps University Archives, Quantico, Virginia; National Archives, Archive II, College Park, Maryland; Naval

Historical Center, Washington, D.C.; U.S. Army Center of Military History, Washington, D.C.; and U.S. Army Military History Institute, Carlisle Barracks, Pennsylvania. I am grateful for the acumen, knowledge, and courteous assistance of the many archivists and librarians at these institutions.

Recognition is also due the U.S. Army Infantry School at Fort Benning, Georgia; Armor School at Fort Knox, Kentucky; 9th Infantry Division (now deactivated), Fort Lewis, Washington; and U.S. Military Academy, West Point, New York. These institutions sharpened my analytical abilities and my understanding of the art and science of war. At Forts Benning and Knox, I learned to assess terrain, battles, and campaigns—at the desk and in the mud. I learned how operations and battles ought to be planned and fought, and the American system of command and control. In the 9th Infantry Division, I had the privilege of serving under an expert in tactical and operational doctrine—General Richard E. Cavazos. General Cavazos critiqued every defense my company dug in, and there were many. At West Point, I had the opportunity to examine the terrain at Omaha Beach in three consecutive years when I took cadets to Europe to trace the path of the U.S. Army from Normandy into Germany. It was on Omaha Beach as I was trying to explain to the cadets and myself the rationale behind the doctrine employed that this book had its origins.

I would like to thank Paula Wald at the University of North Carolina Press. Her knowledge and professionalism made the publication process significantly easier.

Finally, I am indebted to my wife Colleen. Her patience, encouragement, and cheerful attitude made this work possible. She has read every word of it and made countless helpful recommendations. She has been my travel partner and has walked many battlefields with me. She sustains me.

In the preparation of this book, I have examined thousands of documents. I have endeavored to be fair to all concerned. When possible, I have let decision-makers speak for themselves. Nevertheless, if I have erred in judgment or fact, the fault is mine.

I have tried to provide the best explanation for what happened at Omaha Beach. To explain failure or near defeat, we must examine leadership at one or more levels. Leaders may fail in the selection of men, the training of soldiers, the development of technology and doctrine, the planning of operations, the execution of the plan, or the leading of soldiers in battle. In war, it is the soldier who pays the cost for leadership failures, and it is frequently the soldier who makes right on the battlefield failed plans, flawed doctrine, poorly designed equipment, and inadequate leadership. This was the case at Omaha Beach, as in other battles won by soldiers throughout the history of the United States.

Abbreviations

AEAF	Allied Expeditionary Air Force
AFAF	U.S. Navy Amphibious Force, Atlantic Fleet
BAR	Browning automatic rifle
CG	Commanding general
COSSAC	Chief of Staff to the Supreme Allied Commander
CT	Combat team
DD	Duplex-drive
DUKW	2½-ton, 6x6, amphibian truck
ESB	Engineer Special Brigade
ETOUSA	European Theater of Operations, U.S. Army
FM	U.S. Army Field Manual
Force B	Follow-up forces designated for Omaha Beach
Force O	Forces designated for Omaha Beach
Force U	Forces designated for Utah Beach
FTP	Fleet Training Publication

FUSA	First U.S. Army
G-1	Personnel Officer or Division, General Staff
G-2	Intelligence Officer or Division, General Staff
G-3	Operations Officer or Division, General Staff
G-4	Logistics Officer or Division, General Staff
ID	Infantry division
ISTDC	Inter-Services Training and Development Center
LCA	Landing craft, assault
LCF	Landing craft, flak
LCG (L)	Landing craft, gun (large)
LCI	Landing craft, infantry
LCM	Landing craft, mechanized
LCP(L)	Landing craft, personnel (large)
LCT	Landing craft, tank
LCT (A)	Landing craft, tank (armored)
LCT (R)	Landing craft, tank (rocket)
LCVP	Landing craft, vehicle, personnel
LST	Landing ship, tank
M-4	Sherman medium tank
NCO	Noncommissioned officer
RAF	Royal Air Force
RCT	Regimental combat team
RLT	Regimental landing team
SHAEF	Supreme Headquarters, Allied Expeditionary Force
TAC	Tactical air command
USSTAF	U.S. Strategic Air Force

Introduction

Leadership... is the capacity to frame plans which will succeed and the faculty of persuading others to carry them out in the face of death.

Lord Moran, *The Anatomy of Courage*

Walking along Omaha Beach on the coast of Normandy in France, one is struck by four distinct impressions that come in rapid, logical succession. The first impression is one of awe. The magnitude of the 1st Infantry Division's assault in World War II almost defies description. The terrain, the configuration of the ground, greatly increased the difficulty of the task. The length and width of the beach, the dominance of the bluff that overlooks the beach, the concave shape of the shoreline, which permitted the delivery of direct fire from three directions, the concrete remains of the German defense with its numerous fighting positions along the bluff, the cliffs that flank the coast from which artillery observers could deliver indirect fire to any location on the beach, all combine to create the perception of an impenetrable natural and man-made defense. And this initial impression is incomplete since the numerous arrays of obstacles and minefields are now gone.

One can stand on the bluff that overlooks Omaha Beach and visualize thousands of American soldiers and sailors exiting what appear to be tiny landing craft, trying to cross these open stretches of beach in daylight under enemy fire. A basic understanding of the capabilities of modern, rapid-fire weapons suggests the immensity of the task. Of the defense at Omaha Beach, American naval historian Samuel Eliot Morison wrote: 'Altogether, the Germans had provided the best imitation of hell for an invading force that American troops had encountered anywhere. Even the Japanese defense of Iwo Jima, Tarawa and Peleliu are not to be compared with these.'[1]

The second response is emotional. It is a feeling of admiration for the men who fought at Omaha Beach. This is hallowed ground. It would take a poet or a master storyteller, not a historian or a soldier, to describe the spirit of these men. Perhaps the comment of a Union colonel who watched Confederate general George Pickett's division advance on Cemetery Ridge during the third day of the Gettysburg campaign is appropriate. He said: 'It was the most beautiful thing I ever saw.'[2] These words were spoken not to glorify war but to recognize the spirit of the men who advanced. Above Omaha Beach is an American cemetery. There, one feels deep respect for the men who advanced and died at Omaha Beach.

The third thought that comes to mind is, why here? And why this way? A direct infantry assault against a deliberate defense years in the making, in daylight, following a paltry thirty-minute bombardment appears to be a very costly way to take Omaha Beach. The attack had neither the advantage of darkness nor overwhelming firepower. To explain why the American assault on Omaha Beach received such meager fire support, Morison wrote:

> [T]he Allies were invading a continent where the enemy had immense capabilities for reinforcement and counter-attack, not a small island cut

off by sea power from sources of supply. They had to have *tactical surprise*, which a long pre-landing bombing or bombardment would have lost... Even a complete pulverizing of the Atlantic Wall at Omaha would have availed us nothing, if the German command had been given 24 hours' notice to move up reserves for counter-attack. We had to accept the risk of heavy casualties on the beaches to prevent far heavier ones on the plateau and among the hedgerows.[3]

One might ask, if tactical surprise was so important, why didn't the landing take place at night, under the cover of darkness? This would have limited the effects of enemy fire and facilitated achieving tactical surprise. To explain why the landing took place during the early-morning hours of daylight, historian Gordon Harrison, in the official history of the U.S. Army in World War II, wrote: 'The assault was considered as a frontal attack which was unlikely even to have the advantage of *tactical surprise*... The task of smashing through enemy beach defenses was to be facilitated as far as possible by naval fire support and air bombardment.'[4]

In 1944, accurate engagement of targets from the air and sea required daylight. Harrison reinforced his argument by quoting Lieutenant General John T. Crocker, commander of the British I Corps: 'The first essential... was the development of overwhelming fire support from all sources, air, naval, and support craft... to cover the final stage of the approach and to enable us to close the beaches. This required daylight.'[5]

To this, one might respond, was it possible to generate overwhelming firepower in less than thirty minutes? Morison did not believe it was.[6] Didn't the U.S. Marines' experience at Tarawa in November 1943 prove that a three-hour bombing and bombardment was insufficient time to produce the quality of destruction necessary to quickly overcome a deliberate defense and limit casualties? Were the battles for the beaches at Normandy based on 'tactical surprise,' as Morison would have us believe, or on 'overwhelming firepower,' as Harrison would have us believe, or on some combination of the two doctrinal principles? And if some combination of the two was planned, on what experience was it based?

The predominant experience in the Mediterranean theater had been in night landings based on tactical surprise, whereas the vast majority of amphibious operations in the Pacific were based on daylight assaults and overwhelming firepower. The plan for the Normandy invasion did not conform to the British practice of amphibious operations used in North Africa, Sicily, and Italy, nor did it conform to the American practice of amphibious operations used at Tarawa, Kwajalein, Iwo Jima, and other Central Pacific islands. Was it possible to achieve both tactical surprise, which was predicated on no bombardment or a very brief bombardment, and overwhelming firepower, which was based on a sustained, methodical bombing and bombardment? Did Allied commanders Bernard Montgomery and Omar Bradley pursue mutually exclusive operational objectives? How did they plan to win the battles of the beaches?

The fourth thought that comes to mind is that British and American heroes, Dwight Eisenhower, Montgomery, and Bradley, knew their jobs, and if they believed it was necessary to conduct the assault this way, who are we to argue with them? But Robert E. Lee, the Confederacy's most brilliant general, planned and ordered Pickett's charge, one of the most ill-conceived assaults in the Civil War. The American storyteller and historian Shelby Foote stated:

> [Pickett's charge] was an incredible mistake, and there was scarcely a trained soldier who didn't know it was a mistake at the time... [E]very man who looked out over that field, whether it was a sergeant or a lieutenant general, saw that it was a desperate endeavor and I'm sure knew that it should not have been made.[7]

Generals do make mistakes, even very good generals. The plan for the assault at Omaha Beach failed, and American forces had to improvise a new plan under enemy fire. Bradley's own words attest to this fact:

> I was shaken to find that we had gone against Omaha with so thin a margin of safety. At the time of sailing we had thought ourselves cushioned against such reversals as these. Had a less experienced division

than the 1st Infantry stumbled into this crack resistance, it might easily have been thrown back into the Channel... [M]y choice of the 1st to spearhead the invasion probably saved us Omaha Beach and a catastrophe on the landing.[8]

Infantry conducting a frontal assault against a deliberate defense in daylight won the battle for Omaha Beach. The cost of this improvisation was high. Why did the plan fail? Russell Weigley provided the orthodox answer:

The American attack thus stalled throughout D-Day morning, to oblige General Bradley to ponder evacuation. It was painful pondering, in which he might not have had to engage had he himself and all the American planners not so blandly accepted the translation of head-on, power drive strategy into tactics of head-on infantry assault.[9]

The British historian Max Hastings observed:

V Corps's plan for Omaha eschewed tactical subtleties, the use of British specialized armour, and any attempt to seize the five vital beach exits by manoeuvre. Instead, General Gerow committed his men to hurling themselves frontally against the most strongly defended areas in the assault zone. This was an act of *hubris* compounded by the collapse amidst the rough weather.[10]

This argument is not new. The Australian World War II journalist and historian Chester Wilmot first advanced it in his 1952 book, *The Struggle for Europe*.[11] Thus, the current understanding of the battle at Omaha Beach has enjoyed considerable longevity. Wilmot, Weigley, and Hastings have placed the blame on the specific tactical plan for the battle at Omaha Beach, as opposed to the overall operational plan for the Normandy invasion. This has allowed them to place the responsibility on the tactical commanders and the American practice of war instead of on the strategic and operational commanders and the Allied invasion plan. They have argued that it was a uniquely American 'predilection for direct assault' that produced the flawed tactical plan. The terrible casualties suffered at Omaha Beach were thus the results of bad decisions made by tactical commanders. The problem with this argument is that all of the tactical commanders opposed the plan that was put into practice. If the American tactical commanders developed a bad plan, it was because they were directed to produce battle plans that conformed to the operational plan.

The record shows that General Leonard T. Gerow, the commander of the V Corps; General Clarence R. Huebner, the commander of the 1st Infantry Division (ID); General Norman D. Cota, the assistant commander of the 29th ID, which landed with the 1st ID on D-Day; and Admiral John Lesslie Hall, the commander of Amphibious Force O, the naval force that put the 1st ID ashore on D-Day, all disagreed with the plan for the assault and fought to change it. They believed that a landing conducted under the cover of darkness had a better chance of succeeding and would result in fewer casualties.[12] Gerow and Hall argued strenuously to change the time of the landing. The decision, however, went against them.

The operational plan for the Normandy invasion, which was based on a new, hybrid doctrine, was deeply flawed in numerous ways. If the British and Canadian forces at Sword, Juno, and Gold Beaches and the American forces at Utah Beach had fought German forces of the quality and quantity of those at Omaha Beach on similar terrain, they too would have suffered heavy casualties and faced the prospect of defeat.

This work traces the evolution of amphibious warfare doctrine from the interwar period to 6 June 1944 and the development of invasion plans for the continent of Europe from the strategic concept to the tactical battle plans of the regimental combat teams (RCTs) that made the landing. The book begins with a brief narrative of the battle at Omaha Beach. This narrative is not intended to be comprehensive since the battle is discussed in detail in many other works.

This study relies on the analytical framework used by most professional military establishments. Since the wars of Napoleon, the leaders of the armed forces of Western nations have recognized three levels of war: tactical, operational, and strategic.

Tactics is the art and science of applying combat arms—infantry, armor, artillery, and other arms—to destroy enemy forces. Battles take place on a specific piece of terrain. The configuration of the ground can greatly influence the conduct of battle and can vary considerably from one region to another. The variance in terrain requires the creative application of tactical doctrine. Battles are fought ideally by teams. The division is the largest unit in an army trained to fight as a team. Divisions, brigades, regiments, and battalions fight battles. Battles are made up of series of engagements, sometimes referred to as firefights, fought by small units—squads, platoons, and companies. The U.S. Army at Normandy fought two separate battles. The 1st ID fought the battle for Omaha Beach, and the 4th ID fought the battle for Utah Beach. Corps-sized units, organizations of two to five divisions, were sometimes employed as tactical formations in World War II. The V Corps at Omaha Beach deployed three divisions on the same piece of terrain in the same battle to overcome enemy resistance. The tactical commander is responsible for the fighting forces under his command and the forces supporting him. He is responsible for coordinating and synchronizing the employment of air and naval gunfire support in his maneuver plan. Tactical commanders fight battles designed to achieve operational objectives.

At the operational level of war, the campaign takes place. A campaign is a series of battles carried out over a large geographical area, such as Normandy. The five amphibious battles and three airborne battles that took place in Normandy were part of one campaign. The operational commander directs and manages the flow of the battle across a geographical area to achieve strategic objectives. At Normandy, Montgomery was the senior operational commander, the army group commander, and Bradley was the senior American operational commander, the army commander, subordinate to Montgomery. Bradley was responsible to Montgomery for deploying and managing all forces in the American sector. The senior operational commander develops the vision for the conduct of the operation, then tells his subordinate operational and senior tactical commanders how he plans to destroy the enemy. His subordinates develop operational plans for their tactical units—corps and divisions—designed to carry out the vision of the senior operational commander. Operational commanders approve tactical plans and monitor the training and preparation of tactical formations. They oversee the battle and provide the combat support and logistical resources the tactical commander needs to achieve the objectives established by the senior operational commander. They employ operational resources such as strategic bombers and naval gunfire to assist the tactical commander in fighting the battle. The operational commander is not on the ground employing infantry and artillery; he is not personally maneuvering forces on the battlefield—that is the job of the tactical commander. The operational commander directs and manages corps and divisions and, in World War II, armies.

At the strategic level, the commander is concerned with fighting and winning the war. The strategic commander is ideally responsible for all forces—air, sea, and ground—in the entire theater, for example, Western Europe. He is focused on achieving the nation's or coalition's political and military objectives in the most efficient, least costly manner possible. Eisenhower, the supreme Allied commander, was the strategic commander in the Western European theater. The strategic commander develops a vision for winning the war with the forces available to him and is responsible to the political leaders of the nation he serves and to that nation's chief military leader, in the case of the United States, General George C. Marshall.[13] The strategic commander co-ordinates the campaigns that are part of his larger strategic vision, which he imparts to his subordinate senior operational commanders. He then allocates resources to them to accomplish his strategic objectives. Strategic objectives are the destruction of the enemy's armed forces, the destruction of the will of the people, and/or the destruction of the enemy's government. The American practice of war in World War II was to focus on the destruction of the enemy's armed forces; however, the U.S. Eighth Air Force took part in the British strategic bombing campaign designed to destroy the will of the German people by bombing cities.

This system does not always work the way it was designed. Nationalism, disagreements over strategic objectives, personalities and egos, different technologies and doctrines, varying degrees of professional competence, misunderstandings, fear and anger, competition between nations and services, arrogance and contempt, and other factors can erode the effectiveness of this organizational structure, particularly in coalition warfare.

Typically, in modern warfare, the loss of a battle at the tactical level does not jeopardize the entire war effort or greatly influence the strategic level. Since wars are made up of numerous campaigns and campaigns are made up of numerous battles, usually no one battle is decisive in modern warfare. There are, however, exceptions. Some battles are of considerable strategic importance. The five battles fought on the coast of Normandy on 6 June 1944 were of enormous strategic importance to the Anglo–American war effort and ultimately the achievement of established political objectives.

The Anglo–American commanders conducted multiple landings over a broad front, the doctrinal approach employed in North Africa, Sicily, and Italy. This approach permitted the Allies to suffer defeat in one tactical battle and still achieve the campaign and strategic objective of getting ashore. However, if several tactical battles had failed, the entire campaign might have collapsed and the strategy for the conduct of the war might have also failed. Defeat at Omaha Beach would have considerably diminished the margin for success. Each battle at Normandy was of considerable importance to the strategic plans of the United States and Britain.

1

The Battle for Omaha Beach

If you are doing what is right, never mind whether you are freezing
with cold or beside a good fire; heavy-eyed, or fresh from a sound sleep;
reviled or applauded; in the act of dying, or about some other piece of
business. (For even dying is part of the business of life; and there too no
more is required of us than 'to see the moment's work well done.')

Marcus Aurelius

On 5 June 1944 at 1400 hours, General Norman Cota, who was in
charge of a provisional brigade headquarters that was to serve as the
advanced headquarters for the 29th ID, addressed his men:

This is different from any of the other exercises that you've had so far.
The little discrepancies that we tried to correct on Slapton Sands [an
amphibious training center] are going to be magnified and are going

to give way to incidents that you might at first view as chaotic. The air and naval bombardment and the artillery support are reassuring. But you're going to find confusion. The landing craft aren't going in on schedule and people are going to be landed in the wrong place. Some won't be landed at all. The enemy will try, and will have some success, in preventing our gaining 'lodgement.' But we must improvise, carry on, not lose our heads.[1]

General Cota's men were among the few soldiers who received a fair assessment of the coming battle. Cota forecast that naval gunfire would miss its targets, the aerial bombardment would be ineffective, and the beaches would be 'fouled-up.' However, even Cota's D-Day prediction fell far short of reality. One participant later recalled thinking: 'This time we have failed! Nothing has moved from the beach and soon, over the bluff, will come the Germans. They'll come swarming down on us.'[2] According to historian Gordon Harrison:

> To the German officer in command of the fortifications at Pointe et Raz de la Percee it looked in these first hours as though the invasion had been stopped on the beaches. He noted that the Americans were lying on the shore seeking cover behind obstacles, that ten tanks and a 'great many other vehicles' were burning. The fire of his own positions and the artillery, he thought, had been excellent, causing heavy losses. He could see the wounded and dead lying on the sand.[3]

The initial impression of many American and German soldiers was that the assault at Omaha Beach had failed. And, in fact, the plan for the conduct of the battle had failed.

Between two and three o'clock on the morning of 6 June 1944, the Allied invasion fleets arrived off the coast of Normandy. The sixteen transport ships carrying the assault forces took up station in the transport area and immediately commenced landing operations. Admiral John Lesslie Hall commanded the amphibious assault from his headquarters ship, the USS *Ancon*. Aboard with him were Generals

Leonard T. Gerow, commander of the V Corps, and Clarence R. Huebner, commander of the 1st ID, and their staffs. The soldiers of the 1st and 29th IDs were aboard the HMS *Empire Anvil*, HMS *Empire Javelin*, USS *Charles Carroll*, USS *Henrico*, USS *Samuel Chase*, and USS *Thomas Jefferson*. The transport area at Omaha Beach was ten to eleven miles offshore, out of range of enemy artillery. The sea was rough. The 18-knot winds and 3-knot tides produced waves three to four feet high, some reportedly even as high as six feet. The waves made boarding the small landing craft, via the web-like scramble net, a difficult and dangerous task. Soldiers had to time their jump into the smaller craft with the rise and fall of the craft. A mistake in timing could result in serious injury. One soldier misjudged his jump, fell twelve feet, and was knocked unconscious; others received less severe injuries. Heavy, awkward equipment and weapons were loaded over the side of the ships. In the craft, soldiers checked their gear and took up their positions. Some LCVPs (landing craft, vehicle, personnel) hung from the side of the transport ships and were loaded before they were lowered into the water. Once loaded, the LCVPs moved to a designated assembly area and circled until all of the boats in a division were present. In order to land one RCT, 81 LCVPs, 64 DUKWs (2½-ton amphibian trucks), and numerous other landing craft were required.

In an effort to maximize the utilization of space on the landing craft and thereby limit the number of craft required for an assault company, a new organization based on the capacity of the LCVP was put into effect. This organization violated the principle of unit integrity. Major General (retired) Albert H. Smith, who was the executive officer for the 1st Battalion, 16th Infantry, on 6 June 1944 described the new organization:

> To defeat German concrete fortifications it was decided that each assault rifle company would be organized in 5 assault sections, instead of three rifle platoons and one weapons platoon. Each section—totaling 1 officer, and 29 men—would include rifle teams, a wire cutting team, bazooka team, flame thrower team, BAR [Browning automatic rifle] team, 60-mm mortar team and demolition team.[4]

Landing craft were loaded in a specified order, with small-unit leaders at the front of the boat in order to exit first to lead the way. The assault teams were arranged in the following order:

1. Five-man rifle teams carrying M-1s and ninety-six rounds of ammunition each
2. Four-man bangalore and wire-cutting teams carrying M-1s
3. Two-man automatic rifle teams, one man carrying a BAR and the other a carbine rifle; two teams per boat
4. Two-man bazooka teams carrying one bazooka each; two teams per boat
5. Four-man mortar teams carrying one 60 mm mortar and fifteen to twenty mortar rounds
6. Two-man flamethrower teams carrying one flamethrower each
7. Five-man demolition teams carrying satchels of TNT and bangalore torpedoes

Some boats also had medics on board. They exited before the platoon sergeant or a senior noncommissioned officer (NCO), who was the last man to leave to insure that everyone else had disembarked. General Huebner and his subordinate commanders concluded that the new boat organization was unsatisfactory. They believed that unit integrity enhanced combat effectiveness and was more important than the efficient use of boat space: 'Craft must be tactically loaded despite the fact that some space is not used. The assault team based upon craft capacity is impractical. All planning should be built around normal infantry units, squad, platoon, company, battalion and combat team.'[5]

Soldiers wore assault jackets with built-in packs. Each man carried his weapon, a life preserver, a gas mask, five grenades, a half-pound block of TNT, six rations, canteens, an entrenching tool, a first-aid kit, a knife, and whatever special equipment his job required. Soldiers' clothing was treated with a chemical to protect troops against gas attacks. Soldiers also carried comfort items such as cartons of cigarettes and extra socks and various other non-essential items. When fully loaded, each soldier carried between sixty and ninety pounds, depending on the type of weapon and ammunition. Soldiers carried too much. This heavy load diminished soldiers' ability to cross the beach under fire.[6]

Soldiers were soaked to the skin even before their landing craft started for the shore. The dampness and the chill in the air caused men to grow numb in their fingers and hands. The ship-to-shore movement took two to three hours, depending on where a ship was anchored. In transit, a few craft were swamped and sank. Soldiers in these boats discarded their weapons and equipment and swam as best they could until they were picked up by other craft. The rough sea, cramped quarters, and long ride caused seasickness. Many regretted having eaten the heavy breakfast of bacon and eggs aboard the transport ships. Soldiers were given pills for seasickness, but many did not take them because they caused drowsiness. Seasickness sapped the energy of many soldiers, draining the combat power of the assault force.

As the sun rose, starting at 0558, soldiers could see the outline of large ships in the distance, and the feeling of being alone in a small craft on a big ocean was somewhat diminished. When the battleships and cruisers started firing on the German defenses, the thought that everything was going to be all right entered the minds of some soldiers, particularly those who had never conducted an amphibious assault. As the boats continued toward the shore, some passed the crews of DD tanks swimming for their lives. The high waves proved to be too much for the flimsy canvas shrouds that made it possible for the tanks to float. Many of the tanks took on water and sank. Of the thirty-two DD tanks of the 741st Tank Battalion that were to support the 16th RCT, only five reached the shore; the rest sank to the bottom of the Channel.

While still *en route*, some soldiers caught a glimpse of American heavy and medium daylight bombers. The sky was overcast and the cloud ceiling was suspended between 2,000 and 3,000 feet high, but breaks in the coverage occasionally revealed American air power. The bombers flying above the clouds at an altitude of 11,000 feet used radar to determine their bomb release-time, and because of the proximity to friendly troops, they added an extra margin of safety to their calculations.

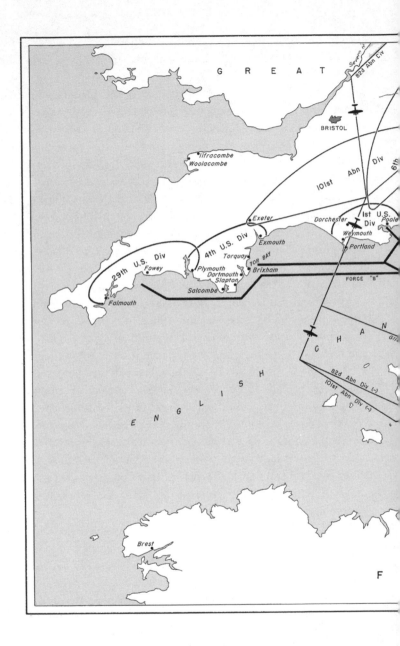

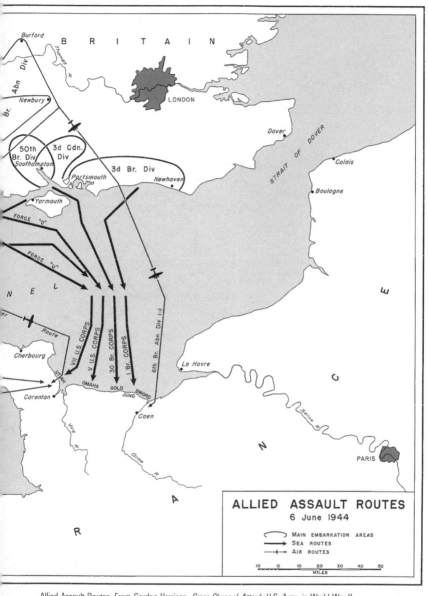

Allied Assault Routes. From Gordon Harrison, *Cross-Channel Attack*, U.S. Army in World War II (Washington, D.C.: Government Printing Office, 1951).

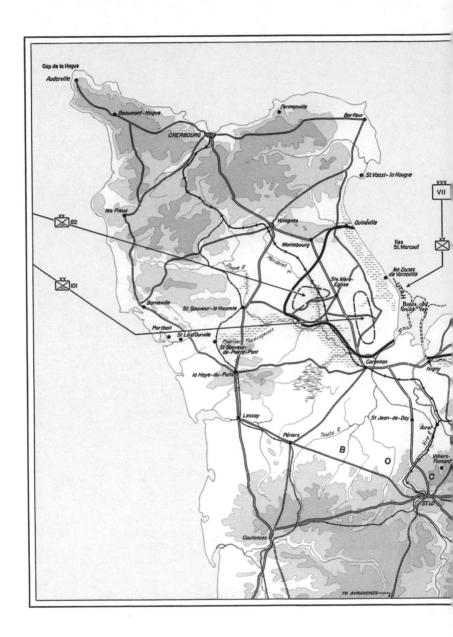

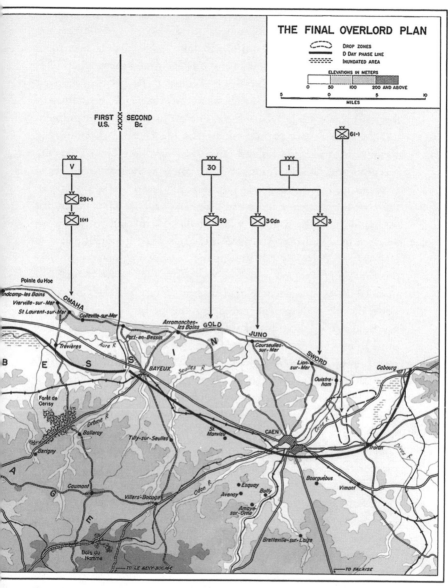

Final Overlord Plan. From Gordon Harrison, *Cross-Channel Attack,* U.S. Army in World War II (Washington, D.C.: Government Printing Office, 1951).

Ten to fifteen minutes before landing, soldiers watched a rocket attack. Thousands of rockets arched into the sky toward the beaches. Because of the high seas and the inability to accurately determine distance and adjust fire, most of the rockets missed their targets. This show was nevertheless impressive and boosted the spirits of the wet, seasick soldiers. But as the beach came into view, soldiers started to realize that something was wrong. The air and naval bombardment had failed to destroy or even neutralize the German defenses. The various arrays of obstacles and wire were clearly visible. The enemy was not stunned or disorganized; fortifications were not broken. There were no ready-made fighting positions produced by bombs, and in the 16th RCT's sector, there was little tank support. The concept for the conduct of the battle – which called for air and sea power to produce the combat power needed to overcome the initial defenses, tanks to provide overwatch and suppressing fire, and infantry to cover the breaching operations of the engineers—fell apart in the first instance. It was immediately evident that the plans of the generals to win the battle with strategic and operational resources had failed. The psychological implications of this cannot be fully comprehended by those of us who were not there. Experienced soldiers probably cursed the planners and leaders of the invasion. Green soldiers were probably confused and uncertain as to what was going on. All were shocked to some degree by the discrepancy between the vision articulated to them and the event transpiring before them.[7] Nothing was as they were told it would be.

Five to six hundred yards from the shore, the assault force began receiving small arms, mortar, antitank gun, artillery, and machine-gun fire. Some landing craft received direct hits and sank. Those men still alive went into the sea and swam as best they could. German machine gunners found their range, zeroed in on the ramps of the landing craft, and fired patterns that killed or wounded the first four to five men down the ramps. Converging fire from multiple automatic weapons produced heavy casualties. Some soldiers jumped overboard to avoid this murderous fire and in the process lost much of their equipment. Small-unit leaders suffered inordinately high casualties because under

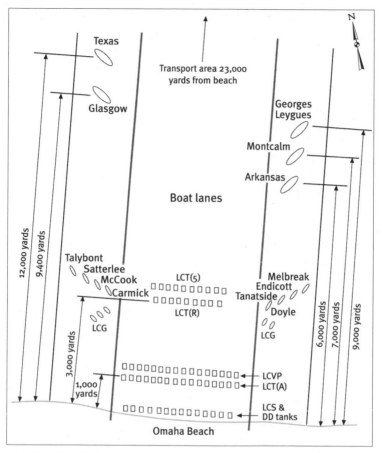

Invasion Plan, Omaha Beach.

the new boat section organization, they were the first off. According to one account from the 116th Infantry:

About seventy-five yards from the beach the ramp was dropped, and the enemy automatic fire then beat a tattoo all over the boat front. Capt. Ettore Zappacosta, the Company Commander, jumped from

the boat and got ten yards through the water. Pfc. Robert Sales saw
him hit in the leg and shoulder. He yelled, 'I'm hit.' T/5 Kenser, a
first-aid man, yelled: 'Try to make it in!' Zappacosta went down and
they did not see him come up again. Then Kenser jumped toward
him and was shot dead. Lt. Tom Dallas, of C [Company], who had
come in to make a reconnaissance also jumped out. He got to the
edge of the sand and fell dead. Sales was fourth in line and it had
come his turn. He started out with the SCR-300 [radio], tripped at
the edge of the ramp and fell, sprawling into the water. It probably
saved his life. Man by man, all of those leaving the ramp behind him
were either killed or wounded.[8]

The tides and winds caused boats to land east of their designated
beaches, so most of the teams encountered terrain they could not
identify. Some boats landed as far as a thousand yards from their
assigned locations. The hours that had been spent making and studying terrain maps were, for the most part, wasted, and the soldiers were
forced to come up with new solutions. The defense to their front was
not the one they had planned to fight.

The fire from the shore intimidated some coxswains. They refused
to go all the way to the beach and dropped their ramps too early. In
some instances, soldiers had to disembark into water over their heads.
Other boats hit runnels and sandbars, and soldiers had to jump into
water too deep for them to wade ashore. These soldiers found themselves struggling to stay above the water. They dropped their weapons
and equipment. Some soldiers who were weak swimmers, unable to
disentangle themselves from their gear, or carrying heavy equipment
such as flamethrowers, drowned. Many of the soldiers who made it to
the shore arrived without weapons and too exhausted to advance.
Others, in the process of dragging themselves, their equipment, and in
some cases their wounded buddies ashore, clogged their weapons with
wet sand, which prevented them from firing. Many remained at the
water's edge among the dead bodies of their friends, frightened,
disoriented, disorganized, seasick, and numb from the cold. Some
were wounded.

LANDING DIAGRAM, OMAHA BEACH
(SECTOR OF 116th RCT)

	EASY GREEN	DOG RED	DOG WHITE	DOG GREEN
H-5			◊◊◊◊ ◊◊◊◊ ◊◊◊◊ ◊◊◊◊ Co C (DD) 743 Tk Bn	◊◊◊◊ ◊◊◊◊ ◊◊◊◊ ◊◊◊◊ Co B (DD) 743 Tk Bn
H HOUR	Co A 743 Tk Bn	Co A 743 Tk Bn		
H+01	Co E 116 Inf	Co F 116 Inf	Co G 116 Inf	Co A 116 Inf
H+03	146 Engr CT	146 Engr CT — Demolitions Control Boat	146 Engr CT	146 Engr CT — Co C 2d Ranger Bn
H+30	AAAW Btry — CoH +HQCoE CoH 116 Inf — AAAW Btry	HQ 2d Bn — CoH CoF 2d Bn 116 Inf — AAAW Btry / 112 Engr	AAAW Btry — CoH HQCoG CoH 116 Inf — AAAW Btry	Co B HQCoA Co B 116 Inf — AAAW Btry
H+40	112 Engr Bn	Co D 81 Cml Wpns Bn — 149 Engr Beach Bn	149 Engr Beach Bn — 121 Engr Bn	HQ 1st Bn 116 — 149 Beach Bn 121 Engr — Co D 116 Inf
H+50	Co L 116 Inf	Co I 116 Inf	Co K 116 Inf	121 Engr Bn — Co C 116 Inf
H+57		HQ Co 3d Bn — Co M 116 Inf		Co B 81 Cml Wpns Bn
H+60	(LCT)	112 Engr Bn	HQ & HQ Co 116 Inf	121 Engr Bn — Co A & B 2d Ranger Bn
H+65				5th Ranger Bn
H+70	149 Engr Beach Bn	112 Engr Bn	Alt HQ & HQ Co 116 Inf	121 Engr Bn — 5th Ranger Bn
H+90			58 FA Bn Armd	
H+100			5th Engr Sp Brig	
H+110	111 FA Bn (3 Btry's in DUKWS)	AT Plat 2d Bn AT Plat 3d Bn — 29 Sig Bn		AT Plat 1st Bn — Co C 116 Inf
H+120	467 AAAW Bn — AT Co 116 Inf — 467 AAAW Bn	AT Co 116 Inf — 467 AAAW Bn 149 Engr Beach Bn	467 AAAW Bn	467 AAAW Bn
H+150		DD Tanks	HQ Co 116 Inf 104 Med Bn	
H+180 to H+215		461 Amphibious Truck Co	Navy Salvage	
H+225	461 Amph Trk Co			

Legend: LCI · LCM · LCA · DD Tank · LCT · LCVP · DUKW

Note: Plan as of 11 May

Landing Diagram, Omaha Beach. From U.S. Army, Headquarters 116th Combat Team, Force 'O,' Field Order, 11 May 1944, RG 407, Box 24373, Files 630–33, NA II.

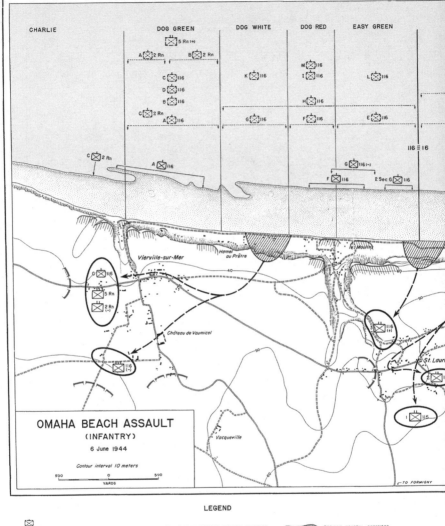

OMAHA BEACH ASSAULT
(INFANTRY)
6 June 1944

Contour interval 10 meters

500   0   500
YARDS

LEGEND

	PLANNED LANDING SECTORS		AXIS OF ADVANCE, ASSAULT REGIMENTS		GERMAN COASTAL DEFENSES
	ACTUAL LANDINGS, FIRST WAVE		AXIS OF ADVANCE, FOLLOW-UP REGIMENTS		GERMAN RESISTANCE, END OF D DAY
	MAIN INITIAL PENETRATIONS		POSITIONS, END OF D DAY		CLIFFS · · · · · · ROCKY CLIFFS
					SLOPES · · · · · · ROCKS

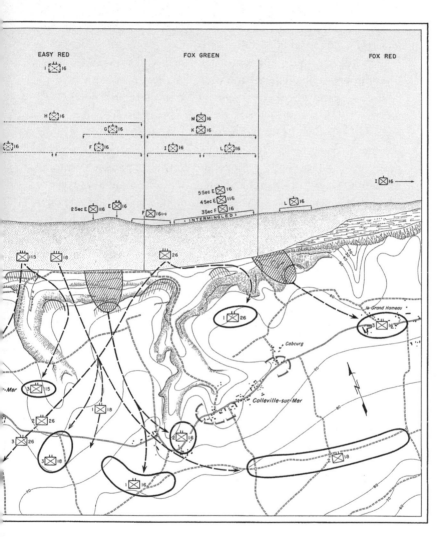

Omaha Beach Assault. From Gordon Harrison, *Cross-Channel Attack*, U.S. Army in World War II (Washington, D.C.: Government Printing Office, 1951).

Most engineers landed behind the infantry. They were transported in larger LCMs (landing craft, mechanized), some of which were immediately targeted and destroyed. Loaded with explosives to clear lanes through the minefields and obstacles, these boats were particularly dangerous. When they were hit by mortars or artillery, even indirectly, they set off a series of explosions that destroyed entire boats and killed whole teams and others nearby. Sixty per cent of the engineers' equipment was destroyed, lost, or damaged on the morning of D-Day.[9] The engineers also had navigation problems, and many of them ended up in the wrong place. Still, some went right to work clearing lanes. Enemy fire, the rising tide, and infantry soldiers impeded their efforts. The tide was already up to the seaward band of obstacles when the last engineer teams, arriving ten minutes late, landed. The infantry and tanks that were supposed to provide overwatch fire were in many cases already out of action. And soldiers who took cover behind obstacles prevented the engineers from clearing several lanes.

The shingle strip on Omaha Beach became the first line of defense. The problem was getting to it. Gordon Gaskill, a war correspondent who landed at Omaha Beach in the first hours of the assault, reported:

> The beach was dotted by crawling bodies – the rest of our 100 men each running his own grim race with death. Sometimes they would stand up and run, falling instantly when a shell came near them. Sometimes they did not rise again. The beach was strewn with abandoned equipment. Almost instantly men had thrown away packs, which averaged little less than 100 pounds each. It was sheer idiocy to think of running such a gantlet with such an enormous burden. The ridge [shingle strip] seemed miles away, a hopeless beautiful paradise I could never possibly reach.[10]

Soldiers who made it to the strip huddled there. They tried to collect themselves and recover from the seasickness and exertion of getting ashore. They tended to the wounded, searched for their units and leaders, attempted to restore some organization to the assault force, cleaned their weapons, and tried to stay alive. Others were in shock and simply stared into space, temporarily out of action.

But decisions had to be made. Should they move down the beach to their designated landing sites or advance from where they were? Should they move forward or go back and try to help the wounded? Should they wait for artillery and tank support or go it alone? Should they stay where they were and wait for someone in authority to come up with a new plan or make their own plan and move out on their own? It took some soldiers time to figure out what to do. The chances of making it to the base of the bluff through minefields, wire, and small arms, artillery, and machine-gun fire seemed almost nil. It was thus easier and may have seemed safer to some soldiers to stay where they were. One account from the operations officer of the 16th Infantry stated:

> Landing craft disgorged more troops onto 7 yard beachhead. The third wave, fourth wave and fifth wave found the first wave assault infantry trapped on the beach. The 7 yard beachhead, jammed with personnel, remained under constant enemy artillery, mortar, AT, MG, and sniper fire. Casualties mounted with each succeeding wave.[11]

The blood and carnage, the burning tanks and landing craft, the smoke and flames, the concussion from exploding shells, the screams of the wounded, the size of the bluff, the cold and exhaustion, and the disparity between what soldiers expected and what was actually taking place combined to drain some soldiers of their initiative, particularly those who were inexperienced. Sergeant Thomas B. Turner recalled:

> We were all surprised to find that we had suddenly gone weak, and we were surprised to discover how much fire men can move through without getting hit. Under fire we learned what we had never been told—that fear and fatigue are about the same in their effect on an advance.[12]

The battle, however, would not stop to give these men time to recover their energy and wits. The 16th Infantry reported:

> Three enemy strongpoints… which were to have been bombed, shelled, and wiped out by the Air Force, Navy and rocket guns, were in action. There were no DD tanks to cover the advance of the assault companies…
>
> Intense fire concentrated on the group; several men struck underwater mines and were blown out of the sea; others continued to cross the obstacle-covered exposed beach to slowly work up the shale at the high water mark to obtain momentary cover. Beach obstacles were numerous…
>
> A hasty firing line was built up along the pile of shale. Company E discovered most of their weapons were jammed with sand. Personnel stripped, cleaned weapons and enemy guns were brought under small arms fire. Despite the fact that enemy MGs and snipers cut down anyone attempting to return to the water to drag wounded up to the lee of the shale, many men pulled casualties out of the water and were wounded. A few succeeded in face of point-blank enemy fire…
>
> With the majority of weapons still jammed, all radio communication gone, an attempt was made to reorganize scattered remnants of Company E for an attack.[13]

Reorganization took place amid the chaos.

Destroyers moved in as close to the beach as possible to provide the supporting fire usually supplied by tanks and artillery. Admiral Hall's naval gunfire support ships had been given the following instructions: 'Commencing at H minus 40 minutes or as soon thereafter as visibility conditions permit, deliver counter-battery, destructive and neutralizing fires on beach defenses as laid down in… schedule of fires. After H-Hour deliver fires called for by assigned Shore Fire Control Parties.'

Shore fire control parties suffered the same losses as the infantry and engineers in the initial assault and were unable to perform their missions during the early hours of D-Day. Hall ordered his destroyers to:

proceed down boat lanes and into inshore sector of fire support area maneuvering so as to maintain as heavy a volume of fire on beach targets as possible and adjusting speed so as to approach close to assault beaches as first waves beach. As far as possible destroyers in fire support areas will remain underway so as to avoid mutual interference with lines of fire. All ships not specifically directed to anchor will close the range as much as possible when delivering neutralizing and destructive fire.[14]

Naval gunfire from destroyers proved to be the only reliable part of the Joint Fire Plan since the Army Air Force's strategic bombers missed the target area and the tactical air force was too poorly trained in close air support to assist. Destroyers were an integral part of the battle for the beach. According to one eyewitness account:

Two destroyers moved in incredibly close, so close we could almost yell to their crews, so close Germans were hitting them with rifle bullets. They fired broadsides directly at us, it seemed, and while their shells were just above our heads, plus the thunderclaps of their 5-inch guns, it was almost as terrifying as the German artillery. Their gunfire was amazingly accurate.[15]

Spotters on the destroyer identified targets. Smoke and fire impeded their efforts, but they knocked out 88mm gun positions, machine gun positions, and pillboxes. Some naval shore fire control parties established radio contact with destroyers and effectively directed fire against enemy strongpoints. The cumulative effect of naval gunfire eventually gave the infantry the break they needed. This was one of the few times in the annals of naval warfare in which ships took direct action in firefights. Had a heavy naval bombardment preceded the landing – even one as short as three hours, the length of the bombardment at Tarawa – Americans would have suffered fewer casualties.

At 0700, the second group of assault troops and engineers approached the shore. These soldiers expected to land on cleared beaches and proceed inland to their objectives. The tide had risen around eight feet, almost completely submerging the seaward band of obstacles and impeding clearing operations. Incoming waves had diffi-culty landing because most of the obstacles were still in place. Only six of the planned sixteen lanes were ready, and of these, only one was completely marked. In the area of the 116th RCTs, only two of the eight lanes were cleared. In the 16th RCT sector, four of the eight lanes were cleared, all on Beach Easy: Red. The volume of enemy fire had not diminished. Because the lanes were not cleared, incoming boats could not land at their designated sites. They moved up and down the shoreline looking for openings. When they could find none, some coxswains simply turned their craft toward the shore and eased their way between the visible obstacles, some of which were mounted with mines. One soldier wrote: 'Something has gone wrong with the plan...; for the plan had provided that by this time – not long after H-hour – the broad front of obstacles covering the beach would be breached in many places. There were the obstacle belts – but where were the breaches?'[16]

The fragmentary reports from the assault forces provided Admiral Hall and General Gerow with the following picture: '[C]raft were being swamped in the heavy seas; …enemy batteries were causing difficulty; obstacles were still troublesome; and covered with enemy small arms and automatic weapons fire.' There was, however, little Gerow and Hall could do. Hall monitored the efforts of his destroyers and pushed them forward. And Gerow and Hall made the decision to land the reserve RCT, the 115th RCT, as soon as possible. As more leaders and units came ashore, reorganization took place:

General Cota was landed in an LCVP at approximately H+57 minutes on Dog White Beach, with the... 116th Infantry... The boat was under heavy machine-gun fire, mortar and light cannon fire. Three persons... were instantly killed as they endeavored to reach the beach when the ramp of the LCVP was lowered. Although the leading elements of the assault had been on the beach for approxi-mately an hour, none had progressed farther than the seawall... Realizing that immediate steps had to be taken, General Cota, expos-

ing himself to enemy fire, went over the seawall giving encouragement, directions and orders to those about him, personally supervised
the placing of a BAR and brought fire to bear on enemy positions.[17]

By 0830, Colonel George Taylor, commander of the 16th Infantry;
Colonel Charles D. W. Canham, commander of the 116th Infantry;
General Willard G. Wyman, the assistant division commander; and the
battalion commanders were ashore directing the reorganization. No
one had advanced off of Omaha Beach.

Soldiers from different companies and even different divisions
organized into new ad hoc units. Buddy systems were worked out.
Brave men crossed the minefields. Many died in the attempt, their
bodies marking the way through which others could pass. Soldiers
crawled forward under enemy fire to blow or cut holes in the wire.
Paths through the minefields and wire were pushed forward incre-
mentally at great risk and high cost. Through these extraordinary
efforts, soldiers reached the base of the bluff. These small but important successes did not take place at the heavily defended beach exits
but between them. Soldiers started working their way up the bluff.

At 0850, the 18th Infantry began landing on Beach Easy: Red. It
was given the mission of the 2nd Battalion, 16th Infantry, which had
landed on Easy: Red in the initial assault and was supposed to seize the
high ground 2,000 yards behind the beach. Lieutenant Colonel
Derrill M. Daniel, commander of the 2nd Battalion, 26th Infantry,
described the landing:

As they neared shore, troops of the 18th had no impression that any
progress had been made from the beach: 'The beach shingle was full
of tractors, tanks, vehicles, bulldozers, and troops – the high ground
was still held by Germans who had all the troops on the beach pinned
down – the beach was still under fire from enemy small arms, mortars,
and artillery.' The first units of the 18th came in where the original
large gap had been left by the assault waves, and they found an enemy
pillbox still in action on the right of the E-1 draw. They immediately
attacked it but were stalled until naval fire was laid on. A destroyer

only 1,000 yards off shore was brought on the target in four rounds and the pillbox quickly surrendered. This cleared the last enemy defenses in front of the E-1 draw, and it was quickly opened for movements off the beach.[18]

Between 0900 and 1000, elements of the 16th Infantry reached the top of the bluff and then moved laterally to attack enemy fortifications. The fighting was at close quarters. Hand grenades and small arms fire were the primary means of destruction. One account from the 16th Infantry stated:

> Working their way to the top of the high ground overlooking the beach the 1st platoon, led by Lt. Spaulding, under covering fire of a platoon from Company G... proceeded west to reduce the strongpoint... consisting of AA Gun, 4 Concrete Shelters, 2 Pillboxes, 5 MGs pillbox by pillbox to wipe out the strongpoint covering the east side of Exit E-1. Extremely stubborn resistance was encountered in this strongpoint with its maze of underground shelter trenches and dugouts. A close exchange of hand grenades ensued and small arms fire until the 1st platoon cornered approximately 20 Germans and an officer who, overpowered, surrendered.[19]

At 1045, the 115th RCT commenced landing on Beach Easy: Red. The breaches in the enemy's defense in this vicinity were now established. The V Corps G-3 Journal for 1155 stated:

> Situation beach exits Easy, Fox and Dog still critical at 1100. 352nd Inf Div (German) identified in area. Has been in position for over a month. 115th Inf directed to clear high ground SW Easy Red beach at 1130. Beachmaster directed to expedite landing of 18th and 115th Inf. 16th and 116th Inf ashore. Fighting continues on beach.

Captured Germans revealed that elements from at least two regiments of the 352nd Division were fighting to retain control of Omaha Beach. At this time, Bradley considered evacuating Omaha Beach. The

115th RCT moved up the bluff to secure the village of Saint Laurent and the road network that ran parallel to the beach. The main effort of the assault was made in the center on Beach Easy: Red, where the first breach was made. By noon of D-Day, there were four major breaches in the German defenses: one on Dog: White, two on Easy: Red, and one on Fox: Green. On the afternoon of D-Day, the breaches were widened and the advance inland progressed.

At 1600, General Huebner and his staff came ashore to personally direct operations on the beach, which was cluttered with tanks, bulldozers, damaged landing craft, and numerous other vehicles and debris. The beach was still under enemy fire, and it was getting late. Huebner needed to put his division in a coherent tactical, defensive configuration before dark to protect it from enemy counter-attack. As night fell, although progress had been made, the division was still in a vulnerable situation. However, because operational and strategic surprise had been achieved, because the air force had isolated the battlefield and interdicted the enemy forces *en route*, and because of the greater success on the other beaches, the Germans were not immediately prepared to counter-attack.

The 1st ID's artillery started landing at 1600. Because of high seas and the overloading of DUKWs, considerable artillery was lost. Still, by dark, Huebner had received organic fire support to stabilize his position. The 26th RCT began landing at 1930. Its mission was also changed. One battalion was sent to 'clean out' Colleville, in the area of the 16th Infantry, and another to advance through Saint Laurent toward Formigny.

By the end of D-Day, it was estimated that the division controlled a section of the Normandy coast 10,000 yards wide and 2,000 to 3,000 yards deep. For this small piece of land, Americans paid dearly. The 1st ID suffered over 2,000 killed, wounded, and missing, each of the two initial assault regiments losing about 1,000 men.[20] Near the end of the war, Huebner praised the men of the 1st ID in a pamphlet entitled 'The First':

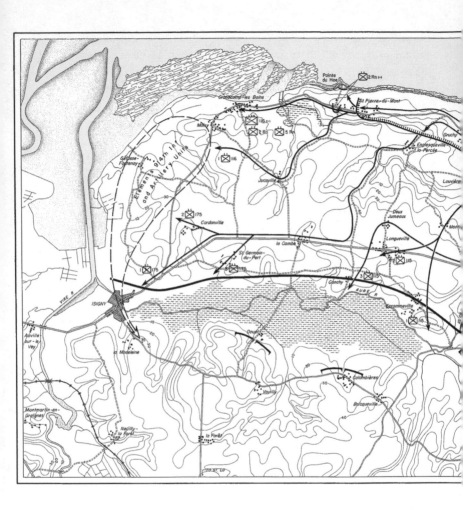

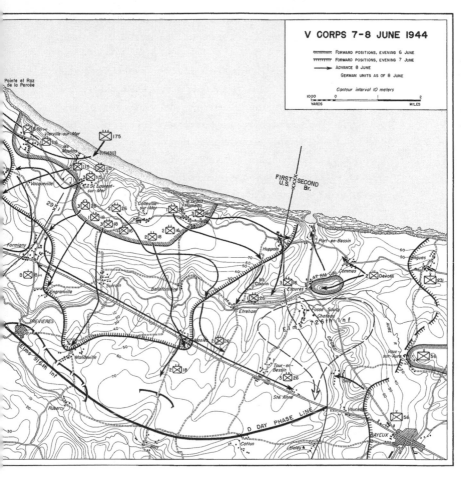

V Corps, 7–8 June 1944. From Gordon Harrison, *Cross-Channel Attack*, U.S. Army in World War II (Washington, D.C.: Government Printing Office, 1951).

The story of the Division and its units is printed herein in factual writing. Our record lives up to our motto: 'No mission too difficult, no sacrifice too great.' The press and the historians have, and will always pay tribute to the 'Fighting First' as a great division; but I want to take this opportunity to recognize you as individual soldiers. Your courage, your caginess, your teamwork, and your spirit are ever present. The German has learned to fear the wearer of the 'Red One.' The unmerciful beating you have given him in many engagements; your desire to close with him and kill have made it so. As long as we continue to have men like you, we will go forward – always forward – forward to the next objective.

Infantrymen, engineers, coxswains, and destroyers improvised success from a failed plan. Why did the plan fail?

2
Amphibious Doctrine
The British and American Visions

Amphibious operations are a complex form of warfare. On the material side they entail technical study, the production of new machines of war, special types of assault craft, both large and small, and the use of these and other devices. On the human side they demand the creation of sailors-soldiers, soldiers-sailors, and airmen-soldiers, who must cooperate with imaginative understanding of each other's methods and problems.

Vice Admiral Lord Louis Mountbatten

Modern amphibious doctrine required the co-operation of air, sea, and land forces to accomplish what each operating alone could not. These forces had to work together to develop a 'joint' doctrine in order to fulfill their missions and achieve the nation's political objectives. World War II marked a departure for the United States in naval and military operations. Never before in the history of the United States had it been necessary for the army and navy to work so closely together to achieve strategic objectives. Joint operations were conducted on a scale never envisioned by either of the services. The cultures of the two services did not merge successfully, and as a consequence, joint operations never achieved synergy.

Modern warfare requires the resources of more than one nation, no matter how great the resources of a given nation. Modern warfare is 'combined' warfare. The human and material resources and geographic circumstances of nations are combined in modern warfare. Combined warfare not only requires a combined strategic vision but also may require the merging of military practices. Combined doctrine may be needed to conduct certain operations. In World War II, the American and British air forces had two distinct doctrines for the execution of the strategic bombing campaign. The British conducted night area bombing with technology designed to fit the British practice of warfare, and the Americans conducted daylight precision bombing with technology designed to fit the American way of war. The air forces of the Anglo-American alliance did not find it necessary to compromise their doctrines to accommodate the military traditions and practices of their ally. The U.S. Navy in the Pacific theater conducted warfare the American way; the U.S. Army and Navy in the Mediterranean and European theaters, however, found it necessary to accommodate the British practice of war in every major operation. The American strategic vision and practice of war were distorted in World War II by the presence of the British, and the British way of war was distorted by the presence of Americans. Neither nation would have conducted operations in World War II the way they were carried out had they been left to their own designs. In 1942, the British way of war dominated the American practice of war, but by 1944, the British were no longer the senior partner. The American practice of war exerted a stronger influence as the war progressed and American manpower and resources came to dominate the war effort. In 1944, the balance of power shifted in favor of the American practice of war, a practice to which the British objected for the remainder of the war. In 1944, Anglo-American forces fought amphibious warfare with a hybrid doctrine. The doctrine employed in the Normandy invasion was the offspring of two genetically different parents, and that doctrine was less effective in combat than either of its parents.

BRITISH AMPHIBIOUS DOCTRINE

The British Empire was conquered and maintained through sea power. The geographical circumstances of Great Britain dictated that sea power was the primary source of national power. Given Britain's geographical circumstances and wide-ranging empire, one might assume that the British were masters of the art of joint, combined amphibious operations. This assessment, however, would be wrong. Britain's relationship with the continental powers of Europe, its policy to act as a balancing force among them, mitigated against the development and practice of large-scale joint amphibious operations. And because the European powers enjoyed a significant superiority in military technology and doctrine over peoples in other parts of the world, such as Africa and Asia, the conquest and maintenance of empires were possible without developing advanced amphibious doctrine and technology.

The British practice of warfare from the sixteenth century to World War I was to employ what Basil H. Liddell-Hart, the British military historian, called the 'indirect grand strategy.'[1] This was a limited-war, exhaustion strategy. The British way of war de-emphasized direct confrontation, concentration, mass, and battle and emphasized surprise, mobility, maneuver, peripheral attacks on enemy weaknesses, dispersion, conservation of resources, and negotiated settlements. War was to be conducted in a 'businesslike' manner and was to be profitable. The British used sea power primarily to achieve their limited strategic objectives. They traditionally fought low-expenditure, high-gain wars that took advantage of Britain's geographic circumstances and exploited those of its enemy. The British way of war was to destroy, when possible, the enemy's fleet; attack enemy trade; blockade the enemy's coast and conduct raids on the enemy's ports, coastal towns, and colonies; seize, when possible, the enemy's colonies; subsidize allies on the Continent; wait for the attacks on the enemy's economy and peripheral areas to erode its capacity to resist; exploit opportunities through the use of surprise made possible by the superior mobility of the fleet; deploy limited expeditionary forces on the Continent to fight alongside the larger forces of allies; and, finally, maneuver the enemy into an untenable position in which it had no other option but to conclude a peace agreement on terms set by the British and their allies. This was the limited-war strategic doctrine that had been employed in the War of the Spanish Succession, the Seven Years' War, and the wars against Napoleon. Through the use of this doctrine, Britain expanded its colonial possessions, trade, wealth, and influence. Liddell-Hart believed that the adoption of the Clausewitzian-style 'continental' strategy in World War I had been a mistake. He argued that the carnage suffered at the Somme and Passchendaele was the result of following the dictates of a strategy foreign to the British tradition.[2]

Technological advances and social changes influenced the British adoption of new strategy and doctrine in the twentieth century. In earlier centuries, because of the vastness and shapes of continents, amphibious assault against hostile shores was, for the most part, an unnecessary military practice.[3] Even though armies have landed on foreign shores for the purpose of conquest for centuries, it was rarely necessary to conduct an opposed landing until the twentieth century. Only in the nineteenth century – with the advent of the modern nation-state, which provided the unifying ideology and bureaucratic structures necessary to harness the energy of a people; the abundance produced by the Industrial Revolution; and the great advances in science and technology – was it possible to defend an entire continent. In the twentieth century, the increased size of armies and advances in technology such as the internal combustion engine, radar, radio communications, airplanes, machine guns, and long-range artillery made it physically possible for armed forces to stretch across an entire continent. Because only littoral regions with certain characteristics were suitable for the landing of troops, the possibility of defending a continent became a reality. This reality made it necessary to develop amphibious assault techniques. In World War I, Britain fielded a mass army to fight on the European continent. In World War II, Britain again fielded a mass army, but this time, it faced the additional task of invading the Continent.

Prior to the twentieth century, the British tradition of amphibious operations was based primarily on amphibious raid. These practices were based on the strategy of the 'indirect approach,' that is, avoiding decisive engagement with the enemy's main army until it was substantially weakened.[4] In *Amphibious Warfare in British History,* published in 1941, when the British were developing their amphibious warfare doctrine, Admiral Sir Herbert Richmond outlined the objectives of traditional British amphibious operations:

i.   To exert economic pressure by the capture or destruction of an oversea source of the enemy's wealth.

ii.   To disable or destroy an enemy's naval forces.

iii. To obtain possession of a new naval base.

iv.   To deprive an enemy of a naval base or prospective base.

v.   To effect a diversion of enemy strength.

vi.   To expel an enemy from a particular territory.

vii. To hamper an enemy by support of local rebellions.[5]

British amphibious doctrine was based on a strategy of limited war and was employed against enemy colonial possessions and occasionally against the continent of Europe. This practice alone was incapable of producing decisive results. The landing forces employed were usually incapable of sustaining themselves and were too small to become decisively engaged; thus, they were frequently confined to the coastal regions, where their lifeline at sea could support them and evacuate them when necessary. From the operations of Sir Francis Drake against the Spanish in 1587; to the operations of General James Wolfe against the French at Quebec in 1757; to the operations of

Admiral Samuel Barrington against the French West Indies in 1778; to the engagement of Admiral Sackville Carden, Admiral John de Robeck, and General Ian Hamilton against the Germans and Turks in the Dardanelles in 1915; to the operations of Lord Louis Mountbatten against the Germans at Dieppe in 1942, the British had amassed a long tradition of amphibious raiding operations against targets of opportunity for limited gains.[6]

Admiral Richmond concluded his analysis by delineating the principles on which successful British amphibious operations were traditionally based:

> First, forethought. For want of thinking ahead, expeditions have suffered and sometimes failed because the necessary means were lacking – bombarding vessels to assist the landings, adequate shipping to carry the army... Next, that the object they desire to attain shall be clear in the minds both of those who order and those who command the operation. In the command there must be full understanding and co-operation between the commanders of the several services engaged... Surprise, either strategical or tactical, or both, is to be sought by every possible means – the passive means of concealment of the preparations and movements and the active means of misleading the enemy.[7]

The principle of war 'surprise' was a fundamental element in the British practice of amphibious warfare.

In World War I, in an operation pushed forward by First Lord of the Admiralty Sir Winston Churchill, the British lost their enthusiasm for amphibious operations. The failed attempt to seize the Dardanelles resulted in heavy casualties. Gallipoli, the site of a particularly horrendous battle, became synonymous with the word 'debacle.' Many military thinkers in Britain and elsewhere came to believe that the awesome combat power that modern rapid-fire weapons added to the strength of the defense made it impossible to force a landing against an organized and well-motivated defense in daylight. Bernard Fergusson, a former director of combined operations, wrote:

The Dardanelles were fought all over again, in printer's ink and at Staff Colleges, in Britain, the United States and Australia. Most people... reckoned that daylight assaults against a defended shore were suicide and folly. Everybody was looking at the past rather than the future; money was tight, and what there was had to be spent on needs more obviously urgent than experiments in Combined Operations.[8]

The development of modern amphibious doctrine required minds capable of breaking with tradition and the practices taught at military schools and academies. Creative thinking was necessary. Personalities capable of divorcing themselves, at least in part, from loyalty to a particular service were also required. The fall of France and Dunkirk created the conditions under which individuals possessing the insights and qualities of character necessary to develop amphibious doctrine could rise to the fore. These events also created the conditions for the funding of experimentation. Much was achieved in the period immediately preceding the outbreak of World War II.

In May 1938, the British chief of staff initiated actions to establish a combined (joint) operations study center.[9] The need for such a center had been recognized two years earlier, but the funding and resolve were lacking. Thus, on the eve of World War II, the Inter-Services Training and Development Center (ISTDC) was established. Officers from the army, navy, and air force were brought together to develop doctrine for amphibious operations. The charter described the center's mission:

i.   To train in all methods for the seizure of defended beaches;

ii. To develop the materiel necessary for such methods, with special regard to protection of troops, *speed of landing, and the attainment of surprise*;

iii. To develop methods and materiel for the destruction or neutralization of enemy defenses, including bombardment and aircraft co-operation;

iv. In time of war, the whole force to be employed for carrying out *minor operations* by itself; or in conjunction with military forces, as the *covering force* to seize and hold beaches for the main landing.[10]

At this time, the need to invade the Continent was not evident. The term 'minor operations'; the concept of a specially trained, elite group of soldiers, or covering force, charged with making the initial break-through; and other aspects of this charter reflected the amphibious raid tradition. Speed and surprise were the principles on which the British based their amphibious doctrine. Surprise was facilitated by darkness. These concepts allowed for a limited initial commitment and gave commanders the option to either follow up success by deploying the main body or cut losses and evacuate. The possibility of failure was more real to the British than to the Americans, who had never lost a war.

The ISTDC, in the short time it had before the outbreak of World War II, produced a functional doctrine that capitalized on British strengths – strengths that were very different from those of the United States:

> By the end of 1938, ...the Brain Trust at the ISTDC had hammered out a broad policy for landing...With variations won by experience, it was broadly the policy that was used in the North African and Sicily [and Salerno] landings...The system provided for an approach under cover of darkness in fast ships carrying special craft; the craft being sent ashore while the ships lay out of sight of land; small-craft smoke and gun protection while the beachhead was seized; the landing of a reserve; the capture of a covering position far enough inland to secure the beach and anchorage from enemy fire; the bringing in of ships carrying the main body; and finally the discharge of vehicles and stores by other craft specially designed to do so directly on to beaches.[11]

This was the basic amphibious practice employed throughout the war in the Mediterranean theater—a practice based on British doctrine. Not until the Normandy invasion did major elements of U.S. Marine and Navy amphibious doctrine emerge. During the war, British doctrine evolved.

The Dieppe raid was given credit for revealing the weaknesses of British amphibious doctrine.[12] Technological problems had to be overcome, and service cultures had to be merged into a workable joint culture. Still, the British entered the war with a doctrine that would be used up to 1944, when the thinking and resources – men and materiel – of the United States began exerting a greater influence. The tenets of British amphibious doctrine were speed, tactical surprise, control of the air and sea in the immediate vicinity of the operation, limited commitment against targets of opportunity, short duration of operations, unopposed assaults on terrain that permitted rapid advance inland, and interservice co-operation as opposed to unity of command. Traditional British practices of amphibious operations were modified by technology and the ability of large national armies to defend the entire coast of a continent. However, the British tended to adhere to the principles delineated before the fall of France, before it became necessary to invade the continent of Europe.

Unopposed landings were no longer possible with the advent of modern professional armies with radar, radio communications, high-speed transportation systems, professional intelligence analysts, and a few small airplanes and boats that could maintain surveillance of large sections of the coast and enemy movements. Tactical surprise became more difficult to achieve and less necessary because the combat power of the landing force was multiplied by technology in the form of battleships, aircraft carriers, close air support, landing craft of all types, and the sheer magnitude of the forces industrialized society could produce. The 'limited commitment of elite troops for short duration' approach could not produce decisive results. This approach could not achieve political objectives and, in the age of nations, was only a minor annoyance. Decisive results required the landing of mass armies on the Continent. Its history of amphibious raids and its lack of resources initially confined British thinking on the conduct of amphibious operations. Habits of mind change slowly. National armies and navies tend to reproduce the practices that brought them success in the past.[13]

In June 1940, after Dunkirk, Prime Minister Winston Churchill directed the armed forces to initiate limited offensive operations against Hitler's Europe. Small elite units, assaulting at night, were to carry out amphibious raids. Churchill's objectives were to restore the offensive spirit of the British armed forces, which was badly bruised by the defeats in France; to compel his commanders to think critically and imaginatively about the amphibious warfare doctrine; and to achieve some limited military successes against the seemingly invincible Germans.[14] Churchill may have also hoped to boost the morale of the British people when he issued this directive. Nevertheless, amphibious raids on the scale envisioned were incapable of producing a decision in the war and were of little strategic value. Strategically, the raids accomplished three objectives, although the degree to which they did so is difficult to determine: they facilitated the restoration of the British offensive spirit; they gave the British armed forces practical experience in joint amphibious operations, reinforcing traditional practices; and they caused the Germans to construct a defense along the coast of France.[15] British experiences in amphibious raids were not directly applicable to large-scale joint amphibious operations. In fact, British experiences in raids hampered their ability to develop effective tactical and operational amphibious doctrine.

Churchill's experiences in World War I made him keenly interested in amphibious operations:

> I had always been fascinated by amphibious warfare, and the idea of using tanks to run ashore from specially constructed landing craft on beaches where they were not expected had long been in my mind... In July I created a separate Combined Operations Command under the Chiefs of Staff for the study and exercise of this form of warfare, and Admiral of the Fleet Sir Roger Keyes became its chief.[16]

The landing-ship tank was one of Churchill's many contributions to the successful conduct of World War II. (The Americans adopted and mass-produced the vessels for operations in both the Pacific and the Mediterranean theaters.) Another of his contributions was the Combined Operations Headquarters, which not only pushed forward the development of doctrine initiated by the ISTDC but also developed the initial plans for the Normandy invasion, including the selection of the invasion site.

In October 1941, Lord Keyes, whose leadership style and vision for the conduct of amphibious raids were too radical for the senior British military leaders, was relieved of his position as director of the Combined Operations Headquarters. His greatest contribution was to create an environment in which officers from all three services could work together to develop doctrine and plans.[17] Lord Louis Mountbatten replaced Keyes.[18] Churchill gave Mountbatten the mission to increase raid activities against the coast, but more important, he directed Mountbatten to prepare for the 're-invasion' of France. Churchill's directives to Mountbatten were broad.[19] He was responsible for planning the invasion of Europe, developing doctrine and technology, implementing a training program in amphibious operations, creating an environment in which interservice co-operation could evolve to a high degree, and conducting raids against the Continent.

The Dieppe raid in August 1942 was another step in the development of a joint amphibious operations doctrine. Mountbatten's Combined Operations Headquarters was responsible for planning the raid, but it had no command responsibility. The raid was designed to be a test of British amphibious doctrine and a rehearsal for an invasion.[20] The raid was a disaster. The Germans were alert and ready to fight, and the Canadians and British suffered heavy casualties. A report on the raid noted:

> The Lesson of Greatest Importance is the need for overwhelming fire support, including close support, during the initial stages of the attack. It is not too much to say that, at present, no standard Naval vessel or craft has the necessary qualities or equipment to provide close inshore support. Without such support any assault on the enemy-occupied coast of Europe is more and more likely to fail as the enemy's defenses are extended and improved.[21]

The report continued:

> The plans for Dieppe did not include high level bombing prior to the assault. Had suitable day bombers such as American Fortresses been

available in sufficient numbers this decision might well have been different. In the circumstances, the main objections to support by night bombing were: Surprise would have been lost.

The Dieppe disaster did not settle the doctrinal issue of surprise versus firepower for the British. The American daylight precision bombers appeared to offer a new opportunity that if properly exploited could save lives and achieve tactical objectives: 'The fair conclusion to draw seems to be that the question whether or not high level bombing should be included in the plan is an open one and that no hard and fast deduction should be drawn. Each case must be judged on it merits.'[22]

On 26 May 1943 at the Assault Training Center Conference, Commodore J. Hughes-Hallett of the Royal Navy, commander of British naval forces at Dieppe, gave his assessment of the operation and the lessons to be learned from it. Hughes-Hallett believed that the Dieppe operation had achieved its main objective of providing a rehearsal for the cross-Channel invasion. He felt that tactical surprise had been attained at Dieppe despite the fact that a naval engagement that took place before the assault had alerted the Germans to the invasion. No common, explicit definition of the term 'surprise' existed among British naval and army leaders, however. Hughes-Hallett noted the following points:

i.   Much stronger forces are needed to break through the stronger parts of the German Fortifications on the coast of FRANCE than those employed at DIEPPE.

ii. Intensive preparations by means of air and sea bombardment are essential in order to soften the defences.

iii. Much heavier support on a carefully organized basis is needed by the troops during the early phases of the landing.

iv. The Military plan must be flexible because the bulk of the military force must not be committed in advance to any particular time or place of landing but must be held as a floating reserve ready to exploit success.

v.   Arising from (iv) above, a very much higher standard of training
     and organization is needed on the part of the landing craft flotillas
     than had previously been thought necessary.[23]

The first lesson was obvious, but the second was problematic. The problem was defining exactly what 'intensive preparations' meant. How much firepower over what length of time was necessary? What quality of damage was required? And how best could the needed firepower be delivered? More time and greater precision in targeting enemy positions were necessary. The fourth lesson was applicable only in small-scale operations. In an invasion in which large armies assaulted side by side in a confined geographic area, it was not possible to significantly change the course of planned events without disrupting the entire invasion plan. Forces had to be committed to an axis of advance the day prior to the landing. The fifth lesson had to be relearned after every invasion – particularly by the Americans. The American personnel administration system tended to move people around too quickly for individuals to participate in more than one actual assault, and as a consequence, Americans were always deploying green soldiers and sailors in assaults.[24]

General Hamilton Roberts of the Canadian Army, commander of military forces in the Dieppe operation, at the Conference on Landing Assaults, 24 May–23 June 1943, set forth his assessment of the Dieppe operation. He answered specific questions from a list prepared by the British Combined Operations, Divisional Headquarters. Asked 'whether any bombardment with H.E. or 4" smoke shell was carried out and, if so, any remarks on its efficiency,' he replied:

I consider the 4" shell is not sufficiently heavy for this type of landing and that you want something really big; more in the nature of a 12", so that when you hit a target something really happens. The chalk walls that go up either side of Dieppe were hollowed out and guns, both antitank and medium machine guns, were in there, really dug right into these holes. They were very difficult to get at, as you can understand. I feel something in the nature of a 12" shell... would probably have brought the whole wall down.[25]

Roberts firmly believed that bigger naval guns in greater quantity were necessary. In this regard, his thinking was in concert with that of naval commander Hughes-Hallett. Roberts's characterization of the German defenses along the coast should also have been of considerable help to the Allies since the German defense at Dieppe possessed many of the same characteristics of the defense at Normandy. Roberts continued:

> We started in with the idea of bombing during the night. At that time, we did not have daylight bombers... [T]he bombers that were available had to bomb at night. They could not guarantee hitting the proper target... We were hoping to get tanks ashore and to get in by surprise. Also bombing would have awakened the defenses; they would have thought something was coming, if we had bombed the place for an hour or so... *Now, of course, with later methods and the fact we can do daylight bombing, we have more machines, more craft, etc. I think that the bomber could, to a large extent, take the place of guns, just to keep the enemy's head down and give you a chance to get in.* On the other hand, of course, guns are very accurate. I think probably a combination of bombs and shells, depending on what you can get, is the ideal. The difficulty at the moment, was that we had not the craft available for a sea bombardment. All we could hope to get were those 'Hunt' class destroyers with 4" guns. There was just nothing else available.[26]

Surprise was not achieved at Dieppe in Roberts's view. Yet to achieve surprise, the British had forgone the employment of night bombing. Would it have been better to employ bombers and sacrifice surprise? Was it even reasonable to assume that tactical surprise could be attained when only a few small boats and airplanes could preclude it? To some British military leaders, the answer was 'yes'; to others, 'no.' Still, in 1944, the American daylight strategic bombers offered a new, potentially decisive solution to the problem with which Roberts and others struggled, a solution that was not available in 1942. However, the effectiveness of the employment of daylight heavy bombers in operations of this type was unknown and remained so until 6 June 1944. Roberts and others could only speculate. The American daylight strategic bombers had never been employed in the manner being discussed, and experimentation and training in the procedures and techniques required for this type of operation were not implemented. The American heavy bombers were too busy conducting the strategic bombing campaign to take part in developing new operational and tactical procedures to facilitate the conduct of an amphibious assault. The American strategic bombing doctrine, however, was called 'daylight precision bombing,' and the American heavy bomber force bragged of being able to put 'a bomb in a pickle barrel.'[27] Thus, ground commanders could assume that the air force was capable of performing this mission without the development of new techniques and procedures. What may not have been fully identified and understood was that 'precision' meant one thing at the strategic level and a very different thing at the tactical level.

Roberts was defensive on the issue of whether heavy bombers should have been employed at night. He stated:

> It has now been accepted that we were wrong in not arranging for heavy air raids before the assault was made. The question has been discussed at length. The advantages of accurate bombing are obvious... To repeat, it [bombing] could only be done in the hours of darkness and would therefore be most inaccurate. Then again, it would have alarmed the defenses and caused more harm than good. Inaccurate bombing would simply have awakened them, which is just about all it would do.[28]

It is difficult to gauge the influence the Dieppe raid had on the development of the plan and doctrine for the Normandy invasion. Roberts's thinking on daylight bombers, however, may have influenced Montgomery. If daylight bombers were not employed and the invasion failed, the operational planners would have been criticized for failing to use all means available against the primary objective. However, if they were given sufficient time to destroy the water's edge defense, along with other fire support systems, such as naval gunfire, tactical surprise would have been lost. And if the bombing was inaccurate, the infantry would have to face an alert enemy in a prepared defense in daylight – the worst-case scenario.

All who took part in the Dieppe operation came away with the assessment that considerably greater firepower was needed for a successful landing. Allied naval gunfire resources in the Atlantic and Mediterranean were believed to be incapable of generating the kind of firepower required in a landing of the size contemplated for the invasion of Europe. The bomber forces were thus seen as a valuable resource. Roberts observed:

> The next question: *Was the frontal attack justified in view of the fact we were not taking any steps to pulverize the defenses before such an attack? My answer is that it is justified.* However, defenses were stronger than anticipated, and failure at the 'Blue' beach... altered the whole situation. The party on 'Blue' Beach, 17 minutes late, which made the difference between first light, when you could just see, and broad daylight. There was not much time to spare, and if you are later you are out of luck. They were 17 minutes late... and they never got in at all. It was a very strongly held beach with a lot of wire and pillboxes.

Roberts had hoped to achieve tactical surprise in an assault before sunrise. When tactical surprise was not attained and part of the landing force was caught in full daylight, the tenets on which the plan was built were proved wrong and the Canadians ran into an active, deliberate defense. Thus, the assault failed, first, because it lacked firepower and, second, because tactical surprise was lost. Which tenet was more important? Roberts continued: '[F]rontal assaults should not be excluded if adequate and dominating close support can be given.'[29] Tactically, on a well-defended coast, there are no flanks. An amphibious assault against a deliberate defense is fundamentally a frontal assault. On poorly defended beaches, other forms of maneuver, such as envelopment and infiltration, are possible. Infiltration techniques are facilitated by darkness.

Fergusson summarized the lessons he drew from the Dieppe operation:

First and foremost, we had learned that our fire support was wholly inadequate. Against strong defences, the light armament of half a dozen destroyers was of little more use than so many pop-guns; and however devoted and daring the fighters might be, *they were no substitute for heavy bombers. The presence of a capital ship at Dieppe might have made all the difference.*

Fergusson believed that '[s]omehow the defenders must be drenched with fire and reduced to a state of gibbering with shock at the last moment.' In regard to surprise, Fergusson wrote:

We know now that the enemy was in an especial state of readiness between the 25th June and 10th July... This vigilance was due not to any leakage nor some masterpiece of espionage; the Germans had put two and one together, and arrived at the reasonable sum of three. First, our propaganda had for some time past been designed to make Germans think that we were plotting some vigorous action across the channel... Secondly, it had been impossible to conceal from enemy air reconnaissance an assembly of shipping and landing craft... And thirdly, any fool with a nautical almanac could work out the most favourable combination of daylight and tides.[30]

Fergusson did not believe the assault force could plan on achieving surprise. In regard to the assaults, Fergusson noted: 'We had learned that a frontal assault on a defended port was impracticable, and we never tried it again. Hughes-Hallett is on record as saying, ..."Well, if we can't capture a port we will have to take one with us."'

The British designed and constructed portable docks for off-loading ships – the Mulberries. Fergusson continued:

We had learned that for tanks to land before tank obstacles had been breached was lethal; they would inevitably be halted, and would become sitting ducks... We had learned that landing-craft were apt, especially if things were going slightly wrong, to land on the wrong beaches or to land late owing to doubt as to which was the right beach.... We had learned that *ad hoc* Headquarters Ships could not handle the signal traffic, nor obtain a clear picture of what was happening either ashore or afloat... Finally... it was obvious that the best results would never be obtained from a number of vessels assembled haphazard for an operation, and dispersed thereafter... that a fleet should be kept permanently in being for such tasks as these.[31]

Various British military leaders learned very different lessons from the Dieppe raid. Roberts believed a direct assault against a deliberate defense was possible, but Fergusson believed it was not. Roberts thought tactical surprise was necessary, but General J.C. Haydon, also of the British Combined Operation Headquarters, and Fergusson did not think it was possible to achieve tactical surprise.[32] Fergusson did not believe tanks should be landed before tank obstacles were breached, but Montgomery disagreed. Differences in time, resources, and technology account for some of the differences in doctrinal thinking. Still, many of the lessons of Dieppe remained unclear. And the raid did not end debate or solidify doctrinal thinking on how the battle for the beaches ought to be won – by firepower with operational assets from the air and sea or by surprise achieved by assaulting at night with tactical formations. American resources, technology, and thinking about war to some degree caused the confusion. In 1942, it was not possible to generate overwhelming combat power and achieve tactical surprise. When Roberts was asked, 'Is a forced landing practicable on defended beaches without the advantage of surprise or great superiority in fire support?', he answered: 'No. You must have surprise or great superiority in fire-power, preferably surprise with fire support available as required.'[33]

Which was more important? This issue was never resolved. British experience was in unopposed raid operations. The British had a cumulative body of knowledge in assaults against poorly defended sectors of a coast – such as in North Africa and Sicily – but little experience in amphibious assaults against deliberate defenses. The major lesson of Dieppe was that greater firepower was needed, but the British inclination from experience and practice was to seek tactical surprise in night operations. The British lacked the naval gunfire and air resources to develop an American-style Pacific theater doctrine. At Normandy, the Allies hoped and planned to achieve both – overwhelming fire superiority and tactical surprise. The problem was that both conditions could not be achieved using traditional methods. New doctrine had to be developed to meet both requirements. Air power was the answer to the British nightmare of insufficient firepower. Haydon observed:

> Now turn to the Air Forces. Direct close support by fighter aircraft must by its nature be very fleeting. On the other hand, heavy bombing can either take the form of a long period of preparation or of a sudden smashing blow or a combination of the two. I always feel that the bombers will be asked to do both in great strength and that the Air Forces by means of its great power and flexibility, can do more to fill the gap in fire support during the initial stages of the assault than any other Service.[34]

Air power, the capabilities and limitations of which were not fully known, offered the Allied commanders, Montgomery and Bradley, a potentially decisive instrument to win the tactical battles for the beaches at Normandy.

The British practice of amphibious warfare until 1944 was based on the experiences of the past five years of war, the British amphibious raid tradition, resources, and geography. The British domination of strategic planning and operations in the early years of the war precluded the adoption of American-style Central Pacific doctrine. British amphibious doctrine was based on local tactical air, naval, and ground superiority; surprise; intelligence; and speed. The assault was made under the cover of darkness, when tactical surprise could best be achieved. Darkness concealed the movement of troops and ships. The British assault was made against 'soft spots,' weakly defended areas, in the enemy's defense. Intelligence on the situation along the coast was necessary to determine the exact location of the assault. The British typically deployed a covering force that cleared the way for the main assault. The British, after Dieppe, preferred infiltration tactics to a direct frontal assault. Infiltration could best be achieved under the cover of darkness. The bombardment fleet was typically small in comparison to those employed by the U.S. Navy in the Pacific. It did not clear the beaches of obstacles and minefields but instead provided direct support and counterbattery fire support. To maintain surprise, the bombardment was typically of short duration. If the cover force encountered substantial enemy resistance, the main assault could either be canceled or be redirected to a secondary objective.

The British practice of amphibious assault was based on a different mental disposition from that of the American practice. British doctrine relied on the thinking that it was possible to fail, that it was possible to be defeated at a given location, and thus measures must be taken to minimize losses. Americans, lacking a history of defeat, tended to be more optimistic. The Americans' mental disposition influenced British thinking, and American resources distorted British doctrine by making possible an operational doctrine based more on the American principles of war mass and firepower. The daylight strategic bombers of the U.S. Eighth Air Force and American thinking about warfare, the direct approach, modified British thinking. British doctrine evolved during the war in the context of small-scale, limited operations directed against poorly defended sectors of a coast. But the doctrinal principles on which British operations were based changed little during the war until the Normandy invasion. Techniques were refined, experience gained, and overall proficiency improved, but the ambiguity remained concerning the choice between surprise or firepower.

AMERICAN AMPHIBIOUS DOCTRINE

The development of U.S. amphibious doctrine was an outgrowth of the great energy and momentum built up during the westward expansion of the United States. Near the end of the nineteenth century, when the juggernaut of American energy reached the West

Coast, it continued to expand into the Pacific to Hawaii, Guam, Samoa, and the Philippine Islands. America acquired a colonial empire and endeavored to influence events in China and Korea. Expansion was fueled by ideologies such as manifest destiny, imperialism, 'navalism,' racism, and capitalism. The geography of the Pacific required a navy capable of carrying America's energy into and across the vast ocean region, and the threat posed by the expansion of the Japanese empire motivated Washington to allocate the funds needed to increase the size of the navy. The navy required forward bases to sustain its fleets. The acquisition and security of these forward bases, called 'advanced bases,' required forces capable of offensive and defensive action. In an extensive memorandum, Major Pete Ellis of the Marine Corps outlined the operational problem in 1921. In a section entitled 'Advanced Base Operations in Micronesia,' Ellis wrote:

> In order to impose our will upon the Japanese, it will be necessary for us to project our fleet and land forces across the Pacific and wage war in Japanese waters. To effect this requires that we have sufficient bases to support the fleet, both during its projection and afterwards. As the matter stands at present, we cannot count upon the use of any bases west of Hawaii except those which we may seize from the enemy after the opening of hostilities.[35]

Ellis accurately predicted the need to seize, secure, and occupy islands held by the Japanese. The terrain required forces capable of deploying from ships, advancing inland, and securing gains. The U.S. Marine Corps, with prodding from the navy, assumed this mission and then set to work developing operational and tactical doctrine. The Marine Corps historian, Allan Millett, observed: '[T]he new naval role was reshaping the Marine Corps in fundamental ways. As important was the fact that the advanced base force concept provided the Marine Corps with a wartime mission important to the navy and a function that encouraged Marine officer reformers and planners.'[36]

The development of American amphibious doctrine was thus a by-product of American expansion into the Pacific and the Marine

Corps' search for a mission. It would be a mistake to argue that the navy and Marine Corps progressed directly from the advanced base concept to fully developed modern amphibious doctrine.[37] The development proceeded in fits and starts, and not until the war was on were the navy and Marine Corps able to work out doctrinal problems. Still, by the time the United States entered World War II, thanks to the forethought of the navy and Marine Corps, the nation had an untested offensive amphibious doctrine.

The army officially adopted marine-navy amphibious doctrine but then chose, for the most part, not to use it. In the Mediterranean, British doctrine was employed. The thinking, makeup, conditions, and practices of the army were sufficiently different from those of the navy-marine team to preclude the complete adoption of the navy-centered doctrine, and the influence of the British in 1942 and 1943 on the conduct of operations, all of which were combined operations, was decisive. The doctrine delineated by the navy-marine team in 1938 was sketchy and more applicable to the smaller-scale operations against atolls and islands in the Pacific than to the 'mighty endeavors' in the Mediterranean and European theaters. Geography, technology, and resources also influenced the acceptance of different doctrinal practices in the two major theaters. The army took bits and pieces of marine doctrine but rewrote it as the war progressed and the army gained experience.[38]

In 1941, the War Department published U.S. Army Field Manual (FM) 31-5, *Landing Operations on Hostile Shores,* which stated: 'This manual is based to a large extent on Landing Operations Doctrine, U.S. Navy, 1938.' The navy's document, written by the Marine Corps, was Fleet Training Publication (FTP) 167. There are two different views of the usefulness of these documents. In *The U.S. Marines and Amphibious War,* Jeter A. Isley and Philip A. Crowl observed: 'The Tentative Manual for Landing Operations published by the Marine Corps Schools in 1934 deserves to be thought of as a sort of combination of the Pentateuch and Four Gospels.'[39] Naval historian E. B. Potter wrote: 'These two publications [FM 31-5 and FTP 167] were refined steadily throughout the war, but remained the basic guides for both planning and training that produced all United States amphibious operations during World War II. The basic doctrine set down in 1934 withstood its prolonged trial by fire without fundamental change.'[40] The Marine Corps' official history, *History of the U.S. Marine Corps Operations in World War II: Pearl Harbor to Guadalcanal,* stated: 'The doctrine laid down in this remarkable document was destined to become the foundation of all amphibious thinking in the United States armed forces.'[41] Marine and naval historians have tended to overstate the significance of U.S. amphibious doctrine in the Mediterranean and European theaters.[42]

Colonel Stanhope Mason, chief of staff of the 1st ID, one of the most experienced army officers in the European theater in amphibious operations, stated the opposing view: 'The Navy's manuals made up for Marine use (FTP 167) went no further than maximum loading of life boats... This was a pure transportation problem that took absolutely no heed of the necessity for ground units to maintain their unit integrity once landed on the beach where they would have to fight.'[43] Mason perhaps understated the usefulness of FTP 167, but he and the division staff had to translate orders into executable invasion plans for the 1st ID – the division that conducted more amphibious assaults than any other division in the European and Mediterranean theaters in World War II. Mason recognized that the doctrine formulated by the navy was incomplete and inadequate for the 1st ID's circumstances. What he may not have recognized at the tactical level was the influence exerted by the British at the operational level.

The doctrinal thinking of the Marine Corps differed from that of the British:

> Night landings, except possibly for small reconnaissance parties going ashore prior to the main attack, were discouraged as too dangerous. Transports carrying the assault troops should approach the transport area under cover of darkness, but the landing should ordinarily be made during the early morning so as to permit the fullest use of all weapons and to afford the landing force ample daylight in which to secure a beachhead. Naval vessels should take position on the flanks of

the landing troops and sweep the beaches during the ship-to-shore movement. Aircraft should be employed in full measure not only for reconnaissance but also for strafing after the troops were landed.[44]

Marine Corps operations were heavily dependent on naval gunfire; surprise played no part. This thinking never developed in the European theater. The British simply lacked the resources to conduct warfare with firepower, and the British tradition of amphibious raids dominated. The marines preferred early-morning landings to maximize the hours of daylight to establish the beachhead with assistance from air and sea forces. British operations involved more phases, and each phase had to be executed sequentially. British operations were more intricate, and because the environment, conditions, and circumstances varied considerably in each landing, combined Mediterranean and European operations required more detailed planning than did operations in the Pacific, where standard operational procedures could be more easily established. British doctrine also required more detailed intelligence on the enemy's situation and terrain than did Pacific doctrine. In the Pacific, it was possible to cut off islands from all outside assistance. This was not possible on a continent. Thus, it was necessary to identify all forces that could influence the situation in a given geographic area and the quality and capacity of all major transportation arteries.

At the start of World War II, neither of the two senior services of the United States was prepared to conduct amphibious operations. Nor were the British. Both British and American doctrines were new and untried. The technology was only partially developed. The training was incomplete and poorly developed, hampered by inadequate resources. The command relationships, the assignment of responsibilities, the manning and acquisition of necessary facilities and equipment, the responsibility for the development of new technologies, the employment of special engineer brigades, and numerous other matters still had to be worked out. Although much had been done before the invasion of North Africa was conducted, there was still a great deal to do.

FM 31-5 outlined American thinking on amphibious operations:

> 17. Operations on Shore. – a. Night attacks are difficult to execute and are rarely attempted in land warfare except under special conditions.
>
> The principal advantages of a night landing are that it tends to secure tactical surprise and reduce the effectiveness of the defender's fire. The principal advantages of a day landing are that air and naval superiority are best obtained, the navigation of ships and boats is facilitated, and shore operations are easier to execute.
>
> Surprise. – a. Darkness increases the chances of securing some measure of tactical surprise. It deprives the defender to a material degree of the information necessary for the proper maneuver of his forces to meet the attack… Landing operations at night are difficult and liable to be attended by greater confusion than during daylight.[45]

The American practice of war at the strategic and operational levels was not to attack the enemy's weakness but to attack its strengths, to seek the enemy's main army and destroy it. This is called the 'direct approach.' To do this, Americans preferred to conduct daylight assaults, which allowed the maximum use of strategic and operational resources, such as battleships and strategic bombers.

> 142. Frontage of Attack. – c. Naval gunfire and combat aviation must be concentrated in support of the landing. Even a relatively small number of enemy machine guns and light artillery pieces firing under favorable conditions have a devastating effect on units as they approach and land on the beach. *Assault units will probably be unable to get ashore and advance against this fire unless adequately supported by ship fire and combat aviation.*[46]

This was a lesson learned from the British campaign in the Dardanelles at Gallipoli in World War I. This tenet became the foundation of marine and navy operations in the Pacific.[47] With each campaign, the significance of the pre-invasion bombardment and bombing increased. Tactical units tend to prefer to follow the path of least resistance and attack the enemy's weaknesses:

> 144. Hostile Dispositions. – *Beaches strongly organized for defense are avoided, if possible, in the initial landings.* Advantage is taken of undefended or lightly defended portions of the shore line, even though they present less favorable landing conditions, in order to outmaneuver the hostile resistance or to gain a position from which flanking artillery or small-arms fire may assist the landing at more favorable beaches.[48]

The nature of the terrain in the Central Pacific made it impossible in many landings to avoid the enemy's main defense, and the great abundance of naval gunfire available made this an unnecessary practice.

> 103. Supporting Fire. – a. Supporting fire is delivered on the enemy defensive position to neutralize personnel and material [minefields and obstacles] most dangerous to our own infantry in overcoming resistance.

> 184. Reduction of Hostile Defenses. – Prior to landing, unless secrecy is the primary consideration, advantage must be taken of every opportunity to deliver air attacks on the hostile defenses. Aircraft, airdromes, aviation materiel, fortifications, gun emplacements, communication and transportation centers, supply bases, and troop movements and concentrations are appropriate targets.[49]

Items 142 and 103 emphasized the importance of firepower from ships and airplanes; however, not until the battles at Guadalcanal and Tarawa did the Marine Corps and navy fully realize the value of these resources. At Guadalcanal and Tarawa, the navy failed to provide the marines with the support that was needed.

American military tradition and Marine Corps tradition emphasized that man was the final determinant of battle, the ultimate weapon. Marine Corps doctrine reflected that culturally imbued norm of the American practice of war, but it also reflected the new role of science and technology. As the war progressed, the role of technology expanded. The exigencies involved in the deployment of the machine became the determining factor in Central Pacific warfare. The turning point was Tarawa, where the marines suffered over 3,000 casualties, 961 of whom were killed, on an atoll roughly two and a quarter miles long and half a mile wide at its widest point. The action report of one unit of the Fifth Amphibious Force stated:

> Recommendations. That the extensive pre-landing bombing and bombardment be conducted during the whole of D-1 day and night; that it be conducted leisurely and deliberately, selecting and obliterating progressively specific targets; that fire cease when smoke interferes; that destroyers give close in and exclusive attention to pillbox defenses along the beaches, particularly where the landing is to take place and that a certain per centage of AP shells be used to penetrate pillboxes; that the bombers fire only at targets they can see, that they concentrate at first on AA positions, air fields and magazines; and later assist in destruction of pillboxes and strong points using at least 1,000 pound bombs; and that the enemy be given not one moment of rest for at least 24 hours prior to the landing. A leisurely, prolonged, and accurate bombardment should greatly reduce the number of these effectives with consequent reduction in casualties to our own landing force.[50]

After Tarawa, the role of naval gunfire and air support increased throughout the war. From the preliminary bombardment – which could last up to ten days – the Marine Corps came to expect the following damage:

a. Destruction of coast-defense installations.
b. Destruction of all weapons which can bring direct fire upon the beaches or transport areas.
c. Destruction of enemy means of air defense (so that our own air strikes may go in unimpeded).

    d. Destruction of fortifications which might obstruct or delay
       landing (such as pillboxes, bunkers and blockhouses on or near
       the beaches).

    e. Stripping of camouflage, sand and vegetation in all critical areas in
       the immediate beachhead.[51]

This was an incredible degree of damage. Obstacles and minefields
were of no consequence; they were destroyed in the bombardment.
The vast majority of the combat power employed to win battles came
from the navy. This was the final evolution of Marine Corps doctrine
in the Pacific in World War II.[52] There was no ambiguity in the
doctrine. Surprise was not significant. Battles were, ideally, to be won
with the deliberate, methodical, sustained use of overwhelming firepower, followed up by a direct, mass infantry assault. A naval gunfire
officer, in reference to the support given the marines at Roi Namur
atoll in the Marshall Islands in Operation Flintlock, reported:

> The main objectives of the atoll were bombarded by six battleships
> and six destroyers on Dog minus one day with the primary mission to
> render the air field inoperative, destroy planes, and then destroy as
> many of the ground installations as possible... The effect of naval
> gunfire here was devastating. It can be said that the accuracy and
> effect of naval gunfire was the prime factor which allowed the troops
> to land on the objective with so few casualties and such little opposi-
> tion. The CG [commanding general], 4th Marine Division has stated
> that at least 50% to 60% of the Japs were killed prior to the landing by
> the air, naval bombardment and artillery... After an inspection of the
> island, it was found that practically every defensive installation above
> the ground had been hit by naval fire.

On the battle for Kwajalein Island, another U.S. Navy observer wrote:

> All of Kwajalein Island was in ruined condition. The ground was so
> torn up that it even made movement by foot difficult... This is another
> strong evidence of the accuracy and effect of the heavy amount of

Naval Gunfire placed on Kwajalein Island. No less amount should be contemplated for any other objective.[53]

The experiences of the Marine Corps and navy in the Pacific proved conclusively that deliberate defenses constructed at the water's edge could be destroyed by firepower. General Holland M. Smith, who commanded Marine Corps forces at Iwo Jima and other landings, explained:

> Given adequate naval and air support, they [the marines] could go ashore on any beach and take any objective. I could have landed them in the mouth of hell if the Joint Chiefs of Staff had picked that target. In this connection, the reader must realize how essential to a landing is the prior naval and air bombardment of enemy positions, which destroys defenses and softens up opposition before the assault waves hit the beach. The stronger the defenses the heavier, more prolonged and more effective should be the bombardment, over periods as short as three days and as long as ten days.[54]

Smith believed that the navy rarely gave his marines the quality and quantity of naval gunfire required, and as a consequence, marines died: 'If the Marines had received better co-operation from the Navy our casualties would have been lower. More naval gunfire would have saved many lives. I had to beg for gunfire and I rarely received what the situation demanded.'[55] Although Smith was not happy with the air and naval gunfire support his marines received at Iwo Jima, the Japanese recognized that these resources were the dominant weapons on the battlefield. Lieutenant General Tadamichi Kuribayashi, the Japanese commander at Iwo Jima, sent the following message to Tokyo in the final days of the campaign: 'However firm and stout pill-boxes you may build at the beach, they will be destroyed by bombardment of main armament of the battleships. Power of the American warships and aircraft makes every landing operation possible to whatever beachhead they like.'[56]

Both British and American doctrines worked. American doctrine, however, offered the best chance of achieving objectives and reducing casualties in an assault against a deliberate defense. British doctrine was not designed to fight a deliberate defense; it won battles primarily with manpower. American doctrine won battles mainly with fire-power. The British lack of resources mitigated against the development of a firepower-based doctrine, and British traditions exerted considerable influence. American resources and thinking caused the British to rethink their doctrine, and in 1944, a new approach was attempted. American doctrine could not be directly applied to the war in Europe; modifications were required. Admiral H. Kent Hewitt of the U.S. Navy undertook the task of adapting Marine Corps doctrine to the Mediterranean and European theaters.

3
Joint and Combined Amphibious Doctrine

The success of a landing depends on three primary factors: (a) The ability of the attacker to land and to overcome the initial beach defense; (b) the ability to support the forces which have been landed; and (c) the ability to maintain the attacking forces in strength superior to anything the enemy can bring against them. This last assumes particular importance in a continental landing against a strong land power, since the attacker must be able, by sea, to build up his force at a more rapid rate than the defender, by land, can bring up opposing force.

Admiral H. Kent Hewitt

In World War II, the Anglo-American team never achieved synergy in the conduct of combined, joint amphibious operations.[1] The operations in North Africa, Sicily, Italy, and Normandy failed to maximize the combat power available. Instead, when faced with strong opposition, the Allies improvised the necessary combat power under emergency conditions in which the landing force faced the threat of defeat. This was the case at Sicily, Salerno, and Omaha Beach. To explain the inability of the armed forces of the United Kingdom and the United States to maximize the combat power of the resources available, the following must be understood. First, doctrine for the conduct of amphibious operations was in its infancy when World War II began. Many lessons had to be learned at places such as Dieppe and Tarawa, and the Anglo-American armies and navies did not always agree on exactly what lessons were most important. Second, the armed forces of the United States possessed no body of experience and knowledge in the conduct of joint operations in 1942. Third, the cultures of the army and navy were significantly different, and each service was unwilling to yield to the superior knowledge of the other service in a particular field. Thus, the army in 1942 started constructing its own amphibious training centers and building its own small-boat navy. Fourth, operations in the Mediterranean were not simply joint operations; they were also combined operations. British practices and traditions of war did not merge well with those of the United States. Fifth, unity of command was never established at the important operational level of war. The presence of a supreme commander at the strategic level of war did not guarantee unity of command in campaigns and battles. The resources of the army, navy, and air force of both nations were never under the command of a single operational commander. And sixth, nationalism and egos damaged the ability of the Allies to generate the quality and quantity of combat power that was possible. Still, even with all of these impediments, one might have expected a more steeply sloped learning curve after two years of planning, training, and fighting together.

JOINT OPERATIONS

Joint operations, that is, operations involving more than one service, in World War II typically meant amphibious operations; however, amphibious operations were not always joint operations. Amphibious operations in the Central Pacific frequently involved air, sea, and land forces belonging exclusively to the navy. The navy had its own ground force and air force and had command and control of all of the resources necessary to conduct modern warfare. Although the Marine Corps was too small to conduct certain operations in the Pacific and thus required army forces, the navy in the Central Pacific enjoyed greater command and control of all of the forces necessary to conduct an operation than did army and navy commands in the Mediterranean and European theaters.

Joint amphibious operations in the Mediterranean and European theaters required co-operation among the military, naval, and air force commanders at all levels − strategic, operational, and tactical. Admiral Alan G. Kirk in his action report on the Normandy invasion wrote:

> A firm tradition of mutual trust and confidence now exists, but this record could easily be marred in special instances by the personal incompatibility of two commanders of different services. There is no effective guarantee of success − it takes one to command and two to cooperate; and the existence at a remotely high level of a supreme commander cannot ensure co-operation against the will of subordinates.[2]

Co-operation and mutual trust were obtained only through experience. Only by working, training, and fighting together could the military and naval cultures and the emerging air force culture be merged into a successful joint command. The actual lines of authority among the services were sometimes unwritten. They changed with every major operation, and they were subject to appeal to a higher authority from another service.

U.S. amphibious doctrine placed command and control of amphibious operations in the hands of the navy. The naval task force commander fought the initial battle for the beaches. The task force consisted of the amphibious forces, which included assault forces, transport ships, landing craft, and naval gunfire support ships. The naval task force commander did not command or control the air power employed and had only a very limited capability to communicate with the Army Air Force. In regard to the employment of air power at Sicily, Admiral Hewitt wrote:

> All air support was to be under the command of the Air Commander in Chief with headquarters in Tunis. There were to be no air units, other than the cruiser observation planes, under the direct control of the tactical commander in the actual operating area, as had been the case with the naval air supporting the landings in Morocco.'[3]

In North Africa, Hewitt had air support from American carriers. According to Hewitt, the problem of air power was also of concern to the army:

> General Patton, mindful of our experiences at Casablanca, repeatedly urged me to secure naval air support. While I realized as much as he the advantage of having tactical air under my immediate control, I did not feel justified in asking for carrier support, considering the proximity for land air fields and the urgent need for carriers at that time in the Pacific.

Problems of command and control were not restricted to the air force. During the assault at Sicily, Lieutenant General George Patton ordered the landing of his floating reserve without consulting Hewitt.[4] The naval commander responsible for landing the force would not proceed until he received orders from Hewitt. The misdirection of orders resulted in delay and confusion.

The armed forces of the United States in the Mediterranean and European theaters violated the principle of unity of command. According to this principle, all resources, naval, air, and ground, should be placed under the command of the individual charged with conducting the operation. That individual should then develop a coherent vision that integrated and synchronized the various strengths of the three services. This meant that the U.S. Army Air Forces and

U.S. Army Ground Forces would be trained and led by a navy officer. The army and air force were incapable of submitting to such a command relationship. They were unable to subordinate themselves to the navy. As Kirk noted, instead of commanding the forces of the other services, the commander had to seek co-operation. Co-operation required compromise, and compromise distorted the vision of the amphibious force commanders.

It is too easy to argue that the armed forces of the United States were unable to work together to produce synergy because of each service's selfish concerns. It is probably more accurate to recognize the significance of the historical evolution of the military and naval cultures. Both cultures evolved over almost two centuries of service to the nation. However, throughout most of its history, the United States has been a continental power, not a naval power. Thus, during the first hundred years of the nation's existence, the dominant culture in war was the military culture. At the end of the nineteenth century, as American energy pushed into the Pacific, the naval culture rose in prominence to rival that of the military culture. At the start of World War II, the United States possessed two cultures with relatively equal strength, vigor, and clout but with different principles, values, traditions, and tenets of war.

In order for armed forces, whether military or naval, to call themselves professionals, they must be effective against the professional armed forces of other nations. The test of the professionalism of armed forces is war.[5] Each service obeyed certain principles, imbued certain values and ethics, and operated under tenets of war particular to a given environment, land, sea, or air. The cultures of the two senior services were thus based on the exigencies of war. The approaches to battles and campaigns were, in part, a function of cultural learning, and because the two services evolved so differently over their histories, they were unable to communicate clearly when they were required to work together. This explains in part why the army in the Mediterranean and European theaters never developed the trust in naval gunfire that the Marine Corps in the Pacific developed. This also explains in part why the army was resistant to turning over amphibious training completely to the navy and initially sought to build its own navy for the conduct of amphibious operations.[6] Because of this distrust, naval amphibious force commanders never enjoyed the level of command and control over operations that amphibious force commanders in the Pacific theater expected and received. And the emergence of a separate air force culture helps explains why the air force was so reluctant to provide close air support or to permit the supreme Allied commander to command its heavy bomber forces. Admiral John Lesslie Hall, who had the unique experience of having commanded amphibious forces in three theaters, the Mediterranean, European, and Central Pacific, wrote:

> I would say that never in my experience in the Mediterranean and in the United Kingdom did we ever approach the efficiency of joint command that existed in the Central Pacific... The U.S. Army Air Force was never willing to be under our command. They just cooperated, and in my opinion any system that doesn't let the fellow who's responsible for winning the battle either ashore or afloat have the aircraft under his command is just like a man trying to fight without his right hand.[7]

Hall also noted that he had difficulty gaining control of amphibious training in North Africa after the invasion, Operation Torch. In fact, Eisenhower refused his request to be assigned command of the army's amphibious warfare training center. Hall wrote:

> During these months from February to July, we started training with the troops for these assaults in Sicily. It was a very interesting time. Gradually we were able to take over this amphibious training base and let them [the army] realize that it was a naval responsibility until we could get the troops firmly established on enemy shores where they could fight. Those decisions and those organizations were arrived at the hard way. Thank God, the United States has gotten past that. We know more about joint command and how to train officers for joint command... But it took a major conflict to force this.[8]

Hall's optimism about the state of joint operations was an acknowledgment that through working, training, and fighting together, the two senior services developed a degree of familiarity and trust that permitted a higher level of professionalism in joint operations. However, this trust was based primarily on personal relationships – friendships developed over time – hence, with the transfer of personnel or the arrival of a new commander, the trust established between the two services was lost. Hall agreed with Kirk that after many difficult years of operating together in the Mediterranean, the army and navy had developed some degree of consensus on the conduct of operations. The two services at the operational level had grown to think more alike, but important differences remained until the end of the war. This development did not take place at the strategic level.

In Washington, where decisions on the allocation of resources were made, the culturally imbued predispositions of senior service leaders influenced operations. The preference for certain types of operations tended to push resources in one direction or another. Hall wrote: 'I'd say we were second fiddle. I'd say the Pacific was the pet of the Navy Department and I'm sure I'm right about that. I don't think it [the Normandy invasion] was uppermost in the heart of Admiral King and the Navy Department.'[9] The predispositions of the Navy Department translated into real military resources, real combat power, being directed into a particular theater of war.

ADMIRAL H. KENT HEWITT

Admiral Hewitt, as the commander of the amphibious force, Atlantic fleet, in the early years of the war was the man most responsible for adapting British amphibious doctrine to American practices and force structure. And later, as the commander of American amphibious forces in the Mediterranean theater, he was the individual most responsible for the evolution of the joint, combined amphibious doctrine. He advanced an amphibious doctrine that was different in significant ways from that employed in the Mediterranean by the Anglo-

American armies, but he was unsuccessful in convincing the commanding generals to adopt his vision. This failure cost many lives.

Hewitt was one of the most highly regarded American naval officers in the Mediterranean and European theaters in World War II. By virtue of his training, experience, study, and accomplishments, he was the smartest man in the Anglo-American navies in the conduct of amphibious operations. He commanded forces in every major landing in the Mediterranean, including Operation Torch in North Africa; Operation Husky in Sicily; Operation Avalanche in Italy; and Operation Anvil/Dragoon in the south of France. Hewitt put more men ashore on hostile ground than any other commander – army, navy, or marine – in World War II. And although he did not command during the Normandy invasion, he had trained both of the senior naval commanders who carried out the operation, Admirals Alan G. Kirk, commander of the Western Naval Task Force, and John Lesslie Hall, commander of Force 'O.' Both men served under Hewitt in the campaigns in the Mediterranean. Despite Hewitt's accomplishments, his name is unknown to most Americans because it has been neglected by historians. No book-length biography of Hewitt exists.

Henry Kent Hewitt was born on 11 February 1887 in Hackensack, New Jersey, the son of Robert Anderson and Mary Kent Hewitt. He entered the U.S. Naval Academy on 29 June 1903 and graduated on 12 September 1906, having received an accelerated pass in order to join the 'Great White Fleet,' which lacked junior officers. His first assignment was on the battleship USS *Missouri,* where he served for three years, during which time he was commissioned ensign in September 1908. On the *Missouri,* he participated in the cruise around the world with the sixteen battleships of the U.S. Atlantic Fleet (1907–9). He subsequently served on the battleships *Connecticut* and *Florida* and the destroyer *Flusser.* While serving on the *Flusser,* Hewitt was promoted to lieutenant (junior grade) in September 1911. In August 1913, Hewitt married Florida Hunt of San Francisco; they had two daughters, Floride Hunt (1915) and Mary Kent (1923). In October 1913, Hewitt took a post at the U.S. Naval Academy in the mathematics department. That December, he was promoted to lieutenant.

In July 1916, Hewitt received his first command, the converted yacht USS *Eagle*. The *Eagle's* first mission under Hewitt's command was to survey areas in the Caribbean. In February 1917, a revolution broke out in Cuba, and the *Eagle* was ordered to protect American lives and property on the island. The ship was very poorly armed and possessed little ability to influence the situation. During this affair, Hewitt displayed the ability to negotiate under difficult circumstances, bluff when he had a poor hand, and focus on achieving objectives no matter what the situation.[10] In the last year of the 'Great War,' Hewitt commanded the destroyer *Cummings,* receiving a temporary promotion to commander. His ship escorted convoys across the Atlantic and patrolled for submarines. After the war, Hewitt returned to the Naval Academy, this time in the Department of Electrical Engineering and Physics.

In 1921, Hewitt was assigned as the gunnery officer on the USS *Pennsylvania*. The ship's captain had recently been relieved because of an unsatisfactory report after an admiral's inspection and failure to qualify in a short-range battle practice. The ship had a poor reputation and, in Hewitt's words, was 'in pretty bad shape.' Hewitt quickly became an expert in naval gunfire, demonstrating time and again his proficiency in the skill that dominated naval thinking at the time. On 5 July 1923, the *Pennsylvania* won the battle-efficiency pennant, enhancing Hewitt's reputation. His success in this position earned him the assignment as head of the Gunnery Section of the Division of Fleet Training in the Office of the Chief of Naval Operations in July 1923 and gunnery officer and aide to the commander, Battleship Divisions, Battle Force, in 1926. In 1924, Hewitt gave a lecture at the Naval War College on naval gunfire, an indication of his professional standing. Hewitt's service with battleships as gunnery officer and his subsequent assignments gave him an understanding and appreciation of the capabilities of naval gunfire that served him well in World War II.

In July 1928, Hewitt was ordered to take the senior course at the Naval War College. Upon completion of the course, he served two years on the Naval War College staff. In June 1931, Hewitt assumed command of Destroyer Division Twelve, and a year later, he was promoted to captain. In July 1933, Hewitt again returned to the Naval Academy, this time as head of the Department of Mathematics. Leo Bachman, an instructor in the department, recalled Hewitt: 'One of the first impressions I had... was his accessibility and his understanding, as well as his complete willingness to consider new ideas.'[11]

In March 1936, Hewitt took command of the heavy cruiser USS *Indianapolis*. While under his command, the ship received the honor of transporting the president of the United States to the Pan-American Conference at Buenos Aires. On 18 November, Hewitt welcomed President Franklin D. Roosevelt on board. Throughout the cruise, the president called Hewitt 'Skipper.' After the cruise, Roosevelt wrote Hewitt a letter that became part of his official record. The letter stated: 'Now that my recent visit to South America is at an end, I retain nothing but the utmost esteem for the fine performance of that vessel so ably commanded by yourself. During the cruise, the ship met every detail of the itinerary with precision and to my complete satisfaction.' Later Hewitt commented: 'It was indeed something to have the head of the nation on board one's ship, and to feel the responsibility for his safety.'[12]

In December 1939, Hewitt was selected for the rank of rear admiral and shortly thereafter was given command of Cruiser Division Eight. By this time, the war was on in Europe, and in 1941, Hewitt was ordered to transfer his division from the Pacific Fleet to the Atlantic Fleet. The Atlantic Fleet was conducting neutrality and convoy-escort patrols to and from the British Isles. Hewitt's task force took part in these operations until the Japanese attacked Pearl Harbor on 7 December 1941 and the United States entered the war.

After the war, Hewitt took part in the Pearl Harbor investigation and commanded the U.S. Twelfth Fleet (U.S. Naval Forces Europe). He retired from the navy a full admiral in March 1949, after more than forty years of service. He died in Middlebury, Vermont, on 15 September 1972.

Hewitt was highly regarded by everyone with whom he served. He was an officer of the highest caliber, but perhaps he could have served his nation and the men under his command better if he had been less cooperative and more combative in advancing his ideas about amphibious doctrine. Hewitt conducted amphibious operations in accordance with the doctrine advanced by the generals of the Anglo-American armies – a doctrine he knew failed to maximize the combat power available. In 1942, 1943, and 1944, Hewitt had a better understanding of amphibious warfare than the generals whose orders he followed. Of Hewitt, Samuel E. Morison, who knew him personally, wrote:

> In amphibious experience he was surpassed by none and equaled by few. And he had qualities of mind and heart that especially fitted him for this particular position; the tact necessary to deal with the French, on whose soil the Allied forces were based; with the Royal Navy, accustomed to supremacy in the Mediterranean; and with the Allied armies and air forces which, in this theater of war, called the tunes.[13]

Had Hewitt been more successful in advancing his approach to amphibious warfare, lives could have been saved at Salerno and Normandy. Not until the invasion of the south of France, the last major amphibious operation in the European and Mediterranean theaters, were landings conducted according to Hewitt's vision.

AMPHIBIOUS FORCE, ATLANTIC FLEET

The evolution of Anglo-American combined amphibious doctrine commenced when Hewitt took command of the U.S. Navy Amphibious Force, Atlantic Fleet (AFAF). In August 1941, Admiral Ernest J. King ordered Hewitt and other flag officers to New River, North Carolina, to witness an amphibious training exercise. Hewitt observed the exercise from the observation plane of his cruiser. He later noted: 'After the beach landing was completed, I joined General Smith in his headquarters ashore to observe the purely military part of the exercise. It was all most interesting and rewarding. And while I was certain of the future probability of such operations, I little realized what was to be my own close connection with them.'[14]

In April 1942, Hewitt assumed command of the AFAF from Admiral Roland E. Brainard. The AFAF was a newly created command, activated in February on the orders of Admiral King. King knew it would be necessary to develop a more significant offensive amphibious warfare capability and to train large forces to conduct these operations. Hewitt later recalled the mission of his command:

> Our mission was the preparation of training and also planning. The amphibious training involved not only the training of the transports and the landing craft that had already been assigned to us but training of officers and crews for large numbers of large landing ships and craft – the LSTs and the LCTs and the LCILs. That was the naval training end of it. Then we had to carry out military training of troops in amphibious landings and all the necessary joint training of shore parties – involving, for instance, navy beach battalions, naval beach master units.., army engineer units..., [and] army and naval communication [units].[15]

After more than thirty years of service, this naval officer – and the vast majority of other naval officers – had not conducted one joint exercise with the U.S. Army. Hewitt had no experience in working with the army, and most army officers had no experience in working with the navy. Now Hewitt was charged with producing combat-ready army and navy amphibious forces for deployment in an operation of considerable strategic importance to the Allied nations. This was no small task.

Hewitt possessed several character traits that helped him succeed in his new position, for which he had no training. He was a fast learner and willing to listen, and his ego did not prevent him from learning from subordinates. Hewitt was willing to exploit the talents of those available to him and to ask for assistance and advice. He was mission-oriented and possessed an unusual ability to get along with others and make things work. He was also a good teacher and knew how to get his ideas across in ways that maximized understanding. These abilities helped Hewitt succeed and communicate effectively with the army.

Hewitt also had the advantage of having worked with General Holland M. Smith of the Marine Corps for a brief period before Smith departed for the Pacific. Smith commanded the Amphibious Corps, a training command that consisted of an army division and a marine division and fell under the command of the AFAF. Smith provided Hewitt with principles that would serve him well in the years to come. Hewitt observed: 'I was very happy to have the initial assistance of Smith and his staff with all their knowledge of the amphibious work they'd done, and the general principles they had laid out from their previous experience were something I followed throughout after that.'[16] Hewitt was one of the few admirals who made a positive impression on the irascible marine general. Smith stated:

> Rear Admiral Hewitt was outstanding as directing head of the new enterprise. While he came to us with little background in amphibious training, he applied himself earnestly to our particular problems and made rapid progress. He was intelligent, sympathetic and willing to accept recommendations. Our relationship was pleasant and "all hands" were happy.[17]

Upon taking command, Hewitt established a joint staff. He persuaded the War Department to assign army personnel to his staff and then reorganized the staff to enable it to better communicate with the army. Hewitt's staff adopted the army's system of functional area specialties, that is, G-1, Personnel; G-2, Intelligence; G-3, Operations, Plans, and Training; and G-4, Supply and Logistics.

Early in June 1942, King ordered Hewitt to report to him immediately. At the meeting, Hewitt was introduced to Admiral Lord Louis Mountbatten, commander of the British Combined Operations Command. Mountbatten was seeking a talented officer to teach the British approach to amphibious warfare – an officer who could return to England with him and receive an education in the British way of war. Mountbatten recorded his initial impressions of Hewitt: 'I came into the room followed closely by a fat, bedraggled figure in khaki, with a shirt covered with dust that I saw to my astonishment had two stars on his collar. He [King] turned around and said, ... "[H]ere you are Admiral, take him with you." This was Admiral Hewitt.'[18] Mountbatten soon developed a great respect for this bedraggled figure. In reference to Hewitt's trip to the United Kingdom, Mountbatten stated:

> Well of course when he came over, he immediately enchanted every-body by his enthusiasm, his desire to fit in with us, he listened to everything, if a young Lt. Commander knew more than him about the job he'd come [and] tell me all about it and everyone went out of their way to help him. They'd [Hewitt and his staff] come over to learn in 3 weeks how to set up a counterpart to my organization to train [the] American Navy. Admiral Hewitt went back to the states where he in fact did miracles in setting up his organization. He made history and he saved the honor of the American Navy.

Hewitt quickly grasped the problems inherent in amphibious warfare, but until he gained experience in actual operations, he could not refine his vision or argue for a particular doctrine.

During the 1930s, the army conducted a number of amphibious train-ing exercises with the navy and Marine Corps, but no base of experi-ence was developed that would facilitate the war effort, and the training value that was received was lost over the long periods between exer-cises. The army did not start training and thinking about amphibious warfare in earnest until 1941. That year, the army's 1st and 9th IDs and the 1st Marine Division, under the direction of Major General Smith, conducted amphibious training in the Caribbean and at New River, North Carolina. The army's 2nd Armor Division, then commanded by General Patton, and 3rd ID also received training under the navy's Amphibious Corps. These were the units that were deployed in Operation Torch in North Africa. The army's experiences in working with the navy and Marine Corps did not persuade it that the Marine Corps doctrine was the best solution to amphibious warfare.

In the summer of 1941, the army was willing to provide the navy with the facilities and resources needed to train army units in amphibious warfare. Army observers monitored the progress of units and the effectiveness of the training. The War Department initially did not question the navy's jurisdiction over amphibious operations and training. However, by late 1941, the army was growing increasingly dissatisfied and distrustful of navy-sponsored amphibious training. In a memorandum to General Marshall on 29 October 1941, General H. J. Malony noted that joint training operations had failed to achieve the desired level of proficiency because of lack of planning and co-ordination, lack of experience, complicated channels of command, and inadequate time for army units to prepare. The slow pace of training, the lack of professionalism, and the small scale of the navy's operations were also causes of dissatisfaction. A report by General Smith on an exercise conducted in January 1942 by the 1st ID brought these problems to the attention of General Marshall:

> The late change of locale... made adequate preparation impossible with the result that the 'excellent plans' of the 1st Division miscarried; the Navy failed to provide suitable transport or adequate combatant vessels and aircraft; combat vessels had not practiced shore bombardment in the past year; naval aircraft were untrained for co-operation with ground troops; and the Navy failed to land troops on designated beaches, so that the ship-to-shore movement was 'from a tactical viewpoint, a complete failure.'[19]

The War Department also had the report of Major General D.C. Cubbison, commanding general of the 1st ID. The report stated:

> The landing was termed 'unsuccessful' by Director Headquarters, by advance mimeograph notice to umpires, date 11 January 1942 (day before). This decision having been based on insufficient naval gunfire and air support, and inadequacy of landing force. However, for purpose of training personnel, the maneuver was to continue...

Unfortunately, the landing of the first waves was faulty in the extreme because the Navy landed troops on the wrong beaches and most seriously crossed two of the battalions. This might well have been fatal in a real operation...

The action of Blue Naval aviators in attacking the Marine Battalion as it was effecting its landing was a capital error whose seriousness could hardly be overemphasized. Taken in conjunction with the faulty landing mentioned above, this action would almost certainly have ruined the landing despite the best plan that could have been devised.[20]

The War Department was also apprised of a difference of opinion between the navy and the Marine Corps over command and control of amphibious operations. A memorandum that summarized Smith's final report on the operation stated: '[General Smith's report] contains a frank criticism of Naval command, constitutes a powerful indictment of the theory and practice of Joint Action, and makes concrete recommendations for unity of command under the Commander of the Landing Force.'[21] The army was naturally inclined to accept Smith's opinion on the issue of command and control. Smith, however, had an agenda of his own. He believed the Marine Corps should be a separate service, even though it was the navy's need for advanced bases that had given the Marine Corps a unique purpose.[22] Smith was highly critical of navy leadership in amphibious operations.

In April 1942, a memorandum prepared by Lieutenant Colonel Floyd L. Parks, who had studied the navy's amphibious training program, delineated a number of significant problems. Parks noted that the navy's training was 'unwieldy, ineffective, and dangerous' and that 'planning, preparation, and training for amphibious operations up to that time had been so deficient that a real operation against a competent enemy could end only in disaster for American forces.' He further stated that '[t]he prevailing Army-Marine amphibious set-up was unsound because only the Army had both the means and the grasp of the problem to plan, prepare, and train the necessary ground forces for joint amphibious operations on the scale envisaged.' Parks recommended that the army abandon its joint amphibious training and 'be charged with the planning, preparation, and training for large-scale amphibious operations; and that the Navy and Marine Corps assist the Army only in procurement of the necessary shipping, landing craft, and special equipment, and with... technical advice and co-operation.'[23]

The result of the army's initial wartime experience with joint operations was the assessment that the army could do it better alone. The General Headquarters, later the Army Ground Forces, under the command of Lieutenant General Lesley J. McNair, thus recommended to General Marshall that the army establish its own amphibious training center.[24]

In April 1942, the navy acknowledged that it was not prepared to train army personnel on the scale required for the conduct of operations in the Mediterranean and European theaters.[25] Hewitt wrote:

> Unfortunately, when the business [of amphibious training] first came up I think the Army wanted the Navy to handle the whole thing but the chief of personnel at that time said he couldn't get personnel enough, so the Army was forced to start some of that on their own.[26]

In the navy's view, this was a temporary measure, and the agreement between the two services noted that the army was assuming responsibility for shore-to-shore amphibious operations and that the navy retained responsibility for ship-to-shore amphibious operations. This part of the agreement, however, was superficial since neither service had the resources in manpower, time, and equipment to make such distinctions. Whatever resources were available were deployed. Hewitt's impression was that

> [t]here was some objection on the part of some of the Army authorities to giving the Navy charge of the amphibious training. The Army seemed to think they should run some of the training themselves and they were a little slow to see what teamwork was required and the absolute necessity of training units jointly, and also the logic of giving that training to the Navy which had to do the actual landing.[27]

In June 1942, the Army Ground Forces established its first Amphibious Training Center at Camp Edwards, Massachusetts. Its mission was:

> to develop the proper organization, equipment, and technique and to whip the first units into shape as operating units capable of success-fully landing troops on enemy shores and then unloading supplies and reinforcements to keep them there… [And] to get amphibian units ready for combined training with infantry divisions and to go over-seas to their combat assignments.[28]

The Army Corps of Engineers was given responsibility for establish-ing the center and developing training, doctrine, and technology. Colonel Daniel Noce was given command of the center. Noce assem-bled a training team made up of individuals from four services – the army, coast guard, navy, and Marine Corps. Noce's task was described as follows:

> to take raw men, in brigade groups, and teach them how to convey fully equipped combat forces to an enemy shore, land them, establish their beachhead supply dumps and communications, and maintain the flow, inland, of the materials and replacements they need to go forward with invasion. And to do this training job quickly.

The *Marine Corps Gazette* reported the experience and assets Noce brought to the task:

> General Noce had several assets to count on. Behind him were three years of experience managing all sorts of small boats in flood-control work on the Mississippi. The river had been a tough adversary to practice on. Behind him also was a successful experiment, back in 1934, in turning raw recruits into skilled soldiers in three months. He had then learned it could be done. At his side was an imaginative Chief of Staff, Colonel Arthur Trudeau, who combed the other armies of the world for precedents on which to base the training

procedure. And before him lay a pool of recruits that included a great many men with experience in running boats or with skill in handling engines and other machinery.[29]

In fact, Noce's experiences on the Mississippi did not prepare him to lead the army's amphibious warfare efforts. Many navy officers knew Noce was in over his head and had a grim view of Noce and his conception of amphibious operations. In a letter to Hewitt, Admiral H. R. Stark, commander of U.S. naval forces in Europe, wrote:

> I am much interested in the developments in your territory and I am wondering what people of ours you are to have with you. I hope they are the best. I regret that General Devers has on his staff anyone like General Noce, who is most dangerous, due to his assumption that he is an amphibious expert. 'A little knowledge is a dangerous thing.' Unfortunately, he passed through this area and did considerable harm, which we had difficulty in correcting... [T]his officer has made a great reputation with the Army and has even been given the Distinguished Service Medal for his development of amphibious training. The pamphlets which he has written are highly elementary and he apparently has no real concept of the actual problems involved in larger landings, which we have now carried out twice.[30]

Stark's final words were in fact true of many army officers involved in the development and conduct of army amphibious operations. Their newness to this task and lack of joint training and experience stymied the development of methods that saved lives and effectively achieved objectives.

On 10 September 1942, the army's second Amphibious Training Center commenced operations at a new facility on the Gulf Coast of Florida, Camp Gordon Johnston. The Florida site was selected because of the ability to train year-round there (winter restricted training at Camp Edwards), the quality of the coastline, and access to offshore islands for use in conducting amphibious training. The camp was commanded by Brigadier General Frank Keating. The army's

1946 study of Amphibious Training Centers described the Florida center: 'The story was the same from start to finish of the Amphibious Training Center – bickering and indecision in higher headquarters; expansion of the training mission and objectives without corresponding expansion of facilities; and attempts on the part of the Center to accomplish its mission with whatever means could be made available. Improvisation and plain Yankee ingenuity frequently saved the day.[31] Both army Amphibious Training Centers suffered from shortages of all types, including trained personnel, landing craft, and other equipment. Successful training was improvised.[32]

Between January and March 1943, General Omar Bradley trained his 28th ID in amphibious operations at Camp Gordon Johnston. He later recorded his impressions:

> Camp Gordon Johnston was the most miserable Army installation I had seen since my days in Yuma, Arizona, ages past. It had been hacked out of palmetto scrub along a bleak stretch of beach. We were forced to scatter our three infantry regiments miles apart and thus could never train as a complete division. Moreover, it was bitterly cold in the northern leg of Florida. Every training exercise in the landing craft was a numbing experience. The man who selected that site should have been court-martialed for stupidity.[33]

Camp Gordon Johnston gave Bradley his first experience in amphibious training.[34] The U.S. 4th ID, which was later to land at Utah Beach, also received its initial amphibious training at Camp Gordon Johnston.

The navy was never satisfied with the army's assumption of responsibilities for amphibious training. A competition for resources developed between the army's and navy's training centers. Throughout the war, the navy would claim jurisdiction over all amphibious operations, but at various stages, it would be unable to fulfill all requirements and would have to make new agreements with the army. Thus, the army lacked experience and know-how, but the navy lacked manpower and resources. This was the case in early 1942, in the spring of 1944, and in the closing days of the war. The clearing of minefields and obstacles at Omaha Beach was an example. The navy did not have sufficient numbers of trained personnel to clear obstacles and minefields up to the high-water mark, and late in the day, the army engineers took on the responsibility. The navy, however, had better ideas on how the task could best be performed but was unable to convince the army of the correctness of its views. Agreements on responsibilities for various aspects of the invasion were renegotiated for every major landing. As the war progressed and navy resources and proficiency in amphibious operations increased, the navy reclaimed jurisdiction over many aspects of amphibious operations and training. However, not until Operation Anvil/Dragoon in August 1944, the invasion of the south of France, would an amphibious operation be conducted in accordance with the navy doctrine advanced by Hewitt.

After the invasion of North Africa, the navy finally convinced the army to turn over the training of boat crews to the navy.[35] In May 1943, the army recognized the navy as the primary agent of basic amphibious training in the United States, and in September, the Army Ground Forces turned over control of Camp Gordon Johnston to the Army Service Forces.[36]

OPERATION TORCH – NORTH AFRICA

In July 1942, the Allies decided to invade North Africa, and Hewitt was given command of the Western Naval Task Force, Task Force 34, which was to land an all-American corps in the vicinity of Casablanca in French Morocco. General George Patton commanded the army forces. The navy commanded the amphibious landing until the ground force commander established a functioning headquarters onshore.

On 8 November, the United States initiated its first significant military operation in the Mediterranean and European theaters. In the North Africa campaign, the mission was not to destroy the enemy. The

Allies hoped that the French would come over to their side without the exchange of fire, but if force was required, the Allies wanted to do as little damage as possible to French forces and French pride. American forces were given strict orders not to fire until fired upon. Thus, no pre-invasion bombardment was planned. The French did not give up, however, and the command for an all-out engagement, 'Play Ball,' was given. The landing was timed to occur at night under the cover of darkness to achieve complete surprise. Tactical surprise was achieved. Still, not until 11 November, three days after the landing, did the French agree to an armistice. During this period, naval gunfire was employed to knock out enemy artillery batteries, armored vehicles, fixed positions, and French warships. Nevertheless, some army commanders resisted the use of naval gunfire. In a report on Operation Torch, Hewitt wrote:

> The fire of the USS *Savannah* and fire support destroyers was effectively used against tanks, shore batteries and personnel. If some Army commanders had failed to appreciate the capabilities of Naval gunfire in supporting landing operations, their doubts were dispelled in this operation. The Army plan called for taking the KASBA Fort 'by the bayonet,' and naval gunfire on this objective was not requested. The delay incident to capture of the KASBA Fort and the coastal defense guns at MEHDIA might have been avoided by having the early support of naval gunfire on these targets.[37]

Hewitt was mistaken in his belief that army commanders gained an appreciation for the capabilities of naval gunfire in the North Africa campaign.

The operation in North Africa was not a real test of Anglo-American amphibious doctrine. Still, the army formed an opinion about the conduct of amphibious operations, the usefulness of naval gunfire, and the proficiency of the navy in amphibious warfare. A report to the commanding general of Allied forces on the lessons learned from Operation Torch, with the signature block of General Patton, stated:

Daylight landings are too costly and will be successful only against weak or no opposition[;] although landings before daylight entail much difficulty in loading landing boats and navigation to beaches, it assures surprise and reduces casualties... Naval gun fire should not be fired on pre-arranged time schedules except as a shore barrage previous to any troops landing. Naval gunfire missions should be 'on call' from naval gunfire support parties.[38]

The operation in North Africa established a pattern of night landings based on tactical surprise that was followed until 1944.

The landings in North Africa did not build trust between the army and navy. In fact, trust between the two services sank to a wartime low. The army did not trust the navy to get its forces to the assault beaches at the right time and place, lacked confidence in naval gunfire, and tended to depend on its own means in an assault.[39] A US Army memorandum on the amphibious operations in North Africa stated:

Army observers and commanders are strongly of the opinion that the Army must control and operate all landing craft; that the Army should take over complete control as soon as the ships arrive in the transport area. Landing craft were very badly handled. Navigation was particularly at fault. Many craft wandered aimlessly, unable to locate their objective. Others landed at the wrong beaches, sometimes as much as twelve miles from the proper place. It would appear that navigators lacked training, experience, equipment, and information essential for either dead reckoning or pilotage.[40]

The navy tended to believe the army was naive and that it overstepped its jurisdiction in joint operations and was too involved in business that should be exclusively the responsibility of the navy.

Through training, an organization can test and refine or reject its tactical doctrine. It can develop standard operational procedures, evaluate and improve battle drills, and build smooth, functioning teams.

Joint operational doctrine, however, typically cannot undergo the same quality of examination because strategic and operational resources are usually not employed in training, particularly during war. Strategic bombers and battleships could not be brought to infantry training facilities to work out and refine procedures and test doctrine. They were involved in real-world operations against the enemy.

Because of the numerous other problems associated with the movement from ship to shore, the army commenced its own training program for boat crews in North Africa. The navy again objected, and the struggle for control of the training for the invasion of Sicily duplicated that which had taken place in the United States prior to the invasion of North Africa. To correct training deficiencies identified in the assault and in subsequent combat operations and to prepare for the invasion of Sicily, the Fifth Army Invasion Training Center was established at Arzew, Algeria, in January 1943.[41] The center was commanded by Brigadier General John W. O'Daniel. O'Daniel had led the 168th Infantry RCT of the 34th ID in the invasion of North Africa, landing with the Eastern Task Force at Algiers. He worked closely with Hall, who was the commander of the Amphibious Force, Northwest African Waters, to train and prepare soldiers and sailors for the invasion of Sicily and to improve procedures and tactical doctrine. The friction between the army and navy over control of training was eventually smoothed out and the training proceeded efficiently.[42]

O'Daniel's operations were not confined to training in previously developed techniques. He and his staff sought to advance new techniques and doctrine.[43] O'Daniel had access to a wide range of army and navy specialists. Experiments in the breaching of beach and underwater obstacles, in technology and methods for unloading vehicles and supplies over the beach, in combat assaults, and in numerous other aspects of amphibious and ground combat were carried out. O'Daniel published a document that described the current thinking on the conduct of amphibious operations on 20 May 1943. This document represented another step in the evolution of U.S. Army-Navy tactical amphibious doctrine in the Mediterranean theater.

From the cumulative experience gained in various amphibious assaults, O'Daniel collected, analyzed, deduced, and delineated the fundamental principles for the conduct of amphibious assaults, given the basic tenets of British operational amphibious doctrine. The doctrine that O'Daniel set forth was based on data from Operation Torch, personal interviews with the leaders who conducted the landing, experimentation at the Invasion Training Center, and the work of a board of officers appointed to analyze the entire body of information collected. O'Daniel wrote:

> The Infantry Regiment as now organized provides an excellent nucleus for an assault landing team... [T]roops should be selected and attached to the Infantry Regiment to form the Combat Team for the particular operation. This combination should then be thoroughly trained as a team to the extent of living together, eating together and fighting together. Such a team might include Field Artillery, Combat Engineers, Medical Collecting Companies, Ranger Battalions or Detachments, Chemical Warfare Troops, Air Corps Support Parties, Anti-Aircraft, Tanks, boat operators of small landing craft and other attachments deemed necessary for a particular operation. All of these should, as the British say, 'Marry up' at the beginning of training for a period of six weeks before the operation.[44]

The regimental landing team (RLT) as conceptualized by O'Daniel and his staff became the basic unit for the assault against hostile shores. The RCTs that landed at Normandy were based on the concept described above. The mix of attached forces could be tailored to a specific operation. The goal was to produce cohesive, proficient teams through a brief, intensive period of training. O'Daniel's vision integrated ground, naval, and air forces. His fire support plan integrated close air and naval gunfire support. O'Daniel wanted to attach air force and navy officers to the regimental staff to assist in the co-ordination of close air and naval gunfire support.

O'Daniel pushed for the principle of unity of command: 'The three services: Army, Navy and Air, should definitely be unified under one command, for planning, training, and operation. In furtherance of this principle; one headquarters in which there is only ONE joint staff should be established.' O'Daniel advanced the following principles:

- Army, Navy, and Air personnel participating in this operation should be together on all planning and training for the operation.
- Any contemplated invasion should be predicated upon accurate and evaluated G-2 information...
- All ships and landing craft should be so loaded that the loss of one or more vessels will not deprive the landing force of any one type of essential troops, weapons, vehicles, or supplies...
- Any component of an assault force, no matter how small, should never be separated from its essential combat equipment.
- All elements of a RLT should be combat loaded.
- It is mandatory that the personnel participating in assault carry only the barest essentials necessary for combat, in food and clothing.
- The striking power of each succeeding wave in the assault should be greater than that of the preceding wave.
- When the assault forces have reached their objectives other troops should be immediately available to exploit the initial success.
- The assault unit should plan for at least 10 days supply combat loaded for the first 48 hours.

Operations:
- Invasions can best be made during the hours of darkness. A complete RLT should be on the beach before daylight.
- An RLT in general should not be required to land on more than two beaches.
- The RLT Commander should make the majority of decisions as to the loading and unloading of the ships assigned to his Landing Team.
- The assault teams of an invading force should be equipped with sufficient boats to land all personnel, equipment and vehicles without recourse to shuttling.

- All craft used in the assault operations, should be armored for protection against small arms fire.
- Troops specially selected and trained should be provided for 'Commando' type operations in conjunction with the main effort...
- The beach head should be adequately protected against enemy air and mechanized threats...
- Armored Divisions should be landed after the assault to exploit a breakthrough...
- Assault boats should be armed.

O'Daniel put forth sound principles, some of which were violated at Normandy. He believed that the mobility of the soldiers, which was inhibited by the task of wading through water, should not be further impeded by carrying unnecessary equipment and comfort items; that unit integrity should be maintained to increase combat effectiveness; that regimental commanders should decide which equipment to take and which to leave behind; and that all forces conducting the fight for a beach should be tactically deployed in LCVPs and combat loaded. At Normandy, the army had to compromise, and in doing so, it violated a number of established principles.

Each RLT was composed of one infantry regiment; one medical collecting company; one company of combat engineers; one field artillery battalion; one signal detachment; one engineer shore battalion; and one coast artillery battalion. Additional assets that could be deployed for specific situations included an engineer bridge company; an armored reconnaissance unit; a company of General Headquarters tanks; and a ranger battalion. The organization and equipment of the army changed slightly after the North Africa campaign to take advantage of the availability of larger, more powerful weapons.

Navy shore fire control parties were to be attached to each RLT to provide on-call naval gunfire. Hall and O'Daniel worked out a system of training that integrated army artillery officers and navy gunnery officers. Such liaison was also sought with the Army Air Force. The air force, however, was unwilling to support these efforts and even at Normandy was incapable of providing close air support to the ground forces.

The tactical doctrine delineated by O'Daniel called for two battalions of an RLT to land abreast. Each battalion would assault with two companies abreast consisting of three rifle platoons apiece at H-Hour. They would assault in LCAs (assault landing craft) and LCVPs. (LCAs and LCVPs were basically the same craft.) At H+3–10, the weapons platoon, company headquarters section, engineer shore company, medical squads, and assistant beachmasters and parties were to land. At H+30, battalion heavy weapons company, two engineer platoons with bulldozers, and field artillery and anti-aircraft artillery reconnaissance parties were to come ashore. At H+60, the regiment's reserve battalion was to commence landing in the same order, starting with three rifle platoons abreast from two assault companies. The sequence for the deployment of forces was not static and could be tailored for specific conditions and enemy situations, but this was the basic tactical organization used to fight amphibious battles for the remainder of the war.

Once the army established the sequence of the invasion and the mix of forces – infantry, armor, artillery, engineers, medics, and so on – the ships were loaded according to that assault matrix. The typical RCT with all of its support elements required fifty-four LCAs, ten LSTs, twelve LCTs, and twelve LCIs.

At Arzew, the U.S. Army and Navy conducted training that produced more proficient units and refined tactical doctrine. The army and navy that fought in Sicily were better organizations than those that fought in North Africa. Lieutenant Colonel Wiegan, commander of the 2nd Battalion, 179th Infantry, and veteran of the campaign in Sicily, recalled: 'Our training at the 5th Army Invasion Training Center in street-fighting and pill box reduction was excellent... The men got the feel of real fighting, and the technique was sound... All infantry units should get the sort of training we had at the 5th Army center.'

OPERATION HUSKY – SICILY

By July 1943, when the invasion of Sicily took place, Admiral Hewitt was convinced that the doctrine employed by the Anglo-American armies was flawed. He later recalled the operation in Sicily:

> The Army was still sticking to night landings in spite of experience in Sicily. They had decided in Sicily that naval bombardment was unsuitable to support troops, and the big defenses had to be knocked out as much as possible by air and that the landing had to be carried out during darkness so that troops would have the cover of darkness, using machine-gun fire and things like that. Then the naval bombardment might be used after that.[46]

Hewitt tried to change the army's concept for the conduct of amphibious assaults, but in the end, he failed. In his action report following the operation in Sicily, he took pains to explain to the army the flaws in its doctrine. He quoted army operation orders and underlined certain passages to point out the fallacies in army thinking. He went step-by-step as if he were explaining a mathematical problem to a young midshipman at the Naval Academy. Hewitt then launched into an extensive lecture on errors in army thinking. First, he highlighted certain points from a document prepared by Eisenhower's headquarters:

> The Appreciation of Force 141, ...the document upon which the Highest Echelon Outline Plan was based, stated:
> 72. To ensure the success of the seaborne assaults, it will be necessary first to neutralize the beach defenses, whether the assault is carried out in darkness, smoke or daylight. There are three possible methods of neutralization:
>
> (a) Naval bombardment.
> (b) Air bombardment.
> (c) Action by airborne troops.

It is considered that the number of ships available and the fact that *naval gun power is not designed for land bombardment make the use of (a) unsuitable.* The primary role of the air forces will be the destruction of enemy air power and therefore (b) will not be available. *Therefore it is essential that airborne troops be used to soften the defenses against which seaborne assaults will be made...*

76. (a) *Airborne troops are necessary to neutralize the beach defenses,* and their maximum employment is required.

(b) Seaborne assault should take place some two hours before first light.[47]

It seems almost inconceivable that a professional military organization would plan to neutralize a beach defense with airborne soldiers. Hewitt pointed out that to facilitate the airborne drop, a date for the landing was selected that provided significant moonlight for the paratroopers, but the moonlight negated the purpose of a night landing:

It will [be] noted in the Appreciation that the selected date would 'afford approach to the coastline the cover of darkness.' An examination of the Astronomical Data above will reveal no such darkness. On the contrary the assault forces were required to make the approach in a brilliant waxing moon which would not set until the vessels had hove-to in the Initial Transport Areas immediately under the coast defense guns of the enemy. These facts were well known to the naval planners who pointed out the fact that the moon phase selected was most unfavorable from naval considerations. The date, however, was not changed because it was reiterated that this phase was most favorable to dropping of the paratroops who were the only means available to 'neutralize the beach defenses opposing the seaborne assault' – 'the most vital part of the whole plan.'

Hewitt had volunteered the navy to do the softening up of the beach defenses: 'Since the softening of the beach defenses prior to the landing was so vital to the success of the whole plan, naval planners then proposed the employment of naval gunfire against the beach defenses.

This was not acceptable to the Army because it was stated 'surprise' was to be achieved in the assault.' Hewitt then outlined eleven reasons why 'surprise' probably would not be achieved: the increased tempo of Allied air attacks, the concentration of Allied landing craft in Tunisian ports, the fact that H-Hour required naval forces to approach within twenty-five miles of the Sicilian coast at twilight, and other factors. Hewitt concluded his analysis of the problems inherent in operations based on surprise by stating: '[T]he preservation of surprise was illusory. Under the circumstance existing, it was the naval viewpoint that surprise on the assault beaches was not feasible. It was, in fact, not necessary providing a proper employment were made to exploit the means available to us.' Hewitt concluded his lecture to the army by emphasizing the awesome power and flexibility of naval gunfire:

> The old-fashioned military concept that naval guns are unsuitable for shore bombardment needs revision. Modern naval guns in cruisers and destroyers are high angle guns capable of ranging on reverse slope targets far in the interior in support of seaborne landings. The firepower in the vessels assigned to gunfire support exceeded that of all the artillery landed in the 7th Army assault. Due to the mobility of these ships, it is possible to bring about a concentration of gunfire on a shore target with greater firepower than is possible with Army artillery... Thus there is available to the Army a mobile artillery concentration of tremendous power capable of being exploited to the advantage of the ground forces.

Tactical surprise was not achieved at Sicily. The convoys were spotted *en route* and attacked by enemy aircraft. An unfortunate incident occurred when several American transport planes flying over the fleet were mistaken for enemy aircraft and shot down. Hewitt believed this accident was caused by the refusal of the Army Air Force to participate in joint planning and the failure to establish a unified command. Neither the tactical nor the operational naval commander responsible for landing the force and fighting the initial battles for the beaches had control over air power. In the Sicily landing, Hewitt did not receive the air plan until his forces were at sea, giving him and his staff no chance to recommend changes.[48] The plan made no reference to naval or ground forces, and after Hewitt reviewed the plan, he could not transmit it to the other ships and landing craft in the fleet because it was necessary to maintain radio silence. The inability of the armed forces of the United States to effectively communicate at all levels had real costs in terms of men and material.

Still, the landing went well. In June, the coast of Sicily was defended by the Italian Sixth Army, which consisted of seven static divisions. Because these forces were of poor quality and low morale, they were incapable of stopping a landing. Their mission was to hold the advance until the main attack was revealed. Six mobile divisions, two high-quality German divisions and four Italian divisions, served as strategic reserves to counter-attack the landing force and push it back into the sea. At Gela, the U.S. 1st ID received the counter-attack of the highly regarded Hermann Göring Division, and naval gunfire took part in the battle. Hewitt wrote:

> It was here that the Seventh Army began to appreciate the true effectiveness of naval gunfire. In this, probably the first cruiser-tank battle, many tanks were destroyed by direct hits, and many others were put out of action by near misses. Dazed survivors, from the famed Herman Göring Division, taken prisoner, wondered what terrible new anti-tank weapon the Americans had. They had never experienced anything like the rapid fire of a 15-gun battery 6" cruiser, and they had no idea that what had hit them came from the sea.[49]

This demonstration of the capabilities of naval gunfire did not change the army's assessment of the correct employment of this weapon. In fact, it reinforced the army's thinking. The 1st ID fought the battle, the navy provided on-call fire support, and the battle was won. Army leaders paid little or no attention to Hewitt's strongly worded report. In Operation Avalanche, the invasion at Salerno, the Anglo-American generals again decided on a night landing to achieve tactical surprise with on-call naval gunfire support.

The invasion of Sicily was unprecedented in both the magnitude of the operation and the technology employed. Eight reinforced infantry divisions were landed almost simultaneously. This was a force larger than that deployed in the assault at Normandy. Over 2,500 vessels took part in the operation, the largest fleet ever assembled up to that time. New technology in the form of landing craft, ships, and amphibious trucks was employed. And the proficiency of both sailors and soldiers was considerably better than that exhibited in the North Africa landings. After the invasion of Sicily – after training, working, and fighting together in two landings – the two senior services had developed a functional relationship, but neither service was completely happy with the state of affairs.

The Sicily campaign was strategically a success. On 25 July 1943, King Victor Emmanuel III dismissed Mussolini from office. The king was now determined to get Italy out of the war. The campaign, however, was not a complete success. The Germans conducted an effective defend-and-delay campaign and evacuated both Italian and German forces. The Italians evacuated 62,000 soldiers, 227 vehicles, and 41 artillery pieces; the Germans evacuated 38,846 soldiers, 10,356 vehicles, and 14,949 tons of supplies.[50] By failing to complete the destruction of the enemy's army in Sicily, the Allies made their task in Italy considerably more difficult. The combat power of these forces was multiplied by the configuration of the Italian peninsula, which impeded efforts to isolate enemy forces. The battle for Italy was slow, arduous, and costly.

OPERATION AVALANCHE – SALERNO

On 9 September 1943, the U.S. 5th Army, under the command of General Mark Clark, invaded the continent of Europe. Admiral Hewitt commanded the landing force. Two corps, the British 10 Corps and the U.S. VI Corps, made the initial landing at 0330. The assaults were based on the same tenets followed in the campaigns in Sicily and North Africa. Surprise was not achieved. Hewitt wrote: 'By the same process of reasoning that led to the Allied selection of Salerno, the Germans deduced that was where the attack would come. Consequently, they were ready – and Salerno became the toughest of Mediterranean operations.'[51] At Salerno, the battle began at the water's edge. The enemy opposition exceeded that encountered in North Africa and Sicily. In the army's official history of World War II, Martin Blumenson estimated that the assault RCTs of the U.S. VI Corps fought two infantry companies of the 16th Panzer Division supported by tanks and six batteries of artillery. Blumenson, however, believed that surprise was achieved.[52] German forces had just recently taken over the coastal defense from the Italians, who only two days earlier had concluded an armistice with the Allies. The 16th Panzer Division was ordered to take over Italian defensive positions. The division was spread thin over a twenty-mile front and was not expecting an attack. Still, the beaches were identified as potential landing sites, German reconnaissance aircraft had spotted the departure of the fleet, German forces were there ready to defend, and a reserve battalion with good road communication was prepared to reinforce.

In the American sector, the decision was made to forgo even a short, preliminary bombardment in order to maximize surprise. The first four hours of the battle were fought without naval gunfire, artillery, or tank support. They were fought at close range with bazookas, grenades, machine guns, bayonets, anti-aircraft guns, and a few artillery pieces that made it ashore. The regimental history of the 141st Infantry recorded the battle:

> Pfc. Juan R. Padilla effectively used his rocket gun against the tanks... Pvt. Manuel C. Gonzalez, in closing in on a tank position, was observed by the enemy and shot through the legs. As he lay helpless to move, one of the tanks ran over him and killed him. Pvt. Harold B. Beaver scored a hit with his antitank grenade by slipping in close to an enemy tank. Pfc. Juan Pruitt placed his Browning automatic rifle on top of a stone wall and maintained a heavy volume of fire against the enemy, until his position was located by a German gunner who opened fire and killed him. Pvt. Ramon G. Gutierrez, although

wounded, moved forward, located an enemy machine gun and knifed the German gunner to death.[53]

These soldiers fought to halt a tank attack that threatened to split their line. Naval gunfire was not available in the early-morning hours of darkness, but at first light, efforts were made to bring fire on enemy positions. Communications, however, broke down, and the big guns of the navy remained silent. Around 0830, artillery and tanks started arriving on the beaches. Around 0900, communications were established with the naval gunfire support ships. Fifteen minutes later, the navy commenced fire: 'By noon the main tank assault on the southern beaches had been brought virtually to a standstill. Naval gunfire and fire from mortars and howitzers had helped to make the operation costly for the enemy, but to a large extent the battle had been fought by the infantrymen, using infantry weapons.'[54]

The landing was difficult but succeeded. By 13 September, the Germans had contained the landing and were threatening to drive a wedge between the British and American corps with an armor attack. The situation so concerned Clark that he considered evacuation. The army rushed in paratrooper and other forces to reinforce, the navy was augmented with additional British battleships, and the air force flew hundreds of sorties. The next two days were critical. The German counter-attack reached its maximum exertion but failed to split Allied forces. The counter-attack was halted, and with the assistance of Montgomery's Eighth Army, the 5th Army advanced to secure the port of Naples on 6 October. Hewitt concluded: 'Only naval gunfire, and air attacks prevented the German tank attack from reaching the shore.'[55]

At Gela in Sicily, Salerno, and Omaha Beach, soldiers heaped great praise on the naval gunfire vessels, going so far as to state that without them the battles would have been lost. The soldiers were extremely grateful for whatever fire support they could get. Naval gunfire saved a lot of lives, and had it been employed more effectively, it could have saved many more. But it is a mistake to argue that the battles would have been lost without naval gunfire. In World War II, American and

British soldiers demonstrated time and again the ability to improvise success from failed plans and to win in direct assaults on deliberate defenses.

Hewitt again wrote an action report that addressed the problems of attempting to achieve tactical surprise in a night landing:

> The Military concept that 'surprise' is essential to achieve a successful seaborne assault was again present in this operation. It was the view of the Army command that troops should land on the beaches by stealth under cover of darkness, and to this end preliminary bombardment of beaches should not be undertaken. This is basically contrary to the naval viewpoint where large forces are being landed over a wide front against prepared defenses.

Hewitt again listed the factors that militated against large convoys reaching assault beaches undetected. He pointed out the existence of enemy radar stations; the concentration of enemy submarines; the presence of Allied landing craft; the phase of the moon, which offered significant light; and numerous other factors. Hewitt observed that in the British sector, a brief fifteen-minute bombardment had preceded the landing and had produced 'noteworthy' results. He noted that the American soldiers of the 36th ID felt 'let down' because they were not provided with a pre-invasion bombardment. Hewitt concluded with another stern lecture for the army:

> The lesson learned in Sicily regarding the proper utilization of naval gunfire support in pre–H-Hour bombardments was re-emphasized at Salerno. One is led to the invariable conclusion that there exists within the Army a considerable lack of appreciation of the effectiveness of the naval gun and its proper employment in amphibious operations. The margin of success in the Salerno landing was carried by the naval gun. This undertaking had forcefully demonstrated that future operations against strongly defended coasts must scrap the outmoded concept of surprise. The coast defenses commanding the assault beaches must be selected as heavy bombing targets for several

days in advance of the landing. Any plan envisaging less than this is unsound.[56]

Hewitt understood that some level of surprise was necessary in an amphibious assault. He probably overstated his case in order to convince the army to change its doctrine and perhaps out of frustration. Admiral Kirk was in agreement with Hewitt. He too believed the battles for the beaches could best be won operationally – as opposed to tactically – with firepower provided from the air and the sea.[57]

Hewitt deserved great credit for the success of the invasion at Salerno. Admiral Sir Andrew Cunningham of the Royal Navy praised him and those under his command for the success of the landing:

> Operation AVALANCHE was the most ambitious amphibious operation so far launched. That it succeeded after many vicissitudes reflects great credit on Vice Admiral Hewitt, U.S.N., his subordinate Commanders and all those who served under them. That there were extremely anxious moments cannot be denied... I am proud to say, however, that throughout the operation, the Navies never faltered and carried out their tasks in accordance with the highest traditions of their services... More cannot be said.[58]

OPERATION ANVIL/DRAGOON – SOUTHERN FRANCE

The last major amphibious operation in the Mediterranean and European theaters was Operation Anvil/Dragoon, the invasion of the south of France on 15 August 1944. In this operation, Hewitt was finally able to implement his vision. In a narrative of his activities from March 1942 to April 1945, Hewitt stated: 'I might mention that at this time it was the first of these landings in which zero hour was made after daylight. This was in accordance with principle which we believe to be correct in that it gave opportunity to exert the full power of the naval artillery prior to the landing in breaking up the coast defenses and the beach defenses. It also permitted an opportunity for air bombing immediately prior to the landing.' Hewitt understood that operational surprise was necessary, but he did not believe that tactical surprise was needed: 'Air preparation for the landing had gone on for some five to ten days prior to the landing by heavy bombing at various points along the coast from the Sète area to Genoa. This area had to be covered in general so as not to point directly at the actual assault area.'[59] Hewitt realized that a five- to ten-day bombardment of the landing site, such as those employed in the Pacific, would compromise operational surprise:

> On the day immediately preceding the landing the actual landing area was concentrated upon. These operations were all successfully carried out and the three landing operations on D-Day were very carefully worked out so as to provide the minimum of interference between the naval artillery and air bombing and also to permit the maximum of destruction being placed on the critical targets in the area. As a result, it is believed... the assaults were carried out as planned with very little loss.[60]

The invasion beaches received sixteen hours of preparatory fire from naval and air sources.[61] By comparison, Omaha Beach received a mere thirty-minute bombardment. Had Hewitt's doctrine been employed at Normandy, it is safe to say that 'bloody Omaha' would have been less bloody. The conditions in the south of France were very different from those at Normandy and Omaha Beach, where the defense was stronger and obstacles covered the beach. Still, the principles Hewitt and the navy advocated were correct. Hewitt's action report for the invasion of southern France stated:

> Aerial bombing before and on D-Day and naval bombardment were so effective that by H Hour all major guns had been damaged and most of the coastal defense crew had deserted their posts, been put out of action, or were willing to expose themselves in order to man their guns properly. The success of pre-D-day pinpoint bombing was

so considerable that the anticipated threat from coastal defenses never materialized and was easily disposed of on D-Day by the closely co-ordinated naval and air attack.[62]

In the final major amphibious campaign of the war in Europe, Hewitt was able to put together a campaign that maximized the combat power of the army, navy, and air force – an operation that had synergy.

BRITISH AMPHIBIOUS DOCTRINE

Throughout 1942 and 1943, the army preferred to conduct night landings, accepting British amphibious doctrine. It believed it was essential to attain a high degree of surprise, and tactical surprise could best be achieved at night. Darkness diminished the effectiveness of enemy fire, provided some concealment for advancing soldiers, and confused the enemy as to the exact location of the landings. Darkness also provided a psychological advantage to the attackers and a disad-vantage to the defenders. The army, in its traditional approach to war, relied more on man than on machine. Army commanders knew they had to quickly overcome a significant disadvantage in firepower at the water's edge. Night provided the best chance for success if the army relied on its own means. The army chose to depend on its own resources to achieve victory and only called on the navy in difficult circumstances. The army did not trust the navy and refused to base success or failure on resources not under army control. Everyone recognized that co-ordination, communication, and navigation were more difficult at night, making missed landings and confusion unavoidable. Still, the army continued to believe that the advantages outweighed the disadvantages – at least until Normandy.

At the start of World War II, the United States did not possess joint doctrine for the employment of the armed forces or for command in the conduct of joint operations. Nevertheless, unified, strategic commands were established in both the European and Pacific theaters, commands that were given the authority to issue orders and directives and to control the operations of all services in a given geographical area. At the operational level, however, new agreements had to be worked out between the army and navy in every major joint operation that took place in the Mediterranean and European theaters from 1942 to 1944. (Years after the war, the system of unified command was institutionalized at both the strategic and the operational level, becoming a permanent part of the American system for the command and control of the armed forces.) At the start of World War II, the branches of the armed forces of the United States were distinct, separate institutions with different thinking, doctrine, equipment, and approaches to war. The fact that the air force was part of the army in World War II did not preclude it from developing and implementing its own doctrine and strategy for winning the war – strategic bombing.[63] The final product of joint service planning in World War II, the operations order, the specific plan of action, did not necessarily reflect the thinking of all of the services. And the relative weight of the influence of the various services differed with each operation. The theater of war, the nature of the operation, the command structure, the personalities and egos involved in the decision-making process, the political importance of the operation, and numerous other factors contributed to or diminished the power of a particular service to influence a specific joint operation.

Because the war in Europe was primarily a ground war and because of the influence of George C. Marshall, army thinking dominated the conduct of joint operations in the European theater. The fact that army thinking exerted the most influence in the overall conduct of joint operations in the European theater did not mean that the thinking of the navy and air force was insignificant. Still, in the case of the Normandy invasion, both the navy and Army Air Force had reservations about the plan for the conduct of the invasion. The army, guided by the British, refused to respond to these concerns. Co-operation between the armed forces of the United States was not what it should have been. The failure of the armed forces to establish joint doctrine and build up a reservoir of trust and respect cost the nation lives and resources in World War II.

After the war, Hall was asked: 'In retrospect, what were its [the Normandy invasion's] real defects?' He responded: 'I should say the worst defect was the lack of joint training of air, ground, and naval forces, and the lack of proper communications among them... I can't think of any more important things.'[64] Hall believed the United States had started a hundred years too late to develop a joint doctrine and 'only the threat of something like world war forced this issue.'[65] His assessment was confirmed by the history of World War II and the Cold War. In the American conduct of joint operations in the European and Mediterranean theaters, the sum of the parts was never greater than the whole and was typically something less than the whole. This was also true at Normandy. The combat power of the armed forces of the United States was never maximized; instead, during periods of urgent need, the services rose to the occasion, improvised, and produced the necessary combat power. This was the typical American pattern during and after World War II. Such instances occurred at Gela, Salerno, Anzio, and Omaha Beach. The combat power that the armed forces of the United States were capable of generating was never organized, co-ordinated, jointly trained, or integrated and synchronized to achieve its maximum potential.

In 1942 and 1943, the British were the senior partners in the Anglo-American alliance and dominated Allied planning. The campaigns in North Africa, Sicily, and Italy were primarily based on British strategic and operational thinking. British tenets of war predominated. The British were able to attain all senior operational command positions and effectively block communication between the supreme commander, Eisenhower, and senior American operational commanders such as Hewitt and Patton, both of whom had different views on the conduct of the Sicily campaign. Hewitt observed: 'With the exception of certain officers temporarily detailed to planning committees, there were no naval officers, either British or American on the Supreme Commander's Staff. Admiral Cunningham felt that the General [Eisenhower] should look to him for naval advice, and that there should be no naval officer on the staff to exert a direct influence on the Supreme Commander's decisions.'[66] Hewitt was two levels of command below Eisenhower. He rarely saw the supreme commander and was of the opinion that Eisenhower did not care to hear what he had to say. The supreme commander made no effort to meet with his subordinate naval commanders or seek their advice. He permitted himself to be separated from the nuts-and-bolts of operational and tactical planning and, as a consequence, failed to learn the complexities of amphibious warfare. When Eisenhower took charge of planning the Normandy invasion, he was a novice in the conduct of amphibious warfare. He had to rely heavily on the experience and knowledge of General Montgomery and other senior British operational commanders.

Hewitt succeeded as an operational commander and deserves great credit for America's accomplishments in the Mediterranean theater. He failed to convince his superiors of the correctness of his vision, however, and apparently did not share his concerns with Admiral King or General Marshall. In this regard, Hewitt failed. The results were high casualties at Salerno and Normandy.

The British Vision for the Invasion of Europe

Sicily had been a sobering experience. For years we had been told that our weapons were superior to any we would encounter. After, all, we were soldiers from the most highly industrialized and richest nation on earth. But the very preoccupation with our advanced technology caused many to assume technology alone would win battles – more emphasis was placed upon victory through airpower than better infantry.'

General James Gavin

The initial planning for the invasion of Western Europe was carried out prior to the issuance of the directive in April 1943 by the American and British Combined Chiefs of Staff establishing the Chief of Staff to the Supreme Allied Commander (COSSAC) staff. Kenneth Edwards of the Royal Navy wrote: 'The invasion of the continent of

Europe from Great Britain was conceived during the darkest days of our history; those days after the withdrawal of our armies from Dunkirk and the fall of France...Yet, while desperately on the defensive, there were in Britain at that time men with such steadfast faith that they began at once to think and plan in terms of a British invasion of the Continent.'[1]

The strategic concept for the invasion of the continent of Europe may have had its genesis in the 'darkest days' of British history, but in strategic, material, manpower, military, and probably moral terms, it was not possible for Britain alone to conduct the invasion of Europe after the fall of France. Two momentous events were required before the invasion of Europe could be seriously considered. After those events occurred, the invasion became a strategic concept that pulled Great Britain inexorably toward the opening of a 'second front' on the European continent. The first event was the German invasion of the Soviet Union in June 1941, Operation Barbarossa, the largest land invasion in human history conducted by over a hundred divisions on a front covering more than a thousand miles. The invasion caused Joseph Stalin to seek relief for his beleaguered army and nation by demanding the opening of a second front in Western Europe, in essence, a return to the strategic situation that destroyed Germany in the First World War.

The second event was the Japanese attack on the United States at Pearl Harbor on 7 December 1941. The success of this attack motivated Adolf Hitler to declare war against the United States and, hence, brought the enormous resources of the United States – 'the arsenal of democracy' – into the war. British political and military leaders, under the able and perspicacious guidance of Sir Winston Churchill, convinced President Franklin D. Roosevelt to adopt a 'Germany first' strategy against the advice of several of his military advisers, most notably Admiral Ernest J. King, America's top naval leader, and the wishes of the majority of the American people, who saw the Japanese as the major threat to the United States. Roosevelt's 'Germany first' strategy gave impetus and direction to the American war effort from December 1941 to the surrender of Germany in May 1945. General

George C. Marshall, America's top army leader, translated coalition and national strategy into military strategy and operations, and it was his belief that a second front should be opened in Western Europe at the earliest possible opportunity, meaning 1942 or 1943. Thus, the strategic concept and the ultimate plan for the invasion of Europe were influenced by the direct and immediate national interests of Great Britain and the Soviet Union, America's interpretation of its own national interest, and the strategic and operational thinking of British and American military leaders.

At the Casablanca Conference in January 1943, the Allies decided to form a staff to advance the planning process and make real what had hitherto been a long-range strategic vision. Prior to this date, volumes of data had been collected and an initial plan developed. The planning and conduct of the failed amphibious raid at Dieppe in August 1942 also caused the accumulation of enormous amounts of valuable information and material on the western coast of France, the conduct of amphibious assaults, and the German defense. Admiral Louis Mountbatten, the director of Combined Operations; Air Marshal Sir Sholto Douglas; and General Sir Bernard Paget were primarily responsible for the evolution of the plan and the collection and assimilation of data necessary to develop the plan. The COSSAC staff inherited this vast store of plans and information, without which the invasion could not have proceeded in June 1944.[2]

COMBINED OPERATIONS

The COSSAC staff was a combined staff, comprised of officers from the United States and Great Britain, and a joint staff, comprised of officers from the three services. Thus, the plan that evolved, in principle, reflected the thinking of both nations and the doctrinal concepts for the employment of forces of the army, navy, and air force. In terms of combined operations, divergent national interests, national character, military traditions and doctrines, staff organization and procedures, philosophy of command and leadership, procedures and philosophy for technology design and innovation, and even language differences had to be reconciled.[3]

The planning process for the invasion of Europe was dominated by the British, and hence, the operational plan for the invasion was more a reflection of British thinking about the conduct of war and amphibious operations than of American thinking. British thinking was evident in the attention to minute details in plans and operations orders.[4] The attention, time, and resources devoted to auxiliary matters such as elaborate deception plans; new devices such as the flailing tank, the duplex-drive (DD) tank, the 'synthetic' harbors, and breakwaters; and numerous other peripheral endeavors were indicative of the British mental processes in the planning of operations. This sort of expansive, excursive thought and planning did not typify the American approach to war, and some American commanders thought it went too far. Admiral John Lesslie Hall, the commander of the Eleventh Amphibious Force and Assault Force 'O,' stated in regard to orders:

> I had been head of the Strategy Section at the Naval War College where my chief duty was to help instruct U.S. Naval officers in how to write operations plans so that they could not be misunderstood, and I'd never seen such complicated misunderstandable operation plans as the British wrote. The objective is the thing: what do you want the picture to look like after the battle is over? That is what you try to tell your subordinates. And we really used to laugh at the long-winded operation plans that would come out of Admiral Ramsay's command, and we thought we knew a lot better how to let our subordinates know what we wanted accomplished.[5]

Admiral A.G. Kirk, the commander of Task Force 122, in a draft of his action report on the Normandy invasion, wrote:[6]

> There exist two fundamental differences between the U.S. and British methods of planning which had a considerable effect on the U.S. planning. These differences are: (1) The British in higher

echelon prescribe details, which in normal U.S. practice are left to responsible commanders in the lower echelons. (2) The British do not use a standard order form. When details are prescribed by higher echelons, the higher echelon is often then put in the position of relying on the lower echelon for information and data, which only lower echelon can supply. This results in delay and a lack of firmness in planning, which in turn greatly complicates the planning of lower echelons employing the U.S. system. In addition the freedom of action of the responsible lower commander is curtailed, as details of his plan became directives from high authority. The U.S. naval order form very effectively fulfills its purpose in contrast to the entire lack of a British system of orders.[7]

In short, the U.S. Navy's complaints about the British system of orders were that it lacked a standard order format, which caused British senior commanders to query subordinate commanders for information that was then issued back to them as orders restricting their range of options; that it lacked standard operating procedures, which made it necessary for British senior commanders to spell out in great detail routine procedures; and that it did not allow initiative on the part of the commander charged with the conduct of the operation. This was no small matter to American navy and army commanders and became a source of disagreement between Admiral Bertram H. Ramsay and Admiral Hall.[8]

Short mission statements were more characteristic of the American practice of issuing orders. The British attitude toward command, approach to orders, and committee system for developing plans left room for maneuver. There was a built-in fudge factor. A conversation between Patton and Montgomery recorded by Bradley immediately following the campaign in Sicily is revealing: 'Weeks later after the Sicilian campaign was ended Patton visited Monty at the latter's CP [command post]. During their conversation George complained of the injustice of Alexander's Army Group directive on the Vizzini–Caltagirone road. Monty looked at him with amusement. "George," he said, "let me give you some advice. If you get an order from Army Group that you don't like, why just ignore it. That's what I do.'" Bradley drew the following conclusions from this discussion and his World War II experience with the British:

> Basically Montgomery's comment to Patton reflected a common atti-
> tude in the British command, a view sometimes difficult for an
> American soldier to understand. Unlike the U.S. Army where an
> order calls for instant compliance, the British viewed an order as a
> basis for discussion between commanders. If a difference of opinion
> developed, it would be ironed out and the order might be amended.
> In contrast, we in the American army sought to work out our differ-
> ences before issuing an order. Once an order was published it could
> not be changed except by the issuing authority.[9]

The American mission statement told a commander what to do and when to do it but not how to do it. The 'how' was left to the initiative of the commander. In the face of strong opposition, Americans tended to trust in the commander's abilities, add more resources, and push harder. In the place of detailed planning, Americans trusted in their ability to improvise; to figure it out as they went; and to learn, build, and create in the process. Americans had to learn to temper their natural inclination to skip the details and get to the bottom line and to overcome all obstacles with more and more resources and greater effort. The British had to learn to move faster, with less caution and circumspection, and to adjust to the great abundance the United States poured into its wars.[10] The British attitude that Americans were naive and inexperienced and simply did not know what they were doing in regard to European war had to be controlled and tempered.[11] And the American belief that the British were obstructionists, too fearful of a return to the carnage of World War I, and a bit arrogant also had to be restrained.[12]

The armed forces of Great Britain operated under a 'committee system.' The British armed forces shared command responsibility in joint operations. The three service heads were equal in rank and authority, and each had his own staff. Most American military leaders believed the British committee system was inefficient and inexpedient and mitigated individual responsibility.[13] The system was slow and tended to produce excess caution. [14]

Many British military leaders came to believe that the American system of unified command was faster and more efficient. Generals Morgan, Montgomery, and Tedder and Admiral Keyes were among the converts.[15] Admiral Sir Roger Keyes, who at one time was the head of the British Combined Operation Command, wrote: 'To be "constitutionally" dependent on a Committee of Experts, who, like all Councils of War, can be relied upon to shrink from responsibility – if there is any possible risk of failure – is a dreadful handicap to labour under, when striving to *make war* against ruthless enemies, who are free from the limitations of democratic Government! Inter-Service Committees were in full swing in Whitehall; irresolution reigned, time passed and golden opportunities were missed.'[16] A document on the planning of Operation Overlord prepared by Montgomery's 21st Army Group noted:

> In retrospect the major drawback in the inter-service planning organ-
> isation (on the Army Group level) prior to D-Day was the lack of a
> single joint service commander. Experience indicated that the speed
> and efficiency of planning the initial phases of the operation might
> have been greatly improved had there been some set-up on the Army
> Group level analogous to the United States Task Force system, with a
> Task Force Commander... The system employed in 'OVERLORD'
> whereby agreement on all points had to be reached by three different
> Commanders-in-Chief, each briefed through their own separate
> staff, was a slow and unsatisfactory one. [17]

Doctrinal differences and the priority given by each service to a particular operation also influenced combined operations. The American and British air forces employed different doctrines – daylight precision versus night area bombing, respectively – and possessed very different capabilities. Senior Allied air force command-ers also believed the employment of strategic bombers in combined operations was a misuse of their resources and slowed the momentum of the strategic bombing campaign. The U.S. Navy preferred to employ Marine Corps amphibious doctrine and gave priority to the Pacific theater for its warships, wrongly believing that the British Navy had the wherewithal to support operations in the Atlantic, Mediterranean, and European theaters. Many British officers believed that the Americans were incompetent in the conduct of ground warfare and amphibious operations and thus argued that the British should retain operational command and have priority for resources.[18] The conflicts between Eisenhower and Montgomery have been well documented, and those pertaining to the invasion at Normandy are examined later. General Marshall recognized that the British were reluctant to re-enter the continent of Europe and thus allocated more resources to the war in the Pacific, where he believed they could be better used. Combined operations thus suffered from the different doctrines of the Allied armed forces and from the importance each service chief placed on a given operation.

Civilian political leaders also influenced the conduct of combined operations, particularly British Prime Minister Winston Churchill. Field Marshal Alan Brooke, chief of the Imperial General Staff, and other British military leaders had a difficult time managing the prime minister. General Raymond W. Barker reported to the War Department:

> One purpose of Morgan's conversation with Brooke was to warn him about the present temper of the American representation, and that he must be prepared for a stiff fight, in comparison with which QUAD-RANT might be 'child's play.' He mentioned to Brooke what he describes as 'the American indignation at certain trends in Allied strategy in the Mediterranean Area.' Morgan states that he was at pains to point out to General Brooke the serious consequences of a continuation of these trends. Brooke's attitude was that, in the first place, he had had lots of experience with the Americans on this line, and, further that it is unfortunate that the people in Washington do not know all of the background of the decisions taken in these matters.

For example, he pointed out that the recent operations in the Dodecanese were undertaken on the instruction of the Prime Minister and contrary to the advice given by his military staff. Also, that the sending to Moscow of the Eisenhower–Alexander Report on the situation in Italy was done by the Prime Minister, contrary to the advice of the C.I.G.S. I think it might be interesting for General Marshall to know these facts.[19]

Churchill exerted considerable influence on operations involving British and American forces in the Mediterranean and European theaters and, as a consequence, caused considerable friction in the Anglo-American relationship. Not only did he make strategic decisions on which operations to conduct, his proper role, but also he made operational decisions on how to carry them out. Churchill's presence was felt in every major operation undertaken in the Mediterranean and European theaters.

Given the makeup of the COSSAC staff, the environment in which it operated, and the nature of the mission it was asked to perform, General Frederick E. Morgan concluded: 'The COSSAC staff, containing as it did men and women of six fighting services of two different nations, was bound to contain all the elements of discord. What is remarkable is not that discord existed, but that it was suppressed and indeed was woven into the great symphony to the strains of which the victorious armies surged across the continent of Europe.'[20]

Without politically astute and conciliatory leadership, the American and British coalition and the 'six fighting services' might not have worked as effectively as they did. The question is, did compromise and politically astute decision-making facilitate the development of the best plan, or was the plan compromised for the sake of international and interservice co-operation? Were the exigencies necessary to produce the most viable and least costly plan in terms of lives adhered to, or did a type of problem-solving conducive to the amalgamation of disparate institutions cause compromise where there should have been none?

THE COSSAC PLAN

In January 1943, the Combined Chiefs of Staff directed that detailed planning be implemented for the purpose of invading Western Europe 'as early as possible' in 1944. Later, a target date of 1 May 1944 was set. The objective for the invasion was stated as follows:

> The object of Operation 'Overlord' is to mount and carry out an operation, with forces and equipment established in the United Kingdom, and with target date the 1st of May, 1944, to secure a lodgment on the Continent from which further offensive operations can be developed. The lodgment area must contain sufficient port facilities to maintain a force of some twenty-six to thirty divisions, and enable that force to be augmented by follow-up shipments from the United States or elsewhere of additional divisions and supporting units at the rate of three to five divisions per month.[21]

In April 1943, the COSSAC staff was formed and issued its first directive. Lieutenant General Frederick Morgan of the British Army was appointed chief of staff. His deputy was an American brigadier general, Raymond W. Barker. Various leaders would represent the navies and air forces throughout the planning process. On 17 April, Morgan addressed the new organization for the first time:

> Before I get down to the real business of this meeting, I think it would be as well if I were to indicate to you something of the historical background behind our meeting...As we are all well aware, ever since the BRITISH Army was ejected from FRANCE ways and means have been sought of getting back once more to the Continent of EUROPE, the only place where this war can be finally settled. Until the UNITED STATES came to our aid with all her immense resources, the study of this question was mainly of an academic nature. Now, thank God, the time is here to descend from the realms of fancy to the levels of practical politics.[22]

In this first meeting, Morgan explained how the staff members should think about the job they were charged with performing:

> In spite of the fact that it is quite clear that neither I nor you have by definition any executive authority, my idea is that we shall regard ourselves in the first instance as primarily a co-ordinating body. We plan mainly by the co-ordination of effort already being exerted in a hundred and one directions. We differ from the ordinary planning staff in that we are... in effect the embryo of the future Supreme Headquarters Staff.[23]

When Morgan spoke these words, it was clearly his understanding that the supreme command would go to a British general. Morgan then listed the mission statements:

> I am charged with planning three operations:
> 1. An operation against the Continent this year on the largest scale that resources will permit.
> 2. I am to plan nothing less than the re-conquest of EUROPE.
> 3. Over and above these other items, I am to plan for a return to the Continent virtually unopposed in the event of GERMANY's resistance collapsing (as it may well do at any time from now on).[24]

Morgan then discussed the limitations they faced. In the early stages of planning, the biggest problem was a lack of information. The number of landing craft, the number of British and American divisions, and the number and location of German divisions were all unknowns. Morgan told his staff to plan on deploying 100 divisions, 15 British and 85 American. He noted that the 'ultimate object is to wage successful war on land in the heart of EUROPE' and that the staff should plan to encounter an army of roughly 100 divisions with air force in proportion. (More realistic figures were soon developed.) Finally, Morgan challenged his staff: 'We face a task without precise precedent. History never repeats itself exactly; we must be guided by the logic of events. I look to you to take the next step in advising me how you propose each to perform his allotted task.'[25]

With these words, the COSSAC staff set about its work. The first major task was the accumulation of specific information. The more accurate and detailed the information, the more thorough and complete the plan. A prerequisite for the development of a comprehensive plan is knowledge of the mission; enemy strength, locations, and capabilities; the types, quantities, and quality of troops and equipment available; and the terrain on which the battles will be fought. The COSSAC staff never had all of the information it needed to put together the most effective plan; what it lacked most was not information on enemy forces but information on the number of Allied forces, ships, and landing craft. Also, as time passed, information changed. Because the COSSAC staff never had an accurate picture of the forces that would be deployed, the plan it developed required significant changes when the commanders for the invasion were finally selected and units assigned.

The COSSAC staff had inherent weaknesses. A general was primarily responsible for planning an operation that had to be carried out in large part by naval forces. Morgan and his staff lacked knowledge and experience in modern amphibious warfare. British thinking was still greatly influenced by the experience of World War I, and the British and Americans did not share a common vision of war. Furthermore, Morgan lacked the rank, position, and executive authority to make firm decisions. Every aspect of the plan developed by the COSSAC staff was subject to change. And since the plan was being formulated in and launched from England, the British Chiefs of Staff had the first look at the plans and the first opportunity to change them.

The inherent strengths of the COSSAC planners were their freedom to use their imagination and the wealth of data they inherited from previous planners. Executive bodies, commands with real troops and real equipment, are typically too preoccupied to carry out the more creative process of planning. The real-world tasks of acquiring, training, organizing, coordinating, and managing real assets can preclude or erode the imaginative process. The COSSAC planners generated an enormous number of ideas, many of which were discarded. The thinking behind the deception plans, the synthetic harbors (the Mulberries), and the asbestos and grease waterproofing compound and numerous other ideas came from this staff. Admiral Kirk in his action report wrote:

> Planners, who were faced with the new problems presented by the Channel Operation and who had only the comparatively easy successes of the Mediterranean or the disastrous casualties of Dieppe on which to base their estimate, were able to consider them in comparative leisure. During this planning period many original concepts were discarded and many of the final concepts of the plans were thus laid. This saved the final planning groups much of the weeding out of ideas they would otherwise have had to face.[26]

The 'weeding' process may not have gone far enough, however. Enormous amounts of time, energy, and resources were spent developing equipment, technology, and techniques with questionable value. Another strength of the COSSAC staff was its knowledge of enemy forces and operations and of the West Coast of France. Some of this information was inherited and some was acquired during the planning process. The intelligence supplied by 'Ultra,' the code name for the secret British intelligence group, and other sources provided the COSSAC staff with essential information on enemy strength and capability that made it possible to select an invasion site.

In July 1943, Morgan's COSSAC staff published the outline plan for the invasion of Europe. This document was the foundation for the final plan that carried Allied forces back to the continent of Europe. Given the requirements and limitations established by the Combined Chiefs of Staff, the COSSAC staff developed and analyzed numerous courses of action, selected the best course of action, and presented its proposal to the Combined Chiefs of Staff. In August 1943, the Combined Chiefs of Staff approved the plan.

The plan was constructed on the following exigencies. First, control of the air and sea at the site of the assault had to be gained and maintained, a prerequisite of any amphibious assault against hostile shores. Second, the landing site had to be within the range of air support flying out of England. Third, the landing sector had to possess port facilities with the capacity to accommodate the arrival of three to five divisions per day and sustain a force of twenty-six to thirty divisions. Fourth, a geographic area with the capacity to provide assault and maneuver space for three divisions and maintenance and build-up space was required. Fifth, terrain suitable for an amphibious assault given the technology available was necessary, that is, terrain that could accommodate landing craft and withstand the ground pressure of armor vehicles. Sixth, the sector selected had to possess communication networks (road and/or rail systems) near the beaches to facilitate a rapid build-up of forces and equipment. Seventh, the sector had to be weakly defended, lacking both the manpower and material required to resist a five-division invasion force. Eighth, the water's edge defense had to be capable of being neutralized with air and sea fire support resources. In addition, the expectation had to exist that the sector selected would remain relatively poorly defended. Finally, the location of the sector in relation to the location of Germany's strategic reserves had to be considered.

Given these considerations, the COSSAC staff developed the plan for a four-phase operation. The first was the preliminary phase, during which air superiority was to be gained by the Allied air forces through the destruction of Germany's air force and its ability to construct, service, and fuel aircraft. This mission was already being carried out by the Allied strategic air forces in Operation Point-Blank. During this phase, every measure possible was to be taken to erode Germany's ability to conduct war. 'All possible means including air and sea action, propaganda, political and economic pressure, and sabotage' were to be integrated into a plan intended to weaken German resistance.[27] Deception plans designed to cause the Germans to believe that the landing would take place at various other sites were to be implemented during this phase. The preliminary phase was to start immediately after approval of the plan by the Combined Chiefs of Staff.

During the second phase, the preparatory phase, the air operations outlined in the first phase would continue, and the effort to isolate the battlefield by destroying communications networks to the invasion site would commence. This effort had to be disguised in order to avoid revealing the landing site to German intelligence. The build-up of materials and troops and special training were also to be carried out during this phase. The ships and port facilities required in southern England were to be secured and made operational. This phase commenced in November 1943 with the selection of units and commanders.

The third phase was the assault phase. The COSSAC plan stated:

> After a very short air bombardment of the beach defences three assault divisions will be landed simultaneously on the Caen beaches, followed up on D-Day by the equivalent of two tank brigades (United States regiments) and a brigade group (United States regimental combat team). At the same time, airborne forces will be used to seize the town of Caen; and subsidiary operations by commandos [U.S. Army rangers] and possibly by airborne forces will be undertaken to neutralise certain coast defences and seize certain important river crossings. The object of the assault forces will be to seize the general line of Grandcamp–Bayeux–Caen.[28]

Fourth was the follow-up and build-up phase, during which the port at Cherbourg, airfields, and major transportation networks would be captured and made operational. Forces would be built up as rapidly as possible. The lodgment area would be secured and preparations made for follow-up operations. Timetables were established for the build-up of troops and supplies based on assumptions about the flow of battle.

Although the preliminary and preparatory phases were preconditions for the assault phase, the primary concern of this study is with the assault phase. What was General Morgan and his COSSAC staff's vision for winning the battles on the beaches of Normandy?

A supplementary directive issued to the COSSAC staff by the Combined Chiefs of Staff on 25 May 1943 specified that:

twenty-nine divisions in all would be available for the assault and
immediate build-up... Of these, five infantry divisions were to be
simultaneously loaded in the landing craft... with two more divisions
in follow-up immediately. We were also to count on two airborne
divisions so that there would be a total of nine divisions in the assault
and immediate follow-up.[29]

The COSSAC planners, however, were limited to three divisions in
the amphibious assault instead of five because of the paucity of
landing craft and ships. The aircraft required to lift airborne divisions
were also in short supply, so the COSSAC staff could plan for only
one airborne division. The mix of Allied forces included substantial air
and naval forces but not enough to conduct the mission as General
Morgan and his staff or the Combined Chiefs of Staff envisioned. The
shortfall in resources of all types would be partially rectified when
commanders for the invasion were finally selected and priority for
ground, naval, and air assets was finally given to Operation Overlord
and Operation Neptune, the amphibious assault. This problem high-
lights one of the inherent weaknesses of the COSSAC staff – the
absence of a commander with executive authority, rank, and priority
for his mission.

The geographic area selected for the invasion was the southwest
coast of France in Normandy in the vicinity of Caen.[30] The Caen
sector was selected for multiple reasons but primarily because German
forces were weakest there. The sector was in range of air power flying
out of England. The capacity and configuration of the beaches and the
terrain behind the beaches were suitable for an amphibious assault and
the subsequent build-up for follow-on operations. The COSSAC staff
studied six sectors along the west coast of Europe from the Dutch–
Belgian Group to the Biscay–Brittany Group. The requirements of the
air force, navy, and army were all analyzed. Through a process of elimination, two sectors in Normandy were chosen, the Caen sector and the
Cotentin peninsula sector. The COSSAC plan noted: 'The Caen and
East Cotentin sectors are in fact, the only sectors within air cover from
England where the defenses at present are such as to offer reasonable

prospects of rapid penetration without long preliminary bombard-ment.'[31] Morgan later recalled: 'As things stood in June of 1943 there was no comparison between the low standard of preparedness of defense in Normandy and the masses of concrete still being poured in the Pas de Calais... Once our attention was focused on Normandy it was satisfactory from our point of view to see work going on in the Pas de Calais. Our hope would be fulfilled as long as work stood still in Normandy.'[32] The COSSAC staff believed it would be unwise to utilize the Cotentin sector because of its configuration as a peninsula. Bordered on three sides by water, a peninsula can restrict ground offensive operations to frontal attacks and considerably strengthen defensive operations. This was the problem that had confronted Allied forces in Italy. The COSSAC staff decided it would be unwise to attack in both the Caen and Cotentin sectors because the Carentan estuary divided the two sectors, thus preventing the rapid linkup of forces and opening the possibility that forces would be destroyed piecemeal. The concentration of forces was one of the principles upon which the COSSAC plan was built: 'In view of the known German policy of immediate counter-attack by formations in reserve, it is clearly desir-able that the limited strength of our assault should be concentrated in one sector, and every temptation to dissipate it by simultaneous attacks in more than one sector of the coast must be resisted.'[33]

The beaches at Caen were thus the final choice of the COSSAC staff. The assault would be made on three beaches:

> Beach 308, plus the western end of beach 307, and 313 are suitable for the assault. From a study of these beaches it is estimated that one divi-sion, on a two brigade front [U.S. regimental front], could assault between St Come de Fresene (8686) and Mont Fleury (9186). A second division on a two brigade front, could assault between Mont Fleury (9186) and Bernières (9985) astride the River Mue. A third division, on a two brigade front, could assault between Colleville-sur-Mer (6888) and St Laurent-sur-Mer (6689).[34]

The latter beach would eventually be code-named 'Omaha.'

The COSSAC invasion plan called for three combat-experienced divisions to make the initial assault, two British-Canadian divisions attacking on the right two beaches (the eastern sector) and an American division attacking on the left beach (the western sector). The Americans were assigned the left beach for command and control reasons, that is, to keep British and American forces separate and because of the anticipated flow of reinforcements. U.S. forces were to be supplied and reinforced directly from the United States initially through the port at Cherbourg, and British forces were to be supplied and reinforced directly across the Channel from England.

The assault would open with a short bombardment from air and sea assets. The divisions would assault simultaneously with two brigades abreast and one brigade in support, followed by the equivalent of two tank brigades, one British and one American. The city of Caen was to be captured by an airborne assault. Special operations units, composed of British commandos and American rangers, were to capture and/or destroy key installations, such as artillery batteries and bridges. By the end of D-Day, the cities of Caen, Bayeux, and Grandcamp were to be in Allied hands and a defensive parameter linking the three cities with the Orne River in the east and the Vire River in the west was to be established.

The COSSAC staff developed a plan to defeat the German defense as it existed in 1943. Under 'Enemy Forces,' the COSSAC plan described the German concept for the conduct of the defense: 'The German policy is based normally on counter-attack of the beaches by panzer divisions held in reserve close behind the coast, and coastal divisions are only expected to hold on for eight to twelve hours until these panzer divisions arrive...The crux of the operation is thus likely to be our ability to drive off the German reserves rather than the initial breaking of the coastal crust.'[35] Morgan believed that the initial assault 'would not present a great difficulty':[36] 'We had little anxiety, comparatively speaking, regarding the early stages, that is, the landing and the capture of Caen and our defensive beachhead in a matter of hours. The weight of supporting fire of all kinds available on the frontage involved seemed undeniable.'[37]

In July 1943, the site selected for the landing was defended by one German division of two regiments stretched across a fifty-mile front, from Carentan in the west to the Dives River in the east. Although inwardly assured that the battle for the beaches would be a relatively minor engagement, Morgan believed that if a major battle was fought on the beaches, the entire operation could fail: 'One hopes and plans for battle as far inland from the beach as may be, for if the invasion battle takes place on the beach, one is already defeated.'[38] Morgan's plan was based on achieving tactical surprise. Local superiority on the beaches was to be attained through tactical surprise and by attacking a poorly defended sector of coast. What concerned Morgan was the possibility that reserve forces would be brought up to counter-attack the vulnerable Allied foothold before it was firmly established ashore. In the view of the COSSAC staff, the most critical and dangerous part of the operation was the expected engagement with local reserves. To build up and establish sufficient force ashore to withstand a major German counter-attack was the intent. Both sides would be engaged in a race to build up overwhelming combat power. To win the race, to overcome weaknesses inherent in amphibious operations against hostile shores, the COSSAC staff based the Overlord plan on three principles: tactical surprise, concentration of force against the enemy's weaknesses, and speed – speed in obtaining, occupying, and establishing the initial defensive parameter to receive the enemy's counter-attack with its local reserves and speed in building up forces to receive the enemy's counter-attack with its operational or strategic reserves. The concentration of force was believed to be necessary to insure adequate air support and to preclude the piecemeal destruction of the landing force.[39]

Tactical surprise was the main tenet of the COSSAC plan. Morgan wrote: 'It was peremptory that absolute surprise be achieved with the first onslaught. If it weren't and if we were caught in the ships and craft off the far coast by a fully prepared enemy, that would indubitably be that.'[40] Morgan at one time believed that the plan would fail if tactical surprise was not achieved, that is, if the enemy had 'eight to twelve hours' notice in which to redeploy its forces.[41] Given the size of the invasion fleets, this was an extraordinary level of surprise. The COSSAC staff believed that tactical surprise could be achieved by attacking at a geographic location where the enemy was not expecting an attack and was poorly prepared for defense. Surprise was not to be sacrificed by a prolonged bombardment of the enemy coast. The COSSAC plan stated: 'There is thus a chance of obtaining some measure of surprise in the operation, provided that we do not give away our intention by long-drawn-out bombardment or other preparatory measures... As preliminary bombardment compromises surprise, it should be confined to the shortest possible duration consistent with the achievement of the required degree of neutralisation.'[42] This thinking was in keeping with the British way of war and amphibious raid tradition and the conduct of the British-led operations in North Africa, Sicily, and Italy.

Closely related to the issue of surprise was the timing of the assault. If the invasion was timed to take place under the cover of darkness, the chance of achieving tactical surprise was enhanced. Tactical surprise was also more likely to be achieved against poorly organized and manned defenses. In 1943, this was one of the advantages of the Normandy site.

The COSSAC planners did not set a time for the invasion of Europe. They did not determine whether the assault should take place during the hours of darkness or light. They delineated the positions of the army and navy. They outlined the requirements for special operations forces, such as airborne, glider, and commando/ranger forces. They specified the conditions required for airborne forces to make a night jump, including at least a quarter-moon. They determined that the navy needed a full day to land the volume of forces and equipment the army wanted on D-Day and noted that the navy preferred a daylight attack to insure the 'density' of force desired in the initial assault waves. (The army wanted 20,000 vehicles landed on D-Day.) The army's position was 'that the main assault should take place just before civil twilight in order to obtain darkness in the approach and daylight for the capture of the beach and exploitation.'[43]

No mention was made of the amount of time needed for naval gunfire support and air power to complete the 'neutralisation' of coastal defenses. The air force was also silent on this issue. However, Morgan later gave his assessment of the problem:

> When both sides could see to shoot, it would become pretty much of a straightforward shooting match. Did we not possess such power that our blow, delivered as we trusted against a surprised enemy, would be decisive even when we were in the disadvantageous position of being afloat, while he was ashore? Were not the profits we hoped to gain by the use of darkness more than offset by the loss of power we should thereby incur? It seemed a devilish close-run thing.[44]

Morgan's statement indicates some degree of uncertainty even after the invasion regarding whether the assault should have been based on firepower or surprise. Morgan tended to believe that the abundance of firepower would more than make up for the advantages gained by assaulting during the hours of darkness – Marine Corps thinking. Yet he was reluctant to allow the air and naval arms the time to neutralize the enemy's defenses because he hoped to achieve tactical surprise. In ideal circumstances, both goals would have been met – tactical surprise and the quality of destruction that could be achieved only in a prolonged bombardment and bombing. In 1943, however, it did not seem possible to achieve both outcomes. Thus, Morgan wrestled with the competing principles of firepower-based assaults and surprise-based assaults. The final decision was not in the hands of Morgan and his staff. The COSSAC staff developed a plan it knew would be modified once the commanders charged with the execution of the mission were appointed. The timing of the assault was left for Eisenhower and Montgomery to decide.

At the same time that the COSSAC staff was developing its plan, in April 1943, Lieutenant Colonel Paul W. Thompson took command of the newly established U.S. Army Assault Training Center at Woolcombe in England. In May 1943, Thompson explained the mission of the Assault Training Center:

The primary and ultimate mission of the Assault Training Center is to provide facilities for, and control of the training of combat teams and assault divisions. This training must cover all phases of the landing-assault operation, under realistic conditions, simulating as closely as possible, those to be encountered by combat teams in an invasion of Western Europe. The Assault Training Center, in addition, has been given certain experimental missions, dealing with testing of assault methods and with the development of tactics and techniques.[45]

The Woolcombe facility was one of eight American invasion training centers in operation between August 1943 and D-Day. The site was selected because its beaches, tides, surf, winds, and weather approximated those on the Normandy coast.[46] At the Woolcombe training center, fortifications were erected to simulate the defenses along the Normandy coast. The physical conditions and facilities at Woolcombe made it one of the most important training centers. It was also important because of its responsibility for advancing amphibious doctrine. A Special Doctrine Board was established under Thompson 'to produce firm recommendations for a definite doctrine for landing-assault operations.'[47] The board's charter was limited. It was to develop solutions to specific problems presented to it. Of the center, historian Gordon Harrison wrote:

> Beside carrying out its primary mission of preparing troops for the assaults, the Assault Training Center made a vital contribution to amphibious doctrine. Through experimentation with new equipment, combined exercises, close liaison with the British, and conferences on tactics, Colonel Thompson's staff learned as well as taught, and their new wisdom not only improved tactical methods but in many important ways modified tactical concepts.[48]

At a conference held between 24 May and 23 June 1943, American and British planners, including members of the COSSAC staff, sought to develop new doctrine for the Normandy invasion based on the experiences of both nations in the European and Pacific theaters.

Thompson stated that the conference 'was aimed at one fundamental goal: that of crossing the English Channel with properly organized and properly trained assault teams, ready to seize, to hold and to maintain beachheads through which might land a major invasion force to advance against the enemy.' One American planner stated at the opening of the conference: 'When we first started to plan the [U.S. Assault Training] Center, there was a problem even deeper than that of selection of proper terrain. What doctrines would we teach? By what methods would we teach them?'[49] Another American said: '[W]e cannot consider this as a classical type of operation. We must examine the "book" carefully to be guided by the doctrine contained therein. But we must go further, in approaching our specific problem – that of training these combat teams for the task ahead of them. We must be willing to open our minds and to prepare to formulate new doctrine, if need be, for this specific and unique type of operation, across the English Channel, for which history gives us no satisfactory precedent.'[50] This mental disposition may have caused the planners of the invasion to overlook or disregard proven procedures and techniques that had evolved in landings in North Africa, Sicily, and the Pacific theater.[51] The planners of the Normandy invasion had a mandate for change. Anglo-American planners were predisposed to novel solutions, many of which were questionable. Examples of new technology and procedures developed specifically for the Normandy invasion include the Mulberries, artificial harbors; the Pluto (Pipe Line Under The Ocean) project, an underwater fuel line that stretched across the English Channel; and the DD tank, a Sherman tank mounted with a waterproof canvas shroud and propeller system to give it amphibious capabilities. Admiral Hall, commander of Amphibious Force 'O,' recalled that when he was shown the plans for the artificial harbors, he anticipated disaster:

> Admiral Cunningham showed us these pictures... these artificial harbors... He said, 'Hall, as one destroyer sailor to another what do you think of these things?' I said, 'Admiral, I think it's the biggest waste of manpower and equipment that I have ever seen... I can

unload a thousand LSTs at a time over the open beaches. Why do you give me something that anybody who's ever seen the sea act upon 150-ton concrete blocks at Casablanca knows the first storm will destroy? What's the use of building them just to have them destroyed and litter up the beaches?' That's exactly what happened. The first storm we had, they just messed up the whole place.[52]

The American artificial harbor was destroyed and the British harbor was damaged in a storm that began on 17 June. After the storm, the U.S. Navy demonstrated it could deliver just as much material using LSTs – the proven, more certain means. The Pluto installation never delivered the volume of fuel anticipated or required, and when it became fully operational, the Allied armies were far beyond the port of entry.[53] The DD tanks proved to be incapable of negotiating heavy seas such as those that existed on the morning of 6 June 1944, and many sank in the landing.[54]

Other ideas and new doctrinal approaches failed to facilitate the achievement of Anglo-American objectives, and the process of new idea development continued into April 1944. After Eisenhower and Montgomery took over, the Assault Training Center developed new tactical doctrine for clearing obstacles and reorganized the standard infantry division into assault teams. The tactical commanders opposed both ideas. These new ideas and approaches were in part the result of a flawed process of joint operational and tactical doctrine development. The participation of the U.S. Navy in the conference was minimal. There is no indication that Hall or Hewitt gave a presentation, and it was Hall who was eventually selected to command the Eleventh Amphibious Force and Forces 'O' and 'B,' which landed at Omaha Beach. He was again responsible for American amphibious training. These new ideas and approaches were also developed in part because of the belief that the cross-Channel attack was so unique that new methods were required. British uncertainties about returning to the Continent – because of the memory of Somme and Dunkirk – may have motivated the desire for new, extraordinary means.

At the Quadrant Conference held in Québec in August 1943, President Roosevelt, Prime Minister Churchill, and the Combined Chiefs of Staff approved COSSAC's Overlord plan. Prior to the conference, the British Joint Chiefs of Staff gave their assessment of the plan:

> The Chiefs of Staff said they were satisfied with the plan. A covering note to 'OVERLORD' was prepared for presentation to the Combined Chiefs of Staff which read as follows:
>
> We have examined carefully the outline plan for operation 'OVERLORD' which General MORGAN has submitted. We have the following observations:
>
> It will be observed that General MORGAN lays down three main conditions which must be created if the operation is to have a reasonable prospect of success. These are:
>
> (i)   There must be an overall reduction in the strength of the German fighter forces between now and the time of the assault.
>
> (ii) German reserves in FRANCE and the Low Countries as a whole, excluding divisions holding the coast, GAF [German Air Force] divisions, and training divisions, should not exceed on the day of the assault 12 full strength, first quality divisions. In addition, the Germans should not be able to transfer more than 15 first quality divisions from RUSSIA during the first two months.
>
> (iii) The problem of beach maintenance over a prolonged period in the Channel must be overcome.
>
> We entirely agree with General MORGAN that these conditions are essential, and we will have certain proposals to make during the 'QUADRANT' discussion.[55]

Field Marshal Alan Brooke, chief of the Imperial General Staff, commented: '[O]ur margin of superiority over the maximum acceptable rate of build-up, particularly during the first two critical days, is small.'[56] He also believed the rate of advance planned by Morgan was too optimistic. He had personal experience in the country behind Caen and knew the terrain in this area was ideal for delaying actions.

Churchill was then briefed on the plan. The minutes of the COSSAC staff conference noted: 'The Prime Minister liked the plan but said that the assault force of 3 divisions was not large enough... [and] that every effort should be made to add at least 25 per cent strength to the initial assault.' Churchill agreed that the Caen area was the best place to land but thought the east Cotentin beaches should be included in the assault area. He also believed diversions were necessary to confuse the enemy. General Barker briefed the American Joint Chiefs of Staff and the president prior to the Quadrant Conference. Barker noted that the plan was well received and that the president and Joint Chiefs of Staff had decided to give it 'their full backing.'[57]

The problem of insufficient numbers of landing craft was also discussed. On 14 August, Admiral King directed his vice chief of naval operations to re-establish priorities for ship construction, giving priority to landing ships and craft. Once the plan was approved, Morgan was authorized to proceed with detailed planning and full preparations.

At this juncture, all were satisfied with the work of the COSSAC staff and the results of the Quadrant Conference. In a letter to Morgan, Barker wrote: 'I am delighted that you had an opportunity to talk with the President and not at all surprised at your reaction to his views on military strategy. We rather felt at Québec that Field Marshal Churchill had been indoctrinating him.'[58]

Morgan's vision was designed to defeat the German defense in 1943, a defense that was poorly developed in sectors that were not close to ports. At that time, the Allies had not conducted a large-scale amphibious assault against a deliberate defense. The Dieppe amphibious raid in 1942 failed in part because tactical surprise was lost, demonstrating that tactical surprise would be difficult to achieve against the coast of Europe.[59] The COSSAC plan was based on the British practice of amphibious operations. Reconnaissance aircraft, radar, small patrol boats, a professional intelligence organization, and a professional army could have upset the plan, which relied on the principle of tactical surprise.[60] However, since the German defense was poorly developed, Morgan's plan was constructed on solid ground. The battle that

Morgan envisioned called for the concentration of forces in a limited geographic area with natural terrain features, rivers, as obstacles to flanking attacks; an assault preceded by a short, intense bombardment from air and naval support to destroy or neutralize the weak enemy crust; the occupation of a hasty defensive parameter along the line of Caen–Bayeux–Grandcamp; a second more significant battle to defeat the enemy's local reserves that were expected to counter-attack in eight to twelve hours; and, finally, the establishment of a stronger defensive boundary behind which preparations would be made to receive the enemy's next counter-attack with operational or possibly strategic reserves or make a breakout attack to seize the port of Cherbourg. According to Morgan:

> The predominant feature of the conduct of the operation we propounded was to be the early capture of Caen and a defensive line running westward there from through the 'bocage' or hedgerow, country. While the enemy was battering his head against this [in the counter-attack], we were to build up behind it our strength in troops, stores and installations at a pace exceeding that at which the enemy could stiffen his resistance. It is the 'rate of build-up' that is decisive in matters of this sort. Then would come the swing to the west then to the north up to Cherbourg.[61]

Morgan's plan came under heavy criticism when Eisenhower and Montgomery took charge of the planning. It was based on the resources he was told would be available. Morgan wrote:

> All doubts, and there were many, stemmed from the meager resources of landing craft and shipping allotted to us. Those who were uncannily expert in handling such matters juggled around with what we were given to get the last ounce out of it. This involved both cutting down allowances of lift made to army units and doing all possible to speed up shipping turn-around... But, even so, the strength of the assault in terms of weapons and men on the ground was pitifully small.[62]

Morgan would have planned to deploy more divisions in the assault had he been given the resources to do so. He was forced to develop a plan with something less than he considered the minimum. Morgan's plan must be viewed differently from the Montgomery Plan. It was based on fighting a 'soft spot' in the German defense, not the deliberate defense that Erwin Rommel constructed in the early months of 1944, and Morgan did not have access to the awesome power of the U.S. Eighth Air Force's daylight strategic bombers. Everything he and his staff planned, everything they believed was critical or essential to the conduct of the operation, was subject to change. The COSSAC staff did not start off with a commander. It started its work with a relatively low-ranking British officer at its head who was accustomed to operating under a committee system that was practiced, in the words of Morgan, in 'muddling through.'[63] The plan for the invasion of Europe started off as a patchwork affair. Bits and pieces were collected from here and there, amassed, and molded into the COSSAC plan. It was a plan put together by officers seasoned in the trench warfare of World War I with limited or no experience in modern amphibious operations. It was a plan constructed primarily on the tenets of the British way of war.

5

The Montgomery Plan

I set out to produce troops who were imbued with that offensive
eagerness and infectious optimism which comes from physical well-
being. And whenever I inspected any unit I used to make the men
remove their steel helmets: not, as many imagined, to see if they had
their hair properly cut, but to see if they had the light of battle in their
eyes.

Field Marshal Bernard L. Montgomery

On 7 December 1943, the president of the United States personally
informed Eisenhower that he would command the invasion of
Europe and the subsequent campaign to destroy the German Army.
He was the supreme commander – the strategic commander.[1]
Eisenhower's thinking on the conduct of the operation is revealed in
the decisions he made on the various options presented to him and

the directives he forwarded to his subordinate commanders.[2] The operational commander, the individual charged with the actual conduct of the operation, under the American system of command should develop the plan he is charged with executing. Detailed planning is in his domain of responsibilities. Higher headquarters, the strategic commander, should study, examine, and question the plan, and if it is acceptable, then do everything possible to support the operational commander. Montgomery was responsible for the detailed planning; Eisenhower made decisions based on the options presented to him. The concept for the invasion – the operational plan – that evolved through the work of the COSSAC staff was substantially revised by Montgomery, and Bradley further refined it in the American landings. Eisenhower approved the modifications to the operational plan, obtained the approval of the Combined Chiefs of Staff and political leaders, and acquired the resources Montgomery needed to carry out the plan. Eisenhower's Supreme Headquarters, Allied Expeditionary Force (SHAEF), produced and transmitted directives to the subordinate commanders but carried out no detailed planning and published no operations orders.[3] Hence, at the strategic level, the system functioned, at least in part, as it was designed.

EISENHOWER AS SUPREME COMMANDER

In the early years of the war, the question of Eisenhower's fitness to command the Anglo-American armies became controversial. It remains so to this day. Nationalism, damaged egos, and service pride have influenced the international debate on Eisenhower's effectiveness as the strategic commander of Anglo-American forces.

When the war started in Europe in September 1939, Eisenhower was a lieutenant colonel serving under General Douglas MacArthur in the Philippines. He had considerable staff and administrative experience but little experience in troop units and no World War I experience. This was a matter of some concern to Eisenhower. In a letter to his friend General Leonard T. Gerow, Eisenhower wrote:

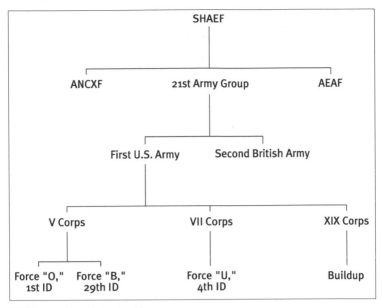

SHAEF organization for the invasion of Europe.

At various times I have had informal reports from Washington, to the effect that I had been requested for positions on certain Corps and Division staffs. My informants have told me that in each such instance the War Department (Chief of Infantry) has declined to give favorable consideration, on the grounds that I needed duty with troops.[4]

In 1940, Eisenhower was assigned to the 3rd Division at Fort Lewis, Washington. He took command of the 1st Battalion, 15th Infantry, and assumed the duties of regimental executive officer. In November, he became a member of the division staff, and in March, he was promoted to colonel. From June to December 1941, Eisenhower served as the chief of staff of the Third Army at San Antonio, Texas. In this capacity, he participated in the Louisiana maneuvers, the largest peacetime training exercise conducted by the army prior to America's entry into the war. During the exercise, Eisenhower earned a reputa-

tion as an outstanding planner and organizer. He received consider-
able credit for the success of the Third Army, and his standing soared.
In September 1941, he was promoted to brigadier general. Five days
after the Japanese attack at Pearl Harbor, Colonel Walter Bedell Smith
directed Eisenhower to report to Washington. In February 1942,
Eisenhower was appointed chief of the War Plans Division, War
Department, and in March, he was promoted to major general. In
April, he was designated assistant chief of staff of the Operations
Division, Office of the Chief of Staff. Two months later, he was
assigned commanding general of the European theater, and the
following month, he was promoted to lieutenant general. On 13
August, after receiving the approval of Churchill, Eisenhower was
appointed Allied supreme commander of Operation Torch. On 8
November, he commanded the invasion of North Africa. Later, he was
appointed commander in chief of Allied forces in North Africa, and as
such, he was senior commander for the conduct of operations in
North Africa, Sicily, and Italy. In February 1943, Eisenhower was
promoted to general. In December, Eisenhower was given command
of Anglo-American forces for the invasion of Europe. Eisenhower
commanded and directed all Anglo-American air, sea, and land forces
in the Normandy invasion and then planned and directed the northwest European theater strategy and served as ground force commander
until the end of the war in May 1945. Thus, he served as the strategic
commander of Allied forces and, after the invasion, when two army
groups were formed, as the senior operational commander – ground
force commander. Eisenhower's rise from lieutenant colonel to
general was nothing less than phenomenal. He achieved senior rank
without commanding major tactical or operational units and without
serving in combat.

In 1960, Morris Janowitz observed: 'A successful military establishment must be run by military managers [the strategic commander],
but must include in its very elite a leaven of heroic leaders [opera-
tional and tactical commanders].' Janowitz recognized that modern
armed forces possess three types of leaders: the traditional heroic type,

the managerial type, and the technologist. According to Janowitz: 'The military manager reflects the scientific and pragmatic dimensions of war-making; he is the professional with effective links to civilian society. The heroic leader is a perpetuation of the warrior type, the mounted officer who embodied the martial spirit and the theme of personal valor.'[5] The advent of the new managerial, political, diplomatic general was brought about by the increased significance of coalition warfare; the huge increase in size and importance of the military in American society; the great cost to the treasury of the United States that the armed forces came to represent during World War II; the increased contact between civilian and military leaders; and the ever-increasing importance of machines, technology, and industry in the ability of the nation to make war. The military manager became important to the modernization and survival of the institution. Still, the heroic type was necessary to lead men in battle. The heroic type imbued warrior values, duty, honor, loyalty, and courage and sought glory. The managerial type sought efficiency, rationality, pragmatism, and utility. General George Patton was a heroic leader; Marshall and Eisenhower were managerial leaders. They established a new precedent, aspects of which remain in the U.S. Army to this day. Martin Blumenson and James L. Stokesbury wrote: 'Eisenhower inaugurated a broader framework of operations more in tune with the nature of modern coalition warfare.'[6]

Few individuals possess the characteristics of both heroic and managerial types. Generals who serve exclusively as technologists and managers do not have to master generalship in the traditional sense. They are not concerned directly with leading men, and they don't fight battles or campaigns. Generals who fight tactical or operational forces or make decisions on the conduct of battles and campaigns, whether they be the managerial or heroic type, need to master generalship.

Generalship is the art and science of employing all available forces to achieve military and ultimately political objectives in the least costly manner to the peoples of a nation or coalition. Generalship requires mastery of the technology employed in war; proficiency in strategic, operational, and tactical doctrine; expertise in skills required to motivate, train, organize, and lead men; knowledge of combined and joint operational doctrine; and mastery of the methods used to manage and supervise large, complex organizations. To become technically competent requires schooling and training. To become an artist, to achieve mastery in any discipline, requires years of practical experience. Because wars are episodic, the practice required to become an artist is seldom acquired; thus, nations typically go to war with only partially skilled and trained generals. The ability to learn fast and to select subordinates with skills that make up for one's own deficiencies is therefore also important.

When Eisenhower was given command of the campaign in North Africa, he had neither the experience nor the knowledge in operational and tactical doctrine to command such an endeavor. During the campaign, Eisenhower's lack of experience was obvious. The British chief of the Imperial General Staff, Field Marshal Lord Alan Brooke, wrote:

> [Eisenhower] had neither the tactical nor strategical experience required for such a task. By bringing Alexander over from the Middle East and appointing him as Deputy to Eisenhower, we were... flattering and pleasing the Americans in so far as we were placing our senior and experienced commander to function under their commander who had no war experience.[7]

Bradley and Blair wrote:

> Ike had now been defeated twice in Africa – in the December race for Tunis and the February German offensive. The latter had cost 6,300 American casualties... Ike led an extraordinarily charmed life. Had the British not already engineered his elevation into the 'stratosphere... I feel certain that after Kasserine Pass he would have been fired. Ike was a political general of rare and valuable gifts, but as his African record clearly demonstrates, he did not know how to manage a battlefield.[8]

Early in the war, the British insulated Eisenhower from the actual conduct of operations. They knew he lacked experience but were reluctant to push for his relief out of fear of offending the American public and political leaders, many of whom wanted to focus on fighting the 'treacherous' Japanese who had attacked American soil.[9] The British, with the approval of U.S. Army Chief of Staff George Marshall, put in place a command structure that in essence elevated Eisenhower to the status of supreme commander and effectively removed him from the battlefield and the conduct of operations while retaining for Americans the top position.[10] The British assumed the positions of deputies for air, sea, and ground and took over the conduct of operations in the Mediterranean theater. These operations were primarily based on British strategic thinking. Air Marshal Sir Arthur Tedder became deputy for air operations, Admiral Sir Andrew Cunningham became deputy for naval operations, and General Sir Harold Alexander became deputy for ground operations. Brooke concluded: 'The main impression I gathered was that Eisenhower was no real director of thought, plans, energy or direction. Just a co-ordinator, a good mixer, a champion of inter-Allied co-operation, and in those respects few can hold the candle to him. But is that enough?'[11] Some American commanders formed similar impressions. In reference to the Sicily campaign, Bradley and Blair wrote:

> The Combined Chiefs named Ike commander in chief for the Sicily operation. But Ike had no direct command responsibility for planning and executing the operation. The Combined Chiefs delegated this responsibility to Ike's deputies for ground, air and sea... Ike had become in his own description, 'chairman of the board,' presiding over a committee of three to run the war.[12]

In the campaign for the invasion of Europe, the British again managed to retain all of the top-level operational command positions: Montgomery was ground commander; Admiral Sir Bertram H. Ramsay was commander in chief of naval forces; and Air Chief Marshal Sir Trafford Leigh-Mallory was commander in chief of air forces. Eisenhower never had the opportunity to mature as a tactical and operational commander in war. He never personally fought a combat unit of any size in battle. Eisenhower was not a traditional American military commander in the vein of Washington, Grant, Sherman, Pershing, or MacArthur. His lack of combat experience prevented him from obtaining the respect automatically given to those who have served in battle. The words of Montgomery – 'nice chap, no general' – Brooke, and other British generals were blunt and often unkind in their appraisal of Eisenhower's abilities as a general.[13]

Certain American generals and admirals were also critical of Eisenhower's leadership. Patton was probably the most critical and, in his diary, accused him of one of the worst sins an American commander can be charged with – that of failing to look after the welfare of his soldiers: 'The U.S. Troops get wholly separated and all chance of being in at the kill [the final battle in Tunisia] and getting some natural credit is lost. Bradley and I explained this to Ike and he said he would stop it. He has done nothing. He is completely sold out to the British... Ike must go. He is a typical case of a beggar on horse-back – could not stand prosperity.' Patton believed Eisenhower was 'too weak in character to be worthy' of his loyal subordinate commanders.[14] In his diary in January 1945, Patton, frustrated at the actions of SHAEF, wrote: 'It is too bad that the highest levels of command have no personal knowledge of war.'[15] Bradley too held a low assessment of Eisenhower's knowledge and understanding of the art of war: 'Ike sent me my first official letter as II Corps commander. It was very long, patronizing in tone, and it contained some specific tactical suggestions which were dangerously ill-conceived and proof to me (if further proof were needed) that Ike had little grasp of sound battlefield tactics.'[16]

After the war, Admiral Hall, the commander of Amphibious Force 'O,' which landed the 1st ID at Omaha Beach, wrote: '[Eisenhower] was one of the most overrated men in military history.'[17] Eisenhower seemed to have never earned the respect and loyalty of some of his most senior subordinate American and British commanders.

Eisenhower, however, was a smart man. He had a keen, analytical mind and was a strategic thinker. He was noted for his foresight and common sense, his ability to express ideas clearly and concisely, and his administrative skills. Major General George Van Horn Moseley, under whom Eisenhower served as a major, wrote Eisenhower: 'You possess one of those exceptional minds which enables you to assemble and to analyze a set of facts, always drawing sound conclusions and equally important, you have the ability to express those conclusions in clear and convincing form. Many officers can take the first two steps of a problem, but few have your ability of expression.'[18] It was this exceptional ability of Eisenhower's that kept him in administrative and staff assignments and away from combat units.

In the Mediterranean and Europe, Eisenhower had an almost impossible task – to merge the egos, cultures, and military traditions of two nations into a workable command structure. Marshall believed that Allied co-operation was one of the most important elements for success, if not the most important element. He recognized Eisenhower's strengths and selected him to go to England to represent the United States because of them. In a speech given at Yale University in February 1944, Marshall stated:

> In my opinion the triumph over Germany in the coming months depends more on a complete accord between the British and American forces than it does on any other single factor, air power, ground power or naval power... The harmful possibilities of... discord have been serious in the past and will continue to be so in the future because of the necessity in the European Theater of combined opera- tions, even involving on occasions the complete intermingling of troops... That we have been able to master these very human difficul- ties, that in fact we have triumphed over them to the disaster of the enemy, is in my opinion the greatest single Allied achievement of the war.[19]

More than any other individual, it was Eisenhower who made this triumph over 'human difficulties' possible. One of Eisenhower's first actions upon taking command in England was to assemble his combined staff to give them his perspective: 'We are not Allies. We have plenty of Allies among the United Nations, but we who are to undertake this great operation are one indivisible force with all its parts more closely integrated than has ever been the case in any force before.'[20] As noted above, Eisenhower's unique perspective did not win him the loyalty and respect of many British senior leaders. Given the command structure put in place, the British did an excellent job of insulating Eisenhower. Above him in England, where the planning for the Normandy invasion took place, were Churchill and the British members of the Combined Chiefs of Staff, and below him were the British senior operational commanders. Still, Eisenhower deserves much credit for maintaining a difficult alliance.

In a letter to his son during the war, Eisenhower wrote: 'This business of warfare is no longer just a question of getting out and teaching the soldier how to shoot... [I]t is partly politics, partly public speaking, partly essay-writing, partly social contact, on to all of which is tacked the business of training and disciplining an army.'[21] Eisenhower understood the importance of public support and the necessity of maintaining a positive public image – issues that were not a problem in non-democratic nations. He also understood the importance of cultivating good relations with peoples of allied nations. Politics, diplomacy, and public speaking were an important part of his job. Without skill in these areas, he would not have been able to secure all of the resources required for the invasion.

Eisenhower also understood that war was a deadly serious business. In a letter to Gerow written after the invasion of North Africa, he expressed his thoughts:

> I wish that every Division Commander in the United States Army could go up there right now and see the consequences, the appalling consequences, of failure to achieve in advance some measure of battlefield discipline, to teach his men the essentials of scouting, patrolling and security, to insist upon initiative on the part of every leader from Corporal up, and finally to harden his men to the point

that the physique of man can achieve no more. We have the greatest material in the world but our men must learn what a serious business this is, they must know that their own lives depend upon the thoroughness with which they learn the lessons taught, and officers that fail to devote themselves completely and exclusively to the task must be ruthlessly weeded out. Considerations of friendship, family, kindliness and nice personality have nothing whatsoever to do with the problem. We owe it to the service to which we belong and certainly we owe it to the men, whose lives depend upon the energy, keenness and thoroughness that we display.[22]

Eisenhower was not a student of war in the vein of Patton, the military historian, or Montgomery, the military trainer and technician. Eisenhower, however, knew how to manage, co-ordinate, and synchronize the many complex organizations that made modern warfare possible. In his book *Crusade in Europe,* Eisenhower wrote:

Our Mediterranean experiences had reaffirmed the truth that unity, co-ordination, and co-operation are the key to successful operations. War is waged in three elements but there is not separate land, air, or naval war. Unless all assets in all elements are efficiently combined and co-ordinated against a properly selected, common objective, their maximum potential power cannot be realized. Physical targets may be separated by the breadth of a continent or an ocean, but their destruction must contribute in maximum degree to the furtherance of the combined plan of operation. That is what co-ordination means.[23]

Eisenhower recognized and understood the importance of synchronizing air, sea, and naval resources to achieve synergy; however, in Allied operations, synergy was not attained. The co-operation needed to conduct professional combined, joint operations was not achieved in World War II. A degree of selflessness was required that too many British and American generals were incapable of displaying. After the war, Eisenhower observed:

Once in Europe during the war, when I was talking to two great soldiers, General George Marshall and Omar Bradley, I asked them what special quality they look for in a man to be given a big job. We talked it over for some time... In the end, the three of us agreed that what we would look for was selflessness. The man who is selfless tackles the job you give him with all his heart and courage and interest. He thinks only of what he can get done for his country, his commander, and his troops. He doesn't begin to think about himself until his job is about finished, if he does so then. He is too busy, too intent on selfless service.

Eisenhower was one of the most selfless leaders in World War II. The same cannot be said for many of his immediate subordinates.

Eisenhower's decision-making in war and peace was greatly influenced by technology. He had a strong measure of the culturally imbued American faith in technology, faith that technology would soon eliminate the need for man on the battlefield.[24] Eisenhower wrote: 'Foremost among the military lessons [of World War II] was the extraordinary and growing influence of the airplane in the waging of war. The European campaign almost daily developed new and valuable uses for air power. Its effect in the weakening of German capacity was decisively felt on both fronts, the Allied and the Russian.'[25] In a speech to Congress on 16 November 1945, Eisenhower stated:

The Normandy invasion was based on a deep-seated faith in the power of the air forces, in overwhelming numbers, to intervene in the land battle. That is, a faith that the air forces, by their action could have the effect on the ground of making it possible for a small force to land troops to invade a continent, a country strongly defended, in which there were 61 enemy divisions and where we could not possibly on the first day of the assault land more than 7 divisions... Without that air force, without the aid of its power, entirely aside from its anticipated ability to sweep the enemy air forces out of the sky, without its power to intervene in the land battle, that invasion would have been fantastic... Unless we had that faith in the air power to intervene and to make safe that landing, it would have been more than fantastic, it would have been criminal.[26]

In Eisenhower's opinion, the decisive element in the Normandy campaign was air power.[27] Eisenhower's view of war during his presidency was based on air power – strategic bombers and nuclear weapons. His vision de-emphasized the role of ground forces and emphasized that of air forces.

Eisenhower did not grasp the complexities of amphibious operations. His lack of experience in amphibious warfare prevented him from accurately assessing the merits of Montgomery's invasion plan. Jeter A. Isley and Philip A. Crowl, in their work *The U.S. Marines and Amphibious War,* quoted Eisenhower:

> General Dwight D. Eisenhower in an interview after the war succinctly stated the navy's responsibility, but he seemed largely to have forgotten the amphibious training and experience his troops needed before setting foot on the coast of Normandy. "You know an amphibious landing is not a particularly difficult thing," he said, "but it's a touchy and delicate thing, and anything can go wrong. In some ways, from the land fellow's viewpoint, it is one of the simplest operations. You put your men in boats and as long as you get well-trained crews to take the boats in, it is the simplest deployment in the world—the men can go nowhere else except to the beach.[28]

This statement is clearly the view of the uninitiated. It indicates that Eisenhower was not tactically and operationally astute in amphibious operations and that he did not talk and/or listen to his American operational and tactical commanders. Admirals Hewitt and Hall and Generals Patton, Gerow, and Huebner were more or less left with the impression that the supreme commander did not care to hear what they had to say. They were unable to share their views with the supreme commander and frequently went to battle with plans they knew were defective.

A further example of Eisenhower's incapacity to make decisions regarding the combat employment of American soldiers was his decision to maximize the loading of landing craft in order to secure sufficient craft to conduct Operation Anvil, the proposed amphibious assault in southern France that was originally to be conducted in conjunction with the Normandy invasion to draw German forces away from the Normandy site. The British believed Operation Anvil should be canceled not only because of the shortage of landing craft but also because the landing site was too far away to act as a diversion. Eisenhower, in an effort to maintain the operation, probably to comply with the wishes of the American chief of staff, Marshall, had his staff develop a loading plan that maximized the capacity of the landing craft. Montgomery initially opposed the new loading plan on the grounds that it would 'compromise tactical flexibility, introduce added complications, bring additional hazards into the operations, and thus generally endanger success.'[29] For some reason, however, perhaps for the sake of Allied co-operation, Montgomery backed down and accepted the proposal.[30] But perhaps Montgomery's initial misgivings were correct.[31] The new organization disrupted unit integrity and thereby diminished combat power. In the army, there is a saying, 'Train the way you fight.' Huebner and the staff of the 1st ID believed that this commonsense principle was violated at considerable cost in the invasion at Normandy.

Eisenhower procured, allocated, and managed resources.[32] He co-ordinated the use of assets. He gained consensus. He informed superiors and political leaders. He placated, cajoled, appeased, compromised, and, when necessary, dictated. On some occasions, he stood his ground and was immovable. Two such instances were over command of the strategic air forces of both nations and Operation Anvil. Eisenhower's primary influences on the plan for the conduct of the Normandy invasion were in tying the American practice of war to the British way of war and securing the strategic bombers of the U.S. Eighth Air Force for deployment by Montgomery. Without them, Montgomery's plan would have been very different. During the war, Eisenhower developed a British outlook. This is not surprising given the fact that all of his operational commanders throughout the war were British. At the strategic level of war, this meant that major campaigns tended to be based on British strategic thinking. At the tactical and operational levels, the British and American armed forces acted independently, each employing their own doctrinal practices, except in combined operations, where the American and British armies had to fight alongside each other. Under these conditions, the American practice of war was subordinate to the British practice of war. The operational vision that prevailed at Normandy was primarily of British conception and design. However, the British practice of war could not be implemented in a pure form. The presence of American technology, resources, and thinking prevented the British from conducting the Normandy campaign in the manner most natural to British inclinations.

In the Normandy invasion, Eisenhower did not exert the type of influence expected of American military leaders for four reasons. First, he did not have the authority to select his subordinate commanders. Political leaders – Roosevelt and Churchill – rightly or wrongly, made these decisions. Second, his primary objective was to maintain the coalition. Third, he adopted, in part, British thinking about war. And fourth, he never mastered the art and science of generalship in the traditional sense. He lacked the tactical and operational experience in amphibious operations to assess and make decisions on the basic principles, the doctrinal considerations, on which the plan was based. This lack of experience also may have caused a lack of confidence that resulted in a tendency to defer to the supposed superior knowledge of others who were more experienced.

MONTGOMERY'S PLAN

On 1 January 1944, Montgomery relinquished command of the British Eighth Army in Italy to assume command of the 21st Army Group and thus operational command of ground forces for the invasion of Europe.[33] In 1948, Montgomery published *Normandy to the*

Baltic, in which he stated: 'The assault was an operation requiring a single co-ordinated plan of action under one commander; I therefore became the overall land force commander responsible to the Supreme Commander for planning and executing the military aspects of the assault and subsequent capture of lodgment area.'[34] On 1 February 1944, the three commanders in chief for land, sea, and air produced the Neptune Initial Joint Plan. Because of his dominant personality, however, Montgomery was largely responsible for the plan. Each commander in chief had his own staff developing his section of the plan. The staffs periodically got together to work out discrepancies, and through this process, the plan for the invasion took final shape.

On New Year's Eve 1943, Churchill had handed Montgomery a copy of the COSSAC plans for the invasion of Europe. Montgomery excused himself early from the company of the prime minister to study the plans. The next day, he gave Churchill his initial assessment. Cautioning that he had not had sufficient time to fully study the plans and consult with his senior staff and commanders, he noted that '[t]he initial landing is on too narrow a front and is confined to too small an area' and that passing arriving divisions through those already ashore would cause extreme difficulties and confusion. He concluded that 'the present plan is impracticable' and proposed an alternate approach:

> The type of plan required is on the following lines:
> a. One British army to land on a front of two, or possibly three corps. One American army similarly.
> b. Follow-up divisions to come in to the corps already on shore.
> c. The available assault craft to be used for the landing troops. Successive flights to follow rapidly in any type of unarmoured craft, and to be poured in.
> d. The air battle must be won before the operation is launched. We must then aim at success in the land battle by speed and violence of our operations.[35]

Montgomery's initial assessment reflected the almost unanimous view of commanders from the Mediterranean theater who participated in

Operation Torch and/or Operation Husky. Greater force over a larger area had been used in both previous invasions. Certainly 'Festung Europa' would require a larger invasion force. Thus began the revisions to the COSSAC Overlord plan as it rapidly evolved into the Neptune operations plan. When Eisenhower returned to England on 15 January after receiving instructions in Washington from the army chief of staff on his new appointment, Montgomery was waiting with a revised plan.

On 21 January, Eisenhower convened a meeting of his senior operational commanders to hear and discuss Montgomery's plan.[36] Present were Tedder, Ramsay, Montgomery, Leigh-Mallory, Lieutenant General Carl A. Spaatz, Morgan, Bradley, Smith, Barker, Kirk, and others. Morgan spoke first. He briefly outlined the COSSAC plan, with which all were familiar. Montgomery then opened his presentation by commenting on the COSSAC plan: 'According to the original plan, we should be attacking on a relatively narrow front; this would make it easier for the enemy to locate and hold us, and more difficult for us to emerge quickly and strike hard and deep. We should be limiting the area in which it was possible for us to discover a soft spot in the enemy's position.' He then outlined his own vision: 'In order to achieve quick success, it would be necessary to have an assault on a five divisional front plus one air-borne division. The expedition should be organised on a front of two armies, each of which would be on a front of two corps. It would be preferable to make the widest possible landing between the areas of heavy fire of the CHERBOURG guns on the right and the HAVRE guns on the left. In this area the U.S. forces should be placed on the right and the British on the left.' Montgomery had expanded the landing to five divisions and extended the invasion area to include the eastern side of the Cotentin peninsula. Instead of concentrating his force, Montgomery planned multiple landings on a broad front. He believed it was essential to capture the port of Cherbourg at the earliest opportunity because he did not want to remain dependent on the artificial harbors for too long. The Americans were given the mission of seizing Cherbourg. To facilitate the capture of Cherbourg, Montgomery planned an airborne assault on the Cotentin peninsula. While the Americans were capturing the port, the British and Canadian forces were to 'deal with the enemy main body approaching from the East and South-East.'[37] Montgomery's plan, at this time, was based on the same tenets as those followed in the landings in North Africa and Sicily.

Eisenhower then spoke. He agreed with Montgomery's plan, but he cautioned against making a premature decision on the invasion of the south of France. The British believed Operation Anvil should be canceled because of insufficient landing craft to conduct the Normandy invasion and because the operation did not fit into their strategic vision. Eisenhower stated: 'We ought to look upon the elimination of the ANVIL attack only as a last resort. We must remember that the RUSSIANS had been led to expect that that Operation would take place, and in addition there would be at least seven AMERICAN and seven FRENCH divisions which would remain idle in the MEDITERRANEAN if ANVIL did not take place.'[38] By March, however, Eisenhower wrote Marshall: 'I firmly believe that ANVIL as we originally visualized it is no longer a possibility.' Eisenhower needed landing craft, and he requested that the bulk of the landing craft planned for use in Anvil 'come here so that we may have the greatest possible chance of success.'[39]

Ramsay followed Eisenhower. He pointed out the implications of expanding the landing. The naval bombardment fleet, minesweeper force, and transport fleet would all have to be enlarged. In regard to the naval bombardment fleet, he stated: 'As for bombarding units, additional cruisers could be made available, but provision of monitors or old battleships was difficult. It appeared that in the new circumstances the SEXTANT decisions would have to be revised and that a measure of U.S. assistance would need to be provided... It had been agreed at SEXTANT that the necessary covering forces (the assault shipping and craft) should be provided from BRITISH sources.' This problem was never resolved to the satisfaction of Hall. Ramsay also noted that '[f]rom the Naval point of view it was desirable that the assault should take place with a moon.'[40] Ramsay believed the Anglo-American generals would continue the practice of night landings used in the Mediterranean theater. He suggested that early May or early June was the best time to land because of the moonlight.

Leigh-Mallory then examined the expanded operation from the point of view of the air forces and discussed Montgomery's plan to isolate the battlefield:

> The tasks at present were to decide when to start bombing for 'OVERLORD' and which were the suitable targets to attack. The Air Chief Marshal's intention was to interfere with enemy communication in North-West EUROPE until there arose a state of paralysis on the railways, as requested by General MONTGOMERY. His plan was to produce an overall falling-off of efficiency on the railway system by a systematic attack on servicing stations... This bombing would be begun some two months or six weeks before D-Day.[41]

On 23 January, Eisenhower formally proposed the 'Montgomery Plan,' the appellation by which it became known, to the Combined Chiefs of Staff. On 1 February, Montgomery's headquarters in conjunction with Leigh-Mallory and Ramsay published the Neptune Initial Joint Plan. This 'initial' plan would be the only plan produced by Montgomery and the commanders in chief for air and sea. At this juncture, the plan went to Bradley's First U.S. Army (FUSA) and General Miles Dempsey's Second British Army. They were directed to submit their Outline Assault Plan to the joint commanders in chief by 15 February.

The Initial Joint Plan for the invasion of 'Festung Europa' called for three phases: the preliminary operations phase, the assault phase, and the build-up phase. The preliminary phase was devoted to naval and air operations. Preliminary naval operations involved acquiring and assembling transport ships and landing craft in southern England and training landing craft crews. Preparations for minesweeping operations to clear the Channel for the invasion fleet were also made. The Allied air forces' first priority was to continue the destruction of the German air force through Operation Pointblank, already under way. Their second priority was to intensify efforts to isolate the battlefield by destroying communication networks – what became known as the Transportation Plan.[42] The assets involved in the preliminary phase were not under Montgomery's command, and the strategic air forces were not under Eisenhower's command. Nevertheless, the Allied air force's efforts to destroy the German air force and isolate the battle-field were a complete success. Air and sea domination – the prerequisite for an amphibious assault against hostile shores – was complete, leaving Montgomery and his subordinate ground and naval amphibious force commanders free to conduct the assault phase.

According to the Initial Joint Plan, in the assault phase,

> [t]he object will be to capture the towns of St. Mère-Eglise 3495, Carentan 3984, Isigny 5085, Bayeux 7879 and Caen 0368 by the evening of D-Day.
>
> First United States Army will assault with one regimental combat team between Varreville 4299 and the Carentan Estuary 4590 [Utah Beach] and two regimental combat teams between Vierville-sur-Mer 6491 and Colleville-sur-Mer 6888 [Omaha Beach]. The tasks of First United States Army in order of priority will be: (a) to capture Cherbourg as quickly as possible, (b) to develop the Vierville-sur-Mer–Colleville-sur-Mer beachhead Southward towards St Lô in conformity with the advance of Second British Army.
>
> Second British Army will assault with five brigades between Asnelles 8784 and Ouistreham 1179. The main task of Second British Army will be to develop the Bridgehead South of the line Caen 0368–St Lo 4963 and South East to Caen in order to secure airfield sites and to protect the flank of First United States Army while the latter is capturing Cherbourg.[43]

Omaha Beach – between Vierville-sur-Mer and Colleville-sur-Mer – was to be attacked by two RCTs of the V Corps, and Utah Beach – between the Carentan estuary and Varreville – was to be attacked by one RCT of the VII Corps. Bombardment of coast artillery batteries and beach defenses was to start before H-Hour, the time at which the first wave of landing craft was scheduled to hit the beach. The final plan for the use of bombers and naval gunfire had not been worked out when the Neptune plan was issued. Close support for the assault forces was to be provided by naval and air resources. The air force was also given the mission to interdict enemy forces attempting to reinforce the coast defense units and to attack enemy reserves.

The mission of airborne forces was as follows:

> One airborne division under command of First United States Army will land in the area behind the Varreville 4299–Carentan 3984 beaches with the main object of assisting the seaborne landing. Two airborne brigades under command of Second British Army will land East of the River Orne with the objects of covering the left flank and delaying the arrival of the enemy reserve divisions from Lisieux. A further airborne division under command of First United States Army, will be landed in the Cotentin peninsula late on D-Day and early on D+1.[44]

Finally, the Initial Joint Plan noted that two other plans were being developed. Air forces, Special Air Service, resistance groups, and the intelligence community were developing a plan to delay the employment of the enemy's strategic reserves. And the Joint Fire Plan was being formulated by all of the services.

The Initial Joint Plan was only a partial plan. Significant portions still had to be worked out. The plan addressed the mechanics of the invasion. It described who, what, when, where, and why, but the crucial how could not be fully apprehended from the text. The plan did not delineate the flow of battle, when and where maximum exertion would be required, when and where the enemy's main element would be engaged, how it would be destroyed, or what elements were crucial to the successful outcome of the campaign.

An operation of the magnitude of the invasion of Europe requires that the commander articulate a vision. Simply amassing and co-ordinating troops and weapons, assigning beaches, and publishing timetables for the assault and build-up of troops and materials is not enough. Soldiers, sailors, and airmen need to know at what point the maximum effort will be required of them, at what point they will be receiving the enemy's maximum effort, and at what point they should plan to destroy the enemy's main body. By understanding the commander's vision of the flow of the battle, subordinate units can prepare themselves for the battle not only physically but also mentally. A commander needs to articulate to his subordinates how he plans to achieve victory so the entire command can focus on the same objectives and surge forward in unison, amplifying the power of the various parts, achieving synergy. In Montgomery's Initial Joint Plan, his thinking on how he planned to defeat the enemy is only partially unveiled.

MONTGOMERY'S APPROACH TO WAR

An examination of Montgomery's philosophy and thinking about war and conduct of battles and campaigns will facilitate the comprehension of the Montgomery Plan. Insight can be gained into Montgomery's approach to war by examining his conduct of the campaigns in North Africa, Sicily, and Italy; what he and others wrote about his battles, campaigns, and art of war; and what general officers who fought with, for, or against Montgomery thought of his practice of war.[45] In regard to Montgomery's writings, several caveats are in order. Montgomery, like other general officers, was concerned about his reputation and about how history would assess his role in World War II. Hence, caution is required when reading his accounts written after the war.[46] Most revealing were Montgomery's words written during the war and his actions, which displayed continuity.

Montgomery was a major general commanding a division in 1939, the year World War II started for Great Britain. He had vast military experience in training and commanding soldiers and had commanded at every level, company, battalion, brigade, and division. In the early stages of the war, he commanded a corps. In World War I, he had fought at the Somme and Passchendaele, the two battles in recent history that formed the lens through which the British viewed all of World War II. At the Somme, while leading a company charge across 'no-man's land,' he was wounded, given up for dead, and almost buried.[47] For his courage, he was awarded the Distinguished Service Order, the second highest British award for bravery.

Nigel Hamilton, the noted biographer of Montgomery, believed that this event was the 'seminal experience of his entire life' and formed his understanding of war, how it should be fought, and what it took to win.[48] It is likely that the seminal events in the lives of the British people in the twentieth century were the six-month battles at the Somme and Passchendaele, in which the 'flower' of a generation of 'British manhood' was slaughtered. It might be argued that Montgomery's conduct of war was in direct opposition to the conduct of war he experienced and witnessed in World War I, which so appalled him (and that Churchill's strategy for the conduct of World War II was in opposition to that used to fight World War I). The unprofessional behavior of British senior commanders – who had no knowledge of the situation on the front and the conditions under which troops fought, lived, and died; did not know how to prepare for and conduct a battle or campaign; failed to train soldiers for the tasks that faced them; and failed to use every measure at hand to limit casualties and save lives – affected Montgomery's character.[49] Pure professionalism was what Montgomery sought and the only thing he would accept. Montgomery was intolerant of the shortcomings of other officers. In war and in training for war, there was no room for mediocrity in his view. He would not tolerate it from his subordinates or from his superiors, and more than once, he got into difficulties for going over the head of his immediate superior, whom he believed was serving in a capacity above his talents and abilities. Montgomery became a zealot, espousing a philosophy of war he thought would minimize the loss of life and achieve objectives. Hamilton wrote:

> Monty learned the lessons that would, one day, help save the democratic world. What can a responsible commander, concerned with human life, ask the men of a democracy to do? Does not a commander carry a responsibility to study his enemy and train his officers and men *in advance of* battle, integrating artillery and infantry,

pivoting both attack and defense upon positions of strength, and streamlining communications to ensure maximum cohesion? Clarity of purpose was imperative, but imaginative rehearsal – by the staff as well as the participating troops – was the secret of waging modern war, Monty became certain.[50]

Although Montgomery was appalled at the way in which World War I was actually carried out, he believed that the principles for the conduct of the war were valid and correct. What angered him was the performance of many British officers who failed to adhere to these principles. A Montgomery campaign was meticulously planned, prepared, and rehearsed and methodically executed. Neither improvisation nor exploitation was tolerated. Not even Churchill could persuade Montgomery to start a battle before he was fully prepared. The principles of mass and simplicity guided Montgomery's thinking on the conduct of war; he implemented a mass artillery preparation before the attack and the mass employment of troops in the attack. Air power, which Montgomery thought could perform the same task as artillery but with more devastating effects, came to dominate his thinking. In a critique entitled 'Montgomery's Tactics,' the British general H. S. Sewell wrote: 'The two factors which Montgomery rates as having the most important bearing on war in general and on battle in particular are (1) use of air power and (2) administration [logistics]. The air battle is a necessary preliminary to land battles, and with air supremacy won, Montgomery's method for the employment of the air force operating with his armies has been to concentrate its full force on selected targets.'[51]

Air power augmented with artillery became the decisive element in Montgomery's practice of war. In the battle of El Alamein, Normandy, and Operation Goodwood, the attempted breakout at Caen, Montgomery used massive artillery preparations and, in the case of the latter two operations, massive strategic air power. (The American daylight strategic bombers were not available to Montgomery at El Alamein.) As in World War I, artillery (and air power) was used to open a hole in the enemy's defense through which the troops could attack. Once the hole was open, the attack had to be conducted vigorously, the goal being to overwhelm the enemy at the point of the breakthrough. Montgomery fought battles that were designed to destroy the enemy methodically and unquestionably.

In 1944, Montgomery published two pamphlets for his subordinate commanders delineating his thinking on the conduct of battles and campaigns: 'Some Notes on the Conduct of War and the Infantry Division in Battle' and 'Some Notes on the Use of Air Power in Support of Land Operations.' In 'Some Notes on the Conduct of War and the Infantry Division in Battle,' under the heading 'The Basic Points of Any Operation,' Montgomery wrote:

12 (b) KEEP YOUR FIRE POWER CONCENTRATED
         UNDER CENTRALIZED CONTROL WHENEVER
         POSSIBLE.
    (c) IN ALL OFFENSIVE OPERATIONS ENDEAVOR TO HIT
         HARD ON A NARROW FRONT AND KEEP ON
         HITTING, PENETRATE DEEPLY, AND THEN TURN
         OUTWARDS, i.e. THE SCHWER-PUNKT AND THE
         AUFROLLEN. THE MOMENTUM OF THE ATTACK
         MUST BE KEPT UP AT ALL COSTS.
    (d) FIGHT YOUR BRIGADES AS BRIGADES, WITH DEFI-
         NITE TASKS AND CLEAR CUT OBJECTIVES.

Under the heading 'The Setpiece Attack,' he wrote:

15. Depth in the attack is necessary... to maintain the momentum of
    the attack; fresh troops must be ready to go through, even if the first
    attacking troops have not got all their objectives. An attack should
    always aim at deep penetration to over-run enemy mortar and gun
    positions...
17. The assaulting troops must be assisted forward by all available
    support from artillery, mortars, machine guns and air...
18. Great fire power is useless unless the assaulting troops are able to
    take quick advantage of it. Infantry and tanks must be right up to

their supporting fire and ready to go in immediately [after] it lifts, and so over-run the defence before the latter can get its 'second wind.'

On amphibious operations, Montgomery observed:

a. SPEED AND ORDER OF LANDING ARE THE FIRST ESSENTIALS.
b. LANDING BEACHES MUST BE FREED FROM OBSERVED SMALL ARMS FIRE.
c. ARMOURED COLUMNS MUST BE PUSHED QUICKLY INLAND.
d. KEEP THE INITIATIVE...

45. It is most important to get enough infantry supporting arms quickly on shore to withstand immediate counter-attack. This will depend largely upon sound preliminary planning...
47. The Division may land on a wide front at several beaches. Once these are firmly joined up, the enemy's chance of isolating them, dealing with them in detail, has gone.[52]

Montgomery's dissertation on war is predominately based on World War I thinking. The operational concepts for armor warfare of the British military theoreticians J.F.C. Fuller and B.H. Liddell-Hart could not be integrated into Montgomery's concept for the conduct of war. Montgomery did not practice the greatest ground-war doctrinal development of World War II – 'Blitzkrieg' operational and tactical doctrine.[53] The fluid battle characterized by multiple fast-moving armor formations supported by close air support, mobile infantry, and artillery conducting breakthrough attacks on a broad front, deep penetrations, and exploitation into the enemy's rear and finally enveloping the enemy's forces was not Montgomery's vision of war. This was not what Montgomery sought in his operations. The German doctrine required that senior commanders relinquish some control of their formations and allow their subordinate commanders to take the initiative. In essence, under German doctrine, the flow and direction of the battle were controlled from the front, where division and corps commanders made the decisions. Montgomery could not tolerate such freedom of operations from his subordinates.

Montgomery's dissertation advanced the concept of deep penetration (item 15) and noted that the enemy's mortars and gun positions 'should always' be the targets. Thus, deep penetration in Montgomery's view was 4–6 kilometers into the enemy's rear. This is World War II verbiage and World War I thinking. A deep penetration for armor formations was 30–40 kilometers into the enemy's rear, and on the Eastern front in 1941 and 1942, penetrations several hundred kilometers deep were conducted. Instead of multiple penetrations along a broad front, a technique that allowed the attacking force to find and exploit weaknesses along the front, Montgomery directed his commanders to 'hit hard on a narrow front' (item 12[c]). Instead of decentralizing, Montgomery wanted his force to keep firepower 'concentrated under centralized control' (item 12[b]). Montgomery's statement that 'fresh troops must be ready to go through, even if the first attacking troops have not got all their objectives' was indicative of trench-warfare methods. This method reinforced failure; it did not exploit success. This was the approach taken at the Somme, Verdun, and other horrendous World War I battles. This was attrition-warfare thinking. Montgomery's vision for offensive operations started with a massive artillery preparation (12[b]) opening a hole through the enemy's defense. Following closely behind this firepower were the assault formations (item 18). Fresh troops were then poured through the break to press the attack (item 15).

Fuller commented during World War II on Montgomery's conduct of the battle of El Alamein: 'One of the many interesting aspects of this battle was the return made to 1916–17 methods of penetration. With the means at General Montgomery's disposal, these methods were only possible of use because the defenses he had to penetrate were insignificant when compared to those normally met in the last war.[54] Nevertheless, if the official map of the battle is correct, the bulge created by the infantry advance varies but slightly from those of

1916–17.' Fuller also noted the lack of speed with which Montgomery's army advanced: 'Another point worth noting is that, had the Eighth Army been equipped with tank mine-sweepers, such as were being produced at the end of the last war, instead of taking eight days to pierce the two minefields, there is no reason to suppose that penetration could not have been effected in twenty-four hours, or even in less.'[55]

Montgomery's vision for amphibious operations was similar to his vision for ground operations. In amphibious operations, however, he was willing to assault on a wide front (item 47). The British Combined Operations Headquarters and the Dieppe raid, which Montgomery helped plan, influenced his thinking on the conduct of amphibious operations. As the commander of the southeastern army in April 1942, Montgomery had been given the mission to conduct the assault at Dieppe; he therefore took part in the planning and became associated with the Combined Operations Headquarters.[56] After the assault was canceled, Montgomery received orders to take command of the Eighth Army in Africa and was thus disassociated from the plan and the disaster. The planners initially considered an airborne assault the night of the landing; commando operations to secure the flanks of the invasion beaches; an intensive preliminary bombardment from the air and sea; and an assault at dawn by the main body supported by tanks and direct and indirect naval gunfire. When the assault was rescheduled, the plan was changed in ways that Montgomery would have opposed. He later wrote: 'The most important were – first, the elimination of the paratroops and their replacement by commando units; secondly, the elimination of any preliminary bombing of the defences from the air. I should not myself have agreed to either of these changes.'[57] Montgomery was taken to task for these words; some believed his memory 'played him false.' Nevertheless, the results of the raid reinforced Montgomery's faith in the importance of air power and the value of the airborne assault.[58]

Transformations in operational doctrine brought about by advances in technology typically take a generation, or a long war, to be realized.

As a result, new technologies are employed to enhance and supplement traditional arms and methods, such as the use of the strategic bomber to support preparatory fire conducted by the artillery. Montgomery was a product of the World War I generation. Hence, when one studies his battles and campaigns, the principles of World War I emerge.

Rommel commented in regard to Montgomery's approach to war in the deserts of North Africa:

> The British Commander risked nothing in any way doubtful and bold solutions were completely foreign to him. So our motorized forces would have to keep up an appearance of constant activity, in order to induce ever greater caution in the British and make them even slower. I was quite satisfied that Montgomery would never take the risk of following up boldly and overrunning us, as he could have done without any danger to himself. Indeed, such a course would have cost him far fewer losses.[59]

Sir Richard McCreery, the British general who commanded the Eighth Army in Italy in the closing months of World War II, touched off a controversy in 1959 when he criticized the generalship of Montgomery in his regimental journal. He concluded that Montgomery's tactics were ill-founded and caused unnecessary losses in infantry and tanks in the battle of El Alamein, that he had been overcautious in his pursuit of the defeated German Army after the battle, and that his intolerance had caused unnecessary difficulties between the First and Eighth Armies in North Africa.[60]

Bradley's assessment of Montgomery's generalship was as follows:

> On the whole, Monty's pursuit of Rommel lacked vigor and imagination; it was more akin to moving trench warfare than the fast open maneuvering of Sherman, or the German blitzkrieg personified by Rommel himself in his better days... British generalship was too slow and too cautious.[61]

Norman Gelb in his study of Montgomery's approach to war concluded that

> in his victory at Alamein, he had displayed perseverance in what had turned into a battle of attrition rather than tactical genius... Montgomery won at Alamein because his much greater resources permitted him to keep feeding tanks and troops into the bloody fray while Rommel's forces were steadily worn down to near-exhaustion.[62]

MONTGOMERY'S VISION

In November 1943, Hitler issued directive 51 giving priority to the Western theater.[63] The geographic circumstances of Europe motivated this decision. The great expanse of territory in the East permitted the Wehrmacht to trade space for time, but a successful landing in the West might bring about a reversal of the German campaign against France and Britain in May 1940, a campaign that was over in less than two months. Rommel was given responsibility for the construction and conduct of the defense along the coast of France. The enemy situation that Montgomery and Bradley were preparing to fight would differ considerably from the enemy situation the COSSAC staff had prepared to fight. Rommel's command, Army Group B, consisted of two armies, the Seventh Army at Normandy and the Fifteenth Army at the Pas-de-Calais. Rommel strengthened the German defense in terms of men and material. Obstacles of all types were added to the defense, and minefields were laid along the coast where landings were possible. He infused a heightened sense of readiness and purpose in the German troops. He started the process of transforming the 'soft spot' the COSSAC staff had planned to fight into a deliberate defense. By June 1944, it was incomplete; still, it was substantially stronger than the defense the COSSAC staff expected to fight. Rommel also changed the German concept for the conduct of the defense. He would not hold back his forces until the situation developed and then conduct a counter-attack. He was determined to win the battle on the beaches, to fight at the water's edge.

Rommel stated: 'The enemy is at his weakest just after landing. The troops are unsure, and possibly even seasick. They are unfamiliar with the terrain. Heavy weapons are not yet available in sufficient quantity. That is the moment to strike at them and defeat them.'[64]

He planned to deploy his reserve forces near the beaches so they would be immediately available to reinforce coastal defense units. If counter-attacks were necessary, Rommel wanted them to be conducted by forces already deployed in the area of operation, forces capable of influencing the battle on D-Day. In Rommel's view, strategic reserves centrally located would be unable to take part in the battle for the beaches, and given Allied material advantages, that was where the battle, and consequently the war, would be won or lost. Rommel believed Allied air power changed the dynamics of the battlefield. The Allies' domination of the air gave them the ability to interdict and destroy forces attempting to counter-attack or reinforce from locations outside the immediate battle area. Rommel concluded that the main effort had to be made on the beaches, and he wanted as many divisions as possible forward deployed.

The theater commander, Field Marshal Gred von Rundstedt, and General Freiherr Leo Geyr von Schweppenburg, commander of Panzer Group West, opposed Rommel's vision for the conduct of the defense.[65] They understood the basic principles of mass and economy of force and believed the battle for the beaches was in essence an economy-of-force mission, that minimum essential force ought to be allocated to the beach defenses because it would be impossible to prevent a landing. In their view, this fact relegated the beach defenses to secondary importance. Schweppenburg argued that the main effort should be made inland with mass armor formations conducting a co-ordinated counter-attack after the situation had developed and the enemy's main effort had been discerned. The initial landings could be a feint or a diversion. By parceling out the mobile divisions along the coast, Rommel violated the principle of mass and deployed armor formations in a manner that restricted their movement. Rundstedt, Schweppenburg, Guderian, and other generals therefore opposed his view. They felt it was necessary to maintain strong forces in strategic reserve until the enemy's main effort was revealed and to use panzer divisions in the type of warfare for which they were designed – open, maneuver warfare. They also did not share Rommel's assessment of the capabilities and effectiveness of Allied air power.

This issue was never resolved, and the German defense was thus based on a series of compromises. One soldier-turned-historian speculated: 'If... Rommel had had his way on all counts, there might well have been one other Panzer division immediately available to counter the Allies on D-Day, and that might have been decisive.'[66] Rommel's assessment of the capabilities of Allied air power was for the most part correct. The Germans' movement of large forces on D-Day and the weeks that followed was greatly impeded by Allied air power.

Rommel lacked the time, co-operation, and resources to build the type of defense he envisioned; nevertheless, he significantly changed the quality and character of the German defense. Intelligence sources provided the Allies with sufficient information to reassess German defensive plans and, thus, the adequacy of their own plans. However, once orders are issued and preparations are being made, it is sometimes difficult to stop and reassess the plan, even in light of new intelligence. Montgomery now should have planned to overcome a deliberate defense constructed at the water's edge, not a soft spot. Rommel's defense – although uneven – was more like those employed by the Japanese in the Central Pacific in 1943 and 1944 before they learned of the awesome power of naval gunfire augmented by aerial bombardment.[67] Montgomery needed to conduct a different fight for the beaches at Normandy than the COSSAC planners had envisioned because the enemy's capabilities and likely courses of action had changed in important ways.

In a presentation given to his subordinate commanders on 7 April 1944, Montgomery assessed Rommel's defense:

> Rommel is likely to hold his mobile divisions back from the coast until he is certain where our main effort is being made. He will then concentrate them quickly and strike a hard blow, his static divisions

will endeavor to hold on defensively to important ground and act as pivots to the counter-attacks. By dusk on D-1 the enemy will be certain that the NEPTUNE area is to be assaulted in strength. By evening of D-Day he will know the width of frontage and the approximate number of our assaulting divisions. The enemy is likely that night to summon his two nearest panzer divisions to assist. By D+5 the enemy can have brought in six panzer type divisions. If he has decided to go the whole NEPTUNE hog, he will continue his efforts to push us into the sea.[68]

Not until the night of D-Day did Montgomery expect Rommel to 'summon his two nearest panzer divisions to assist,' to counter-attack. But if the Germans were certain at 'dusk on D-1' that the 'NEPTUNE' area was the site of the invasion, why would Rommel wait twenty-four hours, until the 'night' of D-Day, to deploy his reserve, mobile divisions? Montgomery knew the Germans would most likely be alerted to the invasion on D-1 because the sea lanes to the invasion beaches would have to be cleared by minesweeper ships the evening before the landing. These vessels would come within clear sight of the invasion beaches.[69] At 0630 on D-Day, Montgomery expected only the coastal defense divisions to be prepared to fight. He expected to achieve tactical surprise. He did not plan to fight the local reserves at the water's edge. He anticipated fighting a counter-attack battle against local reserves later on D-Day. Montgomery's plan, in keeping with the British practice of war, was based in part on the principle of tactical surprise.[70]

Montgomery's assessment of Rommel's defense after the war in his book *Normandy to the Baltic* was quite different:

Rommel, who was no strategist, favoured a plan for the total repulse of an invader on the beaches; his theory was to aim at halting the hostile forces in the immediate beach area by concentrating a great volume of fire on the beaches themselves and to seaward of them; he advocated thickening up the beach defences, and the positioning of all available reserves near the coast.[71]

Montgomery's observations about Rommel's defense during the war were based more on Rundstedt's vision for the conduct of the defense than Rommel's. Prior to the invasion, he did not have a complete understanding of Rommel's plan for the battles at Normandy; as a consequence, he prepared his army group to fight the wrong battles. Montgomery's failure to comprehend the German defense was one of the causes for the near defeat at Omaha Beach, and the outcome could have been much worse. Given Rommel's plans for the conduct of the defense and the probability that he would have at least twenty-four-hour notice of the invasion, Montgomery and his subordinate commanders should have planned to fight every force within a twenty-four-hour range of the invasion beaches.

Intelligence estimates figured the maximum number of German divisions able to reinforce the coast based on their proximity to the invasion beaches. According to the G-2 Estimates of the Enemy Situation issued in December 1943 and February 1944, on D-Day the Allies would face four divisions – two static, poor-quality coastal divisions and two good-quality, mobile reserve divisions. The February estimate stated:

Rate of Enemy Build-up

	Arrival daily of Mechanised Divs	Total arrival by last night
D-Day	2	2
D+1	2	4
D+2	–	4
D+3	–	4
D+4	3	7

a. These timings assume no dislocation by air effort, sabotage, and civilian disturbance.[72]

b. There are believed to be seven mechanised divisions in France and the LOW COUNTRIES at Present. If on D-Day the total exceeds seven, it is expected that the residue could also reach the

NEPTUNE area by last light on D+4. Thereafter further mechanised divisions can be obtained only from other fronts and a gap
in the enemy build-up of such divisions will ensue.[73]

From December 1943 to February 1944, the period during which
Montgomery developed his Initial Joint Plan, intelligence indicated
that two mobile divisions would form the local counter-attack force
on D-Day.

The G-2 estimate on 1 April 1944 showed that from Caen to
Cherbourg, there were three under-strength, low-quality divisions:
the 716th, 709th, and 243rd. (The 711th Division held the sector from
Caen to the Seine River.) The 700 series divisions were low-priority,
static coastal defense divisions. The April G-2 estimate gave the
following assessment of the 700 series divisions:

> Efficiency. a. The morale of coast defense divisions, of which the
> 709th, 711th and 716th are typical, is not good. They contain a good
> 25% of non-Germans and a further 50% of men who in varying
> degrees are elderly, juvenile, tired or unfit. In view of the length of
> time they have been at it, training for their static defense role should
> be reasonably good. Their equipment is generally second rate, motor
> transport is non-existent, and supporting elements and services are
> very inadequate. It is estimated that the value for war of these defen-
> sive divisions... averages not more than 50% of that of a first class
> infantry division, even in static coast defense, and not more than 25%
> in open warfare.[74]

When the landing was expanded from three to five assault divisions
and the Cherbourg region was added, the number of enemy coastal
divisions to be engaged on D-Day increased to three. These poor-
quality, under-strength divisions gave the Allied commanders reason
for optimism.

In the twenty-four hours preceding H-Hour, the period in which
tactical surprise was an issue, the only forces capable of influencing the
assault were the five German divisions identified. If the Allies did not

achieve tactical surprise, given Rommel's concept for the conduct of the defense, all five divisions would have been alert and ready to fight at first light on D-Day.

The G-2 estimate issued just prior to the invasion, on 15 May 1944, showed that four, possibly five, mobile divisions were within a 100-mile radius of the invasion beaches: the 12th SS Panzer ('Hitler Jugend') Division at Evreux, the 84th ID at Rouen, the 352nd ID at Saint-Lô, and the 21st Panzer Division (one of Rommel's two panzer divisions of the Afrika Korps) at Falaise. The 17th SS Panzer Grenadier Division was thought to be located at Thouars, approximately 160 miles from the invasion beaches, on 1 May 1944, but the 15 May G-2 estimate noted that the division might have moved forward to Rennes. If tactical surprise was not achieved, the Allied invasion forces would meet substantial elements of these forces on the morning of D-Day.

The May G-2 estimate predicted the rate of reinforcement to the Normandy beaches:

> The following is an estimate of the optimum time, giving no consideration to air or resistance-group action, for probable reinforcements to be committed against V Corps:
>
>   Afternoon, D-Day – 21st Pz Div – Falaise
>   Evening, D-Day – 12th SS Pz Div – Evreux
>   17th SS Pz Grenadier Div – Rennes
>   Morning, D plus 1 – 352nd Inf Div – St Lô
>   84th Inf Div – Rouen
>   179th Pz Tng Div – Mantes[75]

This schedule of reinforcements assumed that tactical surprise would be achieved. Montgomery expected to fight three poor-quality, under-strength divisions on the morning of D-Day and significant units, for example, regiments, from three 'good'-quality panzer divisions starting on the afternoon of D-Day – the counter-attack with local reserves. He did not plan to fight the 352nd Division on the morning of D-Day at Omaha Beach because he believed tactical surprise would be achieved.

Both the 352nd ID and the 21st Panzer Division were good-quality mobile divisions. According to the G-2 estimate, the 352nd was located at Saint-Lô, twenty miles from Omaha Beach, and the 21st Panzer at Falaise, thirty-five miles from the British beaches. Both divisions had access to good road systems leading to the beaches and had conducted reconnaissance and training in the area. They knew the terrain on which they would fight and Rommel's plan for the conduct of the defense. The 352nd could probably assemble its lead regiment in no more than four hours. Since a regular infantry unit can travel at a rate of four miles per hour without conducting a forced march, the lead elements should have arrived at Omaha Beach in no more than nine hours. With good infantry and an alert chain of command, the lead regiment of the 352nd Division could have been at Omaha Beach in just over five hours. The lead elements of the 21st Panzer Division, with an assembly time of eight hours and a rate of march of ten miles per hour, could have arrived at the Juno and Sword Beaches in less than twelve hours and at Caen, the D-Day objective of the British Second Army, in less than ten hours.[76]

The G-2 estimate included an analysis of alert, assembly, movement, and reconnaissance times:

Entire division (to be ready for a co-ordinated attack)
1. Three hours to be alerted and begin movement.
2. Movement at rate of 20 miles per hour.
3. A mobile division is assumed to require 2 hours to pass a given point, if two routes are available.
4. Two hours for reconnaissance, assembly, and deployment.[77]

Given these estimates, the 352nd deploying from Saint-Lô could have been at Omaha Beach in four hours, less time than it took to conduct landing operations once the fleet dropped anchor in the transport area.

Montgomery and Bradley clearly erred in not planning to fight the 352nd ID at Omaha Beach at 0630 on the morning of 6 June 1944 and in believing that British and Canadian forces would take Caen on

D-Day. An armor division would probably not have been deployed at the water's edge, but given Rommel's plan for the conduct of the defense, in a worst-case scenario, the 21st Panzer Division's combat power should have been factored into the initial assault at 0730. Fortunately for the British, noted David Fraser, the '21st Panzer *as a division* was dispersed and less effective than it might have been.'[78]

Clarence R. Huebner, commanding general of the U.S. 1st ID, also misjudged the situation.[79] The 1st ID should not have been surprised at Omaha Beach by regiments of the 352nd Division. On 15 May, Huebner was aware of the following intelligence:

> The German plan of defense contemplates maximum effort at the beach... At the present time, the German Army is putting forth a great deal of effort to strengthen the coastal crust by placing obstacles along the coastline and by constructing various types of coastal fortifications... [T]he German plan of defense contemplates holding the attacks at the beach until mobile reserves can arrive.[80]

Huebner should have planned to fight the 352nd Division at 0630 on D-Day, no matter what Bradley, Montgomery, and the G-2 intelligence officers said. He knew that the 352nd Division was physically on the battlefield and had enough information to decide for himself. These errors in judgment by the operational and tactical commanders were caused by the belief that tactical surprise was necessary, a failure to understand Rommel's plan for the conduct of the defense, inadequate understanding of amphibious operations and doctrine, and the necessity of conducting combined operations.

Montgomery's plan was based not only on tactical surprise but also on firepower. Eisenhower and Montgomery had access to a resource that did not exist in 1942 when the Dieppe raid was planned and executed. They controlled the only resource in existence that could drop a huge tonnage of bombs in a brief period of time, eliminating the need for the prolonged bombing and bombardment that characterized amphibious operations in the Pacific. The U.S. Army Eighth

Air Force offered an alternative solution to the Mediterranean and Pacific theaters' amphibious doctrines. Both the strategic and operational commanders were convinced that air power would be the decisive element in the battle for the beaches.[81] Montgomery's concept of the operation for the invasion at Normandy relied heavily on fire support provided primarily by the air force. According to one account of the campaign:

> In the last half-hour before the actual landing it would be desirable, General Montgomery's headquarters estimated, to place 7,800 tons of explosive on the shore. Of this amount only 2,500 tons could be delivered by naval guns and 500 tons by medium bombers. Thus it fell to the day-flying heavies of the Eighth Air Force to attack with 4,800 tons, and this duty made it necessary to plan on using the record number of 1,200 heavy bombers.[82]

By May 1944, the Royal Air Force had made significant improvements in its night 'precision' bombing techniques and was able to hit 'small targets' such as gun batteries. On the night of the invasion, the British put 1,136 aircraft in the air to attack coastal batteries. According to Sir Arthur Harris, marshal of the RAF: 'On the night of the invasion ten batteries in the actual area of the landing had to be attacked, and this took more than 5,000 tons of bombs, by far the greatest weight of bombs dropped by Bomber Command in any single attack up till then. In all 14,000 tons of bombs had to be dropped on the defences of the Atlantic wall.'[83] British efforts, however, were not directed at the beach defenses. The vast majority of the firepower on which Montgomery depended to get ashore would come from the U.S. Eighth Air Force. In Montgomery's address to his subordinate commanders just prior to the invasion, he stated: 'We have available to see us on shore, the whole of the allied air power in England, and this air power will continue to support our operations and to bomb Germany. Its strength is terrific. There are some 4,500 fighters and fighter-bombers, and about 6,000 bombers of all types. Nothing has ever been seen like it before.'[84] Montgomery was deeply impressed by the awesome air power available to him. He hoped to win the battle of Normandy with firepower from the air and tactical surprise. The use of these bombers was in keeping with principles of war that require commanders to employ the maximum force available on the primary objective. In short, the enormous combat power of America's heavy bombers could not be left unused; these resources had to be employed on the primary objective.

The timing of the attack was greatly influenced by the require- ments of air power. The assault was scheduled to give the air force just enough time to complete one daylight bombing run with heavy bombers. Montgomery stated: 'The crux of the problem was to decide upon the minimum time required for effective engagement of shore targets by the naval guns and for delivery of the bomb loads by our air formations; eventually the period from nautical twilight (the first sign of morning light) to forty minutes later was accepted as sufficient for our needs.'[85] Given the number of warships employed at Normandy and the experience of the marines and navy at Tarawa, forty minutes was insufficient time for naval gunfire to neutralize a deliberate defense alone. Air power made it possible to combine Pacific theater doctrine and Mediterranean theater doctrine. It was now possible to achieve tactical surprise and a high degree of destruction because prolonged bombing and bombardment were not necessary. The Eighth Air Force had the potential to produce enormous destruction in minutes as opposed to days.

The great expectations for victory with air power were not met at Omaha Beach, on the other beaches, or later in Operation Goodwood. Why did the bombers miss their targets? To insure the safety of assault troops, the heavies, flying straight in from the sea as opposed to parallel to the beaches, delayed the release of their bombs.[86] As a result, the coastline from Omaha Beach east was left untouched.[87] The bombs exploded up to three miles behind the beaches, leaving the German defenses intact. According to one account: 'The cost of taking OMAHA made inevitable the keen disappointment of V Corps that the beach had not been softened by air action, and some of the resulting criticism was sharp. But the prior agreement on the necessity for avoiding all risk of short bombing provides an obvious explanation.'[88] This, however, is only a partial explanation. The Eighth Air Force was asked to conduct a mission it had never performed before that required a level of precision that was not possible at the time flying at high altitudes above the clouds.

On 6 June 1944, the sky over the English Channel and Normandy was overcast. Following air force doctrine, the heavy bombers conducted their attack flying above the clouds using H2X radar to determine the release point. Historian Arthur Ferguson noted that the radar system at the end of 1943 had not been perfected: 'By the end of the year it was becoming clear that radar aids had not worked, and were not likely to work, miracles of accuracy.'[89] The situation was no better in April 1944:

The suggestion that Eighth and Fifteenth Air Force Pathfinder aircraft could detect and accurately attack a marshalling yard... using H2X through 10/10ths Cloud from 25,000 feet assumes target acquisition and bombing accuracy capabilities beyond those that existed. For example, the 29 April 1944 Eighth Air Force attack on Berlin by 570 B-17s and B-24s purportedly aimed at railway facilities in the Friedrichstrasse section in the city centre. Only one of the eleven combat wings placed its bombs closer than five miles from the assigned aiming point.[90]

Using the H2X radar system, the air force could not conduct precision bombing. The best it could achieve was area bombing. With 100 per cent cloud cover, only 0.2 per cent of bombs fell within 1,000 feet of the target, and with 40 to 50 per cent cloud cover, accuracy only improved to 4.4 per cent.[91] In other words, the results at Normandy were typical. Airmen knew they were incapable of the precision required by the army. The U.S. Strategic Bombing Survey noted:

In many cases bombs dropped by instruments in "precision" raids fell over a wide area comparable to... [an] area raid. If the specific target was, for example, a marshalling yard located in a German city, as often happened, such a raid had a practical effect of an area raid against that

city, but on the basis of the declared intention of the attackers it
would go into the air force records as a precision attack on the transportation system.[92]

Technology was not the only problem. The thinking and doctrine of
the airmen thwarted innovation in this type of mission. The airmen
were incapable of developing a satisfactory solution to the problem
of having to fly above the cloud cover at Normandy. The B-17 and
B-24 bomber force was a strategic weapon system. Pilots had little
experience in the tactical support of ground troops. The successful
employment of the strategic bomber force in support of ground
operations in June 1944 would have required a major rethinking of
the mission and purpose of the heavy bomber. In the months leading
up to the invasion, the airmen had no incentive to rethink their role
in the war. By doctrine, training, practice, and technology, American
heavy bomber crews were conditioned to conduct air missions in a
prescribed manner. And because of the air force's preoccupation with
demonstrating that strategic air power was revolutionizing warfare,
such a leap in thinking would only have occurred with considerable
prodding from ground force commanders concerned with exactly
how the bombing would take place and what was and was not
possible.

Air force doctrine called for the conduct of heavy bomber attacks
at altitudes of between 20,000 and 30,000 feet. Crews were trained to
operate at these altitudes, and the weapon system, with its turbo-
supercharged engines, operated at maximum efficiency at these altitudes. In cloud-covered skies, which were fairly normal in Europe, the
Eighth Air Force relied heavily on H2X radar, despite its inaccuracy.[93]
Hence, without considerable effort from some external source, such as
army ground force leaders, the airmen operating heavy bombers
would continue to conduct the business of war from the air in accordance with their doctrine. Thus, the outcome of the bombing at
Normandy, and later at Saint-Lô, where heavy bombers mistakenly
destroyed units of an American division, was not only the result of the
myopia of the air force leadership but also the result of the failure of

ground force commanders to ask the right questions and demand the right answers or their willingness to accept unsatisfactory answers.

In reference to the air support provided at Sicily, Lucian Truscott, one of Bradley's division commanders during the operation, commented: 'When we sailed for operations, we had no information as to what, if any air support we expected on D-Day. We had no knowledge of the extent of fighter protection we would have. We sailed ignorant of when, where, in what numbers, or under what circumstances we would ever see our fighter protection...This lack of air participation in the joint planning at every level was inexcusable.' Bradley stated: 'In southern Tunisia, I had seen what could happen to ground forces when the airmen pursued strategic rather than tactical objectives. The Luftwaffe pasted the hell out of our men... The air support on Sicily was scandalously casual, careless and ineffective.'[94]

In 1944, although joint co-ordination had improved, the objectives and focus of both air forces had not changed. Bradley wrote in reference to the planning for the Normandy invasion:

> [General] Spaatz and [Air Marshal] Harris [the senior strategic bomber commanders for the U.S. and British air forces] were utterly committed to [the strategic bombing campaign]; they sincerely believed that Germany could be defeated by bombers alone, that Overlord was not even necessary. To them it was unthinkable to interrupt the strategic bombing campaign to tactically knock out the French railway and bridge systems.[95]

Given previous experience and the mindset of the airmen, Bradley and Montgomery had sufficient reason to be concerned about the ability of the air forces to conduct the mission required of them on D-Day.

Another way to look at the problems of air power at Normandy is to argue that the expectations of British and American ground force commanders of the effectiveness of air power on fortified defenses were too high:

Much skepticism prevailed in advance as to the value of this last-minute bombardment, and contrary to a common belief it was the air men who held the most conservative views. Ground force commanders tended to overestimate the effect of bomb tonnage on casemated enemy batteries, strongpoints, and the entire hideous apparatus of beach obstacles.[96]

The problem was not the effect of bombs on targets; the size and type of bombs could be varied to produce the desired quality of damage. The problem was that the U.S. Army Air Force claimed an ability it did not possess.[97] It simply was incapable of bombing consistently with the precision it claimed: '[E]ntry of U.S. heavy bomber forces into the fray was surrounded by USAAF characterisation of its capabilities as 'precision,' 'pickle barrel,' and 'pin-point bombing – descriptive terms participants and official USAAF history acknowledge were exaggerations and that of which legends, not history, are made.'[98] American airmen sought to prove themselves and their technology, and in the process, they made excessive claims.[99] The ground commanders, in search of means that reduced casualties, relied on a system that was incapable of producing the desired results.

Montgomery and his subordinate planners and commanders, American and British, discussed two plans of assault. One approach was to rush inland to the first defensible terrain, roughly five miles inland, establish a hasty defense, tie in the flanks of units to form an unbroken perimeter, and prepare to receive the enemy's counter-attack.[100] The problem with this approach was that the invasion beaches would be left in range of German artillery, which could slow the build-up of forces and the logistical build-up and might allow the German defenders time to form their own defensive perimeter to contain the invasion, thereby requiring greater effort on the part of the Allies to break out.

The alternative approach was to advance to a line that placed the invasion beaches out of range of enemy artillery, roughly ten to twelve miles inland. Although this plan facilitated the build-up, it put the assault forces at greater risk because the expected enemy counter-attack force had a greater potential for catching the assault force in movement as opposed to encountering it after it had occupied a hasty defensive perimeter. Montgomery and Bradley believed the air force would significantly cut the flow of enemy reinforcements to the beaches. And the use of airborne troops on both flanks would presumably facilitate the capture of the deeper defensive perimeter by securing the communication line from Caen to Bayeux to Isigny.[101] Thus, air power and the use of airborne forces on both flanks could decrease the risk of being destroyed in separate actions.

Montgomery and Bradley opted for the latter course of action. This decision made tactical surprise of even greater importance and increased the reliance on air power. If Allied forces, which were predominately light infantry supported by armor, were caught advancing independently in open country by panzer formations, they ran the risk of being destroyed piecemeal. Instead of having to fight a partially prepared, cohesive, organized defense, the Germans would have the good fortune of fighting independent actions with units of various sizes at various stages of advance. Thus, the higher the degree of surprise, the deeper the possible penetration.

Montgomery's plan was also based on the rapid build-up of troops and supplies. On D-Day, the tides would cycle twice, once every twelve hours. The third high tide after H-Hour would take place on D+1. High tide was required to get the LSTs sufficiently inshore to be off-loaded without the use of additional time-consuming means, such as the construction of pontoon bridges or other types of intermediate devices designed to bridge the gap between the land and sea.

On D-Day, Montgomery planned to make maximum use of both tides. This required an early-morning assault timed to insure that maximum advantage would be made of the first tide to land the greatest number of men and vehicles. Admiral Kirk believed that the build-up plans influenced the timing of the assault, possibly a bit too much. He wrote: 'One of the reasons against an H-hour longer after daylight was that the amount of remaining daylight would not then permit, on D-Day, a second high water period available for unloading. It is not

believed that this reason is of great importance and certainly not sufficient to alter the desirability of greater time for working on the beach
obstacles.'[102] Kirk clearly thought that too much emphasis was given to
the build-up and, as a result, the operational plan for the invasion
failed to maximize the combat potential of the forces assembled. Navy
underwater demolitions teams and army engineers were given insufficient time to destroy the beach obstacles.

Montgomery's plan was based on tactical surprise, firepower, and
speed in the build-up of men and material. He wrote:

> The overall plan of assault was designed to concentrate the full weight
> of all available resources of all three services in getting the assaulting
> troops ashore and in assisting them in their task of breaking through
> the Atlantic Wall... At H Hour, supported by naval bombardment and
> air action and by the guns, rockets and mortars of close support craft,
> the leading wave of troops was to disembark and force its way
> ashore... We had such preponderance of naval and air resources that
> we counted on stunning the defenders with the weight of our
> bombing and shell fire.[103]

The full potential combat power of the U.S. Army Air Force's daylight
strategic bombers was available to Montgomery. The presence of this
awesome power caused Montgomery to deviate from the British
practice of night assault. American resources distorted the British
practice of war. These bombers were charged with delivering the bulk
of the combat power Montgomery required to get ashore.[104] His plan
to win the battle at the water's edge was built around his expectations
about the capabilities of air power augmented by naval gunfire and his
understanding of the German concept for the conduct of the defense.
Montgomery planned to blast his way ashore with fire support assets
in the minimal time possible, rush troops through the opening made
by firepower, advance inland as rapidly as possible, establish a hasty
defensive perimeter as far inland as possible, build up forces as quickly
as possible, and then defend against the enemy's counter-attack with
local reserves that were to be committed piecemeal starting on the

afternoon of D-Day. Montgomery expected a larger co-ordinated counter-attack at D+4 or D+5 with an 'estimated six panzer divisions':[105]

> We would have to blast our way on shore and get a good lodgment before the enemy could bring up sufficient reserves to turn us out. We must gain space rapidly and peg out claims well inland. And while doing this, the air would have to hold the ring, and hinder and make difficult the movement of enemy reserves by train or road towards the lodgment.[106]

There was considerable agreement with the Montgomery Plan but also considerable disagreement. Some believed it was not possible to achieve tactical surprise, some believed it was not necessary to achieve tactical surprise, and some believed tactical surprise was mandatory for a successful assault. General J.C. Haydon of the British Combined Operations Headquarters commented:

> As to tactical surprise, much depends on your interpretation of the term. If you mean by tactical surprise that the enemy will not be ready for you, then I do not think you will... attain it.[107] Because, as the preparations for mounting the operation get larger and more urgent, so will the enemy's degree of alertness grow. He will, we hope, be ignorant regarding the actual assault areas but, beyond that, ...I do not see that one can expect tactical surprise.[108]

Haydon's assessment was reinforced by the analysis of Lieutenant Colonel H. M. Zeller, U.S. Army, and Lieutenant Colonel Bell Burton, British Army. In a discussion of 'German coastal defenses and defensive doctrine,' they emphasized the following point:

> As for information as to whether the enemy intends to reinforce their main line of resistance, it was stated that there is no question but that the Germans will early discover where our main effort is to be and will move up reserve divisions to reinforce their positions.[109]

Haydon explained why he believed the Germans would be prepared and ready to fight. He gave the German Army credit for being at least as professional as the British Army in 1940, when the Germans were planning the invasion of Britain, Operation Sealion.[110] He believed the Germans would go through the same analysis and thought process the British had gone through in 1940 and come to similar conclusions. The Germans would deduce the most likely time of assault and thus be at a heightened state of readiness. Some American planners drew conclusions similar to those of Haydon.[111] General Norman Cota, U.S. Army, supported Montgomery's view that it was possible to achieve tactical surprise. At the Conference on Landing Assaults, 24 May–23 June 1943, Cota stated:

> There is a lot of talk about whether a landing should be made in the dark or whether it should be made in daylight. It is granted that strategical surprise will be impossible to attain. Tactical surprise is another thing however. General Montgomery says you can always get tactical surprise. I feel that we should always strive for tactical surprise, for there is no question but that tactical surprise is one of the most powerful factors in determining success. I therefore, favor the night landing. I do not believe the daylight assault can succeed.[112]

American veterans of the landings in the Mediterranean theater tended to favor the British practice of amphibious operations.[113] They had grown familiar with it; they knew how it worked and what to expect. They were reluctant to change doctrinal practices this late in the war.

British and American planners disagreed on the basic principles for the invasion of Europe, and plans were developed based on erroneous assumptions of the capabilities of American strategic bombers and an inaccurate assessment of the enemy's concept for the conduct of the defense. The British committee system and the British system of command were used to determine the timing of the assault and to develop the entire plan, a plan that failed to maximize the potential combat power on hand. Montgomery and his planners, both British and American, sought to achieve too many objectives and, in the process, failed to focus on what was most crucial – the destruction of the enemy's army on the coast and the four divisions in local reserve. The process through which the plan was developed permitted too many subsidiary tasks and missions to obfuscate the main objective and the fundamental tenets upon which the plan was based.

Montgomery's plan failed at Omaha Beach and probably would have failed on other beaches had tactical surprise not been achieved, and he had very little reason to believe that tactical surprise would be achieved. Luck, however, is an important part of generalship, and at Normandy, Montgomery was very lucky.

6

The American Vision for the Invasion of Europe

We cannot now rationally hope to be able to cross the Channel and come to grips with our German enemy under a British commander. The Prime Minister and his Chief of the Imperial Staff are frankly at variance with such a proposal. The shadows of Passchendaele and Dunkerque still hang too heavily over the imagination of these leaders.

Secretary of War Henry L. Stimson

American operational and tactical plans were based on the assumptions and prerequisites of the Montgomery Plan. The British selected the geography and terrain on which the assaults would take place. They developed the deception plans and provided most of the intelligence on the enemy's situation, capabilities, and likely reactions. They designed and engineered the DD tanks, the flailing tanks, the engineer vehicles, and numerous other 'Hobart's follies' employed at Normandy on D-Day.[1] The concept and engineering for the Mulberry, the artificial harbor; the Gooseberry, the artificial break-water; and the Pluto operation, the underwater fuel line laid across the Channel, were predominantly British in origin and implementation. As the senior operational commander, Montgomery was responsible for the overall plan for the invasion, and it was his vision that carried the Allies back to Europe. Thus, the Normandy invasion was more a reflection of the British practice of war than the American. Montgomery's plan set the parameters for Bradley's operational plan. American thinking about the conduct of war in Europe up to the battle for Normandy was confined and influenced by British think-ing. The American practice of war and resources did, however, influe-ence planning and British thinking – particularly the American daylight strategic bomber force. American resources created new options and opportunities, causing the development of new doctrine.

BRADLEY'S VISION

In September 1943, General Omar N. Bradley, the newly appointed commander of the FUSA and the First U.S. Army Group (later the 12th Army Group), arrived in London with his staff to begin prepara-tion and planning for the invasion of Europe. When Bradley assumed command, he and Patton were the most experienced operational commanders in the U.S. Army in European warfare – warfare against the German Army. Bradley's experiences in Sicily as the commander of the II Corps, the only corps in Patton's Seventh Army, influenced his decisions in planning the invasion of Europe.[2] At Normandy, Bradley endeavored to re-create the American landings in Sicily.

In Sicily, Bradley's three divisions conducted the assault at night, at 0245, under the cover of darkness. The landing was unopposed in the initial assault, but on D+1 at the coastal town of Gela, one of his divi-sions came under heavy attack by a good-quality German division. The fighting was fierce, and Bradley came to believe that had another division with less experience and tenacity conducted the landing and the subsequent battle, it would have been pushed back into the sea. The 1st ID fought that battle. Bradley wrote: 'Only the perverse Big Red One with its no less perverse commander was both hard and experienced enough to take that assault in stride. A greener division might easily have panicked and seriously embarrassed the landing.'[3] At Normandy, Bradley would again call on the 1st ID, and he would again come to the conclusion that the skill and spirit of that division prevented defeat.

Bradley also recalled the airborne drop made by General Matthew B. Ridgway's 82nd Airborne Division during the Sicily campaign, and he insisted that an airborne division be dropped behind the beaches at Utah to assist in the assault by securing the causeways to the beaches.[4] General Maxwell Taylor's 101st Airborne Division was originally given this mission and, for the assault, became part of 'Lightning Joe' Collins's VII Corps. Later, the airborne mission was expanded, and Ridgway's 82nd Airborne Division was added to the order of battle for D-Day.[5] Bradley's vision for the expanded role of airborne forces was in concert with the view of the army chief of staff, General George Marshall, who made possible the expansion of the airborne mission by securing the additional aircraft needed to drop another division.

Thus, when Bradley became the operational commander of American forces for the invasion of Europe, he based his decisions on the British model of amphibious operations that was employed in Sicily. At Normandy, Bradley sought to duplicate the tenets that brought success in the Sicily campaign. In regard to the timing of the assault, Bradley wrote:

> As far back as December, 1943, the decision was made to launch the attack against the continent of Europe in daylight. This was accepted by CG, First U.S. Army only after it had been stated by commanders of both the American and British Naval Forces involved that unless the assault was made in daylight the navies could not be reasonably certain that assault forces would be landed at the proper point. Also

the Allied Air Commander stated that at least one hour of daylight on D–Day would be required by the Air Forces to accomplish the reduction of coast defense.[6]

Bradley was convinced by Montgomery and the air and naval commanders in chief that the landing had to be made in daylight. This was not in line with Bradley's paradigm, but he accepted the views of his superiors.

Doctrine determined the time of the invasion. Invasions based on British Mediterranean theater doctrine took place in the early-morning hours of darkness. Invasions based on American Pacific theater doctrine took place after a substantial daylight bombardment and bombing. Bradley was schooled in British Mediterranean theater amphibious doctrine. He was not a student of Pacific theater amphibious doctrine. Bradley explained: 'With a daylight assault unavoidable, and with the conditions imposed on the ground commander by the Air and Navy as enumerated above, considerable detailed study was made to determine the best compromise solution. From the Ground Force Commanders' point of view, a landing in the early hours of daylight (while visibility from shore made observed fire difficult) was desirable.' At a conference with his subordinate commanders, Bradley stated: 'Now, they [the joint commanders in chief] have considered all the pros and cons of night attack and day attack… and the final decision was it had to be after daylight, and then, of course, we held out for as short a time after daylight as possible.'[7] Bradley accepted a new doctrinal approach, but he retained the tenets on which British Mediterranean theater doctrine was based. He tried to fit a square peg into a round hole. He hoped to conduct a daylight assault under the same conditions that made a landing under the cover of darkness successful. Bradley's comments indicated that he did not understand the exigencies upon which a daylight assault was built. He did not grasp the lessons of Tarawa, where the navy and Marine Corps learned the type, volume, and quality of firepower required to overcome a deliberate defense. Bradley later realized the importance of allowing the navy and air force sufficient time to neutralize or destroy enemy defensive positions. In *A General's Life,* Bradley and Blair wrote:

> In the British sector, owing to reefs and foul ground, Monty's Second Army under Miles Dempsey had to land on a flood tide an hour to an hour and a half after we landed. This gift of time enabled the warships of the Royal Navy to deliver Monty's beaches a two-hour daylight bombardment, nearly four times as long as the naval bombardment at Omaha. To this was added a massive attack by British heavy bombers. The combined sea and air attacks in the British sector were far more effective than those in the American sector.[8]

This 'gift of time' could have been given to American soldiers at Omaha Beach. Bradley, more than any other American commander, was responsible for the near defeat and heavy losses at Omaha Beach. He came close to admitting this in his first book, *A Soldier's Story,* when he observed: "I was shaken to find that we had gone against Omaha with so thin a margin of safety."[9] It was his job to insure that the doctrine employed maximized the combat power of the forces under his command. He did not do this. Bradley did not share Eisenhower's and Montgomery's faith in air power.

Bradley may have felt somewhat in awe and unprepared at invasion planning conferences with Montgomery and his staff. He realized that the planners of the invasion possessed more knowledge and experience than he had.[10] (Bradley should have taken General Gerow, his subordinate V Corps commander, to these initial meetings. Gerow had worked on the plans since the summer of 1943 and was more knowledgeable than Bradley about the concept for the conduct of the operation.) Bradley probably had a better understanding of the capabilities and limitations of American air power than either Montgomery or Eisenhower. He also had a better understanding of the attitudes and predisposition of American strategic bomber force commanders. Still, he was swayed by the vision and doctrinal thinking of Montgomery. Bradley, like Eisenhower, received his appointment to command late in the planning process. Much had already been decided when he assumed command, and because of the lateness of the hour and his inexperience, Bradley did not exert the influence he later wished he had exerted.

The decision on the doctrine for the assault was made before the extent of Rommel's defense construction program was known. The decision was made before significant numbers of minefields and obstacles were placed on the beaches at Normandy. The fact that the situation and conditions at Omaha Beach changed caused American tactical commanders — Gerow, Huebner, and Cota — to question the decision made by their superiors on the timing of the assault. Bradley's subordinate tactical commanders disagreed with the plan for a daylight assault and argued for a continuation of the Mediterranean practice of night landings, which facilitated achieving tactical surprise. They too had a paradigm of amphibious warfare in mind, but they wanted to adhere more rigorously than Bradley to the tenets of that model. Their arguments, however, fell on deaf ears. The concept for the operation was not changed, a point that Montgomery emphasized in his book *Normandy to the Baltic:* '[T]he basic principles of my plan for delivering the assault and for the subsequent development of operations were decided upon early in the planning stage, and these were never altered or modified but were carried through relentlessly to a successful conclusion.'[11]

Montgomery's approach to command allowed him little room to change after promulgating a plan. This inability to adjust to changing situations was not a weakness in his view but a point of honor. Montgomery, through his experience, knowledge, and personality, was able to decisively influence Bradley. Bradley, for the most part, accepted Montgomery's vision and leadership.

BRADLEY'S GENERALSHIP

Of Bradley, Eisenhower wrote:

> Bradley was the master tactician of our forces and in my opinion will eventually come to be recognized as America's foremost battle

leader... To my mind, Bradley should be the United States Assaulting Army Commander, and become Army Group Commander when necessary... My high opinion of Bradley, dating from our days at West Point, had increased daily during our months together in the Mediterranean... He was a keen judge of men and their capabilities and was absolutely fair and just in his dealing with them. Added to this, he was emotionally stable and possessed a grasp of larger issues that clearly marked him for high office.[12]

Patton's seeming emotional instability and failure to grasp larger issues, such as the importance of maintaining the coalition, lost him the job of FUSA commander and later army group commander. Bradley was next in line for the job. Nigel Hamilton, Montgomery's biographer, believed that Montgomery also developed a high regard for Bradley's ability: 'Bradley's respect and professionalism made a deep impression on Monty, who would come to see him, in the weeks ahead, as by far and away the finest all-round field commander produced by the U.S. Army.'[13]

British historian Alistair Horne also wrote that Montgomery had a high opinion of Bradley: 'Monty always rated Bradley, with his quiet, understated manner and above all his supreme professionalism, highest among all the American top commanders.' Although he claimed that Montgomery considered Bradley a professional, Horne indirectly suggested that Bradley was not proficient at his job. According to Horne, Bradley did not know how to concentrate his forces for the breakout at Saint-Lô. Montgomery found it necessary to explain to him how and where to conduct the breakthrough. Horne described a meeting between Montgomery, Dempsey, and Bradley:

'Monty was wonderful,' recalled General Dempsey of that meeting: 'There were no recriminations – although Bradley had obviously made his own task the more difficult by trying to buck the whole line right along instead of concentrating and punching a hole in one important sector.' In his most comforting and supportive manner Monty said quietly to his much less battle-experienced American subordinate: '...Never mind. Take all the time you need, Brad.' Then he went on tactfully to say: 'If I were you I think I should concentrate my forces a little more' – putting two fingers on the map in his characteristic way. Thus, 'without Bradley realizing it,' Dempsey continued, Monty 'got across to him the idea that he must concentrate his forces for a solid punch at one point.'[14]

Thus, in Dempsey's and Horne's view, Montgomery deserves credit for the breakout at Saint-Lô. Bradley's deferential treatment of Montgomery may have positively influenced Montgomery's opinion of him. Patton's assessment of Bradley's ability tended to support Dempsey's view. In his diary, Patton wrote:

> Brad and Hodges are such nothings. Their one virtue is that they get along by doing nothing. I could break through in three days if I commanded. They try to push all along the front and have no power anywhere. All that is necessary now is to take chances by leading with armored divisions and covering their advance with air bursts. Such an attack would have to be made on a narrow sector, whereas at present we are trying to attack all along the line.[15]

Carlo D'Este, Patton's biographer, concluded:

> Bradley was uncomfortable with those who displayed independence and dash, preferring instead the company of more conservative infantrymen who thought in like terms. The real Omar Bradley was somewhat narrow-minded... As the First Army, and later, 12th Army Group Commander, Bradley was notoriously intolerant of failure, as the numerous division commanders he sacked could attest.[16]

On 12 June 1915, Bradley graduated forty-fourth in his class from the U.S. Military Academy.[17] He was commissioned a second lieutenant of infantry. His first assignment was with the 14th Infantry stationed in Yuma, Arizona. In July 1916, he was promoted to first lieutenant and in May 1917, to captain. Bradley missed World War I. By the time his unit was ready for overseas deployment, the war was over. When the war ended, he was commanding a battalion in the temporary rank of major. In September 1920, Bradley was reassigned to West Point as an instructor of mathematics. In 1924, he attended the Infantry Officer's Advanced Course at Fort Benning, Georgia. The following year, he was promoted to major and assigned to the 27th Infantry of the Hawaiian Division, in which Patton was serving as the division G-2 officer. Thus began one of the most significant relationships in Bradley's career.

In 1928, Bradley attended the Command and General Staff College at Fort Leavenworth, Kansas. Upon graduation, he was assigned to the U.S. Army Infantry School at Fort Benning as an instructor. He served under the assistant commandant, George C. Marshall, and became one of those favored by Marshall. Marshall added Bradley's name to his now-famous black notebook alongside names such as Dwight Eisenhower, Joseph Stilwell, Walter Bedell Smith, and others whom he identified as having the potential for high command. In 1934, after graduating from the War College, Bradley returned to West Point, serving in the Tactical Department. He taught cadets who would later serve under him in World War II, including William C. Westmoreland, Creighton W. Abrams, Bruce Palmer, and Andrew Goodpaster. In 1936, Bradley was promoted to lieutenant colonel. Two years later, he was assigned to the War Department in Washington. He served briefly as the G-1 officer of the General Staff and later as the assistant secretary of the General Staff in the Office of the Army Chief of Staff. In February 1941, Bradley was the first in his class to be promoted to brigadier general. He skipped the rank of colonel. His next assignment was commander of the Infantry School at Fort Benning.

During this period, the army was gearing up for war and Fort Benning was a hub of activity. The newly activated 2nd Armor Division under Patton's command was training, and the airborne force was organizing and training. The Officer Candidate School, which would eventually produce 45,000 second lieutenants, was being developed. With the war on, Bradley took command of the 82nd ID in February 1942. He developed a training program and readied the division for overseas, but a mere four months later, he was ordered to take command of the 28th ID, a National Guard unit in Louisiana. Bradley recalled that it was his job to 'whip those unbalanced units into a trim division and ready it for the field.'[18] Bradley was being groomed for high command and greater responsibilities. While training his division at Camp Gordon Johnston in Florida, one of the army's Amphibious Training Centers, Bradley received word that he had been selected for corps command. However, in February 1943, Marshall sent Bradley to North Africa to serve under Eisenhower following the disaster at Kasserine Pass. Eisenhower relieved Major General Lloyd Fredendall of command of the II Corps and gave Patton that command. Bradley became Patton's deputy corps commander. In April, Bradley took command of the II Corps. He led the corps in the final months of the campaign in North Africa and then in the Sicily campaign under the command of Patton's Seventh Army. In August 1943, the Sicily campaign ended, and in September, Bradley took command of the FUSA.

It was in Sicily that Bradley was dubbed the 'soldier's general' or the 'G.I.'s general' by war correspondent Ernie Pyle. Of Bradley, Pyle wrote:

> The outstanding figure on this western front is Lt. Gen. Omar Nelson Bradley. He is so modest and sincere that he probably will not get his proper credit, except in military textbooks. But he has proved himself a great general in every sense of the word. And as a human being, he is just as great. Having him in command has been a blessed good fortune for America.'[19]

Bradley was not the 'master tactician' Eisenhower believed him to be, which is probably why he never gained the fame that Eisenhower predicted. Nor was he the amateur Dempsey made him out to be. Bradley was average. He was well schooled in infantry operations and tactics, having been the commandant of the Infantry School at Fort Benning, a division commander, an understudy for Patton, and a corps commander in operations against good German units. He fought battles the way Americans expected them to be fought. He fought war with firepower, not with men.

In the 1940s, the United States was an affluent nation with an industrial capacity that rivaled that of Europe. The United States placed great value on the lives of its citizens – particularly its young men. Americans enjoyed a high standard of living and, as a result, had high expectations from life.[20] American culture and its Constitution saw people not as a means to an end, not as an instrument of the state, but as an end in themselves. War distorted this conception. These high expectations, the expectation of 'happiness,' created a high regard for the lives of American citizens that led politicians and military leaders of the United States to expend all other resources lavishly in order to minimize the expenditure of the country's most valued asset, the lives of American men. The American people of the twentieth century have come to expect their political and military leaders to achieve military objectives with a minimum loss of life. By fighting war with technology, machines, and firepower, Bradley and other ground commanders reduced casualties.

Bradley did not take risks. He was a conservative commander, too conservative. His conservative approach caused him not only to miss opportunities but also to restrict the initiative of his subordinate commanders. Bradley found it hard to cut loose Patton's Third Army and let it run free. He felt the need to tightly control the movement of the forces under his command. He was not a practitioner of Guderian-style, Blitzkrieg warfare. He was an average tactician who believed in the American system of war and used it. He was not the best man for the job.

Bradley's meteoric rise to army and army group command, his newness to amphibious warfare, his inexperience in dealing with the British, his arrival in England late in the planning process, his 'quiet, understated manner,' and the sheer magnitude of the operation confronting him may have caused him to defer to the British on matters that gave him and his subordinate commanders second thoughts, matters that perhaps he should have questioned. Bradley did not assert himself up the chain of command. He was too willing to accept, too willing to be convinced.[21] In a matter of months, Bradley advanced from commanding a division to commanding an army and army group, and in the process, he recognized that he had passed by many of his former superiors, including Patton. But Bradley had no difficulty imposing his will down the chain of command. He was quick to relieve corps and division commanders and proved to be unwilling to listen to his subordinates.

The tactical commanders, Gerow, V Corps commander, and Huebner, 1st ID commander, were responsible for preparing their soldiers for the battle at Omaha Beach and the subsequent battles for Europe. They were responsible for developing the tactical plan – within the conceptual framework of the operational plans of Montgomery and Bradley – training their soldiers to perform the missions designated in the plan, and preparing their soldiers psychologically for battle. Some argue that Gerow and Huebner were not entirely successful in planning, training, and psychological preparation. Australian journalist Chester Wilmot observed:

> There were grave defects inherent in the American plan. The first of these was the fruit of the American predilection for direct assault... They scorned the lessons of earlier amphibious operations, which had shown the wisdom of landing between the beach strongpoints, not opposite them, infiltrating and assaulting them from the flank and rear.[22]

British historian Max Hastings wrote: 'General Gerow committed his men to hurling themselves against the most strongly defended areas in the assault zone.'[23] These views are in keeping with the generally accepted assessment of the American practice of war, the direct approach. This argument is sustained by the fact that only at Omaha Beach did the plan of battle fail. The plan put into effect, however, was based less on the vision of Gerow and Huebner, the tactical commanders, and more on the vision of Montgomery and Bradley, the operational commanders, than Hastings's analysis indicates. The battle for Omaha Beach did not demonstrate that the tactical plan for the battle was flawed or that the American approach to war was ill-conceived.[24] It revealed that the operational plan was flawed, that it was built on ill-conceived doctrine and erroneous assumptions about the enemy's capabilities and about air power.

Although Gerow and Huebner argued for significant modifications in the operational plan, they too did not anticipate the battle that confronted them at Omaha Beach. They succumbed to the optimistic belief that air power would clear the way and were surprised by the German 352nd Division located just twenty miles from the beach. Thus, they prepared their soldiers to fight the wrong battle.

Although the V Corps developed the tactical plans for the battle for Omaha Beach, the 1st ID, on Bradley's orders, was actually charged with the conduct of the battle. The reverse planning sequence was not used. The planning started with the requirement to employ major weapon platforms, strategic bombers, and warships. The rest of the plan was built around the criteria for the employment of the weapons that were supposed to provide the majority of the combat power needed to get ashore, the decisive weapons. The tenets and principles of war on which Montgomery and Bradley based their plan vitiated those on which Gerow and Huebner attempted to base their plan.

LEONARD T. GEROW, COMMANDER OF THE V CORPS

Very little has been written about Gerow, and he did not leave a written record of his thoughts on war in general or his assessment of the Normandy invasion. Given the volume of works on the Normandy invasion, it is surprising that so little has been written about the senior tactical commander for the invasion.

The commander of the V Corps was a close friend of Eisenhower's. His career paralleled Eisenhower's until the start of World War II, after which Eisenhower was rocketed to command positions over the heads of many of his seniors. On 6 June 1944, Gerow was totally lacking in command experience at any level against the World War II German

Army. Bradley replaced other inexperienced corps commanders with Eisenhower's approval prior to the invasion.[25] Successful combat commanders were sought for the Normandy campaign. Corps commanders were even brought in from the Pacific theater, such as Generals J. Lawton Collins and Pete Corlett. Gerow, however, was an exception, perhaps because of his relationship with Eisenhower. According to Patton, Gerow 'was one of the leading mediocre corps commanders in Europe and only got the Fifteenth Army because he was General Eisenhower's personal friend.'[26] Upon hearing that Gerow was to take command of the U.S. Army War College after the war, Patton revised his assessment: 'I think giving Gerow the W.C. [War College] is a joke. He was the poorest corps commander in France.'[27]

Gerow was, however, highly regarded by Eisenhower. In a letter to Gerow on 16 July 1942, Eisenhower wrote:

> I knew, of course, that when I got a letter from you it would contain all the nice things you had to say about my appointment here [in England]. Better than that, I knew that in your case they would be honest and sincere. In return, I can only say that there is, as you know, no one else in the whole army whose good opinion means so much to me as yours. I hope also that you will not for one minute, believe that you are stymied in division command. While anyone commanding one of our divisions has a man-sized job and need not be bothering his head about anything else, the fact is that you are so eminently fitted for the highest commands that they will never be able to let you stay there long.[28]

Marshall, under whom Gerow was serving in the War Department at the outbreak of the war, must also, at least initially, have had a positive view of Gerow's ability. Marshall selected Gerow for the position of chief of war plans and then promoted him to general. In September 1942, when Eisenhower was establishing his headquarters in the United Kingdom and preparing for Operation Torch, he requested that Gerow be appointed his deputy commander. In a letter to

Marshall, he wrote:

> In this situation I want to use General Gerow ...as my deputy in command of U.S. forces in the United Kingdom. I am quite well aware that you do not fully share my very high opinion of General Gerow's ability. But I submit that his loyalty, sense of duty, and readiness to devote himself unreservedly to a task, are all outstanding. Moreover, he is a very close personal friend of mine and for that reason alone would strain every nerve to meet any requirement.[29]

Marshall approved Eisenhower's selection, but Eisenhower, aware of Marshall's opinion, decided to withdraw his request.[30]

Bradley's opinion of Gerow's abilities was probably closer to Patton's than Eisenhower's, even though his written comments were positive. Bradley wrote: 'He was an outstanding gentleman and soldier – cool, hard-working, intelligent, well organized, competitive – clearly destined for high rank and responsibility.'[31] He also observed: 'Not only was he conscientious, self-confident, and steady, but he was thoroughly schooled in the OVERLORD plan.'[32] These are guarded words. They are the words of someone who holds a low to moderate opinion of an individual's talents and abilities but has decided to refrain from making negative statements.[33] Gerow was still on active duty when Bradley pointed out in his first book: 'By reason of its early arrival in England, Gerow's V Corps fell heir to the Omaha assault.'[34] Bradley would not have selected Gerow for the command of the assault at Omaha Beach and, in fact, took measures to insure that Gerow did not command the assault. If he had possessed the power to do so, Bradley probably would have relieved Gerow, as he had other inexperienced corps commanders.

The officer corps of the U.S. Army prior to World War II was a small, restricted gentleman's club in which everyone knew each other and crossed paths frequently. Bradley and Gerow were no strangers to each other prior to the war. General Leonard Townsend Gerow (Gee) was four years senior to his boss, Bradley.[35] They had been classmates in the Infantry Officer's Advanced Course at Fort Benning in 1924.

Gerow graduated first in the class, and Bradley second. Gerow was two years senior to Eisenhower, with whom he attended the Command and General Staff College at Fort Leavenworth in 1926 and the U.S. Army War College, then in Washington, in 1931. At the Command and General Staff College, Eisenhower graduated first in his class, and Gerow a close second. The friendship between Eisenhower and Gerow began when they were second lieutenants serving together at Fort Sam Houston in Texas. Gerow played a part in introducing Eisenhower to the woman he would marry, Mamie Geneva Doud.[36] The Eisenhowers and Gerows became close personal friends and exchanged letters when they were not stationed together. This practice continued throughout the war.[37] When Eisenhower assumed command of SHAEF, Gerow came under his command.

Gerow was commissioned a second lieutenant of infantry on 29 September 1911 at the Virginia Military Institute, where he graduated with honors.[38] In 1914, he participated in the occupation of Vera Cruz, Mexico. In 1917, while serving with the 37th Infantry in Texas, he was promoted to captain. In April 1918, he sailed for France, where two months later he was promoted to major. During World War I, he participated in the Saint-Mihiel and Meuse-Argonne offensives as a signal officer. He also served in Paris as assistant to the officer in charge of purchasing and disbursing in the Signal Corps. In October 1918, he was promoted to lieutenant colonel and became the officer in charge. In 1919, he reported to Fort Sam Houston, where he served as the commandant of the Signal Corps School. During this tour, Gerow's friendship with Eisenhower flourished. In July 1923, Gerow was reassigned to the War Plans and Organization Section in Washington. Following this assignment, he attended the Infantry Officer's Advanced Course at Fort Benning and the Command and General Staff School at Fort Leavenworth. From 1926 to 1929, Gerow served as assistant executive in the Office of the Assistant Secretary of War in Washington. Gerow then attended the War College, graduating in 1931. His next assignment was with the 31st Infantry Regiment in the Philippines. During this tour, he served in Shanghai, China.

In 1935, Gerow was assigned to the War Plans Division of the War Department, where he was promoted to colonel in September 1940 and brigadier general the following month. At the War Department, Gerow served as the chief of war plans and later as the assistant chief of staff, holding both positions simultaneously. In July 1941, Gerow predicted that the Russians would be 'licked' before the winter set in and that the Japanese would 'sit tight' after their success in Indochina.[39] He was wrong on both counts. The attack on Pearl Harbor and the fall of the Philippines took place during Gerow's tenure at the War Department. In a secret army report and a minority Senate investigation report, Gerow and his boss, Marshall, were held partially responsible for the poor state of readiness of the U.S. Army in Hawaii.[40] In February 1942, Gerow took command of the 29th ID, a National Guard division that was being reorganized from the World War I square division to the more mobile triangular division of World War II. In a letter to Eisenhower, he stated:

> I am still like a child with a new toy, and feel that I am really accomplishing something. Have lost about ten pounds and feel fine. A.P. Hill [the training site] will give us a wonderful opportunity to get in some real field training. If the War Department will stop stealing my units, personnel and equipment, this Division will be ready to go places by the end of July.[41]

Gerow's replacement at the War Department was his good friend Eisenhower, who at that time was envious of Gerow's new command position.[42]

In October 1942, Gerow sailed with his division for England. He was promoted to commander of the V Corps in July 1943. At that time, the V Corps was the senior field command in the United Kingdom, and as such, it also functioned as the U.S. field forces headquarters in the European theater of operations. Tactical planning, preparation, and training for the invasion of Europe automatically became the responsibility of the V Corps commander and staff.[43] Long before Bradley's FUSA and Eisenhower's SHAEF came into existence, Gerow and his staff worked on the plans for the invasion. Like General Morgan and his COSSAC staff, whose work, position, and prestige were usurped with the appointment of Eisenhower and Montgomery, Gerow and his planning staff, who initially believed they would command the entire ground force, underwent a similar process with the appointment of Bradley.[44] Gerow's position in the invasion was reduced with the establishment of two additional headquarters above him. Gerow and his staff probably felt some apprehension, uncertainty, and even anger.[45] Gerow's lack of experience further diminished his ability to influence events. Bradley was confident that he knew more about operations in general and amphibious warfare in particular than Gerow.[46] Bradley was neither uncomfortable nor hesitant in exercising his authority down the chain of command.

Bradley's vision for the conduct of the battle at Omaha Beach conflicted with Gerow's. On a number of significant issues, Gerow disagreed with his new boss. Gerow, however, proved to be a gentleman. After sustaining heavy casualties at Omaha Beach, after the war, Gerow could have criticized his bosses for their flawed vision of the operation and for failing to maximize the combat power available.[47] Neither Gerow nor Huebner engaged in such reproach, even after retiring. They never fully recorded their thoughts on the Normandy campaign and the battle for Omaha Beach.

At the other end of the chain of command, Gerow had one of the most experienced divisions in the U.S. Army, the 'Big Red One,' the 1st ID. The staff of the 1st ID had remained remarkably stable. The chief of staff, Colonel Stanhope Mason, had been with the division since 1941 when it started amphibious training. The 1st ID had planned and conducted more amphibious assaults than any other division in the European theater. It had an outstanding record in combat, having fought good-quality German units in North Africa at El Guettar and at Gela in Sicily. Bradley knew the 1st ID and its commander well. It was Bradley who had given Huebner command of the division after he relieved General Terry Allen in Sicily. Bradley's relationship with Huebner may have increased the influence of the division. Gerow's ability to influence events was thus blunted at both ends of the chain of command. The experience of his senior commander and subordinate headquarters gave them greater credibility, making it difficult for Gerow to imprint his vision on the operation.

Gerow and his staff planned, developed new doctrine, bargained to acquire needed resources, scheduled and critiqued training, argued with Bradley and his staff over the plans and doctrine for the battle at Omaha Beach, and then carried out the directives and orders they were given. They had some success and some failure in their disagreements with Bradley and his staff. Some degree of discord is to be expected between senior and subordinate headquarters, but Bradley and Gerow disagreed on the fundamental concept for the assault at Omaha Beach. Gerow was unable to convince his boss of the correctness of his vision. Gerow's vision for the conduct of the assault at Omaha Beach was operationally and tactically sounder than Bradley's. He had had more time to study and reflect on the invasion of the Continent, and his plan was based on proven doctrinal practices. Gerow deserves greater credit for the success of the battle at Omaha Beach than historians, soldiers, and sailors have given him. In fact, without Gerow's foresight and understanding of amphibious warfare, the battle for Omaha Beach might have failed.

THE EVOLUTION OF THE AMERICAN OPERATIONAL AND TACTICAL PLAN

On 30 June 1943, the COSSAC planners 'directed' the V Corps to prepare plans for the deployment of the U.S. Army in operations against the continent of Europe. The operation was part of a British deception plan code-named 'Wadham.' The object of the operation was to seize the Brest peninsula:

WADHAM involved an assault by American forces on the Brest Peninsula, following earlier landings on other sections of the French coast by British troops. Rapid advances to seize the port of BREST

...were to be made. The port was to be seized and consolidated for the build-up of the forces, which were to arrive directly from the United States. When this primary mission was accomplished, V Corps was to advance further into the BREST Peninsula, capturing other parts and pushing the Germans from the entire area.[48]

The target date for Operation Wadham was 30 September 1943. The operation called for two infantry divisions and other forces in the assault. An operation of this magnitude had not been conducted in the Western European theater of operations. During the planning process for Operation Wadham, the V Corps carried out extensive research in a number of areas, for example, in the number and types of lifts the assault forces would require; the tonnage and types of supplies that would be required at various stages of the invasion; the availability and capacity of British port facilities; the space requirements in England for assembling such a large force; and numerous other areas. The V Corps action report noted: 'Although never put into operation, the WADHAM plans and the information collected during their preparation proved invaluable in all later planning by the Corps. The ground work done by V Corps in WADHAM provided the basis upon which all future planning was laid.'[49]

The final plan for Operation Wadham was presented to the European Theater of Operations, U.S. Army (ETOUSA), headquarters on 30 August 1943. Shortly thereafter, that headquarters and the COSSAC headquarters accepted it. The V Corps action report stated: 'V Corps was highly complimented for the excellent work done and for the completeness of its compliance with the directive when a critique was held on the planning by General ANDREWS, then Theater Commander.'[50] The success of this planning endeavor was a feather in the cap of the V Corps commander. However, because the preliminary planners and commanders were not the individuals who would actually conduct the invasion of Europe and because of the lack of real combat experience, the V Corps' ability to influence events was only temporarily enhanced. Whatever influence the V Corps might have gained from the successful planning of Operation

Wadham was lost in November and December when the veterans of North Africa and Sicily arrived to take command. Still, as a dress rehearsal for planning the Normandy invasion, Operation Wadham proved to be of considerable value not only to the V Corps but also to the FUSA, which picked up where the V Corps left off. The process used to plan Operation Wadham would be used again by the V Corps to plan Operation Neptune.

On 5 September 1943, the Wadham planning group was disbanded. On 12 September, the V Corps planning group for Operation Overlord was established, including many of the members of the Wadham planning group. The Overlord planning group was given the mission of 'planning the requirements for the V Corps on the assumption that it is to be an assault corps for a landing in Europe.'[51] Colonel Benjamin B. Talley, who had served as the assistant director for Operation Wadham, was designated director of the planning group. Lieutenant Colonel Robert H. Pratt, Lieutenant Colonel Charles F. Sleeper, and Major James K. Gaynor were assigned to the planning group as assistants. Sleeper and Gaynor were veterans of the Wadham plan. The planning group worked with the chiefs of functional sections of the V Corps. This system of forming a planning group separate from the primary staff freed the general staff of the V Corps of the detailed planning, allowing them to conduct daily operations and training. The need to exchange information, however, required that both staffs work closely together.

The planning staff used the reverse planning technique.[52] In reverse planning, the commander first decides how he wants to fight a battle, how he wants his forces arrayed on the field of battle at the moment they engage the enemy, and then all other resources are allocated in reverse sequence to insure that the commander meets the enemy in accordance with his vision of the battle. Although Gerow and his planning staff endeavored to use the reverse planning method, planning was actually centered on the deployment of major weapons systems.

On 24 September, the V Corps planning group was given 'special instructions' for its 'mission':

a. *General.* The mission of the V Corps (Reinf) is the invasion of the continent of Europe as an assault force, either acting alone as a separate task force, or as a part of a larger force, as may be determined by proper authority.

b. *Specific.* The mission of the Planning Group is to determine the requirements of V Corps acting as an assault Corps for a landing in Europe.[53]

The V Corps envisioned landing two divisions in the initial assault – the 29th and 28th IDs. The planning group was charged with determining the following:

> The number and type of large and small craft needed for the operation... Nature of inshore fire support required from the Navy firing from small craft. Nature of inshore fire support required, and feasible from V Corps weapons firing from small craft. Types and number of small fire support craft required (a) by Navy, (b) by V Corps (Reinf). Off shore naval fire support required for the landing operation. Air support required for the landing operation. Desired composition, organization equipment and Standing Operating Procedure for far shore parties, both those attached to V Corps and to the Navy serving with V Corps.[54]

These instructions indicate a lack of standard operating procedures and accepted doctrine for an invasion against a deliberate defense. Instead of going by the book and employing tested doctrine, the planners would have to write substantial parts of the book.

The directive also stated that '[f]ull use will be made of information and assistance from the Assault Training Center, Former Staff of II Corps [Bradley's Sicily command] now in the U.K., Staffs of other forces operating in the Mediterranean when and as they are in the U.K., COSSAC, U.S. Navy, the USAAF, and the Royal Navy in the preparation of plans herein called for.'[55] When this directive was issued, the FUSA and SHAEF did not yet exist, and their commanders had

not been appointed; thus, the V Corps initiated planning in an atmos-
phere of uncertainty, unsure of the role it would ultimately play. It was
not until December that the V Corps received sufficient information
to begin planning.

On 21 December, Bradley held the first Overlord conference with
his subordinate American commanders. He opened the conference by
stating: 'In working on this joint plan for the First Army with the
Navy and Air, I may have to bother Corps Commanders to come into
London for a short time and get their advice and suggestions and also
to keep them posted. As a matter of fact all through this I will try to
keep the Corps Commanders posted as to the progress so that they
can keep up their thoughts and be formulating their plans as much as
we can.'[56] With these words, Bradley was establishing the relationship
he wanted with his subordinate commanders. He clarified the chain
of command – about which the V Corps was uncertain when it
started planning – and noted that for the invasion, the corps came
directly under Bradley's command. At this time, Bradley had two
commands – the 1st Army Group (later designated the 12th Army
Group) and the FUSA. Gerow probably realized early in the conference that he and his staff would no longer operate with the same
degree of freedom they had previously enjoyed and that the new boss
would not permit corps commanders to communicate directly with
senior navy, air force, and British commanders and would more
closely monitor corps planning and operations.

At this conference, Gerow learned something about the thinking of
both Montgomery, the commander of the 21st Army Group, and his
new boss. He also began to realize that his vision for the conduct of the
invasion would probably not come to pass and that the role his corps
would play would be substantially reduced. Early in the conference,
Gerow asked Bradley: 'Are you inferring that we [the Americans] are
limited to two divisions, that that is going to be governed by the lift, I
mean the initial assault?'[57] Gerow had anticipated landing two divisions
from his corps. At this time, Bradley believed that only three divisions,
in accordance with the COSSAC plan, would make the initial assault
and that he would command the entire assault.

After listening to the FUSA's tentative plans for the invasion, Gerow expressed a number of concerns. He was more knowledgeable than Bradley about the details of the operation. He challenged Bradley's thinking on the concept of the operation and questioned the accuracy of some of his information.[58] Gerow and Bradley, with their staffs, discussed a number of issues regarding the makeup of the landing force and the conduct of the landing.

On the issue of the British DD tanks, Gerow did not believe the tanks were reliable and suggested that at least two battalions of medium or light tanks should be put ashore in LCMs during the initial assault. Bradley, who had very limited knowledge about the tanks at the time, supported their use on the basis of the British assessment of the tanks.[59] Gerow nevertheless continued to press for tanks in the initial assault transported by a more certain means. He sought a tank and delivery system that permitted the engagement of beach targets in the approach. (The DD tank could not fire its main gun while at sea.) Bradley thought one battalion of tank destroyers ought to be included in the mix of forces. He noted that these high-velocity guns could 'knock out' the German Mark VI tanks better than any other weapon. Gerow felt that if there were sufficient lifts for tank destroyers, they ought to carry medium tanks instead. Bradley believed two battalions of anti-aircraft guns were necessary. He pointed out that in Sicily they were needed against enemy fighters. Gerow felt that the lifts for anti-aircraft guns should be used for artillery instead. This initial discussion and analysis of the makeup of the landing force covered almost every unit, weapon, and resource available. Engineers, mortars, the new 155 mm gun, trucks, DUKWs, supplies, barges, artificial harbors, the enemy situation, minefields and obstacles, and other aspects of the assault were examined.

Concerning the enemy situation, Bradley noted: 'You have got a new commander (Rommel) over there, and he may upset the whole apple-cart by doing something different.'[60] These were prophetic words, and before the conference ended, Colonel Paul Thompson identified exactly how Rommel would upset the 'apple-cart': 'I think the most dangerous possibility in the time remaining, General, would be to put under-water obstacles along the beach. They could completely block the beach just by driving those piles.' Bradley responded: 'Well, that is going to bring up the question, if they put those in between now and then, whether or not you will have to go somewhere else, or, as someone has suggested, we go in at low tide... *If they put those in, it may change the hour of attack correspondingly.*' [61] In December 1943, six months before the invasion took place, the major problem that would plague the tactical commander up until D-Day was identified – the beach minefields and obstacles. At this point in the planning process, Bradley was willing to consider changing the time and landing site of the assault. He was willing to consider going in at low tide, which would have meant landing under the cover of darkness. At this time, Montgomery had not yet issued his Initial Joint Plan, and Bradley had the time and opportunity to influence his thinking.

During this meeting, the problem of clearing lanes through the minefields, obstacles, and concrete wall on Omaha Beach generated considerable discussion and concern. This problem was directly related to the fire support plan. It was a doctrinal issue. Gerow emphasized the potential problem posed by these obstacles:

> I think it is highly important that we do get something that is going to clear out those thick bands of barbed wire and anti-tank mines. *The thing that concerns me most is the man being held up on that beach by physical obstacles which he can't get by without getting out there with an implement and doing it by hand in daylight.*[62]

This was precisely the situation that developed at Omaha Beach on 6 June 1944 that so impeded the progress of the 1st ID. Six months prior to the battle, Gerow accurately identified the problem that would cost so many American lives and nearly cause defeat. Throughout the preparation phase for the Normandy invasion, Gerow was dissatisfied with the plan for clearing the obstacles and minefields on Omaha Beach. He fought Bradley on this issue but was unsuccessful in pushing his vision. No satisfactory solution was found.

Bradley described his plan for the assault: 'They go in first (DD tanks), followed by engineers, and then with these Churchill tanks with their engineers, and then our infantry comes in at H+25, which gives [the tanks and engineers] time to [clear lanes].' Bradley had the engineers on the beach before the infantry in daylight. The engineers required the protection of the infantry to do their job. Without that protection in daylight, they would be slaughtered. Gerow's thinking on the conduct of the assault at this point was better developed and more tactically sound than Bradley's. Gerow departed the conference with the basic understanding that 'the final decision whether you take this or that' would be left up to him; that the order of battle would be his 29th and 28th IDs followed by the 1st and 9th IDs; that some means would be developed to get his men through the beach obstacles, minefields, and concrete seawall; and that he would command the initial assault at Normandy because Bradley planned to remain in England.[63]

In a directive to Colonel Talley on 28 January, Gerow explained his vision for the invasion:

> Assault with two (2) divisions abreast, X Division on right, Y Division on left. Divisions in column of RCTs. Y Division may come in with 2nd and 3rd CTs [Combat Teams] abreast. The third division of the Corps to be afloat in large craft, and to land as soon as conditions in the assault area permit. Assault to be covered by bombing, Naval gunfire, close support craft and probably, smoke.

The operation was divided into three phases: the assault phase, to secure the high ground; the seize-and-organize phase, to defeat local enemy forces and establish a defensive parameter to receive the enemy's counter-attack; and the extend-the-bridgehead phase, to secure sufficient depth for the buildup of forces. The third phase was tentative since its execution depended on the reaction of German forces and the strength of the anticipated counter-attack. Gerow planned to have two divisions ashore on D-Day and have the third start landing on D+1. The second phase was to commence 'as soon as the initial assault RCTs have reduced the enemy fire to the point that craft can come into the beaches without suffering excessive casualties in craft and personnel.'[64]

In the assault, Gerow envisioned twenty-four assault sections 'supported by two medium tanks per assault section.' He spelled out his concept for the operation:

> The assault sections and tanks should land concurrently, preferably in one wave, or at the most, in two waves, at H Hour. By H+30 this force should have overcome resistance in Areas X-1 and Y-1, or so neutralized it by attacks that only limited fire will be directed against incoming craft. While this is going on, Naval gunfire should neutralize enemy fire coming from Areas X-2 and Y-2. Upon completion of tasks X-1 and Y-1, these task forces, less the one attached company each and reinforced with about one-third of the assault tanks, will organize and defend.[65]

On 1 February 1944, the Initial Joint Plan for Operation Neptune was issued by Montgomery's 21st Army Group and the commanders in chief of naval and air operations to the British Second Army and Bradley's FUSA. The plan was developed with the assistance of a planning group from the FUSA established in London on 17 January 1944. The Initial Joint Plan required that the British Second Army, under the command of General Miles Dempsey, and Bradley's FUSA submit their order of battle and Outline Assault Plan to the joint commanders in chief by 15 February.

On 31 January, the V Corps, VII Corps, 1st ID, 29th ID, and 101st Airborne Division received the FUSA's Planning Directive for Overlord, which stated that they should 'initiate preliminary planning without delay.' The directive delineated the FUSA's concept for the operation:

> The First Army will assault Beach 46 [Omaha] and Beach 49 [Utah] simultaneously on D-Day and capture CHERBOURG with the least possible delay. The British 2nd Army will attack on the left of the

first Army... For the initial assault the 1st Infantry Division with 2 CTs in the assault will capture Beach 46, and the 4th Infantry Division attacking in columns of CTs will capture Beach 49. The 101st Air Borne Division will assist the attack on Beach 49. One follow up Division (29th Inf Div.) in craft will reinforce Beach 46 at the completion of unloading of Assault Division... On Beach 49 the 9th Infantry Division should arrive by D+4 (this will make a total of three (3) Infantry and one (1) Air Borne Division). The 82nd Air Borne Division may be dropped north of LA HAVE DU PUITS on D+1.[66]

Between 21 December 1943 and 31 January 1944, the basic concept for the American assault was formulated. Bradley's vision superseded Gerow's. The 1st ID was to replace the 29th and 28th IDs in the assault at Omaha Beach. Instead of two divisions abreast in column, one division with two RCTs abreast would make the landing. Utah Beach was now part of the American sector, and the VII Corps was added to the order of battle. The 4th ID would lead the assault at Utah Beach, assisted by the 101st Airborne Division, which was to be dropped the night before the landing. The 82nd Airborne Division was also part of the mix of forces, but its exact role had not been worked out. The 1st ID was to assault with one RCT from the 29th ID and one of its own RCTs. Naval forces 'O' and 'U' were designated to transport the divisions and command the amphibious assaults. Naval forces were also given the mission to neutralize enemy coastal defenses with gunfire. The Allied air forces were to support the landings "by prearranged air bombardment of important beach defenses, by saturation bombardment on selected sections of the beaches, by delay of enemy reserves, by bombardment and strafing of targets of opportunity, and by flying strafing-bombing missions on call from assaulting units.'[67]

The directive stated that 'H Hour will be shortly after daylight.' Corps and divisions were to complete their preliminary planning by 10 February, five days before the FUSA plan was due to the 21st Army Group. Their plans were to include the following information:

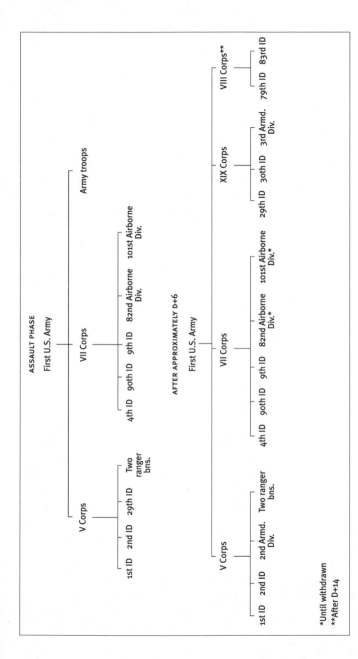

ASSAULT PHASE

First U.S. Army

V Corps — 1st ID, 2nd ID, 29th ID, Two ranger bns.

VII Corps — 4th ID, 90th ID, 9th ID, 82nd Airborne Div., 101st Airborne Div.

Army troops

AFTER APPROXIMATELY D+6

First U.S. Army

V Corps — 1st ID, 2nd ID, 2nd Armd. Div., Two ranger bns.

VII Corps — 4th ID, 90th ID, 9th ID, 82nd Airborne Div.*, 101st Airborne Div.*

XIX Corps — 29th ID, 30th ID, 3rd Armd. Div.

VIII Corps** — 79th ID, 83rd ID

*Until withdrawn
**After D+14

First U.S. Army Organization

a. Assault Plan showing CT frontage and objectives. For V Corps this will include plan for use of two ranger battalions.

b. Provisional list of beach defense targets for pre-arranged Naval and Air fire support, and approximate timing in relation to H Hour.

c. Approximate numbers of men and vehicles to be landed on each RCT beach on each of the first three tides, and the numbers and types of landing ships and craft involved in each case.

d. Tentative list, by type of units, showing the number of men and vehicles allocated to the initial lift of landing ships and craft. (Forces 'O,' 'B' and 'U').

e. Tentative build-up priority lists to include all Division and Corps units.[68]

Bradley's plan indicated that it was possible to destroy the minefields and obstacles on Omaha Beach with air power – 'saturation bombardment on selected sections of the beaches.' Only strategic bombers could saturate an area in a short period of time, and only the American daylight bombers claimed the precision needed to bomb a point target.

On 4 February 1944, the V Corps held one of its many planning conferences with the division commanders and their senior staff. Colonel Henry J. Matchett, chief of staff of V Corps, opened the meeting, explaining that 'the purpose of the conference was to present to the Division Commanders and their staff the planning directive of the Commanding General, V Corps, together with the thoughts of the Corps Commander relative to the initial phase of the assault.'[69] The commanding general of the 1st ID, General Clarence Huebner, and his staff; the assistant division commander of the 29th ID, General Norman D. Cota, and the staff of the 29th ID; Lieutenant Colonel E.D. Adams of the 1st Engineer Special Brigade (ESB); Colonel William D. Bridges of the 5th ESB; Lieutenant Colonel Joseph LaRocque of the Ninth Air Force; Captain M.L. Little of the 11th Amphibious Force; General C.G. Helmick of the 76th Field Artillery Brigade; and other members of the V Corps staff were present.

After the opening remarks, Colonel Talley, deputy chief of staff for planning, explained in detail the V Corps' mission and 'the means the Corps Commander desired be taken to prepare the plans called for by Commanding General, First U.S. Army, in his planning directive for Overlord.' Talley's briefing was based for the most part on the FUSA directive. During the briefing, the corps' staff issued planning instructions and directives to the divisions. Because the V Corps' plan had to be in the hands of the FUSA commander by 10 February, the divisions were advised to establish planning sections with the corps staff. The CG, 1st ID, was instructed to 'prepare detailed plans for the initial assault, subject to the approval of the Commanding General, V Corps.' Gerow made it clear that Huebner was to have 'maximum latitude' in developing his plan for the assault. He also noted that the CG, 1st ID, would command the initial assault until the CG, V Corps, came ashore. The initial objectives, division boundaries, limits of advance, and special instructions were also issued. The CG, 29th ID, was directed to prepare detailed plans for operations in the designated sector immediately following the initial assault. The corps planned to attach the 116th RCT of the 29th ID to the 1st ID in the assault to the right (west) of the corps sector. The other two RCTs of the 29th ID would then come in behind the 116th RCT, and that sector would become the division's zone of action once the corps headquarters was established ashore. One regiment of the 29th ID was designated corps reserve, and it was to be located so that the corps commander could deploy it to influence the situation ashore if needed.

The corps' directive addressed fire support from the air force and navy:

> The success of the initial assault will depend largely on the amount and accuracy of preliminary fire (air and Naval) and close support fires during the actual assault. Therefore, we must insure we have the maximum of such support, using ground weapons in Naval craft, under Naval control, if necessary. DDs cannot fire coming in. Tanks in LCTs are very effective. We may want to use both types of tanks with

the initial assault sections. *One of the air missions should be the destruction of wire.* Every house in the assault area should be listed as a target for destruction by either the air or Naval gunfire. Air bombing and Naval gunfire should continue until troops hit the beach, then shift to inland and flank targets.[70]

General Helmick, V Corps artillery officer, was directed to develop the 'provisional list' of beach defense targets for the prearranged naval and air fire support required by the FUSA. The V Corps identified a mission for the air force that it was totally incapable of carrying out with any degree of precision – 'the destruction of wire.' This mission found its way into operation orders and was expanded to include the clearing of lanes through the obstacles and minefields. The Army Air Forces and Army Ground Forces clearly had different meanings for the term 'precision bombing.' In June 1944, the heavy bombers of the Army Air Forces were incapable of the kind of accuracy required by the Army Ground Forces. Why Gerow and his staff believed the air force possessed such abilities without some demonstration of them is unknown. Bradley's call for 'saturation bombardment on selected sections of the beaches' may have led Gerow to believe that the air force could destroy the minefields and obstacles on Omaha Beach.

Gerow planned to deploy the two ranger battalions at Omaha Beach in the westernmost sectors 'to neutralize the enemy's defenses on the cliffs.'[71] This mission depended on the ability of the navy to land the battalions along the cliffs in landing craft. Since the mission called for the elimination of artillery batteries with the potential to engage naval ships, it was in the best interests of the navy to insure that these guns were taken out of action. Until these guns were neutralized, the navy would remain out of their range, ten miles off the coast.

The corps directive required that the CG of the 1st ID provide the FUSA with specific data, such as the number of units by type and the number of men and vehicles per lift of landing ships and craft. The corps further directed its divisions to specify the units they wanted to deploy in the first three tides, the equipment they planned to take, their build-up priorities, and their attachment and detachment plans.

Thus, part of the corps' duty was to act as a conduit between the divisions and the army. The 1st ID passed along information to the FUSA, and the FUSA used it as a basis for planning. Plans, orders, and directives were then sent down the chain of command from the army level through the corps to the divisions.

After the briefing, the conference was opened to questions and discussion. Huebner stated that he would leave fifteen officers and ten enlisted men with the corps staff for planning purposes. He asked the navy 'what type of ships, the LST and LCT, the APAs [auxiliary personnel attack ships]' would be available to transport the assault forces, information he needed to develop his plan. Captain Little of the U.S. Navy did not have that information. Asked when it would be available, he stated: '[T]hat will depend on London.' Huebner then commented: 'Unless we can get the necessary number of LCVPs it looks like a big hole will be made in our plan right at the start.' Little suggested that Admiral Kirk be contacted to determine the allocation of ships and craft to Amphibious Force 'O.' Cota asked questions along the same lines as those of Huebner. He noted that the plan could not be developed without accurate information on landing craft by type. He asked: 'What should be the basis for planning?' Talley replied: '[I]t is reasonable for General Huebner to indicate the number of LCVPs that he has to have either in the matter of people he has to land or in specific craft.' This approach was supported by Little, who added that 'the number, of course, is subject to the lift assigned to the force carrying General Huebner's command. We cannot increase the capacity of the ships to carry these craft.'[72]

This exchange exemplified the initial negotiation process between the army and the navy. The navy typically did not know what equipment it could make available until late in the planning process. The army asked for what it wanted. The navy responded with what it thought it could provide, which was usually not acceptable. A period of negotiation followed. If the negotiation did not proceed to mutual satisfaction, the problem was pushed up the chain of command, sometimes all the way to Washington. In the end, somehow the navy found the minimum number of ships and craft necessary to do the job.

Agreements of this sort were generally made in writing after a period of negotiation, in which letters were exchanged between the various commands involved. The Joint Fire Plan and the obstacle-clearing plan were assembled in this manner. Joint operations were not based on accepted procedures and techniques; they were based on negotiation.

The issue of the types of craft to be made available to Forces 'O' and 'B' was further discussed. Because Force 'O' was making the initial assault and had to land in a tactical configuration, it was believed that the smaller assault craft carried by Force 'B' could be made available to Force 'O.' Little stated that this was possible but that it depended on a number of factors. He pointed out that it was not desirable to shift craft between forces, even though the navy had done so before, because 'the movement of boats has to be done in the dark with the resulting uncertainties of the craft finding their way to the proper ships and arriving in time.'[73] This problem was not worked out to the satisfaction of the 1st ID. The Report of Operations for the 1st ID noted that this was one of the major deficiencies of the assault plan. Some forces landed in craft that were not designed for a tactical assault. By expanding the size of the landing force in the initial assault, Eisenhower and Montgomery exceeded the number of craft available. The landing was delayed a month to secure additional landing craft, but the final allocation was still unsatisfactory in the view of the assault forces.

The 1st ID and V Corps started their planning in a vacuum. The information they needed was not available when the FUSA required the submission of preliminary plans. However, with the data provided by the 1st ID and other assault divisions, the FUSA could work to get the resources its tactical formations required.

On 9 February 1944, Gerow filed a memorandum for record documenting his first major disagreement with Bradley. The issue was command of the assault force. The purpose of a memorandum for record is to allow an individual to leave a record of a particular action or a position on a given topic. This step is primarily taken when two individuals disagree over an issue whose outcome is uncertain and potential consequences are significant.[74] If the expected results of an endeavor are not realized, a memorandum for record provides proof of the disputant's words and deeds. Gerow's memorandum expressed his disagreement with the organization of the assault forces and the command structure imposed by Bradley. He described what he believed to be the most efficient organization and command structure:

> The V Corps plan formulated in accord with the Army directive, in substance delegates the seizure of the initial bridgehead to a division. The exchange of RCT's between the two leading divisions breaks up the integrity of divisions and complicates the operation both initially and during subsequent phases. Continuity is endangered by the necessity of coordinating the early commitment of additional divisions while the assault is still engaged in D-Day operations. Planning is made more difficult.

The fact that Gerow felt compelled to write this memorandum indicates that he spoke with Bradley about his concerns regarding the organization of the assault forces and his vision for the conduct of the invasion and was not satisfied with Bradley's response. Attached to Gerow's memorandum was a copy of his 28 January 1944 directive to Talley, which outlined Gerow's vision of the invasion. Gerow believed that two divisions side by side should make the assault in column under his command:

> The assault should be made by divisions abreast under the direct command of the Corps Commander. The Corps being a single task force for this purpose, such a plan favors simplicity, speed, power, coordination and continuity in the progressive development of the operation – factors which appreciably influence successful action, particularly in an amphibious operation.[75]

Gerow's assessment that the exchange of RCTs between divisions further complicated an already difficult operation was essentially correct. The exchange of units between organizations can erode the ability of those organizations to function as a team. However, Gerow's plan did not deploy one team; it deployed two divisions.

In *A Soldier's Story*, Bradley explained his reasoning for the seemingly tactically unsound deployment of forces at Omaha Beach:

> The assault force on Omaha was to make contact with the British on its left while at the same time establishing a link with Utah on its right. If one division were to be given both missions, it would have been dispersed across a 25-mile front. And as the follow-up divisions came in, it would have become necessary to reassemble the 1st Division in one corner of Omaha Beach. To avoid the traffic snarl that would otherwise have jammed the beach, I shaped the Omaha attack force with two regiments from the 1st Division, the third from the 29th Division. Thus while the 1st Division concentrated to the left of the beachhead, the 29th would advance to the right. The follow-up division would then come into the line in the hole between them.[76]

Bradley was clearly more concerned with operations following the assault than with the assault itself. What he sought to achieve by placing one RCT from the 29th Division temporarily under the command of the 1st ID could have been accomplished more simply by deploying two divisions abreast, as in Gerow's plan. Divisions in column under corps command would have achieved Bradley's objective of arraying forces on the battlefield in such a manner as to facilitate the link-up with forces on the right and left while preventing a 'traffic snarl.'

Bradley wrote that he employed the 1st ID because it was an 'experienced assault division.' This must have been a secondary consideration because he at least in part negated what he had hoped to achieve by also employing a green RCT from the 29th ID, and at Utah Beach, he deployed the inexperienced 4th ID.[77]

The concept of divisions in column was actually the basis for both Bradley's and Gerow's plans. The real difference between the two plans was in the command structure. Bradley's plan gave command of the assault to the commander of the 1st ID, Huebner, whereas in Gerow's plan, Gerow retained command. Bradley lacked confidence in Gerow's abilities to fight his forces and manage the battlefield. Gerow had never fought his division or corps in battle, and Bradley apparently felt this was no time to train a new corps commander. It was probably only Gerow's 'intimate' relationship with Eisenhower and familiarity with the plan that prevented Bradley from relieving him without prejudice as he had other newcomers.

Bradley's plan provided for greater cohesion in the battle for the beach than Gerow's. A division is the largest unit in the U.S. Army trained to fight as a team, and teamwork can greatly increase combat power. Synergism is achieved when forces are integrated and synchronized to work intimately together. By detaching the 26th RCT of the 1st ID and attaching the 116th RCT of the 29th ID, Bradley eroded the ability of the division to function as a team and lost the efficiency that comes from experience. Bradley's plan nevertheless provided for greater teamwork than Gerow's. One team was responsible for the battle at Omaha Beach as opposed to two teams, and the responsibility for the assault was placed at the appropriate level – the division.

By directing the V Corps to replace its lead division with the 1st ID and by attaching one RCT of the 29th ID to the 1st ID, Bradley achieved a number of goals: he replaced the inexperienced Gerow with the highly regarded Huebner as the commander of the assault; he positioned a veteran staff and one veteran RCT as the lead element; he placed the entire assault under one division commander instead of two; he maintained a role for the National Guard division – possibly for political purposes – that had been training for this mission for two years; and he maintained division boundaries for subsequent operations by placing the regiment from the 29th ID temporarily under the command of the 1st ID for the assault. Once the assault was over and the headquarters of the 29th ID was established ashore, the original division boundary between the 28th and 29th Divisions could be established. Gerow lost this battle with Bradley.

At 1330 hours on 7 February 1944, the V Corps held its second planning conference.[78] This time, Gerow's subordinates would do most of the talking. Gerow wanted to hear their plans. He opened the session by addressing a rumor circulating among the troops that the 'forthcoming operation will be one involving high casualties.' According to the notes of the conference: 'General Gerow impressed the group present with the fact that, in his opinion, the operation is not a too difficult one, and that there should not be the slightest question that our objective will not be reached by D-Day. The Corps Commander emphasized the urgency of hitting as much of the beach as we can, and as quickly as we can.'[79] Whether Gerow believed the landing would not be too difficult or was simply making this statement to quell the rumor is uncertain; however, his words did not help prepare his men psychologically for the battle that lay ahead. Given Gerow's concern about the minefields and obstacles, it is probable that he was attempting to put an end to a rumor that could damage the morale of his soldiers. Nevertheless, if his words were carried back to his soldiers as he intended, they gave the men a false impression of the upcoming battle.

Gerow then succinctly outlined the plan, placing 'great emphasis... on crushing and breaking through the initial "crust."'[80] At this point in the planning process, Gerow was most interested in hearing from his division commanders. He kept his comments brief, leaving most of the time for them. Huebner followed Gerow.

Using a wall map, Huebner pointed out the division's zone of action, the critical areas, and the division's objectives and responsibilities. He discussed terrain, roadways, and lifts. He was primarily concerned about the 'inadequate' number of landing craft and other transport ships allotted for his division. Gerow was also troubled by the paucity of landing craft. He took this issue directly to Bradley on several occasions.

Major General Charles Gerhardt, the commander of the 29th ID, followed Huebner. Perhaps not understanding what Gerow was trying to accomplish with his opening comments, Gerhardt gave an assessment of the operation that came close to contradicting Gerow's view.

He thought the operation presented a number of difficulties. The conference notes stated: 'Gen. Gerhardt then addressed the group, saying that his division approaches this job with nothing but optimism. He then cited, however, that the division mission wasn't an easy one, emphasizing the fact that only the highly skilled soldier has a good chance of survival. The untrained, the lackadaisical, the indifferent soldier, will fall by the wayside. Difficulties will be encountered which are not usually present.'[81] If Gerhardt's troops included untrained, lackadaisical, indifferent soldiers, he should have gotten rid of them – at least for this operation. If he permitted such soldiers to remain in his units while he prepared for the Normandy invasion, he was remiss in his responsibilities. These comments were unnecessary and counterproductive. They did not ease the minds of the soldiers making the assault on D-Day. Neither Gerow's nor Gerhardt's remarks helped the men prepare for battle – Gerow's comments created a false impression, and Gerhardt's placed doubt in the minds of some soldiers.

Gerhardt explained his plan. He analyzed the terrain on which his division would fight and discussed tactics. Gerhardt raised a number of questions concerning tides, the time of landing, and tank battalions. He stated that Cota would command the 116th RCT, which was to be attached to the 1st ID for the assault. After Gerhardt's briefing, the plans and potential problems were discussed, analyzed, and to some degree worked out.

On 10 February, the V Corps Preliminary 'Overlord' Plan was submitted in triplicate to the FUSA in accordance with army directives.[82] The V Corps was constrained to conduct a daylight firepower-based landing at a prescribed time and location. The firepower required to overcome a deliberate defense was not under corps control. The V Corps plan listed a number of deficiencies in the FUSA plan.

Gerow felt it was necessary to put two divisions ashore on D-Day. He thus wanted the 29th ID in Force 'B' to land behind the 1st ID in Force 'O' on D-Day:

'The Tentative V Corps Assault Plan' shows the desired objectives to be reached by late afternoon of D–Day and the likely dispositions of forces at that time. If more than token resistance is encountered beyond the beach crust these objectives could be attained and held only if the 115th RCT of the 29th Division (Force 'B') lands on the heels of the 116th RCT attached to the 1st Division and is immediately followed by the 175th RCT [of the 29th ID]. This requires the foot elements (at least) of the 115th RCT and the 175th RCT to be afloat in the transport area and in position to land behind the 116th RCT when the beaches have been cleared. This requirement makes it necessary for Force 'B' to be close behind Force 'O.' The landing of Force 'B' on D+1... effectively prohibits the employment of the 29th Division on D–day. Inasmuch as present considerations indicate reaching the D–Day objective requires the employment of the 29th Division on D–day, it is requested that action be taken to insure the availability of the 29th Division when it is required.[83]

Gerow and his planning staff believed that if invasion forces met significant resistance, the combat power of the 29th ID would be needed in order to reach specified D–Day terrain objectives, and with two divisions ashore, Gerow would be in command. Ideally, sufficient landing craft would be procured to land tactically the RCTs of the 29th ID in Force 'B.' Gerow wanted these forces configured so they could land fighting if necessary. The resources, however, were not available to tactically load both the 1st and 29th IDs. Still, Gerow persisted in his efforts to have a second division land as close behind the first division as possible. In April, he sent another letter to the CG, FUSA, noting that this issue was of 'grave concern.' He wrote:

If the situation permits, the 115th Infantry should be landed immediately behind the 116th RCT and the 26th Infantry behind the 18th RCT. This will permit their employment during daylight hours on D–Day to complete mopping up the area and to organize the D–Day line preparatory to enemy reaction on the morning of D+1 day. It would seem desirable to position Force 'B' with relation to Force 'O,' prior to the junction of these two forces in the transport area, so that craft loaded with personnel of the 115th and 26th Infantry Regiments can move quickly into the transport area for dispatch to the beach. The complexity of the Naval task involved in the 'NEPTUNE' operation is fully appreciated but the need for getting two regiments in Force 'B' ashore early is considered to be of such major importance as to warrant some adjustment in the Naval Plan.... It is requested that this problem be discussed with CTF [Commander Task Force] 122 with a view to arranging for the landing of the 115th and 26th Infantry Regiment on 3 hours notice given any time after H+3 hours.[84]

This was one of the few times that Bradley yielded to Gerow's request. Gerow's thinking on the employment of the 29th ID was tactically the best solution. He wanted to build up his forces as fast as possible. On D-Day, the 115th RCT was called forward to assist in the battle for the beaches. Before the day was over and the beaches were cleared, the 115th Infantry was fully engaged in battle for Omaha Beach.

The V Corps Preliminary 'Overlord' Plan provided the FUSA with figures on the shortage of landing craft. Force 'O,' which consisted of 24,927 personnel and 2,818 vehicles, would need additional transports for 1,707 personnel and 438 vehicles. Force 'B,' which consisted of 25,394 personnel and 3,890 vehicles, would need additional transports for 2,522 personnel and 412 vehicles.

Gerow was also concerned about the logistical build-up. He noted that he intended to have 'all foot elements of the three RCTs of each division ...ashore by two hours before dark on D-day.' To support these forces, a certain tonnage of materials had to be landed on D-Day. The plan stated: 'First U.S. Army has indicated the number of LSTs and LCTs which can be unloaded on each tide. This restriction seriously handicaps the landing operation, and results in the vehicles of certain craft of the alternate plan landing on the 4th tide [on D+2]. The essential personnel from these craft in both plans must be landed earlier by means of LCVP and other small craft as indicated in the schedules.'[85] Gerow wanted everything done faster and with more forces. The naval aspects of the amphibious assault were of major concern. Gerow's tactical plan depended on the ability of the navy to acquire sufficient resources to deploy the corps in the configuration he deemed tactically sound and to support it once ashore.

Another significant issue discussed in the V Corps plan was the concept for the conduct of the operation. The corps' plan stressed the importance of fire support – the major source of combat power under Bradley's plan: 'Since the landing will be made in daylight the necessity of reducing these targets by pre-arranged Naval and Air fire cannot be emphasized too strongly. Undue delay caused by the necessity for their reduction by assaulting forces may prevent the attainment of the D-Day objectives in the time allotted.'[86]

Gerow and his staff knew they depended on the navy and air force to provide the required firepower to win the battle for the beach. They also knew that as time passed – as the Germans built more obstacles and placed more mines – the importance of naval and air firepower increased. If the navy and air force failed to achieve the expected goals, the burden of winning the battle for the beach would fall heavily on the infantry, and high casualties would be likely. Gerow first voiced this concern on 21 December 1943 at the FUSA's initial planning conference, when the concept for the operation was still sketchy.[87] This fear may have fueled Gerow's tenacious pursuit to put the maximum number of forces ashore in the shortest amount of time.

The plan also addressed the naval command structure. Gerow's corps was divided between two naval forces, Force 'O' and Force 'B.' Gerow would sail aboard Admiral Hall's command ship in Force 'O.' He wanted Hall to have direct command of both forces, making it possible for Gerow to command and control the employment of his entire corps through Hall. He wrote: 'The problem of planning for and landing forces 'O' and 'B' will be simplified if both Naval Force 'B' and Naval Force 'O' could be under a single naval commander, and it is so recommended unless naval considerations unknown to this Headquarters make it inadvisable.' In April, Gerow again requested that Hall command both naval forces: '[T]he commander of Force 'O' should have the authority to direct the movement of these craft [Force 'B'] into the transport area upon request of the Corps Commander if Naval considerations permit.'[88] In this matter, Gerow's view prevailed. Hall commanded both forces at Omaha Beach.

If Montgomery's and Bradley's firepower-based assault failed, Gerow planned to have the maximum number of fighting soldiers ashore in the time given to make up for the deficiency in combat power. As the planning progressed, Gerow's dissatisfaction with Bradley's vision increased.

On 25 February, the FUSA plan for the invasion of Europe was completed. As the date of the invasion grew closer, modifications were made to the plan, but the fundamental tenets remained unchanged. The planning group that helped develop the Initial Joint Plan wrote the FUSA plan. The purpose of the FUSA plan was 'to provide a basis for planning by Task Force Commanders. Should modifications be found necessary or desirable in the course of planning, commanders will make appropriate requests to Commander, First U.S. Army.'[89] Bradley may have sought to allow his subordinate commanders some flexibility in planning the assault.[90] He, however, had little leeway. Although Gerow made requests for changes to the plan, doctrine determined the timing of the assault. If Bradley changed the timing to make a landing in darkness, he in essence would change the doctrine.

On 28 February, the V Corps released its Planning Guide, Operation 'Overlord,' which set forth the corps' plan for the conduct of the invasion. At this stage in the planning process, Gerow had Bradley's approval and guidance and was ready to issue his guidance to his division commanders. Gerow noted: 'Information on some of the aspects of the operation is missing, but this will be supplied as it becomes available.' When this document was distributed, important parts of the plan had not yet been developed, such as the engineer plan for clearing lanes through the minefields and obstacles and the fire support plan.[91]

Bradley and Gerow's exchanges during the planning revealed several points. First, Montgomery and Bradley developed a plan and then tacked on important elements, almost as if they were after-thoughts. For example, the plan for clearing the lanes at Omaha Beach was an addendum to the initial plan. Second, the primary forces for the generation of combat power on Omaha Beach were not in the hands of the tactical commanders conducting the invasion – the division commanders – but two levels above them. The Joint Fire Plan was worked out at the army level with input from the tactical command-ers. The corps did not tailor these resources to support its maneuvers; the divisions were tailored to fit the employment criteria of the fire-power forces.

Although the words 'tentative' and 'outline' were used to describe the 28 February V Corps plan, it was essentially the plan that was put into effect. As the situation on Omaha Beach changed, as Rommel constructed more obstacles and minefields, Gerow endeavored to change the plan, but Bradley held firm to the decisions he had made in January, decisions made before the enemy situation at Omaha Beach was fully assessed and before Rommel's defense took its final form. Bradley did not attempt to defeat the enemy's plan. He sought to dictate the course of the battle and campaign with superior fire-power.

In a memorandum on 21 March 1944, the V Corps commander described his view of the conduct of the operation. The memoran-dum echoed much that was written in the corps Planning Guide, but Gerow had refined his thinking. He explained how he would deploy his battalions, how he would conduct the assault, and the principles on which his vision was based. Gerow wrote:

> Visualizing the operation of the V Corps, it is apparent that the oper-ations from H Hour onward fall naturally into three phases. Phase one, to be accomplished on D-Day, has for its objective, the seizure, by the assault force, of a line which will provide in its rear sufficient room for the landing and assembly of adequate forces for a further advance. The line chosen for this purpose is shown on the map as First Objective, PM, D-day. The second phase consists of an advance from this line to a much deeper line on strong terrain, behind which there

should be adequate room for the landing, assembly, and deployment of the full strength of Corps. This line is shown on the map as Second Objective, 'D' plus 1 day. It is located behind the L'Elle and LA DROINE River and includes a major portion of the dominating terrain in the area of the FORREST DE CERISY. The third phase involves an advance from this second objective, and is dependent upon enemy reactions, forces ashore, and the plan of operations of units on the right and left.[92]

Gerow's plan was constructed on the belief that the Germans could not initiate a serious counter-attack on D-Day. He believed tactical surprise could be achieved and that the 352nd Division, a mere twenty miles away, could not influence the situation on D-Day. On D+1, the corps was to be located on strong defensible terrain, ready to receive the enemy's attack. Gerow explained the maneuver of his battalions:

> The 1st Division will land with two RCT's abreast, the 116th on the right and the 16th on the left, each RCT with two battalions abreast. Taking up first the RCT on the right (the 116th), one battalion will operate along the coast clearing out fixed enemy installations and to it the Ranger Battalion will later be attached. One battalion will move directly inland to the first high ground overlooking the beaches. The third battalion will push forward to the second ridge in the vicinity of LONGUEVILLE and then advance down that ridge on ISIGNY. The left RCT (the 16th) will attack the left sector, one battalion mopping up along the beach in the direction of PORT EN BESSIN. One battalion to move straight forward and occupy the first high ground, the third battalion to move straight forward and occupy the ridge just north of TREVIERES.[93]

The initial effort would be directed at securing the high ground overlooking the beaches, clearing the coast, occupying dominant terrain immediately behind the beaches, and linking up with the British to the east and the rangers at Pointe du Hoe and the VII Corps to the west. Each battalion thus had a different objective. Each battalion was to move in a different direction, with the exception of the two battalions designated to hold the high ground overlooking the beaches. These battalions were to cover the most likely enemy routes to the beach. The terrain that dominated the approaches had to be seized as rapidly as possible. Gerow planned to secure the corps area of operation by first establishing outpost forward positions and then filling in the gaps between them as forces became available. Instead of concentrating forces in a narrowly defined area, Gerow dispersed forces in three directions – south, east, and west. Intelligence on the enemy's strength and expected activities made Gerow's decisions viable.

Gerow also described the concept for the employment of fire support resources:

> The plan for fire support may be broken down into four (4) general phases consisting of (a) counter-battery (b) cutting lanes in wire (c) drenching of beaches in attack of strong points (d) fire on call to support the advance of the assault troops. Enemy batteries which directly affect the mission of the V Corps are specified as counter-battery targets in the support plan. This mission of cutting lanes in wire is one primarily for bombardment aviation. The general schedule of preparation fire is outlined as follows:
>
> H minus 4 hours to H minus 90 minutes – Night heavy bombardment.
> H minus 4 hours to H minus 40 minutes – Medium bombardment.
> H minus 40 to H Hour – Daylight heavy bombardment.
> H minus 40 to H Hour – Counter-battery fire – 1 battleship, 1 monitor, and 7 cruisers.[94]

This plan reveals that Gerow misunderstood the capabilities of the Army Air Force in Europe. It is also evidence of planning and communication problems. The Army Air Force was incapable of cutting lanes through wire or attacking strongpoints with any precision. In June 1944, the tactical air force could not achieve this degree of accuracy and was not adequately trained to conduct close support missions – missions in close proximity to ground forces. The strategic bomber force, by doctrine, training, and technology, was not prepared to perform its D-Day mission. The V Corps and the U.S. Army in Europe typically failed to realistically assess air force capabilities. American faith in technology caused army leaders to place too much confidence in air power. The air force had never demonstrated the capabilities ascribed to it, yet at all levels, with perhaps the exception of the division level, army leaders accepted as a fact the air force's ability to conduct these missions.

The FUSA directives and orders did not specifically state that the air force would clear lanes through the obstacles and minefields on the beaches. This mission was not given to the air force by the FUSA. Although this charge found its way into corps operation orders, Gerow did not believe it could be accomplished in the time allocated, and he continued to seek other solutions.

Gerow further noted:

> For direct support of the assault, there is available, in addition to the above ships, 8 destroyers, 6 LCG(L), 36 155 mm Howitzers on LCT(5)s, 28 medium tanks firing from landing craft, 24 LCS and 9 LCT(R) directing rocket fires. Assault elements will land DD and other medium tanks at H Hour and under the direct fire of these tanks, employ assault teams in the reduction of pill-boxes by *direct assault,* and advance rapidly to secure the first high ground which is approximately one mile south of the beach.[95]

Gerow committed his forces to a direct assault against a deliberate defense in daylight, a maneuver for which he has been criticized. The assault was to be preceded by what was believed to be the heaviest bombing ever employed in an assault. Assault forces were to be protected by direct-fire weapons in close proximity to the beach – destroyers, LCTs mounted with rockets and howitzers, and other weapons. Firing over the heads and on the flanks of the assaulting forces, these weapons were to complete the destruction already started by indirect fire from bombers, battleships, and cruisers. Given the fire-power Gerow expected to be delivered on the enemy's defense, the correct form of maneuver was selected. The Marine Corps and U.S. Army in the Pacific used this method successfully many times. As soon as fires were lifted, the assault took place, giving the enemy no time to recover. The maneuver, direct assault, did not succeed because the firepower that was expected was never produced. Infiltration techniques worked best under the cover of darkness or in dense vegetation. Neither condition existed at Omaha Beach.

Gerow concluded his summary by listing the tactical principles upon which the plan was based:

> In preparing its tactical plan, the Corps has been governed by the following principles:
> 1. Keep all available air and naval gunfire support on enemy beach positions until the initial assault is within two hundred (200) yards thereof.
> 2. Initial assault sections push inland to the high ground, delaying only to take out enemy opposition to their immediate front. Support these sections with DD tanks and tanks landed from LCTAs.
> 3. Objectives during the advance inland to be high ground and enemy observation.
> 4. Keep disposed in depth. Do not leave a defensive position unguarded until the next one inland has been secured.[96]

Gerow's principles indicate that he placed great importance on preparing for the enemy counter-attack. Obtaining the high ground was critical to the corps' ability to withstand a major enemy push.

7

Obstacle and Minefield Clearance Plan

Gerow seemed a bit pessimistic, and finally Ike said to him that he should be optimistic and cheerful because he had behind him the greatest firepower ever assembled on the face of the earth.

Captain Harry C. Butcher

Between February and May 1944, intelligence reports indicated that Rommel continued to construct his defense:

The placing of underwater obstacles on a large scale on open beaches in Northern France has become a general policy since February of this year. The existence of underwater obstacles in the NEPTUNE area was first discovered on a series of oblique sorties of the coastline taken 20 February. So far, the obstacles have been located in... the British area, and in the vicinity of... De Varreville and St Laurent-sur-Mer [Omaha Beach] in the American area.[1]

On 17 March, the FUSA directed the V Corps to develop and submit a plan for army approval for the removal of beach obstacles by 1 April.[2] What had been an army problem was now a corps problem. What had started out as an operational problem to be solved with operational resources ended up as a tactical problem to be solved with tactical resources. Between December 1943 and March 1944, Bradley abandoned his original idea to employ operational assets such as air and naval power to the problem of breaching the minefields and obstacles on Omaha Beach. At the conference on 21 December, he stated:

> I think we are going to have several methods of trying to get through the wire... One of these is the bombing. I am not sure whether or not we are going to be able to make full use of that but for an hour... with H Hour so soon after daylight... We were going to make some tests and I think we may want to go on with them anyway; but whether or not we are going to be able to make use of that bombing to cut this wire at that hour of attack, I am not sure... We are planning on cutting this wire with the Marauders... If they can fly in there with 100-pound bombs (instantaneous fuse) and circle out, they can cut the wire very effectively and set off most of the vehicular mines.[3]

Bradley proceeded to discuss other possible methods of destroying the obstacles on the beach such as using rockets from landing craft and ships, and he reflected on the possibility of changing the time of the assault for breaching operations. Nevertheless, in March, he handed the problem over to Gerow. Then Bradley failed to support Gerow's proposed solution.

What is even more curious about Bradley's decision to turn over the problem to Gerow in March is that the problem became more crucial between February and May than it had been when it was first identified in December 1943. During that period, Rommel greatly strengthened the obstacles and minefields along the Normandy coast to the extent that it was arguably a strategic problem instead of a tactical problem. Without doubt, operational assets stood a better chance of clearing the minefields and obstacles than did tactical assets.

The minefields and obstacles at Normandy required the development of a new subsidiary mission and plan. The obstacles would have to be removed. The question was, how and by whom? By doctrine, the navy was responsible for removing the obstacles up to the high-water mark, which meant that 'underwater' obstacles were the navy's problem. The navy had two means to deal with beach obstacles: destroying them by fire or removing them with underwater demolition teams. In either case, the navy in the Mediterranean and European theaters lacked the resources to breach obstacles and minefields on such a broad front and in such extensive quantities. Between March and April 1944, the army and navy discussed the issue; the discussions were not always amicable. The army's ESBs did not consider beach-clearing operations in the initial assault their responsibility. In response to a message from Admiral Kirk to Admiral Hall's Eleventh Amphibious Force on 25 March 1944 recommending that he request through the FUSA 'the assistance of engineer special brigade,' the Headquarters Provisional ESB Group, commanded by General William M. Hoge, sent a message to the FUSA outlining its objections:[4]

> It is not entirely clear from attached memorandum from the Navy whether the representation by the Navy to FUSA is for the assistance of the Special Brigade Engineer in the assault breaching of underwater obstacles prior to H Hour or in the removal of underwater obstacles during the assault phase, but subsequent to H Hour. It is unlikely that the latter is meant since it is stated in the V Corps under — and in Secret Opn Memo # 5, FUSA, that Special Brigade Engineers do assist Naval beach parties in the removal of underwater obstacles to increase the capacity of the beaches. It is believed therefore, that the Navy is requesting that Special Brigade Engineers assist in the assault breaching of underwater obstacles before H Hour. *This is not in accord with the Army-Navy agreement stated in the FUSA plan and is not an assigned task of Special Brigade Engineers.*[5]

After highlighting a number of reasons why the ESBs could not perform this mission, the message concluded:

Engr Spec Brig have been organized and given certain troops to perform certain tasks, of which assault breaching is not one. If this additional task is attempted, it means a damaging sacrifice in potential to perform regularly assigned and expected tasks. *It requires improvisation at a time when completeness of arrangements is vital.* FUSA plan states that supporting naval forces will transport assault troops to the beaches on the far shore. *It is a clear mission. If obstacles impede such transportation it remains a Navy task to breach them. It is recommended that Special Brigade Engineers not be made available for assault breaching.*[6]

This statement left no doubt that the ESBs did not want to be among the first units on Omaha Beach on D-Day. And the headquarters was doctrinally correct in its protests. The ESB Group had one more appeal that was reinforced by doctrine: 'Lt. Col. Rice states that at conference at Hq, 1st Div, 29 March, he ascertained that 1st Div plan does call for organic and attached combat engineers (not Special Brigade) to breach beach obstacles.'[7] Doctrinally, if the navy could not breach the beach obstacles and minefields, the mission became that of the combat engineer battalions organic to the assault divisions. By doctrine, it was the responsibility of the division's combat engineers to clear minefields and obstacles that impeded the movement of the division.[8] The task at hand, however, was more than the division engineers could handle. Thus, by default, unhappily the mission fell to the ESBs. Two battalions were attached to the 1st ID. They would go in with the first wave.

According to the original concept for the engineer amphibian brigades, a boat regiment and a boat maintenance company were organic to the brigades. Under this organization, the army was responsible for transporting troops to the assault beaches, and since the movement was not simply a transportation problem, the brigades would have been an integral part of the assault. The clearing of obstacles and minefields was one phase of the broader mission of the amphibian brigades. Two such organizations were established early in the war. The idea of the army having a navy rankled some senior naval officers, however, and a revised agreement between the two services gave the navy more control over landing crews, boats, and amphibious training.[9] As a consequence, the 1st Engineer Amphibian Brigade was disbanded and its units reassigned.[10] The need for such an organization remained, however, and after every landing, the missions and tasks for engineers increased. It was thus efficient organizational practice to establish a higher headquarters to co-ordinate the activities and resources of the numerous engineer battalions, which possessed diverse talents and abilities.[11] For the Normandy invasion, the 5th and 6th ESBs (Provisional) were formed to provide landing support to the V Corps. The ESBs were not trained in amphibious assault.[12] They had a different mission and organization from that of the original engineer amphibian brigades. They were, however, trained in the removal of mines and obstacles.

On 28 March, General Hoge was ordered to prepare plans for the employment of the ESBs 'for the purpose of providing a force to eliminate the underwater obstacles that would be encountered in the assault on OMAHA Beach.'[13] These plans were to cover the following:

> (1) Assistance to and co-ordination with Navy in reduction of under-water obstacles. (2) Reduction of beach obstacles above high-water-mark. (3) Removal of mines on the beach. (4) Construction of initial beach roadway. (5) Reduction of road blocks at beach exits and construction of beach exits necessary to exit vehicles landing during the first tide. (6) Breaching of tank walls or filling tank ditches. (7) Removal of mines along CT axis.[14]

Hoge was assisted by Colonel Robert K. McDonough, commander of the 1121st Engineer Combat Group; Lieutenant Colonel Lewis C. Patillo, acting V Corps engineer; and Lieutenant Colonel John T. O'Neill, commander of the Provisional Engineer Group for Special Assault Demolition.[15] Kenneth P. Lord, the assistant G-3 officer for the 1st ID, described the situation:

> Just before we practiced we received an awful blow. We had been closely examining the beaches at Omaha and were quite happy that the

hedgehogs and element C were piled on the beaches and it appeared that the Germans were concentrating on other beaches. One of our bombers happened to jettison some bombs before landing in England. We saw a picture of his bombs exploding but also saw a series of sympathetic detonations of underwater mines. We went to the Navy and pointed out that the official landing operations manual gave the Navy the responsibility up to the high tide mark. They did not disagree but simply said they did not have the troops to clear the mines. We appealed to SHAEF [more likely the FUSA] and they sent us two engineer battalions, one training at Woolcombe in England and the other that was training in Florida. These troops would lead off the division attack. Now we had to change our entire loading plan. *We imagine it was a great shock to those engineers to find that they were the first wave.*[16]

The agreement between the FUSA and the U.S. Navy concerning the clearing of obstacles and minefields stated: 'The U.S. Navy will build Mulberry 'A,' Gooseberries, and Causeways, and clear underwater obstacles and beach mines seaward of the high-water mark. Engineer Special Brigade will connect to naval installations and clear mines and obstacles inshore of the high-water mark. The Engineer Special Brigades will assist the U.S. Navy in mine and obstacle clearance on the beaches between the high water and low-water mark when the beach is dried out.'[17] The agreement was further refined as the time of the invasion drew near:

> Under the principle of mutual co-operation, each service can assist the other in its specific task. The Army can render such assistance to the Navy in the removal of underwater obstacles, as its capabilities will permit. In like manner, should obstacles which are dry at the time of landing become flooded prior to their removal by the Army, the Navy can render such assistance to the Army as lies within its capabilities.'[18]

The friction between the army and navy tended to be between the navy's operational commanders and the army's tactical commanders. Army and navy operational commanders, Bradley and Kirk, tended to work well together, even if they disagreed about doctrine. Army and navy tactical commanders, Gerow and Hall, also tended to work well together and to be in general agreement over the conduct of the operation. Although discord existed between the army and navy, the more substantial difficulties were between the levels of command. Disagreements between the FUSA and the V Corps in regard to the plan for breaching the obstacles, and other matters, continued and intensified as the date of the landing approached.[19]

Between 28 March and 10 April, the basic plan for breaching the obstacles on Omaha Beach was worked out. And on 30 April, the Provisional Engineer Group came into existence. It was made up of the 146th Engineer Combat Battalion and the 299th Engineer Battalion, less one company. Other units were attached. It was decided that sixteen 'gaps' fifty yards wide would be cleared.[20] Each engineer battalion was divided into eight boat teams. The eight boat teams were formed into twelve clearing teams. Three teams had the mission of clearing two gaps. Sixteen tank dozers from the 741st and 743rd Tank Battalions and from the 1st ID's tank battalions supported the engineers. The navy 'estimated' that twenty-one naval combat demolition units would be available to assist in the operation. It dedicated sixteen LCT(A)s to the engineers and made available thirty-six LCMs.

On 10 April, the engineers began training for the invasion at the Assault Training Center in Woolcombe, England.[21] On 20 April, Brigadier General W. B. Kean, Bradley's chief of staff, stated in a memorandum to Bradley: 'Locke is to remain at the ATC [Assault Training Center] and will supervise underwater training until I am assured that the situation is well in hand. I believe the training has finally been set up on a sound basis and is acceptable to both Corps.'[22] Kean noted problems with navy personnel:

> The Senior Naval Commander who reported (Lt. Reiss) has apparently not had any previous experience in the job at hand. He stated that he had been a base commander and had not had experience in clearing of demolitions. He arrived with 16 teams without a training program and without having made any administrative arrangements.[23]

A mere six weeks prior to the invasion of Europe, personnel were still being identified to perform a critical mission, and the army was conducting not only unit training but also individual training to teach soldiers and sailors basic skills and techniques for using explosives to remove obstacles. Kean was concerned that the navy was not giving this mission the priority it warranted: 'I am somewhat concerned about the Navy attitude towards their responsibility and preparation for clearing of underwater obstacles…. [W]e are now training about 4 times the number of personnel than the Navy intended to train. Our part is in preparation for assistance to the Navy in a few feet of water, but the big job is going to the Navy which has the equipment to do it.'[24]

Kean's memorandum indicated that the design of the operation was still being discussed. Changing the time of the assault to allow more time for the clearing of lanes was being considered. This approach would have required landing under the cover of darkness – a change in doctrinal practices. Kean wrote:

> [T]here has been much talk about licking the question of obstacles by making assault on low tide. It seems to me that this is the time to raise the question as to whether or not the High Command intends a low water H Hour. If so, the question of training is vitally affected for all units concerned.[25]

On 24 April, the FUSA G-2 officer distributed Intelligence Note no. 18, in which he stated:

> The placing of underwater obstacles on a large scale on open beaches in Northern France has become a general policy. The progress of construction has been continuous and fast. The fact that short stretches of different types of obstacles are often intermingled and the fact that in some cases obstacles have been moved down from strongpoints back of the beach may indicate the urgency with which the work is being done.[26]

The report also noted that behind Omaha Beach at Colleville, obstacles were being stockpiled and that 'further installation is to be expected.'[27]

On 28 April, the V Corps conducted a rehearsal, Exercise Tiger. Eisenhower, British Air Marshal Tedder, Bradley, and Gerow observed the exercise. The exercise did not proceed as scheduled. Captain Harry C. Butcher, Eisenhower's naval aide, described the drill:

> In this exercise effort was made to get tanks ashore quickly in order to use their firepower. Engineers were brought in as rapidly as possible to demolish obstacles with hand-placed explosives. The tanks had to wait while these operations proceeded. If there had been enemy fire, the tanks, being quite close together, would have been easy targets, as, indeed, would the landing craft. I came away from the exercise feeling depressed.[28]

Gerow was also unhappy with the conduct of the exercise. He was most concerned about the minefields and obstacles. Butcher witnessed the discussion between Gerow, Bradley, Eisenhower, and Tedder after the exercise. He wrote: 'It is the mines that Gerow fears the most for his landing on Omaha Beach. Gerow said he feared the underwater obstacles most of all, and to date no completely satisfactory method of disposal had been found. Gerow seemed a bit pessimistic.'[29] Butcher described Eisenhower's response:

> Ike said to him that he should be optimistic and cheerful because he has behind him the greatest firepower ever assembled on the face of the earth. For the entire landing, there will be six battleships, two monitors, twenty-one cruisers, and an untold number of destroyers. In addition, there will be the greatest amount of air support ever assembled. Then there are the rocket ships and our own artillery, which can be mounted on landing craft.[30]

The naval forces available to Gerow for the assault at Normandy were meager by Pacific theater standards, substantially less than called for by the U.S. Army's own doctrine, and, most important, substantially less than required to quickly defeat a deliberate defense.[31]

Tedder also took part in the discussion: 'Tedder said an agreement had been reached on OVERLORD that there would be mass aerial bombing of the beachhead just before H-Hour. This bombing would start about 200 yards inland from the beach and continue on for eight or nine hundred yards. There would be shorts and longs. The shorts might explode underwater mines.'[32] The American strategic bomber force, the only daylight precision bomber force capable of dropping the tonnage of explosives demanded in the time allotted, was incapable of the level of precision Tedder anticipated. And no training or plan to develop the skills and techniques necessary to conduct this mission was proposed.

Butcher described Gerow's response to Eisenhower: 'Gee said he wasn't pessimistic, he was merely realistic, and he and his staff purposely looked on the worst conditions as being possible so that every preparation that could be thought of would be made.'[33] This exercise confirmed Gerow's doubts about the current plan. In his view, the plan had to be changed. The following day, on 29 April, V Corps headquarters sent a letter to the commanding general of the FUSA entitled 'Breaching Beach Obstacles.' In this memorandum, Gerow requested that the time of the invasion be changed.[34]

The day before the invasion rehearsal, on 27 April, Gerow held a conference at which the obstacle-clearing plan was reexamined. At the conference were Colonels Locke and Emil F. Reinhardt of the FUSA, Captains Little and Welland of the U.S. Navy, Gerow and his V Corps staff, and Huebner and his 1st ID staff. Gerow noted in his memorandum to Bradley that those present 'concurred' with 'the following paragraphs.' Gerow wanted more time for the engineer and navy underwater demolition teams to clear the lanes through the obstacles and minefields. He believed Rommel's construction plan had proceeded to the point that a new solution was needed to deal with obstacles and minefields on Omaha Beach.[35] Gerow wrote Bradley:

Aerial photographs taken on 9 and 19 April, respectively, show obstacles on 'OMAHA' Beach...The photographs of 19 April show a partial row of Element 'C' across the beach at about mid-tide and a considerable strengthening of the hedgehogs. Inasmuch as all of these obstacles were placed during a period of not over three weeks and work is still in progress, it must be expected that the obstacles will be further strengthened. The photographs of 19 April show the sand building up around the hedgerows [hedgehogs], as it has around the groins near the west end of the beach, and as it will probably do around the Element 'C.' This filling in of sand very materially increases the difficulty of breaching and requires special consideration.[36]

The conference recommended that the plan for the conduct of the assault meet the following criteria:

a. Permit the Infantry to land under such conditions that they can proceed ashore without swimming.

b. Permit the rapid inland advance of the assaulting Infantry.

c. Furnish to the assaulting Infantry the maximum fire support, including that of DD tanks.

d. Provide for the touching down of LCTs and other minor landing craft and their retraction.

e. Provide fire support for the personnel engaged in breaching obstacles.

f. Be accomplished in the minimum amount of time.

g. Be sufficiently inclusive and flexible to overcome any likely condition not discovered until just prior to or at the time of commencing the breaching operation.[37]

The final engineer plan failed to meet all of these requirements.

Gerow's memorandum proposed two plans for clearing the sixteen lanes through the obstacles and minefields. Plan 'A' assumed that the clearing operations would take place when the obstacles closest to the sea were 'dried out or... in water *not* more than three feet deep.' Plan 'B' assumed that the seaward band of obstacles was 'in a depth of water more than three feet deep, due either to its location or the stage of the tide at the time of breaching.' Gerow described Plan 'A' as follows:

> Under Plan 'A' the assault would be concurrent with the commencement of the breaching operations. In this case the present assault waves of Infantry, DD tanks, M-4 tanks and tank dozers would touch down at H-Hour with substantially the present Naval and Air support. The assaulting Infantry would advance under cover of tanks and Navy fire, and the demolition parties would land at H+5 minutes to attack obstacles with tanks and armored dozers and with explosives to open sufficient initial gaps for the oncoming waves of landing craft before the rising tide drowned out the obstacles. The supporting Infantry would land at H+30 and the attack would continue.

He described Plan 'B' as follows:

> Under Plan 'B,' it may be necessary, depending on the type of obstacles encountered, to commence breaching operations prior to H Hour... If the seaward band of obstacles does not permit gapping by ramming with LCT(A)s and/or if an intermediary band of heavier obstacles is likewise drowned out, the necessary initial gaps must be opened by the Navy in advance of H-Hour to permit Infantry to get ashore without swimming. In this case, the Army would attack dry obstacles as in Plan 'A,' but such attack can only be launched after the gaps are opened through the flooded bands.[38]

The ability to clear the underwater obstacles was predicated on the conditions and types of obstacles on the beaches. The conditions changed with time. Because explosive mines, Element 'C,' were placed on the seaward bands of obstacles, the possibility of ramming ashore was eliminated. Without this option, Gerow believed it would not be possible to clear and mark the lanes with the resources committed and in the time allotted. Once the obstacles were underwater, or 'drowned out,' the task became substantially more difficult. 'Various estimates' had shown that 'light obstacles' in over three feet of water could be successfully breached in a minimum of thirty minutes. More substantial obstacles, however, required greater time and resources. Thus, Gerow favored a plan that gave the clearing teams the time they needed to do their work while the obstacles were dry. Gerow favored Plan 'B.' He wrote:

> It is obvious that obstacles can be breached easier and faster in the dry than when drowned out. Thus, if certain stages of the tide will permit breaching in the dry, that is the time to attack. Furthermore, the stage of the tide should be such that ample time will be available for breaching before the obstacles become flooded.
>
> Under the present conditions, wherein there is a band of Element 'C' at about mid-tide, the time of H Hour should be advanced sufficiently to allow a minimum of *one hour's work on these obstacles before they become flooded by the rising tide*...
>
> In conclusion, it is further stated that the breaching of obstacles is a difficult task at best, and it must be undertaken only under the most favorable circumstances, which, in the case of present obstacles, is when they are dry. It is considered that the present obstacles warrant changing H Hour at least to low tide, and perhaps to one hour before low tide, depending upon experience gained during the next few days at the Assault Training Center...
>
> The placing of additional obstacles will further emphasize the necessity of landing at low water, and it is recommended that H Hour be changed accordingly. In the event changing H Hour to permit landing at low water on Beach 'OMAHA' presents undue hardship on other beaches, it is considered better to have different H Hours for the several beaches than to attack through obstacles which require breaching underwater.

Gerow concluded by asking that a 'prompt decision' be made.[39]

Admiral Hall was also concerned with the obstacle-clearing plan and attempted to secure more time for this subsidiary mission. He later recalled: 'I was going to Portsmouth to this conference about the time of the H-hour. I was trying to get a staggered attack, since my beaches were the only ones that had underwater obstacles, then I would have adequate time to attack them, and I wanted to attack on a half-falling tide... So, I fought like the deuce at this conference to be allowed to attack on a half-falling tide, and finally the decision was against me.' [40] Hall's comments in his action report were not quite as forceful, but they supported his later statements. He wrote in the report that he 'would have preferred to land at low tide or even one hour before low tide in order to have allowed the demolition parties more time to deal with the obstacles and to afford some leeway in the event that landing was delayed.'[41]

Gerow's and Hall's requests probably never received serious consideration because changing the time of the assault would have changed the entire concept for the conduct of the operation. To secure more time for the engineer operations, H-Hour could be moved to either earlier or later in the day. An earlier landing would have meant landing in darkness before sunrise. This was the approach that the tactical commanders, Gerow, Huebner, and Hall, favored.[42] Beginning the battle for Omaha Beach earlier would have fundamentally changed the premise upon which Montgomery and Bradley based their plan. Bradley and Montgomery intended to win the battle for the beaches with firepower from the air. This mandated a daylight assault. Only in daylight would the air force have a chance to produce the kind of destruction that Montgomery and Bradley hoped for. The air force and navy were given less than thirty minutes of daylight to complete this task. If the assault were moved up just thirty-five minutes, it would have taken place in darkness. If it were moved up even ten minutes, it would have eliminated the bombing mission. (In hindsight, since the sky was overcast and the Eighth Air Force had to use radar to determine the release point, it would not have mattered to the air force if the landing had been moved up an hour or two.)

The tides at Normandy went through a complete cycle every twelve hours, meaning that there were two high tides and two low tides in a twenty-four-hour period. The assault was timed to take place on a low, rising tide. Sunrise would be at 0558 on 6 June 1944.[43] Assaulting at 0630 would mean that the seaward band of obstacles would be underwater within thirty minutes following the landing. The daylight heavy and medium bomber forces had a mere twenty-five minutes to conduct their mission, from H-25 minutes to H-Hour (0605 to 0630).[44] The time allocated to the air forces was already less than they had requested. Thus, allowing any more time for the engineer mission would have eliminated the bombing mission altogether. Bradley and Montgomery could not permit the timing of the assault to be changed without abandoning one of the major tenets, and the major source of combat power, on which their plan was based.

In addition, the timing of the American assault was tied to the timing of the British assault. The British assault was scheduled to take place an hour after the American assault because a higher tide was required to traverse sandbars and runnels on the floor of the Channel in the British sector. If Gerow's and Hall's recommendations were approved, the American assault would take place not one hour but two or more hours before the British assault. Bradley believed that an American assault conducted that far in advance of the British assault would have the effect of drawing all local enemy reserves to the American sector. This was a risk he was not willing to take. Bradley's thinking on the timing of the assault is made clear in a discussion he had with Admiral Kirk in reference to postponing the invasion to 8 or 9 June. Bradley queried his commanders on their assessment of the optimum time. In *A Soldier's Story*, he wrote: 'From Portland came word that Hall and Gerow together favored an earlier H-Hour despite the disadvantage of low tides. But this would put them ashore an hour or more before the British on their left. Because of the rocks on those beaches, the British had no alternative but to go in at high tide.'[45] Bradley continued: '"Good Lord," I exclaimed to Kirk, "do they know what they're doing? If they land that much earlier on Omaha, they'll pull all the enemy fire from the British beach right down on their heads."'[46] Although Bradley believed that Kirk supported his view, Kirk's action report reveals otherwise. In his action report, Kirk reflected:

> It is believed that an H Hour earlier in reference to the tidal conditions would have been preferable, particularly for OMAHA Beach.

On both of the American beaches the conditions at H Hour were satisfactory for landing from low water on, as regards the quality of the beach itself; but in the British Sector there were a couple of beaches with rocks and ledges offshore which made a landing prior to about half-tide undesirable.[47]

It is not clear whether Kirk made his concerns known to Bradley. Hall recalled: 'I don't remember whether Admiral Kirk supported me or not in this plea of mine.'[48] To explain why Bradley was unwilling to change the time of the assault, Kirk wrote:

The military authorities did not consider it desirable that the time for landing should vary more than an hour between the American and British sectors. This dictated an H-Hour for OMAHA and UTAH Beaches which it was estimated would allow about thirty to forty minutes of dry landing on the beach before the water reached the first row of obstacles.

Kirk concluded:

While the Naval Commander, Western Task Force, cannot pass upon the importance of the Army requirement for not over one hour difference between H-Hour on the various beaches, it appears desirable to point out that for a landing conducted with a large tidal range and with considerable obstacles on the beach, it would be most desirable to have the H-hour provide as much time as can be made available to work on the obstacles and to clear the beach before the small landing craft, such as LCTs, come in to land.[49]

Kirk was very diplomatic in his comments. Unlike Gerow and Hall, he favored the doctrinal approach advanced by Admiral Hewitt. This would have given the navy an opportunity to destroy the water's edge defense. Kirk believed the army did not take full advantage of the naval gunfire. However, given the doctrine employed, Kirk supported the assessment of Hall and Gerow that more time was needed.

Bradley also made an issue of the point that the navy required daylight to assure landing at the proper point. Bradley was an experienced soldier, and he knew that night attacks, even when they took place completely on land, invariably suffered from disorganization.[50] What was important was that the units were pointed in the right direction and that cohesive, complete combat units were deployed – units capable of independent action and of sustaining themselves for several hours until daylight, when all would be sorted out. At a conference with Admiral Hewitt prior to the invasion of North Africa, Patton stated: 'Never in history has the Navy landed an army at the planned time and place. If you land us anywhere within fifty miles of Fedhala and within one week of D-day, I'll go ahead and win.'[51] Patton was engaging in hyperbole, but his basic tenet for night operations was correct. Few amphibious assaults conducted at night landed soldiers exactly where they were supposed to be, and Bradley knew not to expect such a level of proficiency from the navy or the army. In addition, because the approach to the beaches of Normandy was initiated during the hours of darkness and most of the eleven-mile movement took place during the hours of darkness, the statement that daylight was necessary to land troops on the 'proper' beaches was contradicted by the facts. The invasion was not initiated in daylight and the troops were not landed at the proper point. Only the final approach and the landing were made during the hours of daylight, and by that time, it was too late to make major course corrections and still land at 0630 hours. Thus, one of the stated reasons for landing during the hours of daylight, the need for navigational accuracy, was negated in the movement phase – that phase of an attack with the greatest potential for confusion and error. The Normandy invasion suffered from the same disadvantages as a night attack – confusion, disorganization, and missed landings – without having the advantages of darkness.

Hall and Gerow tried to gain more time for their underwater demolition teams and engineer battalions to clear the obstacles and minefields on Omaha Beach.[52] Bradley refused their request. He disregarded Rommel's construction and the arguments of his tactical commanders. On D-Day, this mission failed because engineers and underwater demolition teams had insufficient time and attempted to work in daylight under enemy fire. This failure caused the assault to bog down, and the specter of defeat hung over Bradley's head. Bradley thus deserves the greater part of the blame for the near defeat and high casualties at Omaha Beach. He maximized neither his chance for winning the battle with firepower nor his chance for winning the battle with the stealth, secrecy, surprise, and concealment provided by a night landing. The Montgomery-Bradley vision was believed to have significant flaws by Hall, Kirk, Gerow, Huebner, and Cota.

Of the obstacle clearance plan, Colonel Thompson, commander of the Assault Training Center, wrote: 'During the pre-invasion months endless thought and research had been devoted to developing effective ways of attacking the obstacles.' This statement implies that the planners of the Normandy invasion did not believe in the early months of 1944 that the U.S. Army had developed an effective tactical doctrine for breaching minefields and obstacles and thus thought new methods were required. Thompson continued:

> An old axiom of war states that engineers cannot work under heavy fire; but that is exactly what these special engineers set out to do... In substance, the obstacle-clearance plan on Omaha Beach failed. The old axiom of war was confirmed: the special engineers could not operate effectively under that heavy enemy fire.[53]

On 17 May 1944, Gerow conducted a briefing during which he outlined the V Corps plan, his analysis of the flow of the battle, and his thoughts on likely enemy actions. Gerow believed the battle would take place as follows:

a. First, air bombing and gunfire against the transport area and small craft moving into the beaches. This opposition will have to be taken care of by the Air Force and Naval Support fire.

b. Second, obstacles on the beach between low and high water covered by enemy fire from positions on the beach and inland. We propose to overcome these obstacles with combined Engineer and Navy demolition teams, working under cover of the assault tanks, and close support Navy craft. It is essential that D-Day and H-Hour be fixed at a stage of the tide that will permit these demolition teams to have a minimum of twenty minutes to work on the obstacles while dry.

c.   Third, well-organized strongpoints and tank obstacles located on the beach and the high ground in rear thereof. All exits from the beach inland are mined and strongly guarded by wired-in strong points. Additional positions all located on the heights at either extremity of the beach. It is estimated that the beach defenses are garrisoned at the present time with about one (1) infantry battalion reinforced. Preliminary air and naval bombardment will effect some destruction of these defenses, but we are relying on infantry assault teams to finally take them out...

d.   Fourth, counter-attack by mobile forces. There is one (1) battalion in Bayeux. This battalion can operate against either the British or our forces any time after H-Hour. It is not a serious threat. One (1) Infantry Division is located in the vicinity of St Lô. It is possible for at least a part of this division to move up and occupy a defensive position just south of the AURE or to attack across the AURE on the afternoon of D-Day, or later. It is logical to expect this division will be employed against the V Corps. If so employed, it will delay but not stop our advance to the D+1 day positions.[54]

Although Gerow expected the 352nd Division to be deployed against his forces, he did not believe it would start movement until the landing at Omaha took place. He expected to achieve complete tactical surprise. Why he and other American planners expected such a high degree of surprise is a mystery. The water's edge defense at Omaha Beach was believed to be manned by one reinforced infantry battalion – hardly a match for two RCTs. Gerow, for the most part, implemented Bradley's vision. However, his changes and recommendations significantly increased the combat power of the 1st ID on

D-Day. Without Gerow's efforts, the battle for Omaha Beach might very well have failed, and had Bradley accepted his other recommendations, the assault would have proceeded with fewer difficulties and losses.

8
The Joint Fire Plan

[I]n ramming our way ashore against the fortified coast of France, we calculated that firepower would more than compensate for the loss of concealment; stealth could better be sacrificed to more accurate and heavier bombardment.

General Omar N. Bradley

We have proven the precision principle in this war. Our precision however is in a relative not a literal sense. We must assume that our enemies will take this lesson to heart... [W]e must develop bomb sights and bombadiers which, under all weather conditions, cannot only literally drop bombs in a 'pickle barrel' but in the correct barrel.

General Carl A. Spaatz

The Anglo-American leaders planned to win the battle for Normandy with tactical surprise and what was believed to be the greatest firepower ever assembled for an amphibious assault. Neither Eisenhower, Montgomery, nor Bradley had ever conducted an amphibious assault against a deliberate defense. No such large-scale operation was fought in the Mediterranean or European theater. Thus, there was no cumulative body of knowledge, no standard, no yardstick against which the planners could measure the adequacy of their plans or the adequacy of the firepower resources allocated. Still, the Allies could have drawn on two cumulative bodies of experience and knowledge – American Pacific theater doctrine and British Mediterranean theater doctrine. For assaults against deliberate defenses, Marine Corps doctrine was most applicable and effective. The planners of the Normandy invasion, however, decided on a hybrid doctrine. They developed new doctrine, new technology, new tactical organizations, and new units. This emphasis on innovation was a function of lack of experience. The Allies did not fully test their new doctrine, and at Omaha Beach it failed. The air force was untrained and lacked the technology and doctrine to perform the beach-bombing mission in overcast skies. The rocket launchers and artillery mounted in landing craft were inaccurate systems because it was impossible to determine the height of the waves on which the small vessels rode at the instant the weapons were fired. And naval gunfire, the surest means of destruction, was provided in insufficient quantity and given insufficient time to produce the desired effect in the target area. The Allied Joint Fire Plan was flawed, and it failed to produce the quality of damage expected and required to limit casualties.

The operational commanders' high expectations for the Joint Fire Plan created a false mental picture of the battles to be fought on the coast of Normandy. This false picture caused tactical commanders to prepare to fight the wrong battle. It also prepared soldiers psychologically to fight the wrong battle, thereby hurting their chances to succeed. Words such as 'drenching fire' and 'saturation bombing' gave soldiers the impression that they were about the witness 'the greatest show on earth.' But they did not. The gap between expectations and reality was enormous. This, in part, caused the cognitive disjunct that facilitated the onset of shock and paralysis that afflicted many soldiers. The failure of the Joint Fire Plan contributed to the failure of the obstacle and minefield clearance plan. Army engineers and navy underwater demolition teams could not perform their mission under heavy fire. The plan broke down and success had to be improvised. The soldiers on the beaches paid a high cost for this failure in planning and in technology and doctrine development. And what happened at Omaha Beach could have happened on other beaches.

DEVELOPMENT OF THE JOINT FIRE PLAN

The groundwork for the Joint Fire Plan was laid by the FUSA Artillery Planning Group. The FUSA Artillery Office and members of the SHAEF, Allied Expeditionary Air Force (AEAF), Allied Naval Commander in Chief Expeditionary Force, British 21st Army Group, British 2nd Army, and U.S. Navy Task Force 122 made up the planning group. Because modern amphibious warfare was relatively new in World War II, there was a lack of depth and breadth of knowledge and experience, so new doctrine was written and new training manuals were published for the invasion of Europe. The FUSA Report of Operations noted:

> These plans [artillery plans] duly co-ordinated with all interested parties consisted of the following:
> a. Activation, organization and training of Naval Shore Control Parties for the employment with airborne as well as ground troops.
> b. Formulation and publication of a procedure for the accomplishment of naval gunfire support for the assaulting forces.
> c. Draft, co-ordinate, revise and publish the Prearranged Air and Naval Bombardment Plan for the assault.
> d. Draft, co-ordinate, revise and publish the Artillery and Naval Gunfire Support Plan for the assault...

e. Conduct tests in conjunction with the Navy to determine the most practical modification to LCTs when used as support craft. And, so on.[1]

Doctrine was written exclusively for the Normandy invasion. This work was further complicated by the fact that the U.S. Navy and the Royal Navy used different systems to determine grid co-ordinates, which identified precise locations on the ground. Because British warships were to be employed in the pre-invasion bombardment of American beaches, additional training, co-ordination, and procedural development were required.

Bradley's FUSA assumed responsibility for the planning, co-ordination, and use of all fire support assets to be employed in the American sector.[2] The mission of the Joint Fire Plan was stated as follows:

> [T]o destroy the enemy artillery and strong point positions which were capable of firing on the transport areas and the assault beaches. If this destruction were not accomplished, it was believed that effective neutralization would be maintained by continuing some of the air bombardment and gunfire on the targets up to H-5 minutes before lifting to flanking or more distant inland targets.[3]

The fire support for the invasion came from three sources, naval, air, and fire support craft, the latter of which were made up of army and navy forces.

In January, when the Montgomery Plan replaced the COSSAC plan, Admiral Ramsay pointed out that it would be necessary to expand the naval gunfire support fleet to provide coverage to the entire front and that the British lacked the wherewithal to supply the additional vessels. As a result, in March, the U.S. Navy was asked to provide the necessary battleships, cruisers, and destroyers.[4] The initial response of the U.S. Navy was that Eisenhower must get the needed ships from the British. However, after several heated discussions, the navy realized the British did not have the resources and supported the request.

Admiral Hall was particularly concerned about the lack of adequate naval gunfire support for the assault at Omaha Beach. The initial naval bombardment fleet was inferior to that employed in the American sector at Sicily.[5] Hall was ultimately able to secure additional destroyers.[6] The U.S. Navy provided three battleships, two cruisers, and thirty-four destroyers for escort and fire support duty in the Normandy campaign. Naval fire support resources were allocated as follows: Force 'O,' designated to support Omaha Beach, consisted of two battleships, four light cruisers, and twelve destroyers. Force 'U,' designated to support Utah Beach, consisted of one battleship, three heavy cruisers, two light cruisers, one monitor, and ten destroyers. The British, Dutch, and French also supported the American landings with naval vessels.

The Naval Bombardment Plan was divided into three phases. Phase 1 was the counterbattery bombardment, which was to begin at 'first light' and continue until all designated German artillery batteries were 'silenced.' Fourteen batteries were capable of influencing the situation on Omaha Beach. The big guns of the battleships and cruisers were to destroy or neutralize these targets. Intelligence sources identified the batteries and provided co-ordinates. Batteries were assigned target numbers and placed on a priority target list. These targets were to be engaged methodically in accordance with the priority given. Spotter aircraft and spotters aboard ship could also designate targets.

The second phase, the attack of beach defenses, began when cruisers and destroyers moved to locations where they could best support the assault. It was scheduled to begin at H-20 minutes. This 'drenching fire' was to be delivered by close support destroyers and support craft. Battleships and cruisers were to 'augment' this drenching fire upon completion of their counterbattery mission. At H-Hour, close support fire was to shift to targets further inland or on the flanks. A target list was provided for the shifting of fire. The actual preparation of the beach by naval gunfire would last a mere twenty minutes.[7] And the big guns of battleships directed their efforts primarily at the destruction of enemy artillery to the flank and rear of the beaches. Thus, one of the lessons of Dieppe was forgotten.[8]

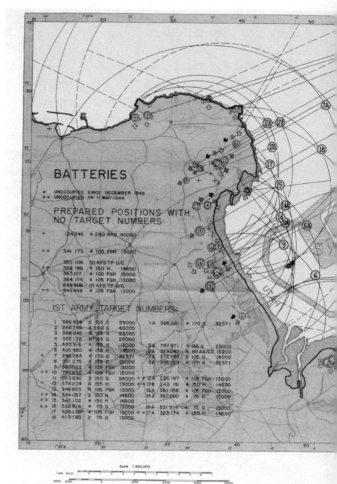

BAT

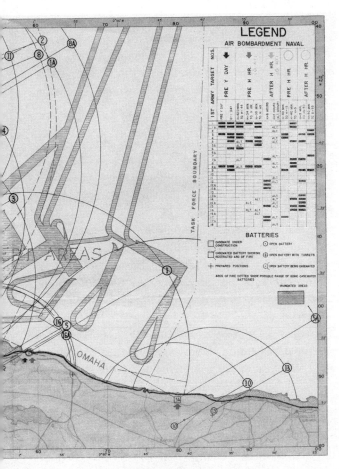

AMERICAN NEPTUNE AREA
...TERY BOMBARDMENT PLAN

American Neptune Area, Battery Bombardment Plan. From U.S. Army, First U.S. Army, Report of Operations, 20 October 1943–1 August 1944, Annex 2, Operations Plan Neptune, USMA.

The final phase was close support fire on call. This phase commenced as soon as naval shore fire control parties were ashore and ready to call for fire, at approximately H+30 minutes. A naval shore fire control party accompanied each battalion. In the initial assault, there were four battalions, and each battalion had two naval vessels in direct support.[9]

Air Chief Marshal Sir Trafford Leigh-Mallory was commander in chief of the AEAF. The U.S. Ninth Tactical Air Force and the RAF Second Tactical Air Force were part of this command. General Carl Spaatz was the senior American airman in the theater. He commanded the U.S. Strategic Air Force (USSTAF). He directed the operation of the Eighth Air Force, administratively controlled the Ninth Air Force, and operationally controlled the strategic forces in the Fifteenth Air Force in Italy. In terms of the employment of American air power in Europe, Spaatz was the most powerful man in the theater. He firmly believed in the strategic bombing campaign and opposed any diversion of resources to support ground operations. Lieutenant General James Doolittle commanded the U.S. Eighth Air Force, a strategic command. America's heavy strategic bombers, B-17s and B-24s, and accompanying day fighters made up the Eighth Air Force. Major General Lewis Brereton commanded the U.S. Ninth Tactical Air Force, which was designed to support army ground forces. It consisted of light and medium bombers, fighter-bombers, fighters, and transport aircraft. Air Chief Marshal Sir Arthur Harris commanded the RAF Bomber Command. He was the British counterpart to Spaatz.

On 14 April 1944, less than two months prior to the invasion, Eisenhower was given 'direction' of the USSTAF and the RAF Bomber Command. Throughout March, the issue of command of these forces was hotly debated. The British Chiefs of Staff objected to the use of the word 'command,' so 'direction' was used instead.[10] Eisenhower exercised his authority primarily through his deputy supreme Allied commander, Air Chief Marshal Sir Arthur Tedder.[11] For operations carried out as part of the Normandy invasion, Leigh-

Mallory was responsible for co-ordinating the activities of the strategic and tactical air forces. No one individual exercised complete authority over the use of air power, and every operation was subject to appeal.

An example of the difficulties inherent in the command structure that was established was the disagreement between Leigh-Mallory and Spaatz over control of the Ninth Air Force. On 10 March, Leigh-Mallory stated in a directive to the Ninth Air Force: 'The Supreme Commander has decided that the time has now come for the operations of U.S. 9th Air Force to be directed toward preparation for OVERLORD. Henceforth 9th Air Force will operate exclusively under the Allied Expeditionary Air Force and will be released from its commitment to assist U.S. 8th Air Force POINTBLANK operations under arrangements made by the force.' Spaatz was employing the long-range day fighters of the Ninth Air Force to accompany his bombers in Europe, and on 18 March, he submitted a memorandum to Eisenhower that stated:

> I think this is a matter of utmost importance in our operations. Unless the 8th Air Force operating out of U.K. can be assured of the availability of all the long range fighters, including P-47s, their deep penetrations will result in greatly increased heavy bomber losses and we will be losing many opportunities to deal punishing blows to the German Air Force.[12]

Eisenhower accepted Spaatz's argument, and Spaatz retained control of the Ninth Air Force's fighters. Had Eisenhower decided against Spaatz, the issue could have gone to General Henry H. (Hap) Arnold, commanding general of the Army Air Forces in Washington. However, the air force typically won interservice and mission priority disputes because of the view that it was necessary to achieve air superiority. No one could disagree with this argument. Everyone accepted the principle that air superiority over the battlefield was a prerequisite for an amphibious operation. The question was, what level of air domination was sufficient – 80 per cent, 90 per cent, 100 per cent? And over how much of the continent of Europe was air superiority required? The close air support mission was last in priority in the minds of American airmen, and as a consequence, the air force was poorly trained in this mission on 6 June 1944. Air force historian Will A. Jacobs observed: 'For a variety of reasons, including personality conflicts, quarrel over strategy, and organizational politics, the Allies never created a single overall air command in northwest Europe. Even Sir Arthur Tedder did not act as Air Commander-in-Chief. He arbitrated in case of conflict between the three air commanders.'[13] To this list of factors causing discord, doctrinal differences, interservice rivalry, opposing mission priorities, and national egos can be added. Each commander had his own staff working on target lists to support operations on the coast of Normandy. This organization was inefficient. Jacobs wrote that the allocation of heavy bombers 'was complicated and awkward, and the final list of targets to be attacked in the prearranged program of close support was not settled until late May... [I]t is hard to escape the conclusion that the Allied air forces would have been more effectively employed had a common plan been developed by a single staff and implemented by the authority of a single commander.'[14]

The Initial Joint Plan estimated that the RAF and the USSTAF would have available the following air forces on 1 June 1944. For operations against the coast of France, the USSTAF would have 163 bomber squadrons with 12 bombers per squadron and 45 fighter squadrons with 25 fighters per squadron. Photo reconnaissance aircraft were also available. The Ninth Air Force was 'associated' with the FUSA.[15] It consisted of 32 squadrons of medium bombers, B-26s, with 16 bombers per squadron; 12 squadrons of light bombers with 16 bombers per squadron; 55 squadrons of day fighters with 25 fighters per squadron; 3 squadrons of night fighters with 12 fighters per squadron; and reconnaissance and troop carrier aircraft. The Ninth Air Force was designated to support Force 'U,' and the Eighth Air Force was designated to support Force 'O' and British and Canadian forces assaulting on Sword, Juno, and Gold Beaches.

It was estimated that the RAF would have available 72 squadrons of heavy bombers with 20 bombers per squadron. Other resources included 18 squadrons of light bombers with 18 to 20 bombers per squadron; 20 squadrons of fighter bombers with 18 bombers per squadron; 64 squadrons of day fighters with 18 fighters per squadron; 22 squadrons of night fighters with 18 fighters per squadron; and numerous squadrons of reconnaissance and transport aircraft.[16]

These were the resources that so impressed Eisenhower, Montgomery, and Bradley. These assets were the crucial factor in determining when the assault would be conducted, thereby determining the doctrine for the invasion. The Air Bombardment Plan stated: 'The air support for Operation Plan 'Neptune,' is based upon the attack of battery positions, beach defense localities, bridges, road embankments, cable junctions – command posts and communication centers.'[17] On the night of the invasion and on D-Day, Bomber Command and the Eighth Air Force gave Montgomery and Bradley their maximum effort and put a record number of bombers in the air. Close air support was not possible from the American air forces because the required level of training and co-ordination had not been achieved.[18] The air force was able to conduct its interdiction mission, however, and isolate the battlefield.

Fire support was also provided by tanks, machine guns, artillery, naval guns, and rockets mounted or loaded onto landing craft of various shapes and sizes.[19] The mission of these forces was '[t]o furnish during the approach to the beaches and prior to touchdown, area fire on and in rear of the beaches, fire on strong points, beach defenses and to take part in the beach drenching.'[20] Captain Lorenzo S. Sabin Jr. commanded the gunfire support craft of the U.S. Navy's Eleventh Amphibious Force. His command consisted of 14 LCT(R)s, 9 LCG(L)s, 11 LCFs, 26 LCT(A)s, and 48 LCP(L)s. These British-built craft were turned over to the U.S. Navy as part of the reverse Lend-Lease agreement in the winter and spring of 1944.[21]

LCT(R)s (landing craft, tank, rocket) were mounted with 5-inch rockets. They were designed to deliver a large volume of preparatory fire on landing beaches at the last moment before the assault. The British constructed twenty-six of these vessels and lent fourteen to the U.S. Navy. The U.S Navy deployed nine at Omaha Beach and five at

Utah Beach. Lieutenant Larry W. Carr commanded the nine LCT(R)s at Omaha Beach. There were two types of LCT(R)s: the LCT(2) carried 792 rockets, and the LCT(3) carried 1,064 rockets. All of the LCT(R)s deployed at Omaha Beach were the newer, larger LCT(3)s. The craft was 196 feet long and 36 feet wide. Rocket racks were fixed to an upper deck at a 45-degree angle, six rockets per rack. Aiming the craft was the only way to aim the rockets. Racks were arranged in the landing craft one behind the other. Each 5-inch rocket carried a 29-pound high explosive warhead to a maximum range of 3,500 yards in 26 seconds. The warhead had a bursting radius of 30 yards. Incendiary and smoke rockets were also deployed. Rockets were fired electrically in 24 to 26 salvos of 39 or 42 rockets per salvo. Because the angle of fire could not be adjusted, the rockets had to be fired at a precise distance from the shore in order to produce the desired effect on the target. The width of the pattern laid by the rockets was 700 yards. This could not be adjusted, but the depth of the pattern could vary from 300 yards to 1,000 yards, depending on the concentration of fire desired. To determine distance, each craft was equipped with radar. In addition, each LCT was equipped with a Brown Gyro Compass. LCT(R)s were to follow 2,700 yards behind the leading assault waves and fire their rockets exactly 26 seconds before the assault wave was 300 yards from the shore. In other words, the rockets were supposed to impact when the leading assault wave was 300 yards from landing. The rockets were supposed to land at the water's edge and clear lanes through the beach obstacles and minefields. The shock power of one LCT(R) was thought to be two and a half times the salvo power of a battleship. The LCT(R)s deployed with enough rockets to reload once. It took the nineteen-man crew (including two officers) four to six hours to reload the entire craft. (On D-Day, an additional officer was assigned to the crews of the nine craft deployed at Omaha Beach.) Of all of the gunfire support craft, the LCT(R)s were the most impor-tant. The expectations for the firepower from these craft were high.

LCG(L)s (landing craft, gun, large) were mounted with two 4.7-inch naval guns and two 20 mm guns or two pompom guns. They were designed to provide direct fire against beach positions and surface attack for first-echelon landing waves. They could also be beached and employed as stationary gun platforms. On D-Day, their mission was to 'take station on flanks of assault waves' and continuously engage fortified beach defenses with direct fire as soon as they became visible and in range. Each LCG(L) had specific targets to neutralize and an area of responsibility. The navy deployed five of these craft at Omaha Beach and four at Utah Beach.

LCFs (landing craft, flak) were mounted with eight pompoms and four 20 mm guns or four pompoms and eight 20 mm guns. There were three types of LCFs, designated as LCF(2) to (4) depending on the armament. These craft were designed to protect assault forces against close-range air and surface attack prior to and during landings. They could also engage beach targets such as concrete emplacements or machine gun positions. The U.S. Navy employed seven of these vessels at Omaha Beach and four at Utah Beach.

In addition, some landing craft carried tanks and artillery. LCT(A)s (landing craft, tank, armored) each carried two M-4 Sherman medium tanks. These vessels were part of the leading assault wave. They were to proceed directly to the beach, disembark their tanks, and return to the transport areas for shuttle duty. The tanks were to open fire as soon as range and visibility permitted, take part in the drenching fire, and then join the assault. The tanks fired over the ramps. Eighteen LCT(A)s were employed at Omaha Beach and eight at Utah Beach. LCT(6)s were used to transport amphibious DD tanks. Although the DD tanks were not part of the Joint Fire Plan, their firepower was an important part of the initial assault. LCTs also carried M-7s, self-propelled 105 mm Howitzers. They followed the boat waves and supported the attack with indirect fire. They were to commence fire when range and visibility permitted and cease fire when the lead boat wave was 1,000 yards from the beach. Upon ceasing fire, the LCTs were to turn back out to sea and circle until their designated landing time. These craft were not under Sabin's command. Finally, LCP(L)s (landing craft, personnel, large) were equipped with smoke generators. Thirty-two 'Smokers' were deployed at Omaha Beach and sixteen at Utah Beach.

The fire support was divided into three phases: phase 1, direct fire on point and area targets by tanks and artillery; phase 2, drenching fire from 2,000 to 3,500 yards at sea; and phase 3, continuous close support fire by artillery, tanks, and LCG(L)s. Thus, fire support craft were to provide direct, indirect, and drenching fire for the assault force.

The target list for the prearranged air and naval bombardment plan included enemy artillery batteries, main roads, road intersections, communication centers, bridges, railway centers, cable junctions, road embankments, telephone exchanges, pillboxes, ammo depots, construction sites, machine gun positions, and troop concentrations. The first priority for the air and naval bombardment was destruction of enemy offensive weapons such as artillery batteries; second, isolation of the battlefield; and third, destruction of enemy defensive positions on the beach. Considering that only forty minutes of bombing and bombardment were available to attack the water's edge defense, the vast majority of the effort was expended elsewhere. Even today, a brief survey of the terrain at Pointe du Hoe, a known enemy artillery position, reveals enormous overkill. The ground is still pocked with huge craters. The concrete emplacements are torn and thrown about. The degree of destruction is excessive. On the morning of D-Day, this battery, which had been previously targeted and attacked, was again targeted and attacked by both the air force and the navy and then assaulted by one of the two ranger battalions employed in the Omaha sector. It was believed that the weapon systems located at Pointe du Hoe – which were not operable at the time of the invasion – posed a threat to the transport fleet. Thus, the navy established the transport area out of range of these guns. If the guns had been in place, the battery at Pointe du Hoe would have been destroyed with a quarter of the tonnage dropped on it. A quarter of the tonnage dropped on the battery at Pointe du Hoe could have destroyed one of the strongly defended beach exits at Omaha. But this type of destruction was intentionally avoided at Omaha Beach because the damage done to the beach surface would have slowed the build-up. The plan for the build-up required the immediate use of the four beach exits.

The actual beaches at Omaha with the obstacles and minefields were not targeted by the heavy bombers and battleships. The reason behind this decision was optimism on the part of senior leaders who simply did not believe the assault would be difficult. They did not want to disfigure the beaches too severely by bombing them with 500- and 1,000-pound bombs and 14-inch shells from battleships. The craters caused by this type of bombing would have so damaged the beach surface that engineers would have been required to repair the damage, slowing the build-up of forces. The air force conducted tests with bombs of various sizes and determined that 100-pound bombs were best used in locations near the assault beaches. Major Kenneth P. Lord, assistant G-3 officer for the 1st ID, explained one reason for employing smaller bombs:

> Since we had a long, flat beach where tides came in very rapidly, we wanted to know what size bombs the Eighth Air Force would be using on the fortifications. He [Major General Elwood 'Pete' Quesada of the Ninth Tactical Air Force] indicated that they would be using 500- and 1,000-pound bombs. We knew that at high altitude some of their bombs would hit on our beaches. Their craters would rapidly fill up with water and many of our laden down foot soldiers would drown. We asked them to use a smaller bomb but he felt that it would not be effective on the fortifications. We agreed that this heavy bombardment would be limited to targets behind the beaches.[22]

Casemated gun positions of reinforced concrete could not be destroyed with 100-pound bombs. The air force had to employ various types of bombs to achieve the quality and character of destruction the army desired, and operational and tactical command-ers wanted different results from the pre-invasion bombardment. The bluff above and behind the beach and the beach exits were targeted. Ten targets were designated on the bluff overlooking Omaha Beach for the air force. They were to be 'attacked from H-30 minutes to H-5' by heavy bombers. None of these targets were engaged by the air force on D-Day because the planes flew too high and employed a method of bombing that was incapable of providing the precision required – blind, radar bombing. Naval gunfire from battleships and cruisers was dedicated to counterbattery fire and other inland targets. That left only the twelve destroyers and fire support craft to attack the beaches. The destroyers and fire support craft were to provide the 'drenching fire' for the attacking infantry that was continuously shifted inland as the infantry advanced across what the British called the 'water gap' – the space between dry land and where the boats came to rest. Drenching fire was not possible given the breadth of the assault beaches, the naval assets dedicated, and the level of joint training acquired in June 1944. After the failed Dieppe raid, the British realized that a considerable amount of accurate well-timed fire support was required to defeat a deliberate enemy defense. Drenching fire was the answer to this problem.[23] Because the British lacked the battleships, cruisers, and destroyers necessary for such fire, given the other missions of the Royal Navy, they developed the various fire support craft.

In the Pacific theater, the navy, marines, and army learned and perfected the technique of providing assaulting infantry with a wall of walking fire.[24] Drenching fire had to be provided by small-caliber weapons such as the 5-inch guns of destroyers and the 105 mm artillery of the army and Marine Corps. (Large-caliber weapons such as those from battleships had a bursting radius and a concussion too great to be closely followed up by infantry. They also had a relatively flat trajectory that limited their use in close proximity to soldiers.) This type of fire was difficult to maintain because of the large quantity of ammunition required. It also required close co-ordination and extensive training between the advancing elements and the supporting units, a level of co-ordination and training that had not been achieved in the European theater between the army and navy partly because of the nature of the war. The Pacific theater demanded joint operations. In the European theater, joint operations were a momentary inconvenience to the independent operations of each service. Whereas veteran organizations had learned to follow up artillery at a distance of 100 to 150 yards, the inexperienced units deployed at

Omaha and Utah Beaches were incapable of this level of combat acumen.[25]

Drenching fire exploded mines before the advancing soldiers, caused enemy soldiers to keep their heads down, caused destruction and disorganization in the enemy's defenses, and allowed the attacking force to close with the enemy. This was not the type of fire that was planned or delivered at Normandy, even though the term 'drenching fire' was used in orders and plans, nor was drenching fire sufficient. Drenching fire did not destroy pillboxes or reinforced positions. Such targets had to be attacked individually and directly. This was one of the lessons of Tarawa. Had this lesson been applied at Omaha Beach, the 1st ID would have suffered considerably fewer casualties.

NAVAL GUNFIRE

Lieutenant Walter C. Ansel of the U.S. Navy wrote in 1932 in 'Naval Gunfire in Support of Landings: Lessons from Gallipoli': 'If the naval guns have not properly done their part the troops will be caught at the mercy of machine guns and other rapid fire weapons.' He continued: 'From manifold experiences of the World War it is possible in land warfare to gauge and with a fair degree of accuracy and reasonable assurance of success, the amount of artillery support needed for an attack on a given position. If a similar procedure could be followed in landing operations one of the knottiest problems would be simplified.' Ansel's study of the Dardanelles campaign of World War I led him to conclude that 'the attacks succeeded in almost the same proportion as the naval artillery support allotted, that is, success followed the strongest artillery.'[26]

Ansel's conclusions and method of analysis, with modifications for air power, were still valid in World War II for a daylight assault against a defended beach. The problem as Ansel saw it was to determine the type and amount of naval gunfire necessary for soldiers to overcome a given defense. The doctrinal approach of daylight assault based on firepower was not at issue. The problem was making firepower-based assaults work by deploying sufficient numbers of forces and by employing naval gunfire more effectively. Based on his analysis of the campaign in the Dardanelles and his study of the employment of artillery in the offense, Ansel concluded that assault landings adequately supported by naval gunfire could and did succeed. Ansel's thinking was consistent with that of other navy and Marine Corps officers who during this period were developing the amphibious doctrine that would be employed in the Pacific theater during the war. It was this type of thinking that formed the basis for the navy and Marine Corps' *Tentative Manual for Landing Operations,* published in 1934.

Ansel considered a number of factors to determine the type and amount of naval gunfire required to do a particular job. He studied terrain, the extent and character of beach defenses, the numerical strength of the defenders, the type of technology employed in the defense, and the acumen of the commander conducting the defense. Based on these and other factors, Ansel compared and assessed the strength of naval gunfire employed against four beaches with varying strengths and weaknesses. He observed: 'Set down in this fashion some arresting facts come to light. We see, for instance, that the strongest effort [at Gallipoli], though directed at the strongest position, was furnished the weakest artillery support... It seems incomprehensible that the main effort should have been launched with such paltry support.'[27]

The two major conclusions of Ansel's study were that battleships, cruisers, and destroyers in sufficient numbers could defeat land fortifications – the stronger the coastal defense, the more naval assets required – and the greatest effectiveness was achieved when warships stood in close to shore. He noted that the *Implacable,* which closed to within 500 yards of the beach at Gallipoli, provided the best naval gunfire support.[28] This was a lesson that would have to be relearned in each major theater in World War II. Nevertheless, navy-marine amphibious doctrine recognized the need for strong, concentrated fire in daylight amphibious assaults. *Landing Operations on Hostile Shores,* the army's version of the navy and Marine Corps' amphibious doctrine, stated: 'Naval gunfire and combat aviation must be concentrated in support of landing. Even a relatively small number of enemy machine guns and light artillery pieces firing under favorable conditions have a devastating effect on units as they approach and land on the beach. Assault units will probably be unable to get ashore and advance against this fire unless adequately supported by ship fire and combat aviation.'[29] The question then was, what quality, character, and volume of naval gunfire support did the U.S. Army in the European theater require in a daylight assault?

In April 1944, Bradley's FUSA published a memorandum that delineated the army's thinking and doctrine for the employment of naval gunfire as that thinking had developed between 1942 and 1944. The first section of the memorandum explained why naval gunfire should accompany air support in amphibious operations:

> Amphibious operations differ from normal land operations in that ground must be gained before field artillery can emplace and support infantry. Field artillery fire support, therefore cannot be expected until at least H+2 hours. During this critical time, only two means of support are available: air bombardment and naval gunfire. Air bombardment will not be sufficient in quantity to meet all the fire support requirements of the infantry. Naval gunfire is the only other source of fire support available... Medium artillery in general support is necessary before the landing force will have sufficient fire power to be independent of naval gunfire. Therefore, naval gunfire will be employed as a minimum until D+1.[30]

The FUSA advocated a concept for amphibious operations that was highly dependent on fire support. It was an approach to war that relied on the vastly superior fire support assets available to the United States in the form of ships and airplanes. To take full advantage of these resources, which literally dictated the course of battle, it was necessary to conduct operations during the hours of daylight to achieve the desired degree of destruction.

Naval gunfire had certain inherent strengths. Support ships could be positioned to achieve lateral angles of fire most beneficial to the destruction of targets. The navy possessed a wide range of weapons, munitions, and calibers to fit specific missions and targets. The navy could provide direct and indirect fire. The rate of fire for naval guns was faster, and the re-supply effort more sure, concise, and rapid than that of army artillery because it was located onboard ship. Navy guns occupied a secure position requiring no infantry protection and were usually ready to fire because they did not have to displace periodically. Finally, the navy could generally be expected to concentrate greater explosives tonnage on a specific target in a shorter period of time than was possible with army artillery.

Naval gunfire also had inherent weaknesses. The navy needed daylight to deliver accurate direct fire on targets. Reliable communications were necessary from ship to shore. The onboard capacity of ships to store ammunition was limited. As forces advanced inland, they moved out of range of the navy's guns. Finally, the trajectory of certain naval weapons was too flat to engage targets that were masked by land formations. Other weaknesses were caused by a lack of joint thinking in policies, priorities, procedures, and training. Planning the use of naval gunfire required, first, good intelligence on enemy fortifications and defensive positions (information that was gained by aerial reconnaissance and other intelligence sources such as the French underground). Second, it required joint training to troubleshoot the tenuous communication systems and educate army personnel on the limitations and capabilities of naval gunfire and navy personnel on the types of uses for naval gunfire the army would require. Third, it required the acquisition of sufficient naval gunfire assets to achieve the degree of damage – the effect on the target – desired by the ground commander in the time period given.

The FUSA believed that an invasion force of regimental size required the following naval gunfire assets:

    a.   One squadron of modern destroyers (8 or 9 ships)

    b.   Two 10,000 ton light cruisers.

    c.   One battleship or heavy cruiser.[31]

These requirements were based on the assumption that a supporting ship could neutralize 100 square yards and provide certain types of support. Hence, the number of naval gunfire support ships required depended on the size of the assault and the capabilities of particular vessels. The assets listed were considered the minimum necessary for an assault conducted with a single RCT. Thus, the two RCTs landing at Omaha Beach on D-Day would have required two squadrons of destroyers (sixteen to eighteen), four light cruisers, and two battleships. Only one RCT made the initial assault at Utah Beach.

Using Ansel's methodology – that is, comparing the strength of the defenses at Omaha Beach and Utah Beach in terms of difficulty by assessing defensive fortifications, minefields, and obstacles; the size and capabilities of the defending forces; and the terrain – it is obvious that the defenses at Omaha Beach were far superior to those at Utah Beach. Even with the absence of accurate intelligence on the size of the enemy forces employed at Omaha, it was evident to American leaders, Bradley, Hall, and Gerow, that the Omaha Beach assault was a much tougher assignment. This may explain the fact that Bradley insisted on deploying a combat-experienced division at Omaha Beach whereas he was willing to risk employing a 'green,' untested division, the 4th ID, at Utah Beach.[32] Nevertheless, the decision on the allocation of naval gunfire support seems to have been based on the principle of equal distribution of resources as opposed to the relative combat power of the enemy at the two locations.

A comparison of the two bombardment groups is revealing. Supporting the VII Corps at Utah Beach was the bombardment group of Rear Admiral Morton L. Deyo. His force consisted of the battleship *Nevada;* the heavy cruisers *Quincy, Tuscaloosa,* and HMS *Hawkins;* the monitor HMS *Erebus;* the light cruisers HMS *Black Prince* and HMS *Enterprise;* and the destroyers *Bates, Butler, Corry, Fitch, Forrest, Gherardi, Herndon, Hobson, Rich,* and *Shubrick.*[33] Supporting the V Corps at Omaha Beach was the bombardment group of Rear Admiral Carleton F. Bryant. His force consisted of the battleships *Arkansas* and *Texas;* the light cruisers HMS *Bellona,* HMS *Glasgow, Georges Leygues* (French), and *Montcalm* (French); the destroyers *Baldwin, Carmick,*

Doyle, Emmons, Frankford, Harding, McCook, Satterlee, Thompson, HMS *Melbreak,* HMS *Talybont,* and HMS *Tanatside.*[33] The two bombardment fleets had the following number of vessels:

	Utah	Omaha
Battleships	1	2
Heavy cruisers	3	0
Light cruisers	2	4
Monitors	1	0
Destroyers	10	12
Total	17	18

It is evident from these figures that an effort was made to divide the available naval gunfire assets equally between the two corps, with Omaha being slightly favored in battleships and destroyers. Samuel Eliot Morison in *The Invasion of France and Germany* did not discuss the relative activity of the two bombardment groups on D-Day. However, his narrative of the battle for Omaha Beach indicates that the destroyers were an integral part of the assault, serving as both tanks and artillery, moving in as close as 800 yards to the shore to engage targets with direct fire. The ammunition expenditure is an indicator of the role destroyers played at Omaha Beach; for example, the *Carmick* expended 1,127 rounds, the *McCook* 975, the *Emmons* 767, and the *Thompson* 638. The role played by destroyers at Utah was not nearly as crucial to the success of the landing. Morison mentioned only a few of the ships employed at Utah, but he noted that they fired half the rounds that were fired by several destroyers at Omaha.

Given the relative strength of the defense at Omaha and Utah Beaches and the deployment of naval bombardment ships in support of the landings, Ansel's comments again seem valid: 'It seems incomprehensible that the main effort should have been launched with such paltry support.' Bradley's FUSA improperly allocated the firepower support ships available to it, and the infantry at Omaha Beach had to make up the difference in firepower.

The FUSA established a doctrinal approach to amphibious assaults that was highly dependent on firepower provided by the air and sea armed services. It then conducted studies to determine how much naval gunfire was needed to succeed against a prepared defense.[35] After having conducted this research, did the FUSA ignore it, or was it simply impossible to obtain such assets from the U.S. Navy? Even if the FUSA had properly allocated the naval gunfire support ships available, it still would have employed considerably fewer ships than called for by army doctrine. Admiral John Lesslie Hall, commander of Amphibious Force 'O,' which put the 1st ID ashore at Omaha, and a veteran of the landings in North Africa, Sicily, and Italy, wrote:

> I was at a conference in London with Admiral King's chief of staff, Admiral Cook, and two or three other American flag officers. I banged my fist on the table, and said, 'It's a crime to send me on the biggest amphibious attack in history with such inadequate support...' I wanted to give my troops the proper support. I fought like hell to do it.[36]

Hall continued:

> 'All I'm asking you to do is to detach a couple of squadrons of destroyers from some transoceanic convoy, give them to me, give me a chance to train them in gunfire support for the American Army on the Omaha beaches.' And I got them. Thank God I did.

Hall received only part of what he believed was necessary and went into battle believing his naval gunfire forces were 'inadequate.' He apparently also felt he was alone in his effort to secure additional naval gunfire support: 'I remember telling General Bradley that I wasn't getting sufficient naval gunfire support, and telling Admiral Kirk, but we attacked in Normandy with pretty much of a shoe string naval force, in the most important attack in the history of the United States, in my opinion.'[37] Bradley would have disagreed with this statement. In *A Soldier's Story,* he wrote:

During spring planning Kirk and I had battled side by side in a stren-
uous effort to coax additional naval gunfire support from naval operations in Washington. For originally the bombardment fleet assigned
the invasion looked woefully inadequate for its task. As late as April,
the U.S. Navy could spare only two battleships, four cruisers, 12
destroyers, and a variety of small craft to support the American
Landing... I would gladly have swapped a dozen B-17s for each 12-
inch gun I could wrangle... I begged the navy to stack the odds more
heavily on our side. Eventually Washington agreed and Kirk's
bombardment fleet was enlarged to four battleships (two of which
holdovers from World War I), four cruisers, and 26 destroyers. It could
not be called a formidable force in terms of Pacific naval campaigns,
but at least our pinchpenny days were ended.[38]

Thus, initially, Bradley too was dissatisfied with the naval gunfire
support allocated by the U.S. Navy. Although he was not overly
impressed, however, Bradley was satisfied with the final allocation of
naval gunfire support ships, even though it was considerably less than
the quantity his own doctrine told him was necessary.

At Omaha Beach, the FUSA improperly allocated resources, fought
the battle with a 'shoe string' naval bombardment fleet, and failed to
provide sufficient time for naval gunfire to do its work. The navy had
less than forty minutes to attack German defenses years in the
making. The desire to achieve tactical surprise precluded a more
substantial bombardment. Later, Bradley wrote: 'I was shaken to find
that we had gone against Omaha with so thin a margin of safety.' At
the time of sailing, Bradley believed he possessed overwhelming
combat power.[39] He was wrong.

The Allied plan for winning the battle of the beaches was based on
firepower. Every other aspect of the landing was sacrificed to firepower. Bradley stated:

From the army's point of view there could be no choice. We would
stick with the tides and compromise on daylight [in favor of a later
landing], if necessary take a chance on forming our assault waves

under daylight observation of the enemy's guns. The disadvantages
would have to be overcome by fire-power.[40]

The vast majority of the firepower on which the Allies depended was
to be delivered by the Army Air Force.[41] The air force was required to
conduct pinpoint bombing, flying above the clouds, using an
unproven, experimental radar system.[42] This mission had never been
conducted before. The air force did not train for the mission and thus
did not develop effective procedures for employing an instrument
designed to conduct strategic, high-altitude area bombing in close
tactical support of troops on the ground. This was a mission air force
leaders would have preferred not to perform.[43] The mission was a
failure. As a consequence, the Allied plan to win the battle for Omaha
Beach with firepower failed.

The naval forces at Normandy lacked the time and resources necessary to destroy or neutralize enemy defenses at Omaha Beach. The
minimum number of support ships per RCT determined by the
FUSA estimate were not deployed at Omaha Beach. And the forces
available were divided almost equally between Omaha and Utah.
Thus, the same mistakes in the distribution of limited forces made by
the British at Gallipoli were repeated by the Americans at Normandy.

A comparison of the number of naval gunfire support ships
employed at Omaha Beach with the number employed at an atoll in
the Central Pacific is revealing. In the Flintlock Operation in the
Marshall Islands, thirty ships fired eight scheduled bombardments,
some ships firing several exercises.[44] At Namur, the 4th Marine
Division was supported by six battleships, two heavy cruisers, three
light cruisers, and eleven destroyers.[45] At Kwajalein Island, the 7th ID
was supported by seven battleships, three heavy cruisers, and eighteen
destroyers.[46] The resources and time allocated and the procedures
instituted by the navy in the Pacific insured the destruction, not
simply the neutralization, of the water's edge defense. At Normandy,
the navy could not be given two days to destroy the target area
because operational surprise was essential to the success of the invasion; the time and resources allocated were paltry in comparison to

those employed at Namur and Kwajalein. They were also paltry by the standards established in army doctrine and by the estimate of one of the navy's most experienced commanders in amphibious operations, the man most responsible for the conduct of the amphibious battle at Omaha Beach – Admiral Hall.

Although Bradley noted his preference for naval gunfire over heavy bombers, he and Montgomery put into effect a plan based primarily on air power.[47] At Normandy, naval gunfire, which was the most accurate, direct, and efficient means of destroying the water's edge defense, was not the primary means of destruction. The air power of the U.S. Eighth Air Force was the principal means for the neutralization of the German defenses at Normandy by the design of the Allied operational commanders, with the concurrence of the U.S. Navy, which was preoccupied with the war in the Pacific, and the acquiescence of the Army Air Force, which was too busy conducting the strategic bombing campaign to train for the beach preparation mission. The presence of the awesome potential combat power of the American daylight strategic bombers distorted Allied amphibious doctrine and skewed Montgomery's and Bradley's vision of the conduct of amphibious operations.[48] Montgomery and Bradley rested their hopes on means that were untried and less certain to achieve their objectives.[49]

The World War II journalist and author Hanson Baldwin wrote: 'Pacific amphibious technique is more advanced than that used in the invasion of France.'[50] It is more accurate to state that the Allied leaders and planners of the Normandy invasion did not display the level of professionalism that should be expected this late in the war. In this theater, Admirals Hewitt, Kirk, and Hall all advocated a doctrine based heavily on naval gunfire. For the Normandy invasion, the Allied commanders ignored tested doctrine and the warnings of Admirals Hewitt and Hall. They thus ignored the cumulative body of knowledge in amphibious operations gained through hard-fought battles in North Africa, Sicily, and Tarawa. Montgomery and Bradley put into effect an unproven means to deliver the vast majority of the combat power needed to overcome the defense. They failed to troubleshoot their primary plan – air power – and to fully develop a backup plan – naval gunfire.[51] As a consequence, the Allied battle plan failed at the most heavily defended beach. Victory at Omaha Beach had to be improvised by the soldiers of the 1st and 29th IDs and the sailors who brought their destroyers in so close they were able to function as tanks and artillery. The cost of this improvisation was high, and the risks taken were extreme.

AIR SUPPORT

Studies of the role, doctrine, capabilities, and effectiveness of U.S. air power in World War II abound.[52] Although opinions on the effectiveness vary, generally students of the air war conclude that the results from the application of air power, while satisfactory, were less than expected. It may well have been that too much was expected from the young service and that air force leaders exaggerated the capabilities of air power and thus fostered the development of unrealistic expectations.[53] According to James A. Huston:

> One of the ironies of World War II was that, when operating against a first-class adversary on a continental land mass, air units assigned or attached to ground forces proved incapable of providing effective support of ground forces... The value of any of the major attempts at massive carpet bombing may be seriously questioned. Certainly it is difficult to justify, in terms of immediate results, the tremendous expenditure of resources in the tonnage of bombs dropped at Cassino, at Caen, or at St Lô. Perhaps this simply was the logical extreme of the principle of mass. [54]

To this list of battles with disappointing applications of strategic air power at the tactical level of war can be added the Normandy invasion. The U.S. Army's Eighth and Ninth Air Forces had three missions to perform on the morning of D-Day: to continue to isolate the battlefield by destroying communication channels and interdicting forces reinforcing the front; to destroy or neutralize the water's edge defense to facilitate the amphibious assault; and to provide close air support – scheduled and on-call. The battle for air supremacy had already been won.

The British and American air forces performed their first mission with great skill, effectively isolating the battlefield, but the American air forces were considerably less successful in the latter two missions. The thinking of air force officers – delineated in air force doctrine – on the role of air power in modern warfare was in part responsible for the air force's inability to conduct 'massive carpet bombing' and close air support missions.

The doctrine of the U.S. Army Air Force in 1944 was greatly influenced by the British.[55] In fact, General Robert C. Candee suggested that the air force had 'swallowed the RAF solution of a local situation in Africa hook, line and sinker, without stopping to analyze it or report it in 'Americanese' instead of British speech.'[56] Air force doctrine was set forth in *Command and Employment of Air Power*, FM 100-20, published in July 1943. Robert Frank Futrell wrote: 'Since the War Department had published Field Manual 100-20 without soliciting its concurrence, the Army Ground Forces viewed the manual with "dismay" and described it as the "Army Air Forces' Declaration of Independence."'[57] The manual was based in part on the thinking of Montgomery in 'Some Notes on High Command in War,' a pamphlet he wrote in January 1943 about his experiences while in command of the British Eighth Army in North Africa.[58] General Pete Quesada, who commanded the IX Tactical Air Command, which supported the FUSA at Normandy, in a discussion with Richard H. Kohn gave credit to RAF Vice Air Marshal Sir Arthur 'Maori' Coningham for molding Montgomery's thinking on the tactical employment of air power and for advancing American tactical air doctrine. Coningham's air force supported Montgomery in North Africa. Quesada stated: 'If there was a creator for the concept of tactical air operation in a manner that is removed somewhat from the Army, we have to say it was 'Maori' Coningham.'[59]

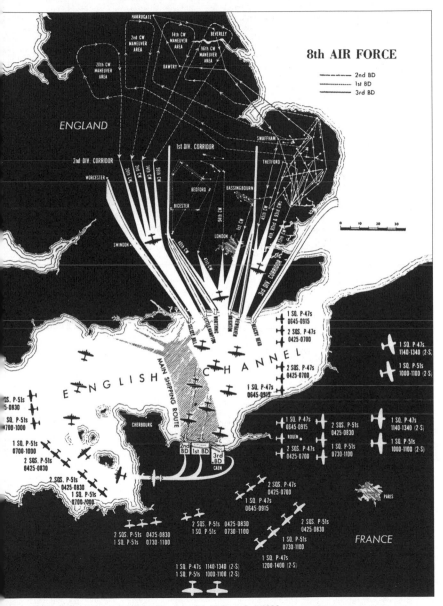

Eighth Air Force, Normandy Invasion Plan. From *8th AF News,* April 1990.

Given that Montgomery's thinking on the employment of air power shaped and influenced American tactical air doctrine and that it was in part his vision that was the basis for the invasion plan that took the Allies back to Europe, it is useful to examine his thinking on the use of air power. Montgomery produced two pamphlets documenting his thoughts on air power: 'Some Notes on the Use of Air Power in Support of Land Operations' and 'Some Notes on Direct Air Support.' In the former, Montgomery wrote:

> The greatest asset of air power is its flexibility. Whereas to shift the weight of effort on the ground from one point to another takes time, the flexibility inherent in Air Forces permits them without change of base to be switched quickly from one objective to another in the theater of operations. So long as this is realised, then the whole weight of the available air power can be used in selected areas in turn. This concentrated use of air striking force is a battle winning factor of the first importance.[60]

These words were paraphrased in the air force's field manual.[61] Air force thinking was guided by two beliefs that dominated all others. The first was that war could be won through air power using daylight precision strategic bombing. The second was that the air force must be autonomous, separate from the army's command and control.[62] Montgomery's thinking supported these two beliefs. The concentration of force meant that air force assets would not be divided up to support army corps and divisions. It meant that the air force would retain operational command and control of all air resources. It also meant that the air force would not acquire the training, develop the procedures, or achieve the necessary level of integration with army units to effectively conduct on-call close air support missions in close proximity to ground forces until well after the Normandy invasion.

Montgomery's belief that air power when concentrated was a 'battle-winning factor' was also accepted by the air force. Montgomery's plan to win the battle for the beaches at Normandy, his plan for the breakout at Caen, and Bradley's plan for the breakout at

Saint-Lô were based on the belief that air power could achieve battle-field success cheaply. Montgomery wrote: 'Nothing could be more fatal to successful results than to dissipate the air resources into small packets placed under command of Army formation commanders with each packet working on its own plan. The soldier must not expect or wish to exercise direct command over air-striking forces.'[63] Montgomery advanced the concept that the two services, air and ground, were 'independent,' with a 'common task.' Because they were independent, satisfactory solutions to military problems had to be based on a 'process of negotiation.' And the process of negotiation had to be based on knowledge of the strength, limitations, and capabilities of the respective services and on 'mutual trust and honesty.'[64] The fact that this had to be written is indicative of a problem in the command structure.

In his section 'Some Notes on Direct Air Support,' Montgomery advanced the idea of a tactical air force, an idea he had proposed in 'Some Notes on High Command in War' and that was put into effect for the Normandy invasion. Montgomery wrote:

An Army Group in the field gets direct air support through the agency of a Tactical Air Force. The Tactical Air Force is an independent air command organised and equipped for its particular task and comprises: (a) A Headquarters, (b) Tactical Groups on the scale of one per army, (c) A Light/Medium Bomber Group, (d) A Strategical Reconnaissance Wing, (e) A Base Defence Group.

Montgomery continued:

The Tactical Group consists of fighter type aircraft exclusively, all trained in air combat and ground attack... The Light/Medium Bomber Group is equipped and trained for day and night operations...The HQ of the Tactical Air Force is associated with and works with HQ of the Army Group. Each Tactical Group is associated with and works with an army. [65]

This was the organizational structure the U.S. Army Ninth Tactical Air Force in Europe adopted prior to the invasion. Its heavy bombers (B-17s and B-24s) were reassigned to the Eighth Air Force. By creating a tactical air force, Army Air Force leaders satisfied the demands of operational and strategic ground commanders and created the conditions under which their strategic aims could be achieved: 'General Arnold... wished to insure a freedom of action for the strategic air force, and he was willing to provide the tactical air force in order to free the strategic air force from a routine requirement of supporting ground forces.'[66]

Montgomery believed that '[t]he focus of all direct air support both in the planning stages and in the conduct of operations is at the Army/Tactical Group level.'[67] The U.S. Air Force created tactical air commands (TACs) and associated one with each U.S. Army. Thus, the IX TAC was attached to the FUSA, the XIX TAC was attached to the Third Army, and the XXIX TAC was attached to the Ninth Army. All were under the command of the Ninth Air Force, which was associated with Bradley's Twelfth Army Group. Of the reorganization of air force resources, Richard H. Kohn wrote:

> During the first few months after its reconstitution in the United Kingdom... the Ninth Air Force concentrated on activating, organizing, training and equipping the many specialized tactical, technical and service units which would function as a huge, smoothly working team in Operation OVERLORD and thereafter. Planned to be a major air component of the Allied invasion forces, the Ninth from 16 October 1943 until D-Day had a remarkably rapid physical growth: from 4 to 45 tactical groups, from less than 300 to more than 1,100 bombers, from zero to more than 3,000 troop-carrier aircraft and gliders and from fewer than 50,000 to considerably more than 200,000 personnel. The job of the Ninth Air Force was not primarily to fit organized, trained and equipped units into its structure but rather to construct these units from casual personnel, to struggle for their aircraft or other equipment and to train and retain all personnel for functions quite often entirely foreign to those for which they were originally trained and equipped.[68]

Given the nature of its conception, the magnitude of the endeavor, and the time available to become operational, it was perhaps impossible for the Ninth Air Force to conduct close support missions in close proximity to friendly ground forces on D-Day.

Montgomery identified three applications for air power: the set-piece battle, daily prearranged support, and immediate support. The battles at Normandy, Caen, and Saint-Lô were set-piece battles. These efforts required the combined strength of the tactical and strategic air forces of both nations.[69] Montgomery concluded his dissertation on air support with a warning and a prediction: 'On a purely selfish basis then, it will pay any army formation or unit to reach a high standard in this business. From the wider angle, it is abundantly clear that all modern land operations are combined Army/Air operations. Technical developments in the air weapon continue apace and their possibilities are bounded only by imagination. It follows that land operations are likely to be influenced more and more by air action.'[70] By doctrine, the air force accepted the two missions it was to conduct on D-Day. Close air support and massive carpet bombing to facilitate a breakout attack were legitimate uses for air power. The question was more one of priority. And the air force made it clear what its priorities were in air force doctrine.[71] The first priority was to gain and maintain air superiority. This was achieved through the employment of both the strategic and tactical air forces. The second priority was isolation of the battlefield. This was primarily the mission of the tactical air force, augmented by the strategic air force. The third priority was close air support 'combined actions with ground.' It was believed that these operations had to take place sequentially; thus, air superiority had to be achieved before the battlefield could be isolated and close air support could be provided. And if the isolation of the battlefield was achieved, the final close air operations would require significantly less air effort.

The campaign to destroy the German Air Force was closely related to the strategic bombing campaign, which sought to destroy Germany's industrial ability to make war. The question then was, when was the German Air Force rendered combat ineffective? The answer to this question would determine when it would be possible to reallocate forces to subsequent, lower-priority operations. The army, while not disagreeing with the air force's doctrine, considered the isolation of the battlefield essential to the invasion. The Transportation Plan was thus put into effect, a plan that interfered with the Allied air forces' strategic bombing campaign. Nevertheless, the Transportation Plan greatly reduced the ability of the German Army to reinforce the Normandy front.[72] With the resources of the strategic and tactical air forces fully committed to the Transportation Plan and the strategic bombing campaign, there was little time to think in an innovative manner about bombing the coast of Normandy with heavy bombers in a way to maximize the chance of destroying or neutralizing the water's edge defense. And there was little time to learn the techniques and establish the relationships required to conduct close air support operations. Bradley wrote:

> The Ninth Air Force had been formed in England in October, 1943, when the tactical air command was separated from the Eighth. In January, 1944, it joined the air battle over Europe under Leigh-Mallory as commander-in-chief of the Allied Expeditionary Air Force. Since the Ninth's ground-support mission would not begin until the invasion, it flew throughout that spring in support of the heavy bombers and helped to drive the Luftwaffe out of its forward airfields. Finally, just one month before we were to sail, the Ninth Air Force reported that it had at last caught up with its shooting war and could thereafter devote time to training with the ground. 'Too bad,' I answered, 'but we've completed our training. Troops are already moving into the sausages.' As a result of our inability to get together with air in England, we went into France almost totally untrained in air-ground co-operation.[73]

The Eighth Air Force went to Normandy unfamiliar with the task it was required to perform. Quite simply, the Eighth and Ninth Air Forces did not develop the proficiency they needed to perform the breakout bombing mission and the close air support mission until well after D-Day. They considered these missions too low priority to warrant the time necessary to develop the required skill level. The air forces also evinced distaste for army support missions, which they felt interfered with their autonomy and were generally considered the least productive use of air power. The assistant secretary of war in 1942, John J. McCloy, stated: 'It is my firm belief that the Air Forces are not interested in this type of work, think it is unsound, and are very much concerned lest it result in control of air units by ground forces. Their interest, enthusiasm, and energy is directed to different fields.'[74]

To provide close air support, the air force deployed air support parties with each RCT. They carried VHF radios but were not permitted to talk directly with aircraft. Jacobs wrote: '[T]hey were enjoined from contacting aircraft overhead unless specifically authorized to do so. Nor were they allowed to intervene in stopping attacks on friendly troops or the wrong targets. This writer has been unable to find reasons for such inhibitions.'[75] To request fire support, the air support parties called a headquarters ship, and the request was relayed to a central control facility in Uxbridge, England. There the decision was made whether to support the request. Obviously this process took time, time that precluded direct intervention of the air force in the battle for the beaches. On the morning of D-Day, the V Corps at Omaha Beach made only six requests, and during all of D-Day, Uxbridge received only thirteen requests. Targets of opportunity were attacked by aircraft on station above the battlefield; however, these forces too could not communicate with ground units and thus were unable to assist in a particular firefight.

The air forces were incapable of improvising success from failed plans. They were too poorly trained in direct support of ground forces. Whereas the army and navy almost made it a policy to improvise, to rise to the occasion, the air forces totally lacked this capability on 6 June 1944. It is one of the ironies of World War II that the Army Air Force was less able to conduct joint operations on D-Day than the army and navy.

GUNFIRE SUPPORT CRAFT

On 12 December 1943, Captain L.S. Sabin Jr. assumed command of the gunfire support craft, Eleventh Amphibious Force. Sabin wrote:

> Gunfire Support Craft as used in this operation were an innovation in the United States Navy. Although various types of smaller craft had been used for close support of landing, this operation was the first in which the U.S. Navy used the British type of shallow water major landing craft converted to gun fire support.[76]

Sabin's command was supposed to saturate the beach with fire in the last instant before the assault, protect against air attack, provide direct fire on the beaches in support of the infantry assault, deliver tanks directly onto the beaches in the first wave of the assault, and lay down smoke to conceal the assault forces, if necessary.

Gunfire support craft were a cheap form of firepower. The shallow draft of the craft permitted close-in support of landing. These small vessels freed larger, more important naval ships from amphibious landing support duty, and because they were relatively easy to produce, they could assume greater risk in close-in engagements with shore batteries. Thus, landing craft converted to gunfire support appeared to be a cheap fix for the difficult problem of fire support in amphibious assaults.

The unit that was to provide fire support to the 1st ID at Omaha and the 4th ID at Utah was organized in September 1943 at Little Creek, Virginia. It was designated a special support group. The group conducted its initial training in the United States and in November sailed for Scotland aboard the *Queen Elizabeth*. At the time of sailing, the unit consisted of 144 officers and 1,537 enlisted men. In December, the group was re-designated a gunfire support craft unit, and Captain Sabin took command.

After conducting his initial interviews with his subordinate officers, inspecting enlisted personnel, and checking the records, Sabin determined that '[o]nly a very small percentage of the officers and men had ever been to sea before and the number who had had any combat experience was practically negligible.' He concluded: '[W]e cannot expect civilians with only a short indoctrination course to be finished naval officers in every sense of the word or that the enlisted man with three weeks of recruit training can be the highly skilled petty officer and man-of-wars man we know in peace time.'[77] Sabin started well behind in the chain of events necessary to prepare his sailors for battle. He had training, equipment, maintenance, and planning problems.

Sabin lacked sufficient craft to train his personnel. Many of Sabin's landing craft arrived months behind schedule, and five craft arrived only a few days before the invasion. As a consequence, training was delayed, and crews had little or no opportunity to participate in the full-scale training exercises conducted at the Assault Training Center in the south of England. In regard to training, Sabin concluded:

> When the time came to assemble for the assault, I was distinctly dissatisfied with the overall status of training in spite of the fact that every opportunity had been taken to prepare the Group for action. The bare fact was that late deliveries had so curtailed the time available for training that it was impossible to bring the personnel to a high state of readiness. Two rocket craft joined their assault force without ever having handled their craft except in passage from BASE TWO and without ever having fired rockets except at the Assault Gunnery School. *The fact that insufficient time remained between deliveries and assault for adequate training was small comfort when viewed in the light of the possible importance of the craft in contributing to the success of the combat mission.* The direct result of the late deliveries was an overall unsatisfactory condition of readiness on the part of the Group both as to material and training of personnel.[78]

Thus, the commander of the U.S. Navy gunfire support craft believed his troops were insufficiently trained for the missions they were to perform on D-Day. Sabin recorded the training status of each type of craft:

LCF – Good (First craft to complete deliveries)

LCG(L) – Fair

LCT(R) – Generally poor except for two or three early deliveries which reached a satisfactory state of training.

CT(HE) – Definitely poor – The captains of many of these craft beached their ships for the first time on the Normandy Coast of France.

LCP(L) – Fair as to training – Very bad as to material condition.[79]

Sabin's forces were divided to support the landing at Omaha and Utah Beaches. Sabin commanded the forces at Omaha Beach, and his executive officer, Lieutenant Commander L.E. Hart Jr., commanded the forces at Utah Beach. Force 'Oboe' consisted of 9 LCT(R)s, 7 LCFs, 5 LCG(L)s, 18 LCT(A)s, and 32 LCP(L)s. Its destination was Omaha Beach. Force 'Uncle' consisted of 5 LCT(R)s, 4 LCFs, 4 LCG(L)s, 8 LCT(A)s, and 16 LCP(L)s. Its destination was Utah Beach.

In planning for the operation, Sabin experienced difficulties in receiving and distributing plans and orders. In his action report, he wrote:

Operation Plans and Orders of the Task Force Commander, Force OBOE, were not received in time for the Task Group Commanders to estimate the situation, form their own orders and issue sound directives to their subordinates. The need for security is recognized. But there is much that could have been imparted without releasing the 'where' and the 'when.' Everybody knew the invasion was planned.

Sabin believed there was a gap between the 'planners and doers.'[80] Finally, Sabin had maintenance problems. The requisition of parts was slow and complicated. The craft were British built, but requests for parts initially had to go through U.S. Navy channels.

Between 0230 and 0300 on 5 June, Sabin's forces left anchorage from ports in southern England. In transit across the Channel, the lack of training showed. Lieutenant Larry W. Carr, commanding the

LCT(R)s, wrote: 'There is no excuse for the craft failing to stay close up. Part of the miserable station keeping was perhaps due to the inexperience of some officers on the conn. It was without a doubt, the worst station keeping ever done by LCT(R)s.'[81] Sabin's convoy stretched twelve miles. The convoy speed was five knots. The maximum speed of most LCTs was nine knots, but the necessity of towing LCMs, the demolition units, caused some vessels to fall behind. Towing reduced the speed and maneuverability of the craft. Sabin worked feverishly to get his vessels in formation and keep them there, but the high seas, rough weather, poor communications, and inexperience took their toll. Two of his craft foundered and sank.

Sabin arrived in the transport area at 0300. Here too the situation was confused. Hundreds of clumsy landing ships and craft were maneuvering to get into position in darkness. LCT(DD)s, LCT(A)s, LCG(L)s, and LCT(R)s were widely dispersed. Some were lost; others were late. The LCT(R)s detached the towed LCMs. One LCG(L) went to the wrong beach – Utah. When the captain realized his mistake, he turned back toward Omaha, but he arrived too late to support the landing. Through extraordinary efforts, Sabin and Carr rounded up most of their vessels and had them roughly where they were supposed to be in time for the landing. Sabin observed:

> We went in towards the beach, there was no sign of life or resistance. Approaching closer, the concrete wall just to the east of Dog Green [Beach] became plainly visible. Some structures appeared to be pill boxes, a few houses, and the church steeple of Vierville were sighted. At exactly H-40 [minutes], the naval bombardment commenced... Gun craft moved inshore to take up their positions... Several squadrons of fighters roared overhead but no bombers. We waited. That aerial beach drenching was to be sorely needed. But it never came. Not one bomb was seen to drop on Omaha Beach... LCT(A)-LCT(HE) were scattered. Reports indicated that most of this type of craft hit the beach between 0635 and 0700. All were taken under terrific fire. Gun ships... were generally in proper position and engaged pre-arranged targets on schedule.[82]

Sabin's forces took their positions and commenced operations. The flak ships, LCFs, had 'little or nothing to do.' Allied air superiority was over-whelming. These craft performed no significant task on D-Day. The LCG(L)s took up positions on the flanks of the beaches and opened fire on fixed enemy positions and prearranged targets. These vessels were not tied into the naval gunfire control system, and as a consequence, army forward observers and naval shore fire control parties on the beaches could not request fire support from these craft. Spotters on the craft had to identify targets. Because spotters lacked information on targets and because they could not provide indirect fire without forward observers, the effectiveness of these vessels was limited. LCG(L)s could adjust fire and thus performed more like a tank turret and gun.

The LCT(R)s took up station and fired their rockets so that they impacted when the leading assault wave was 300 yards from the beach. Three craft opened fire early. The rockets from two LCT(R)s impacted when the assault wave was 500 yards from the shore. Some of the rockets from these craft were observed falling into the sea. A number of rockets were defective and exploded almost immediately after launch. To verify the range to the target, all craft fired a ranging salvo, but low visibility on most of the beaches made accurate calcula-tion of the point of impact impossible. Thus the ranging salvos were used only to check approximately the accuracy of the radar. Radar at this time was still in its infancy and could not produce the level of accuracy required for this mission. And although the captains of these craft believed they were relatively accurate, there was no way for them to know. Lieutenant Carr in his action report recorded that '[o]fficers-in-charge believe they fired on target in all instances.' However, he also noted that '[t]he majority of the craft did not see their targets.'[83] Some rockets fell short, others flew over the beach, and some hit their targets. Some of those that hit the beach started grass fires. The smoke from these fires obscured observation, making the delivery of close fire support more difficult. The rockets did not produce the desired effect on the target area. The German defense was virtually untouched by rocket fire, and the obstacles and minefields were still intact when the infantry, engineers, and tanks assaulted.

At H+6 hours on D-Day, Sabin surveyed the situation on Omaha Beach: 'Craft of all description were on fire...Tanks were being ruined and hit by gunfire. Troops were plainly visible on the beach lying in the sand. So were the dead. Heavy machine-gun fire was coming from enemy positions half way up the hill. Troops were unable to advance.' Sabin reported his observations to the task force commander and to Generals Gerow and Huebner. He requested permission to lay down a second rocket barrage. This was the second time Sabin made the request, and for the second time, the decision went against him. The fear of hitting friendly troops was the overriding consideration. Sabin believed his superiors made a bad decision in this case.[84]

Sabin concluded: 'Rocket craft are the most useful and important of close gunfire support craft. Properly trained and used, they can be of great assistance. It is recommended that additional high speed, shallow draft, short range rocket craft be developed.' In regard to the LCFs, he wrote: 'I believe, and am fairly well convinced, that the flak craft are hardly worth the time, trouble, and money to convert them. It is recommended that none of this type be constructed.' In reference to the LCG(L)s, he concluded: 'Gun ships have a definite value for close inshore work but their fire control system is too crude.' The Smokers were not used. Sabin, however, recommended that 'LCP(L)... be lifted, ...if taken on another trip. Some of them sunk *en route*. The remainder were in such bad material condition after their arrival in the assault area that many could not be used.' Finally, Sabin rendered his assessment of the operation:

> The landing of tanks as the initial assault wave against a well-defended beach with obstacles to cut through is not believed to be sound procedure. This operation pretty well proved that demolition units under heavy fire cannot cut paths through the obstacles. LCTs get caught easily. They and their tanks are 'sitting ducks.' And, in addition to the initial obstacles, we find our LCTs and tanks cluttered off and on the beach to form an extra hazard to the small boats bringing in the assault wave. Naval gunfire, rocket fire, and air bombardment will never completely silence a well-fortified beach. Troops on the beach

are going to have to take care of what remains. The beach head must be established and I do not believe it can be done efficiently unless troops are put on the beach first.[85]

On D–Day, Sabin lost six LCT(A)s, and many more were damaged in the assault. He believed the plan for the conduct of the operation was flawed. He was right.

In reference to the LCT(R)s, Colonel Thompson wrote:

> No considered estimate of effects can yet be made; but it is likely that the high hopes held for the rockets were not completely realized and even that the returns did not compensate for the cost (which included the diverting to rocket use of perhaps a dozen badly needed LCT(5)s).[86]

Thompson's initial assessment was correct – the rockets were considerably less effective than had been hoped, and overall the gunfire support craft contributed little to the battle for Omaha Beach. The potential of the various systems employed was not realized. It was not the fault of the sailors and their officers. The systems simply had too many bugs – bugs that additional training would not have corrected. The system used to engage the target area with radar and rockets fixed to the deck of a small, shallow-draft craft was incapable of producing the quality of accuracy required. The captains of these vessels were dependent on crude radar systems, and there was no way for them to compensate for the rise and fall of the sea. The movement of the seas made the accurate engagement of the target area a matter of luck. It was simply not possible to ascertain the height or angle of a wave or swell on which an LCT(R) rode at the instant of firing. The rougher the seas, the slimmer the chance of hitting the target area, and the conditions on June 6 were not ideal. Finally, even if all of the rockets had hit their targets, it is doubtful that they would have caused the quality of damage desired. They could not have destroyed hard targets, positions such as pillboxes or individual steel beach obstacles. Such targets had to be destroyed deliberately with aimed fire or demolitions. Rockets could explode mines and destroy wire obstacles. The LCG(L)s were useful, but there were too few to make a significant contribution in the invasion. As Sabin noted, 'The Gunfire Support Craft as used in this operation were an innovation in the United States Navy.' The U.S. Navy adopted and deployed these systems without adequately testing them and training personnel to operate them.

The Joint Fire Plan allocated the majority of gunfire craft resources to Omaha Beach, yet it divided naval gunfire ships almost equally between the two beaches. Omaha Beach was allocated four additional LCT(R)s. Was it believed that these four craft made up for the difference in the strength of the enemy defenses on the two beaches?

THE DUPLEX-DRIVE TANK

Part of the firepower on which the Allies depended to get ashore on D-Day came from amphibious tanks. The thinking that went into the development of this technology and the doctrine for its employment is indicative of the thinking that permeated the entire planning process.

Three years prior to the Normandy invasion, the British started work on designing an amphibious tank. The failed Dieppe raid reinforced the need for a reliable amphibious tank. At Dieppe, tanks fitted with snorkels were dropped into the Channel. Some of them never came up. The amphibious tank the British came up with was called the duplex-drive tank. It used a nine-foot canvas shroud containing thirty-six airtight pillars held up by collapsible metal struts for flotation. The shroud was attached to an American-built M-4 Sherman tank. The basic physics were sound. It is possible to float almost any size vehicle no matter the tonnage as long as the shroud wrapping is high enough. However, the higher the shroud, the more unstable and fragile the vehicle is in the water. When at sea, the bulk of the DD tank hung below the surface of the water. The canvas shroud was all that protruded out of the water. The vehicle was propelled and steered by two 18-inch propellers – the duplex drive – which were movable and acted as rudders. Under ideal conditions, the DD tank could maintain a maximum speed of 4.5 to 5 knots. Each DD tank was equipped with a directional gyroscopic compass for navigation, a periscope that enabled the tank commander to see from inside the tank with the shroud extended, a bilge pump with a fifteen-gallon-per-minute capacity, and safety gear. The safety gear included one inflatable life raft per tank; one submarine escape device – a modified version of the Davis lung – per man; and one inflatable safety belt per man. The DD tank, like other Sherman tanks, had a crew of five.

To launch the tanks at sea, LCTs were modified. A specially designed ramp was mounted to these craft. Four DD tanks could be loaded aboard an LCT(DD). A trained tank crew could have a DD tank ready to launch in less than five minutes, and the navy, during the hours of darkness and under blackout conditions, could launch four tanks from each LCT in less than eight minutes. In daylight, the navy could cut this time in half. During the joint training drill, Exercise Tiger, in April 1944, the navy launched thirty-one DD tanks in five minutes in the early-morning hours of darkness. The DD tank could traverse 4,000 yards in calm seas in twenty-eight minutes. In tests, DD tanks were deployed from as far out as 6,000 yards; however, most testing and training were carried out at a distance of 3,000 to 4,000 yards. In calm seas, the canvas shroud could be dropped in three seconds, and the tank's main gun fired instantly.

The DD tank gave the Allies the capacity to land fully functional tank forces, possessing all of the capabilities of regular M-4 tank battalions, on hostile shores. The Allies believed the DD tanks had the advantages of surprise, shock effect, dispersion, firepower, and size (the DD tank presented the enemy with a smaller target than an LCT loaded with four tanks).[87] Lieutenant Colonel J.S. Upham, who commanded the 743rd Tank Battalion at Omaha Beach, described the advantages of the DD tank: 'The DD Tank, when afloat looks very much like a canvas duck boat. With this deceptive appearance they would be indeed a surprise to an enemy unaware of their identity. It was realized that if their existence could be kept secret, the Germans would be surprised when confronted with blazing tanks instead of innocent canvas boats.'[88] Upham believed that the sight of the tanks would shock the defending German forces, giving the Allies a significant advantage. He and others who supported the use of this tank believed the defending German forces would be psychologically impaired by the sudden appearance of these machines.

How effective were the elements of surprise and shock produced by DD tanks at Omaha Beach? Did the presence of tanks delivered ashore on their own power reduce the combat effectiveness of the German Army more than tanks delivered in LCTs? Probably not. Although tactical surprise was achieved, what might be called 'local surprise' was not. At 0630, when the surviving DD tanks touched down, the German defense was fully manned, weapons were loaded and at the ready, and the German soldiers were in a psychological disposition to kill Americans, which they very effectively proceeded to do. The bluff that overlooked Omaha Beach and the obstacles and minefields on the beach were effective barriers to tanks. The inability of the tanks to close with the enemy – something the German defenders understood better than the American attackers – diminished the shock effect of the tanks. Shock and local surprise did not disconcert the German Army to any measurable degree. Tanks did, however, provide a psychological advantage.

After the battle at Anzio, Lieutenant Colonel A.O. Connor assessed the lessons learned from employing tanks in the battle: 'The division had, throughout this operation, some attached tanks. Two points were brought out forcefully. First, if there is a tank near an Infantry position, regardless of how much or how little damage it has done, or might be able to do to the enemy, it bolsters green troops into holding on to positions. Secondly, German Infantry has an exaggerated idea of the capabilities of their own armor, and the sight of our tanks seems to instill considerable fear and awe.'[89] The psychological influence of tanks on both the enemy and inexperienced American soldiers was positive. (Given Connor's assessment, it was fortuitous that the DD tanks supporting the inexperienced 116th RCT were landed by LCTs. The 16th RCT, the veterans of the 1st ID, had to fight their battle without significant tank support.) The mere presence of tanks increased Allied combat power and may have diminished the enemy's combat power after the initial assault. The psychological advantages noted by Connor, however, were also achieved by deploying regular tanks in LCTs.

Amphibious tanks permitted the Allies to land with greater dispersion. They were thus able to engage more targets over a wider range than tanks deployed in LCTs. Amphibious tanks dispersed along the shore presented the defenders with more numerous targets. An LCT with four tanks onboard was not only an easier target to hit but also a more lucrative target. One round from a German 88 mm gun, mortar, or artillery piece might damage or destroy two or more tanks and the landing craft. The landing craft in the initial stages of the assault was a more valuable resource than the tanks it carried. These craft were needed to run the course between the transport area and the beaches. Damaged or destroyed craft blocked lanes through the obstacles, and with only a limited number of lanes open in the early hours of the assault, such blockages were a serious impediment to the success of the landing. There were, therefore, a number of real advantages to deploying amphibious tanks in the assault.

On 4 February 1944, Colonel S.S. MacLaughlin, commanding the 3rd Armored Group, contacted the V Corps Headquarters to discuss with Colonel Henry Matchett, V Corps chief of staff, the assignment of tank battalions to corps for the Normandy invasion.[90] MacLaughlin assigned two tank battalions, the 741st and 743rd. A third battalion, the 745th, was to support V Corps if another battalion was needed. The battalions originally consisted of three companies of medium M-4 tanks and one company of light tanks. The plan called for two medium companies from each battalion to train on the DD tanks – Companies B and C. Operation of the DD tank and the LCT (DD) required extensive training.

In late February, the DD tank crews began six weeks of training under British instructors. They received classes on the Davis lung, operation of the vehicle, navigation at sea, launching the vehicle, engaging targets on the beach, and other related subjects. On 10 March 1944, MacLaughlin directed Major William D. Dungan, who had trained with the British since January 1944, to locate a site and set up a school to train two medium tank companies on the DD tank.[91] A school was established at Slapton Sands in Devon, England. On 15 March, Dungan commenced training. In the final training exercise, tanks were launched from 4,000 yards out in the early-morning hours of darkness. The exercise was designed to test the crew's navigational skills, ability to maintain formation, and assault techniques. The exercise was a success. The vehicles touched down at first light, and most of them were in the right place.

The Tank Employment Plan for the 116th RCT called for Companies B and C, the DD tank companies, to proceed in column to within 1,000 yards of the beach. The DD tanks were to land at H-5 minutes (0625). If no underwater obstacles were encountered, they were to deploy laterally into line formation and advance. If under-water obstacles were encountered, they were to remain at the water's edge until the engineers could prepare and mark lanes through the seaward band of obstacles. They were then to deploy laterally to attack the pillboxes and other fixed installations. Company B was to advance along Beach Dog: Green, and Company C along Beach Dog: White. Company A, a regular M-4 tank company, while still afloat in LCTs was to place 'drenching fire' on fixed enemy positions on Beaches Easy: Green and Dog: Green.[92] Company A was then to land at H-Hour (0630) on these beaches and give priority to knocking out the pillboxes and concrete emplacements and supporting the advance of the 2nd Battalion. When the lanes were clear, it was to move through beach exit D-3. The 16th RCT's plan for the employment of tanks was for the most part the same.[93]

The DD tanks were to attack fixed installations. The main gun of the tank was to be used to knock out pillboxes on the beach and posi-tions dug into the sides of the bluff and cliffs. The range, accuracy, and effect on targets of the main tank gun exceeded those of all infantry weapons. Tanks were to provide overwatch fire for the assaulting troops. The tank's machine gun was to suppress enemy fire. Tanks were thus to open the battle and to provide cover fire until the infantry closed to engagement range and the engineers and underwater demo-lition teams cleared the lanes.

The DD tank had a number of limitations. Studies conducted by the U.S. Army and Navy noted that the canvas shroud was easily torn and that a tear greater than one foot could cause the tank to sink. Research revealed that the DD tank could not negotiate high seas. It 'could be sunk by the wash of LCT, LCS, and larger craft passing within a few yards of the tank,' a fact that was proven during the Normandy invasion, and the concussion from nearby explosions could cause the metal frame to collapse.[94] The tank's main gun could not be fired while the tank was at sea. Only the .50-caliber machine gun could be employed while the vehicle was afloat. It was believed that carbon monoxide poisoning was possible. In cases where the DD tank had to traverse more than 4,000 yards of sea, some crews were poisoned. Finally, visibility was limited to one periscope, and the navigational ability of the DD tank was questionable.[95]

Lieutenant Dean L. Rockwell, a naval officer who conducted a study of the DD tank and would command a flotilla of sixteen LCT(DD)s on D-Day, concluded that the DD tanks were 'basically sound' and recommended that they be deployed on D-Day.[96] However, because of the tanks' limitations, Rockwell made a number of recommendations for their deployment. He advised that the navy not take responsibility for determining whether conditions were right for launching the DD tanks. He believed that responsibility belonged to the army:

> Inasmuch as the Army is desirous of launching, if at all possible and feasible, the DD tanks on D-day, an Army officer who is thoroughly cognizant of the limitations and peculiarities of said tanks should make the decision, in case of rough sea, whether or not the tanks shall be launched or taken directly to the beach.[97]

He believed that an escort vessel 'with the latest and most accurate navigational equipment' should accompany each company of tanks (sixteen tanks) to within 1,000 yards of the shore. He recommended that no other cargo be placed on the LCTs carrying the DD tanks due to the fragile nature of the canvas shroud and that all LCT(DD) personnel receive the maximum amount of training possible in the time left. Rockwell stated that LCT(DD) personnel should be stabilized, LCT vessels should be identified, tanks and LCTs should be matched up, army and navy teams should be formed for training and deployment purposes, and personnel and resources should be protected from external requirements and other missions.

Major William Dungan, commandant of the school established to train, test, and evaluate the tactical capabilities of the DD tanks, conducted a study of the tanks for the army. Dungan possessed considerable knowledge of the DD tanks. He also supported the use of DD tanks and made a number of recommendations, several of which were the same as those in the navy's study. Dungan recommended that because of the limited capacity of the bilge pump and the possibility of carbon monoxide poisoning, DD tanks should 'not be launched more than 4,000 yards from the beach'[98] and that an experienced army officer who understood the capabilities and limitations of the DD tank should accompany the assault companies and make the decision on whether the conditions were favorable for deployment of the tanks. He also recommended that this officer have access to radio equipment that allowed him to advise higher commanders of his decision. He suggested that a guide craft with an experienced navigator escort the tank force. He believed this procedure would allow tank commanders to concentrate on fighting their tanks as they approached the shore. Dungan also recommended that one LCVP accompany every sixteen tanks to serve as a lifeboat because of the frail nature of the tank's flotation device. He expressed concerns about personnel and training that were similar to those of Rockwell.[99] At Omaha Beach, important recommendations for the employment of the DD tanks were ignored.

Between 0530 and 0600, the DD tanks of the 741st Tank Battalion deployed as planned. The officers and men of Companies B and C realized that the conditions exceeded the capabilities of their amphibious tanks, yet the decision was made to go: 'At H-1 hour 16 DD tanks from Company C, ...and 16 DD tanks from Company B,

741st Tank Battalion, 6000 yards from beach OMAHA proceeded toward [Beaches] FOX GREEN, and EASY RED... 26 of the 32 DD tanks sank, some the instant they submerged, because of rough seas.'[100] As the tanks rolled off the ramps, some immediately began to sink. Tank crews waiting their turn to debark could see their buddies struggling to get out of the rapidly sinking tanks. Still they too made the decision to go. The cumulative weight of months of planning, training, and preparation; the knowledge that the men of the 16th Infantry were depending on their firepower to get ashore; the culturally imbued American sense of manhood; the cohesion that binds men together in war; an optimistic 'I can make it' attitude; and the desire to follow orders made the decision to go easier than the decision not to go for the men of 741st Tank Battalion.[101] Training may simply have taken over, and the men responded automatically. Operations have a way of taking on a momentum all their own, and it becomes easier to follow the plan than to abort it, particularly if there is any possibility of success.

Some tanks took on water and sank more slowly than tanks whose canvas shrouds collapsed. The men in these tanks were fortunate enough to be able to use the safety devices provided. Other crews only had enough time to get out of the tanks. These men struggled in the water, supported only by their life vests. Some crews were able to deploy their inflatable life rafts. There is no evidence that the army's modified version of the Davis lung saved any lives on the morning of 6 June 1944. Only five of the thirty-two DD tanks of the 741st Tank Battalion, which supported the 16th RCT, made it to the beach. Most sank upon launch; others sank *en route*. Of the five that made it to the beach, three were brought in on an LCT because of difficulties with the ramp.

A mile offshore, the LCVPs transporting the men of the 16th Infantry passed the men of Companies B and C struggling in the water. It may not have dawned on them initially that these men were their tank support for the invasion, but when the beach came into sight, this realization hit hard and heavy. This was one of the many failures that impeded the efforts of the 16th Infantry at Omaha Beach.

Rockwell commanded the LCT(DD) flotilla transporting the 743rd Tank Battalion. He too attempted to launch his tanks, but after watching 'one or two tanks... go down,' he, along with Captain Elder of the 743rd, 'decided that it would be foolish to launch any more tanks.'[102] The 743rd tanks were taken into the beach. The DD tanks at Utah, Sword, Juno, and Gold Beaches met with varying degrees of success. At Utah Beach, one LCT(DD) struck an underwater mine and sank with all four DD tanks. The conditions at Utah Beach were not as severe as those at Omaha Beach; thus, the overall performance of the tanks was better. On the British beach, passing LCTs swamped some DD tanks. Many arrived late because of the slow speed of the vehicles and the strong winds and tides. Other tanks experienced the same problems that confronted the tanks of the 741st. Still, some tanks made it to the beach and fought as planned. Overall, the deployment of DD tanks in the British sector was more successful than in the American sector, which caused some historians to argue that it was the American deployment of the vehicles that was at fault for the disaster.[103]

The weather conditions at Normandy on D-Day exceeded the amphibious capabilities of the DD tank. Some tanks started taking on water immediately after launch and sank within sight of their LCTs. Others sank within the first 1,000 yards. Only two tanks made it to shore under their own power. The original American employment plan specified that the tanks be released at 6,000 yards. The plan was later revised and the release point was set at 5,000 yards.[104] This, however, was still beyond the recommended deployment range of 4,000 yards set by both army and navy experts. Still, the results of launching at 4,000 yards would have been the same. Given the sea and weather conditions required for the deployment of the tanks, they should not have been deployed at Omaha Beach as amphibious vehicles. The technology was too poorly designed to stand up against the forces of the open sea. The launch should have been called off and the tanks taken to their designated beaches. On D-Day, the winds were 18 knots and the tide was running at 3 knots. This produced waves of three to four feet, and some as high as six feet. Upham wrote:

[T]he training periods on the DD Sherman Tanks proved conclusively that a calm sea was essential to the success of the tank mission.
Even a fairly rough sea in which the waves were forming whitecaps
would collapse the canvas screen and down would go the tank.
History records that on 6 June 1944 the sea was anything but calm. In
fact it was rougher than at any previous time the DD Tanks had been
launched.

According to Rockwell, the DD tanks never trained in rough seas.
Training was canceled when conditions were not ideal.[105]

General Gerow and other senior army tactical commanders were
not impressed with the DD tank. At a planning conference with
Bradley, Gerow stated: 'You have got to have some leeway, say, two
battalions of lights [tanks] armed with 57s and I hate to rely too much
on that DD tank.'[106] Gerow questioned the seaworthiness of the DD
tank given the currents off the Normandy coast and the difficulties of
navigating at night. Bradley, however, was more optimistic about the
capabilities of the DD tank. He stated: 'The British have a very whole-
some respect for this tank and here it is unduly pessimistic.'[107] Bradley
and Eisenhower believed in the vehicle and supported its employment. Based on experiences in the Mediterranean, they tended to
favor British solutions. After the war, in 1948, Gerow commented that
'more DD tanks landed than he ever expected.'[108]

The DD tanks failed to meet American standards for reliability –
and probably British standards as well. They were a quick fix to a
knotty technological problem made more urgent by the failed Dieppe
amphibious raid. They were an inexpensive, poorly designed solution
to the problem of deploying armor in an amphibious assault. World
War II stretched British resources very close to the limit. On the scale
of total to limited war, the British came much closer to the extreme of
total war – the commitment of the total resources of a nation – than
the Americans ever did. The DD tank thus represented a temporary,
urgently needed solution to a doctrinal problem that was not recognized before the war. Still, the DD tank is an example of the British
philosophy for the design and production of military technology.

Instead of designing an amphibious tank from scratch, the British tinkered with existing tanks and attempted to fit them to the current need, to new situations and conditions.

The quality of the technology was not the only problem with the DD tank. Admiral Hall, the commander of Amphibious Forces 'O' and 'B,' was unimpressed not only with DD tank technology but also with the concept for the employment of the tanks. In his action report, he wrote that he was then, and still is doubtful of the efficacy of DD tanks and tanks from LCT(A)s landing in the first wave on strongly defended beaches. In unopposed landings – or landings on beaches against light opposition – where strong counter-attack may be expected early in assault, such tactics may be sound; against beaches obstructed by obstacles and strongly defended, however, it is believed that naval gunfire must supply close support to replace tanks and artillery until the beaches can be cleared sufficiently to permit their landing.

Hall 'acquiesced' to the use of these tanks because he realized he lacked the necessary naval gunfire support. He wrote that he 'ultimately agreed because he recognized the necessity for more fire power at this stage of the assault than could be supplied by the Naval craft then available.'[109] At Omaha Beach, the terrain limited the role played by tanks.[110] Insufficient maneuver room restricted tanks to the function of static fortifications. At Omaha Beach, only three cuts through the bluff were capable of supporting tank movement. Until these beach exits were opened, there was no room for tanks to advance. They could only move laterally along the length of the beach. They were in essence armored pillboxes, which made excellent targets.

Tanks have five attributes: speed, mobility, firepower, survivability (or protection), and shock effect. Some would add that they also have a morale effect on enemy and friendly forces. The terrain at Omaha Beach negated three of the attributes of the weapon – mobility, survivability, and shock effect. Given the terrain and enemy disposition at Omaha Beach, Hall's doctrinal argument appears to be valid. In terms of technology and doctrine, the DD tank proved to be inadequate for the conditions at Omaha Beach.

One hundred and thirty-five men from Companies B and C, 741st Tank Battalion, went into the Channel the morning of D–Day. Remarkably, most of them survived. Thirty-three men drowned. Immediately after the battle for Omaha Beach, the bodies of twenty-five soldiers were recovered. They were permanently interred either in the United States or in one of four American military cemeteries in Europe, depending on the choice of their families.[111] Later in June, two more bodies were recovered and buried at sea. After V.E. Day, the American Graves Registration Service mounted a major campaign to recover and identify the bodies of American soldiers killed in World War II. No more bodies were found off the Normandy coast.

In 1987, the U.S. Army in Europe mounted a third campaign to recover bodies from the watery tank graveyard. Early that year, a French scuba diver claimed to have seen skeletal remains in a tank off the Normandy coast. The claim was credible, and the army took it seriously. A joint army and navy task force was formed to search for the remains. The tank in question was located, but no remains were found. The task force conducted a thorough search of other tanks and concluded that there were no remains. The U.S. Army officially accepted this conclusion. No effort was made to recover the tanks, and they remain at the bottom of the Channel.

CONCLUSION

The armed forces of the United States began operations in World War II with a dearth of doctrine and tactical and operational knowledge and experience, particularly in joint and combined operations such as amphibious assaults. Advances in technology between the world wars rendered much of the doctrine of the horse-drawn armies obsolete. Between 1940 and 1944, the armed forces learned the hard way by trial and error. They gained valuable experience in the Mediterranean theater in amphibious operations. The army and navy amassed a body of knowledge on techniques and operational procedures. The army developed tactical doctrine for breaching minefields and obstacles.

The navy learned the capabilities and limitations of naval gunfire against ground forces. The army developed a degree of respect and trust in the capabilities of the navy, not as simply a means of transportation but as a combat arm. The army established minimum naval gunfire requirements for opposed amphibious assaults. In short, in 1944, there existed a proven body of knowledge with fundamental principles for the conduct of amphibious assaults against hostile shores. This body of knowledge was primarily built on the capabilities of the two senior services. The combat power of the air force in regard to the battle at the water's edge had not been demonstrated in any landing conducted by the Allies in World War II, yet Montgomery and Bradley constructed their battle plan around the exigencies for the employment of air power. The potential combat power of the air force greatly influenced the planners of the Normandy invasion. That potential combat power was never realized.

The planners of the Normandy invasion were energized by the magnitude of the task that confronted them, and perhaps the enormity of the task blocked their view. There was a tendency to believe that nothing quite like this had ever happened before. This belief caused them to seek new solutions to problems that had previously been identified and studied, problems for which there were established procedures, techniques, and materials. What was new was the size of the invasion. The fundamentals for an assault against hostile shores, however, were unchanged. The planners of the invasion believed they had to be innovative and develop new procedures, technology, and doctrine. In doing so, they discarded many lessons of the past.

9

The 1st Infantry Division's Battle Plan

We must succeed in the short time left until the large offensive starts, in bringing all defenses to such a standard that they will hold up against the strongest attack. Never in history was there a defense of such an extent with such an obstacle as the sea. The enemy must be annihilated before he reaches our main battlefield.

Field Marshal Erwin Rommel

As commander of the 1st ID, General Huebner was responsible for deploying and fighting his battalions and companies in the battle for Omaha Beach. His primary objective was to attain a lodgment through which follow-on forces could advance. It was his duty to develop tactical plans that achieved army and corps objectives and minimized the risk to the lives of his soldiers. These were weighty responsibilities that could not simply be passed up the chain of command by attributing everything that happened or failed to happen to the operational commanders, Montgomery and Bradley. In other words, as the division commander, Huebner deserves credit for both what happened at Omaha Beach and what failed to happen.

Gerow and Huebner were for the most part in agreement on the concept for the conduct of the battle. Because the staffs of the V Corps and the 1st ID worked closely together to develop the plan and because of the continuous exchange of information between the two headquarters, there was a high degree of consensus between Gerow and Huebner. When Gerow sought to change the operational plans for the invasion, he noted that Huebner supported his recommendations. In the records, there is no indication that Huebner disagreed with Gerow's vision of the assault at Omaha Beach. And in his after action report, Huebner confirmed that he agreed with Gerow's assessment that the assault should have taken place under the cover of darkness.[1] Huebner may not have supported Gerow's efforts to maintain command of the assault, but he did support Gerow's attempts to change the approach to the invasion at Omaha. Gerow's V Corps took it upon itself to relieve the division of the burden of much of the planning, allowing Huebner and his staff to concentrate on training. If battles had to be fought over the vision for the conduct of the invasion, the corps was the proper place for such efforts. Because of the considerable experience of the 1st ID in amphibious assault, the V Corps staff was probably more willing to consult with and accept ideas and recommendations from the division staff. However, because of its comprehensive understanding of how things worked in England and the plan for the invasion, the corps staff was more effective and efficient at getting things done.

Huebner had very little latitude in developing the plan for the assault at Omaha Beach. The when, where, who, and how – the doctrine – were dictated to him and his subordinate regiment and battalion commanders in considerable detail. One battalion commander complained in his after action report that he had been given no say in determining what equipment his battalion would carry, and as a result, his men carried things they did not need and left behind things they needed.[2] Huebner was told he would assault with two regiments abreast, two battalions abreast in each regiment. He was told how to load the landing craft, how to configure his platoons into boat teams, what equipment each boat team would carry, and how to exit the landing craft. He was given the engineer plan for clearing lanes and the Joint Fire Plan. It is difficult to find any aspect of the American plan and doctrine for the battle at Omaha that conformed to standard organizational and doctrinal procedures. Almost the entire book was rewritten for the campaign at Normandy. Not even the principle of unit integrity was maintained.[3] The concept for the conduct of the invasion was not Huebner's, and the resources upon which the success at the water's edge was supposed to be built were not under his control. Yet it was Huebner's 1st ID that improvised the combat power necessary to defeat the German defense. And if Huebner and Gerow had been allowed to exert greater influence in developing the plans for the assault, they would have fought a very different battle.

Huebner's battle plan was constructed on false information and assumptions. It was based on Montgomery's and Bradley's erroneous assessment of the firepower capabilities of the air force and navy; erroneous assessments of the enemy's strength, capabilities, and concept for the conduct of the defense; the assumption that a high degree of tactical surprise would be achieved; and unproven tactical doctrines, such as the plan for the employment of engineers in daylight to clear lanes through the obstacles and minefields under enemy fire.[4] Miscalculations and erroneous information and assumptions caused Huebner to prepare his division to fight the wrong battle. As a result, the men of the 1st ID were deployed in a manner that failed to maximize their chances of success and survival. They were deployed in a direct frontal assault against the most heavily defended sectors of the German defense in daylight. Gerow's and Huebner's flawed plan made the cost of taking Omaha Beach high. However, Huebner's leadership and the magnificent effort of his soldiers improvised success.

GENERAL CLARENCE RALPH HUEBNER

Of General Huebner, the veteran World War II journalist Don Whitehead wrote:

> I looked closely at this man whose division had been given the tremendous responsibility of leading the invasion assault. I saw a kindly face with a square jaw and direct blue eyes that twinkled with humor. I judged he was in his early fifties. He was physically fit and there was an air of confidence about him that I liked. I found that Huebner had a great love for his 1st Division. [He was] one of the finest soldiers and gentlemen I've ever known.[5]

General Clarence Ralph Huebner commanded the U.S. 1st ID in what was strategically the most important operation in World War II for the British and Americans, yet the story of his life has only been sketched. Historians have given little time and space to the lives and achievements of America's division and corps commanders in World War II. This is particularly noteworthy in the cases of Huebner and V Corps commander Leonard Gerow. Numerous works are devoted to the Normandy invasion and the battle for Omaha Beach, but the two men most responsible for developing the tactical plans for the battle and fighting at Omaha Beach are all but neglected by history. In *Masters of the Art of Command,* Martin Blumenson devoted nine pages to Huebner, and only the last three pages address his command of the 1st ID in World War II.[6] *The D-Day Encyclopedia* devoted only two pages to Huebner.[7] Gerow typically receives only a sentence or two in most works on the Normandy invasion, but it was his V Corps that actually wrote the orders for the invasion.

In 1965, Major Ronald Joe Rogers wrote a master's thesis at the U.S. Army Command and General Staff College at Fort Leavenworth, Kansas, entitled 'A Study of Leadership in the First Infantry Division during World War II: Terry De La Mesa Allen and Clarence Ralph Huebner.'[8] The purpose of this study was to compare, contrast, and assess the leadership styles and abilities of two successful World War II division commanders. To prepare his thesis, Rogers conducted personal interviews and corresponded with Huebner and his senior subordinate commanders. Huebner died on 23 September 1972. He left no personal papers and wrote no summary of his career or experiences at Normandy. Thus, Rogers's work may be the only primary source of information on Huebner. We also have the comments of those who served under him, the records of the 1st ID, and the observations of his senior commanders. Through these sources, we can gain some understanding of the man who fought one of the most significant battles in World War II.

Of Huebner, Blumenson wrote:

> Clarence Ralph Huebner personifies what will power, native intelligence, and natural aptitude – helped by luck and hard work – can do in the way of fashioning an outstanding military career... Of all the great American soldiers of the twentieth century, including many far better known to the public, none better exemplifies the fundamental strength of a citizen army in a democratic society – the career open to talent.[9]

Huebner's life story represents the American dream. He entered the service a private and retired forty years later a lieutenant general. He did not benefit from the prestige, clout, and connections that went along with graduation from the U.S. Military Academy; Huebner rose through the ranks. He enlisted in the army on 17 January 1910 and advanced through the enlisted ranks from private to master sergeant.[10] In the 18th Infantry, while serving as the regimental supply sergeant, he was recognized for his talents, abilities, and potential and given the opportunity to compete for a commission through objective examinations. On 26 November 1916, Huebner was commissioned a second lieutenant of infantry.

Huebner received his infantry training at Fort Leavenworth, graduating in April 1917. The same month, the United States entered World War I. On 25 May, the First Expeditionary Division, which eventually became known as the 'Big Red One,' was organized. Huebner was a

charter member. He took command of a rifle company in the 28th
Infantry Regiment and, a few weeks later, sailed for France. Huebner
led his company at Beaumont in March and April 1918. During the
battle, he was wounded and reported killed.[11] Huebner later saw
action at Cantigny from April through July. When his battalion
commander was killed, he took charge and led the battalion, an act for
which he was promoted and awarded the Distinguished Service
Cross. The citation read:

> For three days near Cantigny, France... he withstood German assaults
> under intense bombardment, heroically exposing himself to fire
> constantly in order to command his battalion effectively, and although
> his command lost half its officers and 30 per cent of its men, he held
> the position and prevented a break in the line at that point.[12]

In May, Huebner was promoted to captain, and in June, to major.
While serving as the battalion commander in the Aisne-Marne offensive in July, Huebner was again wounded and noted for his actions
under fire. He was awarded an Oak Leaf Cluster on his Distinguished
Service Cross. The commendation read:

> South of Soisson, France, July 18–23, 1918, he displayed great
> gallantry and, after all the officers of his battalion had become casual-
> ties, he reorganized his battalion while advancing, captured his objec-
> tive and again reorganized his own and another battalion, carrying the
> line forward. He remained continuously on duty until wounded the
> second day of action.[13]

Huebner fought in the Saizerais sector in August, the Saint Mihiel
offensive in September, and the Meuse-Argonne offensive in
September and November. In October, while commanding the 28th
Infantry Regiment, he was promoted to lieutenant colonel. When the
war ended, Huebner was one of the most highly decorated officers in
the army. In less than a year, he had risen through the ranks from lieutenant to lieutenant colonel and had commanded at every level from

company to regiment. Huebner was fully tested in World War I. He was an officer of proven courage and leadership abilities. For his service during the war, he was awarded the Distinguished Service Medal, which stated:

> As captain, major, and lieutenant colonel of the 28th Infantry, 1st Division, throughout its training and active operations in France, he successfully commanded all echelons of the regiment, participating with distinction in every engagement from Cantigny to Sedan, reorganizing his regiment after its heavy losses in the first phase of the Meuse-Argonne Offensive, and inspiring it with the will and dash that carried it to the heights of Sedan. By his sound tactical judgment, his unusual leadership and indefatigable energy he contributed in a marked manner to the various successes of his regiment and of the 1st Division and rendered to the American Expeditionary Forces most conspicuous services in a position of great responsibility.[14]

Huebner also received the Silver Star, the Purple Heart with one Oak Leaf Cluster, the French Légion d'Honneur, the French Croix de Guerre, and the Italian Croce di Guerra. Huebner was a genuine American hero.

World War I had little influence on the American practice of war and on American officers' views of how war should be fought.[15] The U.S. Army never suffered a Somme or Verdun, and it fought in Europe for less than a year before the war ended. The impact World War I had on Montgomery, the British Army, and the British people was not felt by the American people and the U.S. Army.[16] Although technological developments greatly influenced American strategy and doctrine in World War II, America's optimism about its ability to wage war, its proclivity for fast-moving offensive warfare waged on a mass scale with lots of firepower, and its inclination toward fighting and defeating the enemy's main army and pursuing total solutions were unchanged by the nation's first experience in European war outside the United States.[17] Huebner was a practitioner of the American way of war.

During the interwar period, Huebner served in a number of positions and attended several service schools, where he had the opportunity to develop his thinking about doctrine, technology, and the training of soldiers. In America's small peacetime army (200,000 to 280,000 officers and men), most officers moved between field units, staff positions, and service schools. Because the army was small, command positions were few and far between.

At the end of the war, Huebner took command of a battalion in the 16th Infantry and then command of the regiment. He led the 16th Infantry in the victory parades in New York and Washington. Huebner then returned to the 28th Regiment and served as the executive officer and the regimental commander. He gave up command in June 1920.[18] From 1920 to 1922, Huebner served as an instructor at the Infantry School at Fort Benning, Georgia. In 1923, he graduated from the Infantry Officer's Advanced Course at Fort Benning. In 1924, following an assignment as a staff officer in the 11th Infantry at Fort Knox, Kentucky, he attended the Command and General Staff College at Fort Leavenworth. He was an honors graduate. Following Leavenworth, Huebner was reassigned to the Infantry School at Fort Benning as an instructor. In 1928 and 1929, he attended the U.S. Army War College in Washington. Upon graduation, he was assigned to the Command and General Staff College as an instructor. In the early 1930s, he served as a member of the Infantry Board at Fort Benning and in the Office of the Chief of Infantry in Washington. Following this assignment, he reported to the 19th Infantry at Schofield Barracks, Hawaii, where he served as the executive officer.[19] In July 1940, Huebner became the chief of the Training Branch of the Operations and Training Division of the Office of the War Department General Staff in Washington. In January 1941, he was promoted to brigadier general.[20] On 7 December 1941, the Japanese attack at Pearl Harbor brought the United States into its second major conflict on the European continent. In 1942, following an assignment as commandant of the Infantry Replacement Training Center at Camp Croft, South Carolina, Huebner was appointed director of the Training Division at Army Service Forces Headquarters. He held this position until March 1943.

During the interwar period, Huebner earned the nickname 'Coach' because of his reputation for developing and executing outstanding training. When World War II started, Huebner was one of the nation's greatest resources. By experience, education, and training, he was superbly qualified for high command.

Huebner can best be described as an officer in the vein of Matthew B. Ridgway, not exclusively a managerial type like Eisenhower or Bradley and not exclusively a heroic type like Patton.[21] He was one of those rare individuals who performed well in both capacities and had the ability to move between the two schools of leadership. He used the objective, managerial, scientific approach, which might be called the General Marshall school, to solve problems, but he also recognized the limitations of this approach. Huebner had personally led soldiers in battle at the small-unit level. He understood better than most of his superiors what it took to succeed at the point of the sword, where firefights took place. Huebner had a strong moral center. He was not a political general and was not afraid to speak his mind.[22]

In March 1943, the newly promoted Major General Huebner was assigned to the Mediterranean theater as the operations officer. After a month in the theater, he was reassigned to serve as the deputy chief of staff to British general Sir Harold Alexander. Because of friction between British and American leadership involving the abuse of American units by Alexander, Huebner was relieved of his position.[23] Blumenson wrote:

> Huebner joined Alexander's staff to prevent further favoritism based on nationality and to provide a genuinely Allied outlook. The tacit understanding was that Alexander would consult with him before issuing directives concerning the United States units in his area. Huebner did not last long in this position. He embarrassed Alexander by coming in his quiet way to dominate the entire staff.[24]

Huebner was angered by the British superiority complex. Rogers wrote:

Alexander, like many British officers, missed few opportunities to disparage the fighting ability of the American troops in North Africa. Since General Huebner stood firm in his defense of the U.S. Army's fighting ability, considerable friction developed between them. It was a happy day for both Huebner and Alexander when Huebner was nominated to command the First Division.[25]

In August 1943, during the campaign in Sicily, Bradley relieved Generals Terry Allen, the commander, and Theodore Roosevelt, the assistant division commander, and gave Huebner command of the 1st ID.[26]

Under the best of conditions, taking command can be a difficult task. The men do not know their new boss, his habits, likes and dislikes, and idiosyncrasies. They do not know what he thinks is important and what he thinks is unimportant, whether he knows his job or how he goes about his business, or the strengths and weaknesses of his character. The new commander has to create the environment he wants to prevail, but first, he has to let everyone know who is in charge. He can then go about the business of gaining their confidence and respect. Legal authority – authority vested by the Constitution, rank, and position – works under most conditions, but under the conditions of heavy, sustained combat, a more secure basis of authority is needed. Authority based on proven, tested ability and the knowledge that the boss is looking after the best interests of his soldiers is needed. This type of authority is not automatically given. Time is required to develop and nurture it.

In the case of Huebner, this process was particularly difficult because of the way he received command. Allen had fought the division through North Africa and Sicily and was highly regarded by his men.[27] His relationship with his men was special because it was formed and tempered under enemy fire in numerous fights. No matter who took Allen's place, the men were likely to feel considerable resentment. The division operations officer, Colonel Stanhope B. Mason, wrote: 'Throughout the Division there was a sense of hurt at the loss of Allen and Roosevelt who were respected and beloved leaders.'[28] Blumenson wrote:

It [taking command] was a difficult task, for the men revered their former commanders and resented the newcomer who quickly abolished the informality of his predecessors. Within a brief time, however, Huebner had overcome this handicap, won the affection of his troops, and placed his own stamp on them. They were shaped once again into a cohesive, top-notch, and highly disciplined unit. So successful was Huebner that in England the 1st Division was selected to join the D-Day landing, and he commanded it, along with two regiments of the 29th Division, going ashore at Omaha Beach.[29]

The task of taking command was more arduous than Blumenson's account indicates, and the men of the 1st ID would have rejected his thesis that the division had lost its cohesion, its 'top-notch' status, and its discipline while under the command of Allen. Patton understood what it took to succeed in battle, and his selection of the 1st ID to lead the assault on Sicily speaks volumes about his confidence in the division's ability to fight. Patton was proven correct in this decision. At Gela on the coast of Sicily, the division fought gallantly and tenaciously against a highly regarded German division. Even Bradley would have disagreed for the most part with Blumenson's assessment. Bradley wrote: '[W]hile the 1st might be the best division in the U.S. Army – it nevertheless was *a part* of the army, a fact it sometimes forgot...This relief was not to be a reprimand for ineptness or for ineffective command. For in Sicily as in Tunisia the 1st Division had set the pace for the ground campaign.'[30] Bradley wanted a different kind of discipline than that displayed by the men of the 1st ID and their commander. He wanted conformists like himself, not unorthodox rebels like Allen. Yet he too recognized that the division had performed well under the most difficult circumstances.

Bradley also would have disagreed with Blumenson's assessment that in a 'brief time' Huebner 'won the affection of his troops, and placed his own stamp on them.' Bradley wrote: 'A more sensitive man than Huebner might have cracked under the strain, for it was not until after the Normandy invasion, one year later, that the last resentful adherents to Terry Allen conceded Huebner the right to wear the Big Red One.'[31]

Finally, Bradley would have disagreed with Blumenson's assessment of why the 1st ID was selected for the Normandy invasion. Bradley wrote: 'The division had already been selected for the Normandy campaign. If it was to fight well there at the side of inexperienced divisions and under the command of an inexperienced corps, the division desperately needed a change in its perspective.' Bradley continued with an assessment of the importance of the 1st ID: 'A division represents not only the lives of 15,000 men and millions of dollars worth of equipment, but it also represents a priceless investment in months and years of training. In the 1st Division that investment had been multiplied beyond measure by its long experience in battle. Thus in quality the 1st was worth the equal of several inexperienced divisions. It had become an almost irreplaceable weapon for the Normandy invasion.'[32] Of Huebner, Bradley wrote:

As Allen's successor in the 1st Division we picked Major General Clarence R. Huebner, known to the army as a flinty disciplinarian. He was no stranger to the Big Red One, for he had already worn its patch in every rank from a private to colonel. In returning to command the division, however, he had come from a desk in the Pentagon, an assignment which did not tend to ease his succession to Allen's post.[33]

Allen, displaying no bitterness, personally introduced Huebner to the commanders and staff of every regiment and battalion command post and gave Huebner his personal endorsement.[34] Huebner later stated 'that if it had not been for Allen's personal endorsement and his acquaintance with a number of lieutenants and warrant officers of the unit, he doubted that he would ever have been accepted by the division.'[35]

On taking command, Huebner immediately initiated programs to get the soldiers' minds off the division command problems, to inform the division in no uncertain terms that he was in charge, to assess the division's state of training and readiness, to determine the abilities of key subordinate leaders, to test the flow of information down the chain of command, and to shape the division to his vision of a combat-ready unit. These programs also gave the new boss the oppor-tunity to demonstrate that he knew his business and that things were going to be different. Huebner did not fire people to get the division's attention, even though he had Bradley's permission to do so.[36] He did, however, make many soldiers angry. Bradley wrote: "'Keerist' the combat veteran exclaimed in undisguised disgust, "here they send us a stateside Johnny to teach us how to march through the hills where we've been killing Krauts. How stupid can this sonuvabitch get.'"[37]

Anger, however, when properly used, can facilitate the process of taking command. Anger cannot be sustained over a long period of time, but until the boss has earned the respect of his men, it can provoke soldiers to do things strictly by the book. If things go wrong, the book protects them. Anger can divert the attention of soldiers away from problems they have no control over and can be a strong motivator for action. The 'I'll show you' attitude when properly channeled can move units forward rapidly. Huebner worked through his staff and subordinate commanders to achieve his objectives. His superiors wisely gave him the time and leeway to make the division his. Mason stated: '[I]t took us a while to make the change to his type of command and we all were chewed out frequently and beautifully in the process of learning.'[38] Colonel John W. Bowen, a battalion and later regiment commander in the 1st ID, wrote: 'He gave his staff and commanders a hard time with his querulous questioning and his rejection out of hand of many of their ideas, concepts and plans. It was his way of starting out tough to show who was boss and disci-plinarian.'[39]

According to Rogers:

> Although General Huebner had inherited a division which had great pride and a magnificent fighting spirit, he was convinced that they needed more training in fundamentals – especially rifle marksman-ship. At the same time he did not want to do anything that would injure the fine qualities which the division had, nor did he want to undermine the confidence which the men had in their officers.[40]

Huebner was an astute leader. On checking training records, he discovered that over 2,000 soldiers were not qualified in rifle marksmanship, so he had a rifle range constructed on which he served as instructor.[41] Huebner was known to be a stickler for detail. Rogers wrote:

> When he found a deficiency in a soldier's position or firing technique, he would ask the squad leader what was wrong. If the squad leader did not know the answer, he would ask the platoon leader, and, if necessary the company commander. This had an immediate effect on the NCOs and officers. They not only took great interest in the training of their men, but rapidly became very knowledgeable of proper firing techniques.[42]

These measures did not make Huebner popular. He stated: 'I got the reputation of being an unreasonable and mean old bastard.'[43] After this period of training, Huebner requested an inspection by the corps commander. Rogers wrote:

> He specifically requested a 'tough' inspection, where nothing would be found to be right. He asked further that the corps commander strongly express his dissatisfaction with General Huebner in front of the troops. He felt that this psychology would accomplish a dual purpose: first, it would let the men see that they were not the only ones subject to criticism; and second, that it was not only their own Commanding General who was dissatisfied with their state of discipline and training.[44]

Huebner clearly understood human nature. He created situations and conditions to encourage specific behavioral patterns and to enhance soldiers' understanding of how and why things worked the way they did.

On 23 October 1943, Huebner sailed with his division for England, where the 1st ID's training program assumed a new significance, direction, and intensity. The 1st ID began training for the Normandy invasion. Amphibious assault and combined arms training consumed most of the division's time, and physical conditioning took the rest. Long road marches were frequent. General Clift Andrus, who would later command the division, wrote:

> All of General Huebner's activities were directed at the Infantry and every detail in every unit was carefully supervised. He personally handled the various Infantry weapons and he even went into a foxhole and let a tank run over him. As one Infantry G.I. told me; "The 'Old Man' surely knows his business."[45]

Don Whitehead, a journalist who observed Huebner and his division prior to the Normandy invasion, wrote:

> He knew the job of every man in his division as well as or better than the men knew the jobs... The general wanted his division to be the best in the entire Army. It wasn't entirely a matter of personal pride because Huebner knew that the toughest, straightest-shooting division won its objectives with the least loss of life. And if he was stern in his discipline, it was because battle casualties have a direct relation to discipline.[46]

After the battle of Omaha Beach, during one of Eisenhower's inspection tours, his naval aide, Captain Harry C. Butcher, recorded a conversation with Huebner in his diary:

> The next day we drove to headquarters of the U.S. 1st Division, which had just taken Aachen. General Clarence R. Huebner, my friend from the Mediterranean, invited us to lunch, during which I asked him how he had managed to gain the confidence of his division after his relief of the popular Terry Allen in Sicily. He said it had been simple. He required all of them to practice shooting, and ample ammunition was furnished. He said that there wasn't a man in the division who hadn't improved his shooting. There's nothing the GIs like better than to shoot, particularly if they are not supervised too closely. He said he had the 'shootinest' division in the Army.[47]

Taking command was not as 'simple' as Huebner would have had
Butcher believe, but it was in character for Huebner to say it was.
Making the difficult look easy was part of his job as the commanding
general. Still, after the battle for Omaha Beach, Huebner realized that
his relationship with the men of the 1st ID had changed. Rogers
wrote: 'By this time a genuine feeling of mutual respect and confidence had developed between Huebner and the Division. For the first
time, many of its members accorded him the right to wear the 'Big
Red One' on his shoulder.'[48]

Huebner developed programs that took advantage of natural
human emotions, attitudes, and responses to facilitate the process of
taking command. The way a commander commands when he is new
to a unit is very different from the way he commands when everyone
knows the capabilities, strengths, and weaknesses of all major compo-
nents of the division. Huebner's understanding of humanity more
than his knowledge of rifle marksmanship gave him the wherewithal
to efficiently and expeditiously take command of the 1st ID.

Huebner's efforts paid dividends for the U.S. Army at Normandy.
The Oak Leaf Cluster on the Distinguished Service Medal awarded
Huebner after the battle at Omaha Beach stated:

> He organized and commanded the force which was assigned the
> extremely difficult mission of making the initial assault on the coast of
> France. In spite of the fact that this force was assigned the most
> heavily defended sector of the invasion coast and met almost insur-
> mountable obstacles, it carried through its mission of gaining control
> of the beach... The success of the greatest amphibious operation in
> history against a strongly fortified and almost impregnable coastal
> barrier was in large measure due to the organizing ability and fore-
> sight, indomitable determination and inspiring leadership of General
> Huebner.[49]

Huebner was commander of the V Corps under Patton when
Germany surrendered.[50]

TACTICAL ANALYSIS OF THE TERRAIN

At each level of command from army to division, a terrain analysis is carried out prior to an invasion. Models of the terrain are constructed and provided to the assaulting infantry and engineer units for study. Tactical plans are based in part on the configuration of the terrain, the enemy's situation, and an analysis of the enemy's probable actions – that is, projections of how an enemy commander will most likely fight his forces on a particular piece of ground. The more detailed the terrain analysis, the more accurate the intelligence on the enemy's situation, and the better the estimate of likely enemy actions, the better the plan of battle. The flow of battle across a particular piece of ground cannot be thoroughly analyzed, however, until it has been walked over and studied by the commander who has to conduct battle. Minor variations in terrain and small nuances typically go undetected by photos and other two-dimensional depictions, and a small rise or depression can change the conduct and course of a battle. The advantage of being able to walk and study a piece of ground on which a battle may be fought typically falls to the defender. Thus, the commander of a unit charged with the defense of a particular piece of ground has the opportunity to plan the conduct of the battle on that terrain in light of the strengths and weaknesses of his unit. He has the opportunity to walk that piece of terrain with his subordinate leaders and explain to them his concept for the conduct of the battle. This can be a significant advantage.

One of the principles of the defense is that it should never cease improving and developing. A defense should evolve over time. The longer a unit is located on a given piece of terrain, the stronger its defense. Constant refinement, constant analysis, constant 'what iffing' are the secrets of a successful defense. A unit occupying a piece of ground for several days should have well-marked fields of fire; should know the range to every significant fold that might protect or hide a man; should have the means for firing into dead space, areas masked from flat trajectory weapons because of variations in the ground; should have analyzed every possible approach from the view of the attacker; should know the ground so well it is able to fight and engage targets at night nearly as well as during hours of daylight; should have employed all of the material means available to erode the attackers' combat power, for example, wire, mines, and tank ditches; should have plans to channel the enemy into specially prepared areas, or kill zones, to complete the destruction; should have in-depth positions and contingency positions to cover alternate avenues of approach; and should have rehearsed contingencies to counter every imaginable enemy move, including counter-attack forces with planned routes of advance and prepared fighting positions. The conduct of the defense is not a mechanical process. It is not an endeavor for engineers or technicians. It involves science, but it also involves art. And art calls for creativity. Because every piece of terrain is unique, there are no textbook solutions. There are, however, principles. The commander charged with the conduct of the defense is required to create a work of art that maximizes the strengths of his unit, minimizes its weaknesses, and exploits every advantage of the terrain. A well-planned, well-developed, well-fought defense is a work of art.

The German generals of World War II were not the artists in the conduct of the defense that German generals in World War I were. Given the time and resources available to the German Army, the defense in the West clearly evinced a low level of attainment in this art. This lack of talent in defensive warfare was an advantage for the Allies. The British had deep-rooted memories and fears of World War I defenses carried out by Generals Paul von Hindenburg and Erich Ludendorff. The British, therefore, had a greater appreciation of German capabilities and potential than did the Americans. However, in North Africa and Sicily, the Germans did not demonstrate a mastery of defensive warfare, and perhaps the veterans of the Mediterranean theater came to expect poor performance in the conduct of the defense.

On 17 February 1944, the FUSA released Beach Study Overlord. The purpose of the study was to 'evaluate currently available engineer intelligence relative to Neptune Beaches and pertinent to the mission stated hereinafter.' This document described the American invasion beaches. It explained the tidal conditions, specified landing characteristics, analyzed communications networks off the beaches, described natural and man-made obstacles, and discussed the possible effects of terrain on operations. Omaha Beach was described as follows:

> One and one-quarter miles west of Ste Honorine, the chalk cliffs give way to a sand beach backed by low cultivated country. This beach extends westward 7900 yards to the Pointe de la Percee just beyond Vierville. The westernmost quarter-mile narrows and is backed by steeply rising chalk cliffs continuing almost to Grandcamp. The beach has a narrow 15-yard strip of shingle at high water, with hard sand to seaward, cut by runnels below half-tide. The gentle beach slope continues for some 250 yards to seaward below low water. Clearance or over running of the shingle strip with a mat... may be required for the exit of wheeled and truck vehicles. Except for the cliffs to the extreme west, the beach is backed by a low grassy bank or shingle ledges, topped by a 4 to 10 foot seawall from the western side of St Laurent to the rising cliffs at Vierville. Minefields have been reported as located just above the high water line and extending all the way from Vierville to St. Laurent... Observation from the beach is somewhat limited, but the cliffs on the flanks and the edge of the high escarpment inland provide excellent sites for observation posts.

The FUSA's terrain analysis was somewhat lacking in detail, but as the day of the assault drew near, the information on the terrain became more detailed and the analysis more thorough. The study concluded: 'Beach 46 [Omaha Beach] Ste Honorine to Vierville, with a length of 7900 yards, is the only suitable landing area between Bayeux and Isigny.'[51] This was a conclusion the Germans had also drawn.

On 25 March, the 1st ID released its Tactical Study of Terrain. The purpose of the study was 'to give a brief general description of the area of the NEPTUNE operation, and detailed analysis of Beach 46 [Omaha Beach] and the area behind it from the assault viewpoint.' The 1st ID did not have to draw conclusions on the acceptability of the landing site; that decision had already been made. Under the section entitled 'Tactical Effect of the Terrain,' the influence of terrain on the division's operations was discussed and analyzed. The 1st ID's study noted many of the same characteristics described in the FUSA's study and the V Corps' study, but its analysis was more detailed.[52]

The 1st ID's study identified the advantages of the terrain at Omaha Beach. First, the bluff at the rear of the beach prevented the enemy from deploying its coastal defense units in depth. In order to see to shoot, defending forces had to be located well forward. Flat trajectory weapons could only be employed from positions on the very edge of the top of the bluff, the face of the bluff, and the beach itself; hence, the enemy's defenses lacked depth in the initial assault. And direct-fire weapons positioned at the top of the bluff could only engage targets using 'plunging fire,' the least desirable form of fire because range as well as deflection had to be accurately determined in order to successfully engage targets. Second, 'winding corridors and narrow draws leading from the beach' created folds in the ground through which soldiers could 'infiltrate.' It was believed that pillboxes located on the beach could be taken from the rear by infiltrating through cuts in the ground. Third, the shingle strip and concrete seawall along Omaha Beach were viewed not only as obstacles but also as the first defensible pieces of terrain. The study noted that '[t]he only cover or concealment in the area is the limited amount provided by the seawall, the grayness and the cliffs.'[53] The seawall and shingle strip provided an initial defensive position with some protection from small arms fire. These relatively minor features saved many lives on D-Day.

The study also listed the disadvantages of the Omaha Beach terrain. First, the 'shingle strip' was a possible obstacle to armored vehicles. However, the study cited a German report that stated that the heavy gravel at Dieppe did not prevent British tanks from landing, although it did render the landing 'more difficult.' Second, the concave shape of Omaha Beach permitted 'grazing fire' from the defending forces' 'flat trajectory weapons sited anywhere along the beach.' (With grazing fire, it was not necessary to accurately determine range.) The study noted: 'Since the beach is slightly concave, the heights on either end command its entire length.'[54] This meant the defenders could achieve not only grazing fire but also 'enfilade fire' – the ability to fire down the length of an array of targets from a flanking position – from both ends of the beach. Weapons could therefore be mounted in a manner to prevent observation from the seaward approach. Instead of pointing the barrels of weapons out to sea, they were pointed down the length of the beach. This made the weapons more lethal and more difficult to spot from ships. It also meant that artillery and mortar spotters had excellent positions from which to view the battle and call for fire.

Third, only two of the five beach exits permitted armored vehicles to advance inland off the beach through the bluff. This fact favored enemy antitank weapons: 'Due to the steepness of the slope directly in rear of the beach west of Le Ruquet River..., tanks accompanying troops in the assault will have to use the two corridors in this sector as exits from the beach. Since these corridors are narrow and are provided with concrete road blocks, enemy tank defense in this sector is greatly facilitated.'[55] The bluff that overlooked Omaha Beach restricted the movement of vehicles. Mobility, one of the great attributes of tanks, was effectively eliminated until the beach exits were opened.

Fourth, the terrain in the rear of the beach was considered 'excellent' for artillery and mortar. At a V Corps planning conference on 7 February, General C.G. Helmick, the V Corps artillery officer, reportedly said, 'on the development of fire power, ...that this area from the point of view of hostile batteries, is the most favorable on the whole coast. Terrain indicates five batteries that are capable of firing on the landing beaches, and really only one that can control the transport area.'[56] Defilade positions, positions capable of concealing and protecting artillery batteries and mortar platoons from direct observation and fire, abounded in the terrain behind the bluff.[57]

Fifth, the next significant terrain feature behind Omaha Beach was a ridgeline running about 2,000 yards to the rear of the beach. This position could provide the enemy with a second line of defense or a location from which to counter-attack. The fact that 2,000 yards was out of range of small arms fire from the initial position was an advantage. If the next defensible piece of terrain was only 1,000 yards to the rear, the battle would have been one continuous assault.

A brief summary of the tactical aspects and defensive potential of the terrain at Omaha Beach might have read as follows. Omaha Beach is concave, shaped sort of like a banana. The beach is approximately six miles in length and flanked on both sides by cliffs that cannot be traversed without climbing equipment. Behind Omaha Beach approximately 300 yards from the water's edge at high tide is a bluff that rises to a height of 100 to 170 feet. The bluff has a commanding presence over the entire range of the beach surface. Nothing can move on Omaha Beach that cannot be observed from the bluff towering above it and the cliffs flanking it. Anything that can be observed can be targeted and killed. The shape of the beach gives the defender the ability to position weapons at both ends and aim them inward toward the center of the beach. This placement of weapons has two advantages: it allows the defender to cover the entire length of the beach to the maximum effective range of weapons with grazing, enfilade fire, and it facilitates hiding the weapons from observation from the sea, which means naval spotters will find it difficult to identify targets.

The bluff has five cuts for minor roads that lead off the beaches.[58] Only two are capable of supporting tanks. These roads are the keys to a successful assault at Omaha Beach. They have to be taken at the earliest opportunity and kept open in order to win the race of the build-up of forces. If these exits are not taken in the first hour of the assault, the four battalions of tanks and numerous engineer vehicles will pile up on the beach and become sitting ducks, and the FUSA's plan for the build-up will fall behind schedule. The Germans realize the significance of these beach exits. They are the most heavily defended positions on the beach. They are defended by fixed, reinforced installations, blocked with concrete and wire emplacements, and overwatched by machine guns and antitank positions.

Pillboxes, machine gun positions, and antitank gun positions are located on the beach and the cliffs. They are arrayed to deliver high volumes of accurate fire on the assault force. These positions represent formidable obstacles. Air and naval resources are to knock them out prior to the landing.

The size of the tidal range can make the task of the infantry more difficult. At Omaha Beach, the tidal range varies from 250 to 300 yards. At low tide, soldiers have to traverse 500 to 600 yards of beach surface in the open. Soldiers would prefer to land at high tide to eliminate the extra distance they have to cross in the open; however, because obstacles have been emplaced near the low-water mark and because the landing craft cannot pass over them or defeat them by ramming, the landing has to take place at low tide.

Obstacles and minefields cover the beach. No means have been devised to rapidly destroy them, so they will have to be removed by hand, the slowest and least desirable method. The engineers, in order to do their jobs, will have to be protected by high volumes of naval gunfire, LCT fire, and infantry fire. Close support from the air force cannot be expected. Until the lane-clearing operations are complete, the assault cannot proceed as planned.

The terrain at Omaha Beach greatly multiplies the combat power of the defenders. In an assault in which the infantry is required to generate the combat power necessary to defeat the enemy's defense, it is believed that if the beach is defended by a full division of three regiments, it ought to be considered impregnable and another site less well defended selected for the invasion or another means of generating the necessary combat power considered. If the beach is defended by a full regiment of three battalions, the defense becomes formidable, and the attackers can expect to suffer heavy losses. Although this mission is 'doable,' it is advisable to consider other means of generating the necessary combat power. If the beach is defended by anything less than a regiment, the task is 'doable.' However, if infantry is expected to generate the combat power necessary to overcome the defense, a landing under the cover of darkness is considered preferable.

This summary is by no means complete. The terrain analysis prepared by the operational and tactical headquarters was nearly forty pages long and included numerous maps and diagrams. Still, it covers the major points discussed and analyzed by the planners and leaders of the assault.

General Morgan and his COSSAC staff first selected Omaha Beach as a landing site because it was virtually undefended. In the months leading up to the invasion, however, Rommel changed the character, quality, and strength of the defense. When the German defense and concept for the conduct of that defense changed, the Anglo-American leaders had a reason and an opportunity to reconsider Omaha Beach as landing site. Early in the planning process, Bradley was willing to consider changing the site or the doctrinal approach.[59] Omaha Beach was not the only viable assault beach. By doctrine and practice, the Anglo-American alliance had conducted multiple landings over broad fronts in North Africa, Sicily, and Italy. Hundreds of miles separated the landing sites. When Montgomery developed his plan, one of the tenets on which it was based was greater dispersion of forces over a broader front.[60] He added the Cotentin peninsula landing. Rommel's construction at Omaha Beach made the task of taking the beach considerably more difficult. At this juncture, the operational commanders might have considered another location. Still, even with all of the disadvantages of the terrain at Omaha Beach, an assault was thought to be well within the capabilities of the 1st ID because of the size and quality of the German forces it expected to fight.

ALLIED INTELLIGENCE

Gordon Harrison wrote: 'Allied intelligence had otherwise a remarkably detailed and accurate picture of the German defenses and troop dispositions.' 'Otherwise' was a reference to the failure of intelligence sources to identify the location of the German 352nd Division. Harrison commented: 'Reasons for this failure remain one of the more interesting mysteries of the war.'[61] Since 1951, when Harrison's book was published, the mystery has unraveled a bit. In the 1970s, the British revealed that throughout the war, they were able to read secret German radio transmissions through the efforts of an organization known as Ultra. This intelligence-collecting and deciphering organization used the Germans' Enigma encoding machine against them to break German codes. Thus, the British knew the locations of most of the major German units with a high degree of certainty. According to Ralph Bennett, who worked in the British Intelligence Corps decoding and translating German transmissions during the war:

> Ultra had identified (and in a good many cases located) well over half the garrison type divisions which would be the first line of resistance to the landings. In addition, all the army and corps commands along the coast had been identified at least once, many of them together with evidence showing what units or formations each controlled. This probably did not provide more than a hard core to other information about the tactical disposition of German troops manning the coastal defences, and it no doubt fell a good deal short of what was desirable. Thus 352 Division, a field division of good quality which moved into the Cotentin in March and right up to Omaha Beach a few days before the landings, received only a single mention in ultra before the fighting began.[62]

Although this statement does not solve the mystery, it does indicate that one source of intelligence on the enemy failed to identify the location of all maneuver divisions that could have influenced the situation on D-Day.

More recently, declassified sources revealed that Allied intelligence acquired considerable information on the German defense by intercepting, decoding, and translating telegraphed messages from Japan's ambassador Hiroshi Oshima in Berlin to Japan. Of this source of intelligence, Marshall observed: 'Our main basis of information regarding Hitler's intentions in Europe was obtained from Baron Oshima's messages from Berlin.'[63] Although these messages provided large quantities of valuable detailed information on German war plans, they did not give the location of the 352nd in the month prior to the invasion. Other sources of intelligence, such as French underground organizations and aerial reconnaissance, also failed to reveal the exact location of the 352nd. Thus, none of the intelligence sources detected the exact location of the 352nd until after the invasion forces sailed for Europe.

It was not necessary for American and British military leaders and planners to know the exact location of the 352nd division or any other mobile division. All they needed to know was the general location of the division, and then they could calculate its ability to influence the situation under various conditions given road networks, transportation assets, and other factors. Allied intelligence discovered that the 352nd was twenty miles from Omaha Beach. In other words, the Allies knew the 352nd was already on the battlefield. Although Huebner's battle plan was based on incorrect and incomplete information on the enemy's situation, the worst mistake was the faulty analysis of the information available. In April 1944, the V Corps had the following information on the German Army in the West:

There are 56 divisions in France and the Low Countries. Of these 42 are defensive divisions and 14 are offensive divisions. Twenty-six of the defensive divisions are holding coastal sectors and, since they are not provided with transportation and are definitely tied down to coastal defenses, these divisions do not constitute mobile reserves for early employment against an invading force. The other defensive divisions are either in the interior of France or are unlocated...

Divisions in reserve are not held centrally, but disposed at fairly regular intervals some twenty miles inland from the coast, around centers of communications. During the past few weeks, several Infantry Divisions have been identified immediately behind static coastal divisions along the ENGLISH CHANNEL; these include three static divisions in the CALAIS–DIEPPE area, a static division and *an unidentified division (believed offensive infantry) in the* CHERBOURG–ST LÔ, *area* [the 352nd Division], and an offensive Infantry Division on the BREST Peninsula. *It may be expected that in an emergency the two divisions nearest the area assaulted will move toward it at once, preferably by road. Every effort will be made to bring at least one division into counter-attack on the afternoon of the day of the assault.*[64]

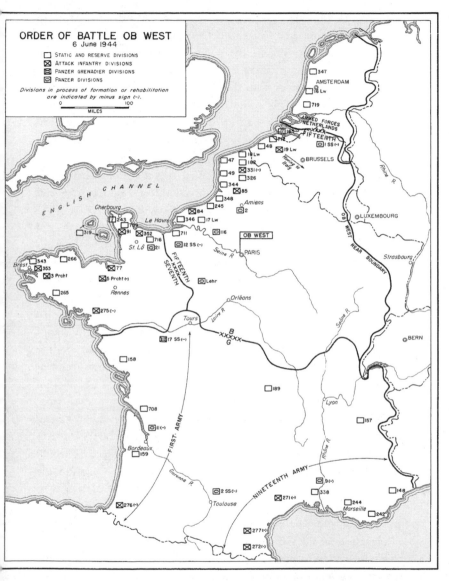

German Army, Order of Battle. From Gordon Harrison, *Cross-Channel Attack*, U.S. Army in World War II (Washington, D.C.: Government Printing Office, 1951).

This report indicates that in April the Allies had a fair picture of Rommel's defense. The German defense had three echelons. First, a thin coastal defense force – the static divisions – and local mobile reserve forces – the offensive infantry and panzer divisions – were located 20 to 100 miles from the coast. Second, operational reserves were located 100 to 150 miles from the coast. And third, strategic reserve forces – primarily panzer divisions – were located over 150 miles from the front, depending on where along the coast the invasion took place. Forces considered in strategic reserve were not limited to divisions in Panzer Group West. Any division that could be redeployed from other fronts was included; for example, the 2nd Panzer Division in the Pas-de-Calais in four days time was part of the strategic reserves for a landing in Normandy. The strength and quality of these units varied; however, the mobile offensive divisions were believed to be of relatively high quality. Thus, the invasion of Normandy can be seen as a sequence of battles: the battle for the beaches with static defense divisions and local reinforcing reserve divisions; the counter-attack battle fought against operational reserves probably on D+1 or D+2; and the final battle fought against strategic reserves probably on or about D+4, depending on the response time of the German leadership in the West, the success of the Allied deception plans, the success of the air force's interdiction mission, and numerous other factors.

Gerow and Huebner had to determine where the enemy's main effort would be made. Would the battle for the beaches be the enemy's main effort before the strategic reserves could be employed, or would the counter-attack be the main effort? They had to analyze the German defense and determine an order of battle and exactly how to array their forces on the battlefield. The final G-2 Estimate of the Enemy Situation before the invasion provided accurate, detailed information on the German defenses. The tactical commanders used this information to produce their own detailed plans. The following information on the enemy's situation was available:

The 716th Division is defending a 53-mile front and a single battalion of this division is defending 21 miles of the coast line in the V Corps assault area. This is not much for a strong coastal defense...

Defense at Beach. The German plan of defense contemplates maximum effort at the beach. The coast defense line is not in great depth; in the V Corps assault area there is no evidence of the construction of an organized system of defenses in rear of the beach crust... In the V Corps assault area the defending battalion is disposed with three rifle companies holding coastal sectors and with the fourth company (heavy weapons) completely broken up and integrated into forward combat groups of the rifle companies... [T]he weapons of both infantry and artillery units are positioned to bring maximum frontal and enfilading fire on the beaches at the instant of landing. At the present time, the German Army is putting forth a great deal of effort to strengthen the coastal crust by placing obstacles along the coastline and by constructing various types of coastal fortifications. Almost nothing along this line is being done in the interior. *All of these things indicate that the enemy intends to defend the coast line as strongly as possible in an effort to hold the attackers until mobile reserves can arrive.*

Counter-attack. (1) *As stated above, the German plan of defense contemplates holding the attacks at the beach until mobile reserves can arrive.* The 716th Division has two regiments forward and probably a divisional battalion (Georgian) in reserve. Each of the forward regiments has a battalion in reserve. Two battalions of light artillery and one of medium are disposed in coastal positions in the divisional sector. Thus, in the sector held by the 716th three infantry battalions are available as local reserves, and these reserves must suffice for local counter-attack until the arrival of elements of mobile divisions... (4) In view of his desire to limit the penetration of the hostile forces and the difficulties to be expected in their rapid deployment, initially the enemy will undoubtedly commit his panzer and panzergrenadier combat teams as they arrive. *He may also commandeer local transportation and send one combat team of the 352nd Division into action on the afternoon of D-day.* As other elements appear on the scene and time becomes available for regrouping, co-ordinated attacks will be the general rule.[65]

This analysis was based on the belief that tactical surprise would be achieved. If tactical surprise had not been expected, the G-2 should have figured that given the distance of the 352nd Division from Omaha Beach, twenty miles, the lead elements of the division would have arrived within nine hours and that if indeed vehicular transportation was 'commandeered,' elements of the division could have been in place within three to four hours after notification of the pending invasion.

The leaders of the 1st ID and V Corps had enough information available on the location and capability of the 352nd Division to plan to fight it on D-Day at H-Hour. Given the relatively slim chance of such a vast armada crossing the Channel undetected and given the fact that sea lane-clearing operations took place in sight of the invasion beaches a day prior to the assault, it is difficult to understand how any other conclusion could have been drawn. If the invasion fleet dropped anchor at 0200 and was not detected until that time, the Germans still would have won the race to the water's edge. The G-2 estimate also delineated the capabilities of German air power:

> *Air Action.* The German Air Force is capable of making 1,500 sorties per day in the Channel area... Although enemy air attacks against the United Kingdom have been increasing in recent weeks, it is not likely that heavy commitments will be made against strongly protected concentration and embarkation areas, but when the cross-channel movement is detected the German Air Force may be expected to employ its maximum strength against convoys and against the actual landing operations.[66]

Only one airplane was needed to detect the movement of the Allied fleet. There is no good explanation for the failure of the United States to plan to fight the 352nd Division at Omaha Beach. It was not an intelligence failure, as commonly believed. It was a failure to properly analyze available intelligence. It was a failure to ascribe to the enemy the same level of competency the Allies ascribed to themselves. The Germans possessed the aircraft and small boats to conduct reconnaissance of British ports in the south of England. Thus, it should have been taken as a fact that the German forces would have a minimum of twelve hours notice – the time it took to cross the Channel with the invasion fleet – and that all forces within a twelve-hour radius of the invasion beaches would have to be defeated at the water's edge, given the German concept for the conduct of the defense. And a worst-case scenario would have extended this period to twenty-four hours.

However, the real intelligence failure was on the part of Germans. They allowed the Allies to achieve tactical surprise in an operation that threatened the very existence of Germany. The G-2 estimate continued:

> *Defense in Successive positions.* [A] major counter-attack will not be possible until the arrival of mobile forces which are at least five hours away. Pending the arrival of mobile elements the defending forces in the coastal sector will most likely seek to prevent our establishment and expansion of a beachhead by defense in successive positions. Since the mobile forces which are nearest the assault area will probably arrive in small combat groups on widely separated roads, it is expected that they will attempt to continue the defense along successive lines to prevent expansion of the beachhead until the arrival of a sufficient mobile force to stage a co-ordinated counter-attack.[67]

This was the information on which Gerow and Huebner built their plans for the assault at Omaha Beach and the subsequent battles with enemy reserves. They believed that the enemy's main effort would be made on the beach and that the enemy forces located on the beaches would be alert and ready to fight at H-Hour but would be too meager to put up a sustained defense. They believed that the 716th Division's organic reserve battalions would have to be called forward and would arrive piecemeal one or two hours after the initiation of the invasion.

They thought elements of the 352nd Division would not be in action until the 'afternoon' of D-Day. Thus, at H-Hour on D-Day, the tactical commanders expected to fight one poor-quality German battalion, and during the morning of D-Day, they expected to fight one poor-quality German regiment committed to the battle piecemeal. Because of the perceived weakness of the German defense at Omaha and because of the high expectations of Allied air and naval firepower, the initial assault to defeat the water's edge defense was considered a *fait accompli*.

BATTLE PLANS OF THE 1ST INFANTRY DIVISION

The initial assault at Omaha Beach can be divided into two phases. Phase 1 was the first 1,000 yards, the assault on the beach defense, and Phase 2 was the advance inland to the D-Day Phase Line.

In Phase 1, Huebner and Gerow had to choose between five forms of maneuver: envelopment, turning movement, penetration, frontal attack, and infiltration.[68] It was not possible to conduct an envelopment or a turning movement because of the terrain and enemy defense. A penetration maneuver masses forces to break through on a narrow front. This maneuver was not feasible because of the dispersion required by the numerous landing ships, landing craft, DD tanks, and other vessels. Huebner and Gerow had two choices: frontal attack or infiltration. They could land directly in front of the beach exits and conduct a frontal attack or land between the heavily fortified beach exits and attempt to infiltrate between them. They decided to conduct a frontal assault against the most heavily fortified sectors of the defense, the beach exits. Thompson, in an article written in June 1944, delineated the principles upon which the tactical plans for battle were based:

> Pursuant to a bold decision to make this a daylight landing, H-hour was to be 0630 in the morning an hour after sunrise... The grand tactics of the Normandy invasion operation consisted of applying

overwhelming force at the critical point... Virtually four infantry companies [in a given sector] heavily reinforced by tanks would land at H-hour. Thus the landing-assault was a case of throwing regiments against battalions and even companies. That there was any doubt at all about the outcome was due to the obstacles and fortifications which augmented greatly the strength of the outnumbered defenders.[69]

The plan Thompson outlined was primarily an infantry assault; the battle was to be won by applying overwhelming numbers of men in daylight against a deliberate defense. Thompson and other American planners should have considered the assessment of the defense at Gallipoli in the *British Official Military History:* 'So strong were the defenses of this beach that, even though the garrison was but one company of infantry, the Turks may well have considered them impregnable to an attack from open boats.'[70] A well-prepared defense, one with good terrain, protection from enemy fire, and sufficient automatic and rapid-fire weapons, could defeat a force many times its strength. If the battles for the beaches were to be won by infantry, the invasion should have started under the cover of darkness and infiltration tactics should have been employed. If the battles were to be won by firepower resources, conditions that maximized the effectiveness of those resources should have been sought and frontal attack tactics should have been employed.

Thompson's description of the battle calls to mind battles of the American Civil War such as Fredericksburg or assaults such as Pickett's Charge at Gettysburg, in which infantry attacked fortified positions across an open stretch of terrain. Thompson's comments support the assessment of Russell Weigley and Chester Wilmot that it was folly for the U.S. Army to commit troops in a direct, frontal assault against the most heavily fortified positions in daylight when the maximum effectiveness of weapons could have been brought to bear against them.

Thompson's view was that of a tactical commander. During the invasion, he commanded the 6th ESB.[71] At each level of war, commanders have to plan to win battles with the resources they control under the orders they are given and the conditions that exist.

Thompson's perspective emphasized a daylight assault based on human waves. Operational and strategic commanders could bring other resources to bear. They had a different perspective, a different vision.

The battle was not won with the frontal attack maneuver. Most of the men who attacked the beach exits were slaughtered before they could reach the obstacles and minefields. Entire companies were rendered combat ineffective moments after landing. The battle was eventually won with infiltration tactics, attacking through the area between the strongpoints. Huebner's assault plan failed, and the soldiers had to improvise new tactical solutions in the midst of battle. However, Gerow and Huebner selected the correct maneuver given the operational plans of Montgomery and Bradley.

In hindsight, it has been argued that the tactical commanders erred in judgment in planning the Normandy invasion; however, that error was based on improperly conceived doctrine, unproven techniques and technology, and a flawed operational plan. Infiltration techniques called for covert movement of the assault force through enemy lines. This approach was most effective under conditions of limited visibility, in dense terrain where movement could be concealed, in poorly defended areas where the enemy's defense was incapable of covering the entire front, or in areas where any combination of these conditions prevailed.[72]

Infiltration at Omaha Beach would have been impossible if the entire 352nd Division had been prepared to fight at H-Hour on D-Day. Given the range of modern weapons and the number of soldiers in a typical German infantry division, the entire width of Omaha Beach could have been covered, with at least one battalion left in reserve.[73]

The infiltration approach was probably initially rejected for the following reasons. First, the expectation that strategic bombers and naval gunfire would clear the way was extremely high. Eisenhower, Montgomery, and Bradley told Gerow, Huebner, and the soldiers of the 1st ID that these forces would effectively destroy the enemy's defenses. Second, the Allies evinced a low regard for the capabilities of the German Army, particularly the static coastal divisions. Third, the Allies were impatient to begin the build-up.[74] There was a rush to open the beach exits and start moving vehicles through them. Fourth, incomplete intelligence and faulty analysis of available intelligence told Gerow and Huebner that the enemy's defense was inadequately manned by poor-quality troops. Therefore, they concluded it was not necessary to use infiltration tactics. And fifth, by achieving tactical surprise, they hoped to catch the enemy in a poor state of readiness. During this period, the Allied armies could advance with relative ease. If Montgomery and Bradley had been correct in their assessment of the course and conduct of the battle, Huebner and Gerow would also have been correct in their selection of the maneuver. In fact, given the operational plan, Gerow and Huebner selected the appropriate maneuver.

In Phase 2, the advance inland, there were two possible approaches. Huebner and Gerow could have concentrated their forces or dispersed them. They decided to disperse their forces in a semicircle, conduct link-up movements to the east and west, establish strongpoint defenses to the south on the high ground, and then fill in the gaps in the defense and move it forward as force became available. Huebner's approach was based on the assumption that tactical surprise would be achieved. Greater risk could be taken if surprise was achieved. By dispersing his forces to the west, southwest, south, southeast, and east, Huebner assumed greater risk. If he was attacked while his forces were so distributed, small, independent, company-size battles would have taken place across the division's front. A more conservative approach would have been to concentrate his forces in one sector of the beach-head, form an unbroken line, and conduct a division or regimental defense.

Huebner, however, had an insurance policy. The 2nd Battalion, 116th Infantry, and 2nd Battalion, 16th Infantry, were to move rapidly to occupy the most defensible terrain in the vicinity, and the reserve battalions were to come in behind them. If the advance became too difficult, if enemy opposition was stronger than the initial forces could overcome, instead of passing through the defending battalions, the

reserve battalions could fill in the gaps and form a defensive perimeter. The two regiments could be linked up, and a division perimeter
formed. Thus, with few additional maneuvers, the division could
quickly form a fairly strong defense. Of course, the two battalions that
were conducting the linkup to the east and west would be pretty
much on their own.

The 1st ID's orders to its RCTs specified how the regimental
commanders were to deploy their battalions and companies to
achieve the division's objectives. Omaha Beach was divided roughly
down the middle. Each RCT had approximately three kilometers of
beach on which to land. The boundary between the 116th and the
16th RCTs ran southwest through the village of Saint Laurent-sur-
Mer, through Formigny, to the Aure River. This would eventually
become the boundary between the 1st and 29th Divisions. The plan
for the capture of Omaha Beach, the coastline to the west and east,
and the high ground behind Omaha Beach divided the area into
battalion-size objectives. Demarcation lines called the Beachhead
Maintenance Line and the D-Day Phase Line were used to establish
the limits to which battalions were to advance during a particular
phase of the assault. With these measures, the division headquarters
could control the movement of forces. The limit of advance, the D-
Day Phase Line, ran roughly from Isigny in the west, to Canchy, to
Trévières, to the Isigny–Bayeux road in the east.

The 1st ID's coastal 'zone of action,' Omaha Beach, was divided first
into areas designated Baker, Charlie, Dog, Easy, Fox, and George. The
main assault would take place in areas Dog, Easy, and Fox. These areas
varied from two and a half to three and a half kilometers in length and
were further divided into areas designated Green, White, and Red.
The 116th RCT was to assault on Beaches Dog: Green, Dog: White,
Dog: Red, and Easy: Green, and the 16th RCT was to assault on
Beaches Easy: Red and Fox: Green.

The 116th RCT was to deploy one ranger company and two battalion landing teams in the initial assault. The third battalion landing team
was to follow. The 116th RCT was to '[r]educe beach defenses in its

zone of action, seize and secure that portion of the Beachhead Maintenance Line in its zone of action, capture POINTE DU HOE, and seize and secure that portion of D-Day phase line in its zone of action by two hours before dark on D-day.[75] Additional D-Day missions called for the 116th RCT to gain and maintain contact with the U.S. VII Corps on the right; capture Isigny, Vierville-sur-Mer, Longueville, Grandcamp, and several small villages; and carry out patrolling to the D-Day Phase Line. Thus, the 116th was responsible for capturing and/or destroying all enemy forces in the area west to the Vire River and south to the Aure River, an area of approximately fifty square miles, on D-Day. It was also responsible for the capture of Pointe du Hoe. For this mission, it was given two ranger battalions. The linkup with units landing at Pointe du Hoe, a distance of roughly five and a half miles, also had to be accomplished on D-Day.

The 1st Battalion, 116th RCT, was to land on Beach Dog: Green with five companies in column, including one company from the attached ranger battalions. Its mission was to reduce the beach defenses, turn west to capture the fortifications along the coast from the western limits of Omaha Beach to Pointe du Hoe, and capture the town of Vierville-sur-Mer. Once these missions were accomplished, the battalion was to assist the rangers in capturing the beach fortifications between Pointe du Hoe and Isigny and then prepare to capture Isigny. The 1st Battalion landed in one of the most heavily fortified sectors of the beach. The beach exit to Vierville was directly in front of Beach Dog: Green. A reinforced company, it was believed, defended the beach exit.

The 2nd Battalion, 116th RCT, was to land on Beaches Dog: White, Dog: Red, and Easy: Green with three companies abreast. Its mission was to reduce the beach defenses in its sector, capture the village of Saint Laurent-sur-Mer, seize the high ground 2,500 yards southwest of Saint Laurent, and then construct a hasty defensive position with all-around defensive capabilities. The beach exit to Saint Laurent was also believed to be defended by a reinforced company. In order to achieve its D-Day objectives, the 116th RCT first had to take control of the two beach exits in its vicinity.

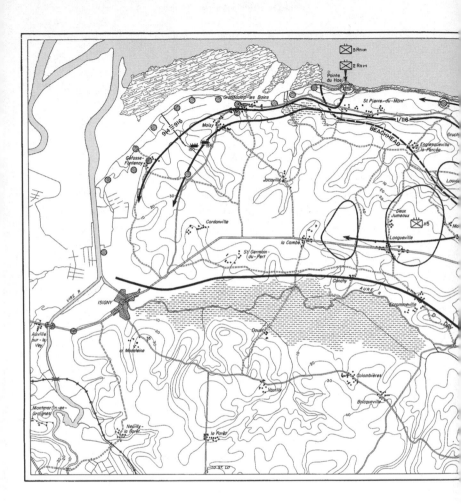

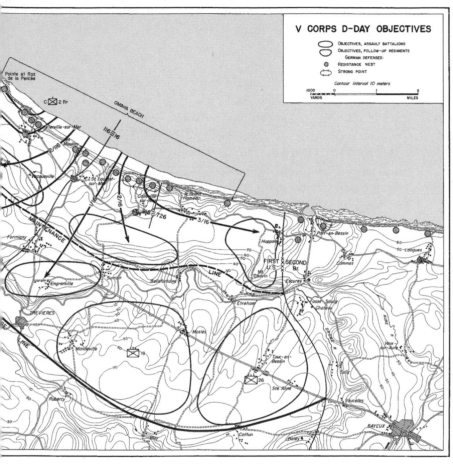

V Corps, D-Day Objectives. From Gordon Harrison, *Cross-Channel Attack,* U.S. Army in World War II (Washington, D.C.: Government Printing Office, 1951).

Huebner ordered the concentration of forces on Beach Dog: Green, directly in front of the enemy's strongest defense. On this beach alone, Huebner assaulted with four companies in column, including one ranger company. The results were disastrous and led to charges of incompetence by British and American students of the invasion.

The 3rd Battalion, 116th RCT, was designated the reserve battalion. It was to land with companies abreast behind the 2nd Battalion on Beaches Dog: White, Dog: Red, and Easy: Green. It was to pass through the 2nd Battalion, capture the village of Longueville and the high ground 2,500 yards west of the village, dig in and establish a hasty defense with all-around security, and then send out patrols to conduct reconnaissance of the town of Isigny in preparation for capturing it.

The 16th RCT was to land on Beaches Easy: Red and Fox: Green with two battalions abreast. Its mission was to '[r]educe the beach defenses in its zone of action, seize and secure that portion of the Beachhead Maintenance Line in its zone of action, and the high ground north of TREVIERES, gain and maintain contact with 116th Combat Team on the right and British 50th Division on the left.'[76]

The 2nd Battalion was to land on Beach Easy: Red with two companies abreast followed by two companies abreast. Its mission was to reduce the beach defenses, capture the village of Colleville-sur-Mer, capture the high ground approximately 2,500 yards south of Beach Easy: Red – the commanding terrain feature – dig in and establish an all-around defensive position, prepare to repel an enemy counter-attack, gain and maintain contact with the 2nd Battalion, 116th RCT, and patrol to Trévières, located near the D-Day Phase Line.

The 3rd Battalion was to land on Beach Fox: Green with two companies abreast followed by two companies abreast. Its mission was to reduce the beach defenses; turn east to reduce the coastal defenses between Omaha Beach and the British sector; gain and maintain contact with the British 50th Division; capture the high ground 3,000 yards to the southwest; seize the villages of Le Grand Hameau, La Vailee, and Saint Honorine-Despertes; dig in and establish an all-around defensive position; prepare to repel a counter-attack; and patrol to Huppain and Tour en Bessin.

The 1st Battalion was designated the reserve unit. It was to land on Beach Easy: Red behind the 2nd Battalion, pass through the 2nd Battalion, gain and maintain contact with the 116th RCT on the right and the 18th RCT on the left when it landed, capture the villages of Formigny and Surrain, seize the high ground north of Trévières, secure the bridges across the Aure River south and south-west of Trévières, establish a defensive position with all-around security, prepare to repel a counter-attack, and conduct patrols to the Bayeux–Saint-Lô Road.

The expectations for D-Day were impressive by any standards. To conduct the planned movement without encountering and fighting the enemy made major demands on the soldiers. These expectations make it clear that the Americans grossly underestimated the capabilities of the German Army. The Americans did not believe German soldiers were capable of the same level of exertion as American soldiers. If they had, they would have expected to fight the 352nd Division, a mere twenty miles away, on Omaha Beach at H-Hour.

Epilogue
The Question of American Military Skill

Mission and concept-of-operation statements must be developed that put subordinates into the mind of the commander and enable freedom of action by subordinates in harmony with each other and in harmony with the commander's intent. The German Army calls this aftragstaktik, that is, the promotion of harmonious thinking at all echelons of command, which enables subordinates to understand and carry out the mission concept of their superiors.

General Richard E. Cavazos

The necessity to integrate two very different practices of war, two very different military traditions, and two very different amphibious doctrines in combined operations caused in part the near disaster at Omaha Beach. The Anglo-American planners developed and employed a hybrid amphibious doctrine that operationally and tactically was not as sound as either British Mediterranean doctrine or American Pacific doctrine. Montgomery was so impressed with the potential combat power of the strategic bomber force that he partially adopted the American vision of war, a vision based on overwhelming firepower. By failing to adhere to the tested tenets of either doctrine, he eroded the potential combat power available to him – maximizing neither firepower nor the advantages of darkness.

A commander charged with the conduct of offensive actions against a prepared enemy defense can conduct the operation during the hours of darkness, daylight, or 'half-light' (half-light being the period of transition from night to day or day to night). A commander's decision on the time of attack is based on his estimate of relative combat power and the types and mix of forces available to him. The Chinese Army in Korea preferred night attacks because the darkness concealed their movements; limited the effectiveness of American weapons; maximized the chance of achieving some degree of surprise; and caused some degree of fear, uncertainty, and confusion among the defenders. The Chinese lacked the quality and quantity of artillery, air power, and naval gunfire available to the Americans; therefore, the logical choice for them was the night attack. During the hours of daylight, they could not achieve the necessary fire superiority to succeed in attacks against the U.S. Army without suffering extraordinarily high casualties.

In the Pacific theater during World War II, the U.S. Marine Corps conducted all of its major assault landings during the hours of daylight. The mix of forces available in Admiral Chester Nimitz's Central Pacific theater included the vast majority of America's most lethal naval weapon systems: battleships, cruisers, destroyers, and aircraft carriers. Marines always enjoyed a substantial firepower advantage over their Japanese opponents. And as the marine-navy team became more proficient in the conduct of amphibious assaults, the length of its bombardments from air and sea increased. At Tarawa in November 1943, the pre-invasion bombardment was three hours in duration. At Iwo Jima in February 1945, the pre-invasion bombardment was three days in duration. And at Okinawa in April 1945, the pre-invasion bombardment went on for seven days.

A commander with conspicuously superior fire support will give up the element of surprise and the concealment of darkness to insure the accurate delivery and concentration of fire on the objective, whereas a commander who lacks fire superiority 'must be expected to close with the enemy under cover of darkness or unfavorable weather' to achieve his objectives, according to a 1951 article published in the *Military Review* by Lieutenant Colonel William Shanahan, artillery instructor at the U.S. Army Command and General Staff College. Shanahan observed:

> In general, a force that is dependent largely for success on superior air and artillery support will favor daylight attacks in order to exploit these means most advantageously. Conversely, a force that lacks this superiority must be expected to close with the enemy under cover of darkness or unfavorable weather... The commander, in his estimate, must consider whether he can better accomplish his mission by attacking in daylight, using the full effect of his air and artillery to blast his way into the enemy position, or whether he is more apt to obtain success, with fewer casualties, by attempting to capitalize on surprise by attacking at night or during bad weather.[1]

U.S. Navy commanders believed the army did not take full advantage of naval gunfire to support landing operations, primarily because of a lack of trust.[2]

The problem with the plan for the invasion of Europe was that the planners pursued two incompatible doctrines, believing that air power made possible the combination of the decisive elements in both doctrines. As a result, they failed to maximize the firepower available by attacking in daylight after a substantial bombardment had destroyed the water's edge defense, and they failed to maximize the elements of surprise, confusion, and concealment provided by attacking during the hours of darkness. The planners of the Normandy invasion sought three objectives, two of which could not be reconciled. They sought to maximize the hours of daylight for the build-up, achieve tactical surprise, and achieve overwhelming firepower superiority. They sought too many objectives, and as a consequence, compromises were made that failed to maximize the potential of either a day or a night attack in terms of combat power. The plan was compromised to the point of diminishing their chances for success, and at Omaha Beach, the situation was not as fortuitous as it was on the other beaches.

The battle for Omaha Beach had to be won in the most costly manner conceivable – infantry assault against a prepared, deliberate defensive position in daylight, with all of the disadvantages inherent to an amphibious assault. The combat power necessary to overcome the defense at Omaha Beach had to be generated by the infantry and Admiral Hall's destroyers. Lieutenant General Raymond S. McLain, who served two years with combat units in the Mediterranean and European theaters, commented in the *Military Review* in 1947:

> In this day of multiplicity of means of procuring fire power, the infantryman should never be required, unless in very exceptional cases, to develop the fire power necessary for his advance. It can much better be developed by mortars, by machine guns using overhead or flanking fire; by artillery and by air support. The infantryman has an infinitely greater problem in working his way forward behind this fire support, and any attempt on his part to use his rifle prematurely or to secure a superiority of fire by his own means will only subtract from his effort to get forward, slow his advance and cause great casualties.[3]

After the shocking battle of Omaha Beach, questions were asked: 'Why did not the planners for NEPTUNE provide several days bombing and bombardment of German strongpoints, as later at Iwo Jima and Okinawa, instead of a scant half-hour at break of day? Why didn't bombers and naval guns pulverize the German defenses? Hadn't the Navy learned the value of its own support? Did there have to be all that carnage on the beaches?' Samuel Eliot Morison provides the answer to this question: '[O]wing to the imperative need for tactical surprise very little had been done to bomb the immediate beach defenses and the Navy was not given time enough to do it.'[4] This is only a partial explanation. The thinking of the operational planners of the Normandy invasion was also influenced by the overly optimistic expectations concerning air power, a low regard for German intelligence and military capability, a lack of recognition of the combat power necessary to overcome a deliberate defense, a lack of appreciation of the capabilities of naval gunfire, an incomplete understanding of Rommel's concept for the conduct of the defense, and an inaccurate analysis of the intelligence available. The tenets on which the plan was based failed to maximize the combat power of the Allied forces assembled.

Not only was the Allied plan for the invasion of Europe flawed, but the German plan for the defense of Europe was also flawed. The German system for intelligence gathering and analysis broke down completely. And the German defense at Normandy was not of the quality of a German World War I defense. Had the Anglo-American alliance fought a defense of the design and quality of those constructed by Hindenburg and Ludendorff, Churchill's worst nightmares would have been realized and the battle for Normandy would have failed. The Wehrmacht that had pioneered Blitzkrieg warfare and restored mobility to the battlefield forgot many of the hard-learned lessons of World War I defensive doctrine. The German defense lacked depth and elasticity.

Simply put, the decision to assault at 'half-light' was a bad one. It was a decision that ignored years of experience gained at high cost in the Mediterranean and Pacific theaters and failed to maximize the 1st ID's chances for success as well as the chances of other assault divisions. The reasons for this decision were systemic. The exigencies upon which the planning process was based corrupted the vision of the assault. Operational decisions made in planning the Normandy invasion were the result of an emphasis on Allied co-operation, the British vision of war, American resources, the inability of the Allies to put in place a single operational commander, service arrogance, the lack of joint doctrine, and the belief that the operation was so unique that new doctrine and techniques were required. This thinking caused Americans to violate basic principles, such as 'Train the way you fight.'

The decision-making process used in World War II represented a break from the American and U.S. Army tradition. In World War II, the decision-making process became more complex. Coalition warfare became the norm, and the navy and air force came to play a more significant and larger role in warfare. The exigencies of preserving the coalition and of appeasing the egos of the individual services became part of the decision-making process. The exigencies for decision making in World War II represented a change in the military tradition of the United States, and although the political objective typically remained foremost in the minds of commanders at the strategic level, the most efficient use of the army became subject to the needs of the coalition, the needs of the other services, and the needs of the machines – technology. This type of decision-making later became the norm during the Cold War era.

It can be argued that by maintaining the coalition, by placing the exigencies of coalition warfare before those of the army, the interests of the army and its soldiers are attended to because the burden of war is shared by all nations involved. It can be argued that competition between the services is a good thing, that by competing, the best of all of the armed forces is realized. Still, the decision-making process is more complex, and where to draw the line between competing interests is problematic. The danger is that tenets vital to the success of the operation can be masked or compromised by peripheral issues important to a given service or foreign nation. The vision for the operation can be so eroded as to make the plan unworkable. The plan for the Normandy invasion is an example of the problems inherent in coalition warfare and joint operations. The Anglo-American planning team put together and executed a plan that had the very real potential of failing.

SOLDIERS

Both inexperienced and veteran soldiers were shocked by the situation that developed at Omaha Beach. What they had been told to expect and what they saw, felt, and heard were categorically different. John W. Baumgartner of the 16th Infantry later wrote:

> A tragic fact became apparent, immediately. The three enemy strong points in this vicinity [the area of operation of the 16th Infantry], which were supposed to have been destroyed, or neutralized by Air Force bombardment and naval guns and rockets, were still in action... The fact that coastal batteries had not been silenced by the terrific pre-landing bombardment had a demoralizing effect on the surviving troops.[5]

Statements similar to this can be found in all of the unit histories. The authors of *Danger Forward: The Story of the First Division in World War II* noted: 'The assault troops experienced their worst disappointment of the day when they found the beach untouched by air bombardment and soon realized that the air bombardment had little effect on the beach defenses.' Joseph Balkoski wrote of the 29th ID:

> They were assured that the Germans on the beach would be blasted with bombs and naval gunfire prior to landing... Bradley emphasized that the 116th was not alone; the navy and Army Air Force, he said, would prepare the way. He concluded with a prediction the men would remember: *"You men should consider yourselves lucky. You are going to have ringside seats for the greatest show on earth."*[6]

The most telling account of the state of mind of the soldiers comes from the 115th Infantry, which was scheduled to begin movement toward the shore at 0930:

> It came as quite a shock to many when, just prior to going ashore, the men assembled on the decks of the landing craft and heard that they might have to land fighting. *Briefing had stressed the fact that the landing itself would be relatively simple; that the troops would merely walk ashore, make for the high ground, and then walk until the objective was reached.* Many of the men had put on clean socks the night before in anticipation of a long hike their first day ashore.[7]

The military historian Max Hastings quoted Private Lindley Higgins of the 4th ID, which landed at Utah Beach:

> [I was] dumb enough not to feel the slightest trepidation. We really thought that at any moment the whole Reich was going to collapse. We saw what we had, heard what they didn't have. We really thought that we only had to step off that beach and all the krauts would put up their hands.[8]

Prior to the invasion, American soldiers and sailors were conditioned to believe that the assault would not be 'too difficult,' that the German defenders were of lesser quality and in a poor state of preparation and readiness, and that American air and naval power would be decisive. American leaders began to downplay the fighting quality of the German Army and overemphasize the capabilities of air power prior to the invasion of Europe. A veteran of the Sicily campaign, Captain Reed, executive officer of the 1st Battalion, 180th Infantry, warned: '[W]e have got to stop belittling the fighting ability of the German. The enemy is vicious, clever, and ruthless. It is going to take leadership of the highest order to whip him for good and all.'[9] General James Gavin explained:

> Sicily had been a sobering experience. For years we had been told that our weapons were superior to any we would encounter. After all, we were soldiers from the most highly industrialized and richest nation on earth. But the very preoccupation with our advanced technology caused many to assume technology alone would win battles – more emphasis was placed upon victory through airpower than better infantry.[10]

The lack of contact of many American leaders with good-quality German units prior to the invasion of Europe may account for this tendency of senior American leaders to belittle the fighting ability of the German Army. In North Africa and Sicily, the U.S. Army, with some exceptions, did not meet the best German organizations, and in both campaigns, the Germans were already on the defensive and in the process of withdrawing.

The American enthusiasm for air power was infectious. The navy also came to believe air power would be decisive. Prior to sending the navy's underwater demolition teams to clear the obstacles at Omaha Beach, Hall met with the men to inspire them by expressing his confidence in their ability to accomplish this important mission, the plan for the invasion, and the air support they would receive. He later recalled: 'I knew they had a tough job and I wanted to be with them. I went in and told them that I'd like to go ashore with them but I couldn't. I told them they were being supported by the greatest air support in history because I had been told that 10,000 aircraft were supporting my forces... I was sucker enough to believe it... I told them that they had this job to do which sounded difficult but which *I didn't think was too difficult because they had the greatest air support in history.*'[11] Hall echoed the comments of V Corps commander General Gerow, who months earlier, in an effort to suppress rumors that the landing force would suffer 'high casualties,' told his subordinate leaders that 'in his opinion, the operation is not a too difficult one, and that there should not be the slightest question that our objective will not be reached.'[12] In an address to the men of the V Corps prior to the invasion, Gerow emphasized the weakness of the enemy and the strength of Allied naval and air forces:

Officers and Men of the V Corps:

You have been selected by the Supreme Allied Commander to perform the most important military operation in the history of the world. Your task will be to destroy the Nazi defenders of the gate to Western Europe and to lead our victorious forces on to Berlin. The way has been prepared for you – the Hun has been driven from the sea, annihilated by the Russians, kicked out of Africa, bombed from the air and is now nervously and hopelessly waiting for you to deliver the knockout blow.

You are well prepared to do the job. No troops have ever entered battle better trained or more magnificently equipped. Supporting us will be the tremendous resources of the Allied Naval and Air Forces. Success is assured. With victory will come the eternal gratitude of freedom-loving nations the world over.

I have implicit confidence in your professional ability, your courage and your determination. Hit hard and keep going forward. We fight on God's side and cannot fail. Good luck to all of you.[13]

By emphasizing the reduced state of the enemy and the 'tremendous' naval and air support, Gerow and other American and British commanders created expectations that were proven to be false on Omaha Beach. In *Army Talk,* Montgomery told American soldiers:

We have got this war absolutely gripped in a firm hold and the enemy cannot escape. The only uncertain thing now is when the war is going to end. You can choose your own date and put your money on it. I have not the slightest doubt that if the battle front and the home front really get down to it this year we can get the thing almost finished – held so tightly that next year we just topple it over. At the end of this year, if not sooner, we shall have it just about right for toppling over.[14]

Thus, the senior operational commander told American soldiers that the war was essentially over. It was a *fait accompli.* Montgomery's words may have had unintended effects.

The American dream, adopted by the British, of winning battles and wars with technology, the allure of air power, and assumptions about the low quality of the German Army created a false sense of security in commanders that caused them to fail to adequately prepare American soldiers and sailors psychologically for the battle ahead. They painted a false picture, and in the process, they may have contributed to the paralysis that afflicted some soldiers. The overly optimistic expectations of operational commanders, which were allowed to persist by some tactical commanders (although there is evidence that some small-unit leaders in the battle-tested 16th Infantry gave their soldiers a more precise understanding of the coming battle), probably damaged the fighting ability of the divisions. Captain Richard F. Bush gave an eyewitness account of the battle:

> They lay there motionless and staring into space. They were so thoroughly shocked that they had no consciousness of what went on. Many had forgotten they had firearms to use. Others who had lost their arms didn't seem to see that there were weapons lying all around them. Some could not hold a weapon after it was forced into their hands. Others, when told to start cleaning a rifle, simply stared as if they had never heard such an order before. Their nerves were spent and nothing could be done about them. The fire continued to search for them, and if they were hit, they slumped lower into the sands and did not even call out for an aid man.[15]

A report from the 29th ID read:

> The tide was coming in very fast and the beach was crowded with men, most of whom were immobilized and seemed incapable of action... At that point I saw a large number of men and officers lying around and doing nothing. Some were wounded but most of them appeared to be dazed.[16]

One soldier from the 16th Infantry recalled:

> When that shell burst, I got up and I guess I panicked. I started crying. There was a ship to our right that had dry docked, tied at one end, and my buddies got me behind that ship, where I cried for what seemed like hours. I cried until tears would no longer come. Suddenly, I felt something, I can't explain it, but a feeling went through my body a warm feeling went through my body, and I stopped crying and came to my senses.[17]

More soldiers probably had such experiences than were willing to admit, and green soldiers were probably more afflicted than veteran soldiers.

This story of soldiers being temporarily paralyzed by fear was told over and over again. It appears that a significant number of men experienced shock and were initially incapable of advancing. This paralysis eroded the combat power of the division and led to many casualties. Only by advancing and seeking the cover available could men expect to survive the hail of well-aimed missiles launched at them.

The configuration of the German defense and the nature of the terrain at Omaha Beach facilitated the onset of the shock and paralysis that afflicted some of the men of the 1st and 29th IDs. Action can mitigate the influence of fear and forestall the development of shock and paralysis by limiting exposure and providing an alternative outcome to the obvious one taking place before a soldier.[18] Amphibious operations preclude movement to the rear, and at Omaha Beach, the 400- to 500-meter stretch of beach covered with numerous obstacles and, most significant, the 150- to 170-foot bluff from which enemy fire rained down and which eliminated the possibility of immediately closing with the enemy, seemed to preclude forward movement. The inability to retreat and the seeming inability to advance, to get at the enemy, immobilized soldiers and thus facilitated the onset of shock and paralysis.[19] Colonel John Kelly, who fought in Patton's Third Army, observed: 'Once men stop and seek cover under heavy enemy fire, it's a tough job getting them out and going again. A man under fire usually feels safer staying wherever he is, even with inadequate cover, than in moving forward.'[20]

The shock and subsequent paralysis were caused by the mind's failure to accept the situation the eyes beheld. They were caused by sensory and cognitive overload, a condition known as psychological dislocation. In more recent times, the term 'acute stress-induced psychosis' has been used to describe this phenomenon.[21] The dead mangled bodies of friends, the concussion and noise of artillery rounds and other ordnance exploding nearby, the whistle of bullets, and the ever-present threat of death were, in many cases, too much for the uninitiated mind to comprehend. The citation awarded the 16th Infantry after the battle stated:

Within a few hours almost a third of the assault strength were casualties. Men dragged themselves shoreward leaderless and scattered by the loss of key personnel. Blocked from advancing by minefields, pinned down by annihilating fire, wave after wave piled up on a seven yard beachhead until thousands of men lay huddled on the fire swept shore. In the face of an apparently hopeless situation the 16th Infantry began its reorganization. Officers and men gathered the remnant of their unit together, and slowly, with groups being cut down almost as soon as formed, began to develop from a confused, hurt mass into a cohesive, determined fighting force.[22]

The author of this citation, perhaps the regimental commander, recognized that something transformed many of the men on that beach on D-Day. He realized that some soldiers required a period of adjustment, during which they came to accept the situation and the fact that they might die and then resolved to act. The time required for this adjustment varied from soldier to soldier. Some soldiers were permanently scarred psychologically by the experience – as is the case in every major hard-fought battle.[23] What is clear is that the period of adjustment could be dramatically shortened or even eliminated by the presence of strong leaders.[24] Men like General Norman D. Cota of the 29th ID, Colonel George A. Taylor of the 16th Infantry, and numerous lieutenants, sergeants, and privates were able to spur others into action. Paralysis was therefore caused in part by a lack of strong leadership. In the initial landing, a large number of primary leaders, that is, company commanders and platoon leaders, were killed or wounded in their attempt to lead from the front by exiting the landing craft first. The standing division order 'that an officer be the first man to go off the boat' eliminated many leaders in the first moments of the battle.[25] In the various narratives of the battle, it is not uncommon to read statements such as: 'No leaders were there to give orders, and none was given. Each man made his own decision.'[26] Natural leaders, some of whom were privates, had to rise to the fore and fight their individual battles with those men who would follow.

The 'greenness' of many soldiers may also have slowed the development of an improvised offense. Colonel Henry J. Matchett, an observer and leader of men in combat in World War II, noted:

> In combat we found that green troops would invariably freeze when first coming under fire. They would stop, seek cover, and then try to find the enemy. They could not see any clear distinct targets. Therefore they did not fire. Their casualties increased. The conditions under which they had been trained to open fire simply did not exist... I recall one instance in particular. A rifle squad, under fire for the first time had sought cover behind a small fold of ground. One German sniper was holding up approximately twenty men. No one was firing. The squad leader showed me where he thought the sniper was hiding. Still no firing. The sergeant was waiting for the sniper to fire again in order to locate the target, estimate the range, and give the fire order. And this was not an isolated incident.[27]

At Omaha Beach, over half of the initial assault force was inexperienced, and at Utah Beach, the entire assault force, the 4th ID, was green. Inexperienced lieutenants and sergeants – platoon and squad leaders – led inexperienced soldiers. Yet Bradley credited his decision to deploy the veteran 1st ID for the success at Omaha.[28] He noted that '[i]n all of England there was only one experienced assault division... The Big Red One.'[29] He was wrong. There was another combat-experienced assault division in England prior to the invasion, the 9th ID, the 'Old Reliables.' The 9th ID took part in the invasion of North Africa, fought in Sicily, and was one of the few army divisions trained along with the 1st Marine Division and the 1st ID in amphibious operations and techniques in 1941. Two experienced combat divisions were available for the Normandy invasion, but Bradley deployed only one veteran RCT in the initial assault.

In the development of the Overlord plan in May 1943, General Morgan and his COSSAC staff determined that veteran divisions should make the initial assault. Morgan told his principal staff officers that 'battle-inoculation' and intensive training could not achieve the same results as actual fighting experience.

> As those of us know who have taken part in battle, it is one thing to manoeuvre freely when secure in the knowledge that the man behind the gun is doing his best to miss us, but it is quite another thing when that same man is doing his utmost to liquidate you.[30]

At the Quadrant Conference in August 1943, the COSSAC staff proposed to the Combined Chiefs of Staff that combat-experienced divisions be redeployed to the United Kingdom to lead the assault at Normandy. The proposal was approved. Three British and four American combat-experienced divisions were to be redeployed to conduct the invasion.[31]

Many senior British and American officers considered previous experience one of the most important factors in determining performance in combat. The *Infantry Journal* and the *Marine Corps Gazette* published a wealth of material on controlling battle fear during the war. Articles with titles such as 'Twelve Rules for Meeting Battle Fear,' 'Meeting Battle Fear,' 'Preparing the Mind for Battle,' 'Fear,' 'Causes and Conquest of Fear,' 'Why Warriors Fight,' and 'Conquering Fear' confirm the significance of this issue to the two principal infantry arms of the armed forces of the United States. A common theme in these articles was that '[a] great part of courage is the courage of having done a thing before.' The author of 'Why Warriors Fight' concluded that 'no amount of pre-battle training and lecturing can approach the seasoning gained in actual combat.'[32]

After the U.S. Army suffered two defeats in North Africa, Bradley commented: 'I came to the conclusion that it was fortunate that the British view prevailed, that the U.S. Army first met the enemy on the periphery in Africa rather than on the beaches of France. In Africa we learned to crawl, to walk – then run. Had that learning process been launched in France, it would surely have... resulted in an unthinkable disaster.'[33] In his history of World War II, Eisenhower also concluded that combat experience was an important factor in combat performance:

Veteran organizations are normally more capable than those entering battle for the first time. However, experience in fighting does not engender any love of the battlefield; veterans have no greater desire to enter the bullet-swept areas than have green troops. They do become more skillful in the utilization of every advantage offered by fire power, maneuver and terrain. They acquire a steadiness that is not shaken by the confusion and destruction of battle.[34]

Hastings observed: 'One of Montgomery's outstanding contributions before D-Day was his careful meshing of experienced veterans from Eighth Army with the keen, green formations that had been training and languishing for so long in England.'[35] Montgomery addressed the problem of the lack of battle experience in both of his books. He described the steps he took to integrate the veterans of his Eighth Army with green formations:

> The army then in England lacked battle experience and had tended to become theoretical rather than practical. Officers did not understand those tricks of the battlefield which mean so much to junior leaders and which save so many lives. In the last resort the battle is won by the initiative and skill of regimental officers and men, and without these assets you fail – however good the higher command. Some very experienced fighting formations had returned to England however from the Mediterranean theatre at the end of the Sicily campaign. By exchanging officers between these formations and those which had never left the country, I tried to spread such battle experience as was available over the widest possible area. Again, this was unpopular, but was more readily accepted when I had explained the reason.[36]

Bradley also took limited measures to place combat-experienced personnel in key leadership positions, relieving two corps commanders, without prejudice, because 'neither had as yet experienced combat command in World War II.' Bradley would later note: 'Not until the principal commander got ashore did the men begin to move toward the cover of the seawall and bluffs.'[37]

The 4th and 29th IDs started their war 'running,' without the benefit of the courage that comes from having done something before. If Bradley was correct and it was the experience factor that made the difference at Omaha, it was within his means to improve his chances for success by using all of the 1st ID in the initial assault, by following Montgomery's approach and exchanging officers between veteran and green formations, or by employing the veteran 9th ID.

To ascertain why after two and a half years of fighting the United States could not find four experienced assault divisions to conduct the invasion of Normandy, one has to look back at the evolution of Anglo-American strategy.[38] The disagreements among British and American political and military leaders over the strategic vision for the conduct of the war caused the continuous diversion of resources and forces to other theaters and too often led to cursory planning. The British chairman of the Joint Chiefs of Staff, Alan Brooke, argued forcefully for a Mediterranean strategy.[39] General George C. Marshall favored a plan that took the Allies immediately into the European continent. And Admiral Ernest J. King, chief of naval operations, argued for more resources and forces for the Pacific theater. This three-way pull for limited resources and forces continued throughout the war and affected the allocation of not only army divisions but also landing craft, naval gunfire ships, and other resources. Brooke won the first three rounds of combined planning, and the British Mediterranean strategy was carried out; however, his success caused significant forces to be tied up in a slugging match for Italy and motivated the United States to send more forces and resources to the Pacific theater. Late in 1943, when preparations for the Normandy invasion were well under way, this three-way pull continued to divert forces and resources away from the Normandy invasion. Brooke was not willing to halt operations in Italy, and King was not willing to halt operations in the Pacific. As a consequence, only two of the four American combat-experienced divisions designated for the Normandy invasion were redeployed to Britain.

Priority for the landing at Normandy came late in the war when assets were tied up across the planet, and the circumstances in the

Mediterranean and Pacific theaters precluded the redeployment of seven combat-experienced divisions, which the COSSAC staff had proposed and the Combined Chiefs of Staff had approved. This, however, is only a partial explanation. Strategic-level commanders and planners have an obligation to provide operational and tactical commanders with soldiers possessing the level of experience and expertise commensurate with the operation to be undertaken. If Bradley was correct in his initial assessment, the U.S. Army failed to maximize its chances for success on the coast of France by deploying green troops in the initial assault.

However, the belief that prior combat experience is a determinant of performance is not universally held. Stephen Ambrose in his book *D-Day* argued that under certain conditions, inexperienced troops are preferable to veteran soldiers:

> For a direct frontal assault on a prepared enemy position, men who have not seen what a bullet or land mine or an exploding mortar round can do to a human body are preferable to men who have seen the carnage. Men in their late teens or early twenties have a feeling of invulnerability... Men like [these]... – and there were thousands of them in the American army – could overcome the problem of inexperience with zeal and daredevil attitudes.[40]

Zeal and a daredevil attitude may help soldiers overcome the fear of entering the army and becoming infantry soldiers, but it is doubtful that they sustain soldiers on the battlefield. Zeal and a daredevil attitude are stripped away in the first moments of combat. Veteran soldiers have at least three advantages over green soldiers that ought to be considered in particularly difficult operations and operations of strategic importance.

First, the soldier who has advanced under enemy fire in the past is likely to move forward again. It is a fact that not all soldiers advance, not all paratroopers exit the aircraft. Lord Moran, an astute observer of men in war, wrote: 'There seemed to be four degrees of courage and four orders of men measured by that standard. Men who did not feel fear; men who felt fear but did not show it; men who felt fear and showed it but did their job; men who felt fear, showed it and shirked.'[41] The middle of a difficult battle is not the time to determine who will and who will not advance. Battles are made up of a series of firefights. If a soldier who is carrying a particularly crucial weapon, such as a machine gun or antitank weapon, will not advance, he can cause a small unit to lose a firefight. He may not only endanger the lives of the soldiers in his unit but also cause the loss of the battle. Second, veterans have seen the effects of bullets and shrapnel on the human body. They have seen dead, torn, mutilated bodies. They no longer stop and stare when faced with such images. Most humans experience at least a moment of shock when they encounter distorted bodies for the first time. In that moment of paralysis, a soldier can be targeted and killed. Third, successful veteran soldiers have overcome their culturally imbued disposition against killing. They are more likely to employ their weapons to kill the enemy.

Some soldiers quickly overcome these obstacles; others require more time and stronger leadership. Nevertheless, in battles, upon which the outcome of the war rests, it seems prudent to employ tested, proven soldiers. The selection and deployment of soldiers for the Normandy invasion proceeded much like the development of the rest of the plan. Morgan got the approval of the Combined Chiefs of Staff for the deployment of seven combat-experienced divisions, yet both the United States and Britain deployed inexperienced formations in the initial assault, even though all of the senior commanders believed combat experience was an important determinant of performance.

It can be argued that veteran soldiers have learned the tricks of the trade that save lives and accomplish missions. Balkoski wrote:

> No matter how repetitive or realistic the 29th Division's tactical exercises were, the 29ers knew that they would have to learn the subtleties of real combat the hard way, on the battlefield. In combat, however, it took a few weeks for the squad leaders to grasp the significant differences between real war and war 'by the books,' and by then many of them were dead.[42]

Because there are many types of combat, the value of lessons learned through experience is questionable. Experience gained in Sicily may not have been useful in the Bocage country of Normandy. The experience of battle at Tarawa was very different from that at Okinawa. Variations in terrain and the enemy situation can make previous experience of little value. It is more likely that the psychological adjustments are more important than the specific techniques learned in combat. Still, it can be argued that although battle does not change the character of an individual, experience in battle teaches soldiers something about their character, the character of their unit, and the character of the enemy. A marine who fought at Tarawa probably learned something about the character of Japanese soldiers that helped him succeed at Okinawa. This type of knowledge may well have been more important than the tricks a soldier masters on a particular piece of terrain.

There was probably no way to completely prevent the incapacitation that struck many members of both divisions. Even combat-experienced soldiers were shocked at the situation that developed at Omaha Beach. Prior experience was no guarantee against temporary paralysis. Nevertheless, the psychological preparation of the soldiers that emphasized that the assault would not be 'too difficult,' that the enemy was of poor quality, and that air and naval assets would win the battle in essence told soldiers that their power to influence the situation was dwarfed by the greater and more plentiful power generated by technology. They were told they had nothing to worry about, that they should consider themselves 'lucky' because they were 'going to have ringside seats for the greatest show on earth.'

Not all soldiers went into battle with this belief. Some did not believe what they were told and expected the worst. Theo G. Aufort, a sergeant in the 16th Infantry and a veteran of North Africa and Sicily, stated: 'All NCOs were called into a large tent for instructions and briefings. There we were told what our objectives were and what to expect on Normandy. And we were also told that a lot of men would die.'[43] These sergeants told their soldiers what to expect so they had a greater opportunity to prepare themselves mentally for the battle. The disjunct between expectation and reality was minimized in the minds of these soldiers because of knowledgeable leadership. The senior leaders not only missed an opportunity to better prepare their soldiers for combat but also may have contributed to the mental paralysis that afflicted some soldiers.

On Omaha Beach, following the initial shock and a period of recovery, small groups of men formed, crossed the beaches, scaled the bluff, and engaged the defenders in battle. The citation for the 16th Infantry read:

> Leaderless men attached themselves to the forming of groups. A breach was blown in the wire and the Regiment advanced. Human mine markers lay in the mine fields guiding the passage of the battling troops. With grim determination, suffering terrible casualties, the Regiment forced its way forward in a frontal assault on five principal enemy strong points. They engaged the enemy and in a magnificent display of courage and will to win, destroyed them.[44]

Notes

The following abbreviations are used throughout the notes, in addition to the abbreviations listed on pp.10 and 11.

CMH	U.S. Army Center of Military History, Washington, D.C.
COS (43)	British Army, Office of the War Cabinet, Chiefs of Staff Committee, Operation 'Overlord' Report and Appreciation, COS (43) 416 (0), 30 July 1943, Omar Bradley Papers, Main Library, U.S. Military Academy, West Point, N.Y.
CWM	College of William and Mary, Manuscript and Rare Books Department, Swem Library, Williamsburg, Va.
EL	Eisenhower Library, Abilene, Kans.
FDM	First Division Museum, Wheaton, Ill.
MHI	U.S. Army Military History Institute, Carlisle Barracks, Pa.
NA II	National Archives, Archive II, College Park, Md.
NHC	Naval Historical Center, Washington, D.C.
NWC	Naval War College, Newport, R.I.
USMA	U.S. Military Academy, Main Library, West Point, N.Y.
VMI	Virginia Military Institute, Preston Library, Lexington, Va.

INTRODUCTION

1   Samuel Eliot Morison, *The Invasion of France and Germany, 1944–1945* (Boston: Little, Brown, 1957), 115.

2   *The Civil War: An Illustrated History* (New York: Alfred A. Knopf, 1990), 232.

3   Morison, *Invasion of France and Germany,* 152 (emphasis added).

4   Gordon Harrison, *Cross-Channel Attack,* U.S. Army in World War II (Washington, D.C.: Government Printing Office, 1951), 191, 193, 188 (emphasis added).

5   Ibid., 189.

6   Morison, *Invasion of France and Germany,* 116: 'This "sealing off" of the combat area was very effective and essential for victory; but – owing to the imperative need for tactical surprise – very little had been done to bomb the immediate beach defenses and the Navy was not given time enough to do it.'

7   Shelby Foote, in *The Civil War: An Illustrated History,* 268, 269.

8   Omar Bradley, *A Soldier's Story* (New York: Henry Holt, 1951), 271, 272.

9   Russell F. Weigley, *Eisenhower's Lieutenants* (Bloomington: Indiana University Press, 1981), 89.

10   Max Hastings, *Overlord: D-Day and the Battle for Normandy* (New York: Simon and Schuster, 1984), 90.

11   Chester Wilmot, *The Struggle for Europe* (New York: Harper and Brothers, 1952), 264.

12   Harrison, *Cross-Channel Attack,* 188: 'A considerable body of Army opinion favored continuing the pattern of surprise landings under cover of darkness in the attack against the Continent. The whole experience of the Mediterranean theater had been with night assaults.'

13   Following the Sicily campaign, Marshall wrote Eisenhower: 'My interest is to give you what you need, support you in every way possible, and... leave you free to go about the business of crushing the Germans and gaining us great victories' (Ed Cray, *General of the Army, George C. Marshall* [New York: W.W. Norton, 1990], 384).

CHAPTER ONE

1   U.S. Army, Historical Service, Personal Recollections of General Norman Cota, Norman Cota Papers, Box 2, File Lieutenant Jack Shea, EL.

2   Don Whitehead, 'Normandy: As I Saw It,' in H.R. Knickerbocker *et al., Danger Forward: The Story of the First Division in World War II* (Washington, D.C.: Society of the First Division, 1947), 212.

3   Gordon Harrison, *Cross-Channel Attack* (Washington, D.C.: Government Printing Office, 1951), 319, 320.

4   Albert H. Smith, 'Lecture Transcript: Operation Overlord and D-Day, 6 June 1944,' presented to Armor School, Fort Knox, Ky., 16 August 1984, EL.

5   U.S. Army, 1st Infantry Division, G-3 Report of Operations, 31 May–30 June 1944, General Huebner, 45, FDM.

6   S.L.A. Marshall, *The Soldier's Load and the Mobility of a Nation* (Quantico, Va.: Marine Corps Association, 1980), 35: 'But when I had concluded my work with the survivors of the companies which had landed during the initial Omaha assault, the impression was inescapable that weight and water – directly and indirectly – were the cause of the greater part of our losses at the beach.'

7   Ibid., 41.

8   Joseph H. Ewing, *29th Let's Go!: A History of the 29th Division in World War II* (Washington, D.C.: Infantry Journal Press, 1948), 43.

9   Barry W. Fowle, ed., *Builders and Fighters: U.S. Army Engineers in World War II* (Fort Belvoir, Va.: Office of History, U.S. Army Corps of Engineers, 1992), 437.

10   Gordon Gaskill, 'Bloody Beach,' *American Magazine,* September 1944, 101.

11   U.S. Army, 16th Infantry Combat Team, S-3 Combat Report, 6 June 1944, 2, FDM.

12   Marshall, *Soldier's Load,* 44.

13   S-3 Combat Report, 3.

14   Admiral John Lesslie Hall, Operation Plan Neptune, Western Naval Task Force, Assault Force 'O' (Task Force One Two Four), USS *Ancon,* Flagship, Annex E, Gunfire Support Plan, 20 May 1944, 4, 8, John Lesslie Hall Papers, 78 H14, Box 13, Folder 4, CWM.

15   Gaskill, 'Bloody Beach,' 106.

16   Anonymous, 'D-Day Diary,' *Infantry Journal,* November 1944, 27.

17   U.S. Army, Headquarters 29th Infantry Division, Lieutenant Shea, Letter to Colonel Mason, 16 June 1944, Norman Cota Papers, Box 1, File 201, EL.

18   Derrill M. Daniel, Lieutenant Colonel U.S. Army, Infantry, Commander 2nd Battalion, 26th Infantry, 1st Infantry Division, 'Landings at Oran, Gela, and Omaha Beach: An Infantry Battalion Commander's Observations,' 9 November 1950, 26, Accession no. 16759.2, MHI.

19   S-3 Combat Report, 3.

20   Knickerbocker, *Danger Forward,* 190.

CHAPTER TWO

1   Basil H. Liddell-Hart, *When Britain Goes to War: Adaptability and Mobility* (London: Faber and Faber, 1932), 29–42: 'Our historical practice... was based on economic pressure exercised through sea-power. This naval body had two arms; one financial, which embraced the subsidizing and military provisioning of allies; the other military, which embraced sea-borne expeditions against the enemy's vulnerable extremities. By our practice we safeguarded ourselves where we were weakest, and exerted our strength where the enemy was weakest.' See also Alfred Thayer Mahan, *The Influence of Sea Power upon History* (New York: Hill and Wang, 1957).

2   Liddell-Hart, *When Britain Goes to War,* 18: 'If the adoption of this fight-to-a-finish formula was the hall-mark of the last war, its visible embodiment was our vast citizen army. For the first time in our history we poured the nation into the army. Here was the great cleavage between this and our past wars. We are apt to take for granted its necessity. But it is worth while to ask if it was a necessity.'

3   C.E. Callwell, *Military Operations and Maritime Preponderance: Their Relations and Interdependence* (Edinburgh: William Blackwood and Sons, 1905), 343: '[T]he first landing of a military force in a country which is in occupation of the enemy seldom takes place within a harbour. It is safe to assume that the seaports situated on the adversary's coast will be occupied by detachments of hostile troops, and that they will be found to be prepared for defence. The initial disembarkation is therefore generally perforce carried out in some more or less open bay, where there is a stretch of foreshore convenient for boats to be beached, and where the transports which bring the troops across the ocean can ride at anchor within a reasonable distance of the landing-place.' This thinking was evident in British amphibious doctrine in World War II.

4   See Liddell-Hart, *When Britain Goes to War.*

5   Herbert Richmond, *Amphibious Warfare in British History,* Historical Association Pamphlet no. 119 (Cambridge, Eng., 1941), 4.

6   Ernest Dupuy and Trevor N. Dupuy, *The Encyclopedia of Military History: From 3500 B.C. to the Present,* 2nd ed. (New York: Harper and Row, 1986).

7   Richmond, *Amphibious Warfare in British History,* 31.

8   Bernard Fergusson, *The Watery Maze: The Story of Combined Operations* (New York: Holt, Rinehart and Winston, 1961), 35.

9   In World War II, the British term for joint operations was 'combined operations.'

10   Fergusson, *Watery Maze,* 38 (emphasis added).

11   Ibid., 40.

12   Ibid., 182. See also Terence Robertson, *Dieppe: The Shame and the Glory* (Boston: Little, Brown, 1962), 385.

13   John Shy, 'The American Military Experience: History and Learning,' in *A People Numerous and Armed* (Ann Arbor: University of Michigan Press, 1990), 270–73.

14   Winston S. Churchill, *The Second World War,* vol. 2, *Their Finest Hour* (Boston: Houghton Mifflin, 1949), 243: 'If it is so easy for the Germans to invade us in spite of sea-power, some may feel inclined to ask the question, "why should it be thought impossible for us to do anything of the same kind to them?" The completely defensive habit of mind which has ruined the French must not be allowed to ruin all our initiative. It is of the highest consequence to keep the largest numbers of German forces all along the coasts of the countries they have conquered, and we should immediately set to work to organise raiding forces on these coasts where the populations are friendly. Such forces might be composed of self-contained, thoroughly equipped units of say one thousand up to not more than ten thousand when combined. Surprise would be ensured by the fact that the destination would be concealed until the last moment. What we have seen at Dunkirk shows how quickly troops can be moved off (and I supposed on) to selected points if need be. How wonderful it would be if the Germans could be made to wonder where they were going to be struck next, instead of forcing us to try to wall in the island and roof it over! An effort must be made to shake off the mental and moral prostration to the will and initiative of the enemy from which we suffer.'

15   Why in June 1940, when Britain stood alone in the war, the prime minister wanted the Germans to construct a defense along the coast he one day hoped to invade is an interesting question. He may have hoped to produce a defensive frame of mind in the German Army – an unlikely eventuality given the magnitude of German successes. More likely, he hoped to distract and divert German units and resources from the planned invasion of England – Operation Sealion.

16   Winston S. Churchill, *The Second World War,* vol. 2, *Their Finest Hour,* 243, 249.

17   Fergusson, *Watery Maze,* 85: 'His biggest achievement was the actual setting up of C.O.H.Q.... C.O.H.Q. could never have flourished in infancy under the roof of any one of the Service Ministries, nor under an officer of whatever calibre who restricted his allegiance to any one Service.'

18   Winston S. Churchill, *The Second World War,* vol. 3, *The Grand Alliance* (Boston: Houghton Mifflin, 1950), 542; Fergusson, *Watery Maze,* 84, 87.

19   Fergusson, *Watery Maze,* 88. Churchill told Mountbatten: 'Your main object must be the re-invasion of France. You must create the machine which will make it possible for us to beat Hitler on land. You must devise the appurtenances and appliances which will make the invasion possible. You must select and build up the bases from which the assault will be launched. Before that you must create the various Training Centers at which the soldiers can be trained in the amphibious assault. I want you to bring in the Air Force as well and create a proper inter-service organisation to produce the technique of the modern assault. I want you to consider the great problem of the follow-up, and finally, I want you to select the area in which you feel the assault should take place and start bending all your energies towards getting ready for this great day' (ibid.).

20   Ibid., 168: 'The force that sailed for Dieppe, on the evening of the 18th August, 1942, was intended to land, to destroy a number of targets, to capture prisoners, and to re-embark... But the real purpose was to gain experience; to test certain tactical concep-

tions, and to learn more of the technique required to breach what Hitler called the Atlantic Wall.' See also U.S. Army, Assault Training Center, 'Conference on Landing Assaults, 24 May–23 June 1943,' Commander J. Hughes-Hallet, Royal Navy, Naval Force Commander at Dieppe, p. Hallet 1, D756.3.C66 1943, v. 2, c. 3, MHI: 'The reason for taking this risk was that the DIEPPE Operation differed in one important respect from all the other raids planned in 1942. It was definitely intended as a small-scale rehearsal for the major cross-Channel Operation which it had always been felt would eventually have to be undertaken. Accordingly, it was deliberately planned on the lines of a try-out on the form of attack, which was then believed to be likely on a number of separate sectors in the 'ROUND-UP' Plans.'

21 Combined Operations Headquarters, Combined Report on the Dieppe Raid, 1942, 38, RG 38, Box 1708, NA II.

22 Ibid., 43.

23 'Conference on Landing Assaults,' p. Hallet 6: 'There is no doubt whatever that the operation achieved its main object to a more complete degree than had been fore-seen. The lessons learnt cause a drastic re-casting of our ideas concerning amphibi-ous operations in face of a heavy scale of resistance. In the absence of the experience gained at Dieppe there is not the slightest doubt that a major disaster would have occurred had we proceeded to attack in North Western EUROPE on the lines hitherto visualised.'

24 Derrill M. Daniel, Lieutenant Colonel U.S. Army, Infantry, Commander 2nd Battalion, 26th Infantry, 1st Infantry Division, 'Landings at Oran, Gela, and Omaha Beach: An Infantry Battalion Commander's Observations,' 9 November 1950, 21, Accession no. 16759.2, MHI. In reference to the Normandy invasion, Daniel wrote: 'The rehearsal proceeded very smoothly. One glaring weakness noted was that the Naval control offi-cers and boat crews were *not* the ones who would land the 16th Infantry on Omaha Beach. The control officers and boat crews who did land the 16th Infantry on Omaha Beach were untrained and inexperienced, and for the most part arrived in England too late to take part in the rehearsal. It seems incredible, but in the dress rehearsal for the most important assault in all history, the control officers and boat crews who were to land the units on what proved to be the most critical beach *were not even present.*'

25 'Conference on Landing Assaults,' p. Roberts 2.

26 Ibid., p. Roberts 3 (emphasis added).

27 U.S. Army Air Force, *The Development of the Heavy Bomber, 1918–1944,* Historical Study no. 6 (Maxwell Air Force Base, Ala.: Air University, 1951). See also Richard Overy, *Why the Allies Won* (New York: W. W. Norton, 1995), 115.

28 'Conference on Landing Assaults,' p. Roberts 4.

29 Ibid., p. Roberts 3.

30 Fergusson, *Watery Maze,* 172.

31 Ibid., 182–84.

32 'Conference on Landing Assaults,' p. Haydon 3.

33 Robertson, *Dieppe,* 405.

34 'Conference on Landing Assaults,' p. Haydon 4.

35 Headquarters U.S. Marine Corps, Division of Operations and Training, 'Memorandum for the Major General Commandant,' 23 July 1921, 1, Marine Corps University Archives, Quantico, Va.

36 Allan Millett, *Semper Fidelis: The History of the United States Marine Corps,* rev. ed. (New York: Free Press, 1991), 284.

37 For a more complete history of the navy and Marine Corps' development of amphibious doctrine, see ibid.; Dirk A. Ballandorf and Merrill L. Bartlett, *Pete Ellis:*

An Amphibious Warfare Prophet, 1880–1923 (Annapolis, Md.: Naval Institute Press, 1997); Jack Shulimson, *The Marine Corps' Search for a Mission, 1880–1898* (Lawrence: University Press of Kansas, 1993); Edward S. Miller, *War Plan ORANGE: The U.S. Strategy to Defeat Japan, 1897–1945* (Annapolis, Md.: Naval Institute Press, 1991); and Merrill L. Bartlett, ed., *Assault from the Sea: Essays on the History of Amphibious Warfare* (Annapolis, Md.: Naval Institute Press, 1983).

38   Doctrine is the body of authoritative, fundamental principles by which armed forces guide their actions to achieve objectives. Doctrine influences organization, equipment, training, and research and development. Technology, resources, national character, national policy, and strategy influence doctrine.

39   Jeter A. Isley and Philip A. Crowl, *The U.S. Marines and Amphibious War* (Princeton, N.J.: Princeton University Press, 1951), 36.

40   E.B. Potter, *The United States and World Sea Power* (Englewood Cliffs, N.J.: Prentice Hall, 1955), 586. See also Samuel Eliot Morison, *Operations in North African Waters, October 1942–June 1943* (Boston: Little, Brown, 1954), 20: 'As a result of these exercises, a manual on landing operations was issued to the Fleet and the Marine Corps in 1938. This laid down organization and doctrine of amphibious warfare on such sound lines that it could be followed, with amplification rather than alteration, throughout the entire course of World War II.'

41   Frank O. Hough, Verle E. Ludwig, and Henry I. Shaw, *History of the U.S. Marine Corps Operations in World War II: Pearl Harbor to Guadalcanal,* vol. 1, FMFRP 12-34-I (Washington, D.C.: Historical Branch, G-3 Division, Headquarters, U.S. Marine Corps, 1989), 14.

42   It is an occupational hazard that naval and military historians tend to adopt the views, and in some cases become part of the culture, of the service they study. The distorted assessment of marine and navy amphibious doctrine may be a function of this phenomenon.

43   Stanhope Brasfield Mason, Major General U.S. Army retired, 'Reminiscences and Anecdotes of World War II,' 11, Birmingham, Ala., 1988, FDM. See also Roger A. Beaumont, *Joint Military Operations: A Short History* (Westport, Conn.: Greenwood Press, 1993), 69: 'In spite of all the efforts over two decades, the United States had no amphibious force per se, or doctrine allowing either a firm base for quick mobilization or for quick deployment at a high level of effectiveness. A year into the war, training exercises fell well short of an acceptable level of performance, and the Army had begun to build its own major amphibious command.'

44   Isley and Crowl, *U.S. Marines and Amphibious War,* 26. See also Kenneth J. Clifford, *Progress and Purpose: A Developmental History of the U.S. Marine Corps, 1900–1970* (Washington, D.C.: U.S. Marine Corps, 1973), 64, 65.

45   U.S. Army, *Landing Operations on Hostile Shores,* FM 31-5 (Washington, D.C.: War Department, 1941), 17, 16.

46   Ibid., 97 (emphasis added).

47   Robert D. Heinl Jr., 'Naval Gunfire Support,' *Military Review,* December 1946, 19: 'Without naval gunfire support, Tarawa could not have been stormed, the Marshalls and Marianas might still be Japanese outposts, and the assault of Iwo Jima would be unthinkable.'

48   FM 31-5, 98 (emphasis added).

49   Ibid., 117.

50   H.B. Knowles, Captain, Commander Task Force 53.1, Transportation Group, Action Report on Tarawa Operation, 1 December 1943, 14, RG 38, Box 545, NA II.

51   Heinl, 'Naval Gunfire Support,' 21. See also Robert D. Heinl Jr., 'Naval Gunfire Support in Landings,' *Marine Corps Gazette,* September 1945, 40.

52 George M. Harvey, 'Iwo Jima and Amphibious Operations in the Central Pacific,' *Military Review,* September 1945, 24.

53 U.S. Navy, U.S. Fleet, Headquarters of Commander in Chief, Navy Department, Memorandum, Subject: Distribution of Naval Gunfire Officer, Headquarters V Amphibious Corps, Serial 00671 letter of 7 March 1944, Subject: Naval Gunfire Report on the Marshalls Operation, 22 March 1944, 6, 7, 12, RG 407, Files 6-12.060/45, 6-12.0703/44, NA II.

54 Holland M. Smith, *Coral and Brass* (New York: Charles Scribner's Sons, 1949), 14.

55 Ibid., 17.

56 Donald M. Weller, 'The Development of Naval Gunfire Support in World War II,' in Bartlett, *Assault from the Sea,* 261.

CHAPTER THREE

1 Adrian R. Lewis, 'The Failure of Allied Planning and Doctrine for Operation Overlord: The Case of Minefield and Obstacle Clearance,' *Journal of Military History* 62, no. 4 (October 1998): 787–807. See also Adrian R. Lewis, 'The Navy Falls Short at Normandy,' *Naval History* 12, no. 6 (December 1998): 34–39.

2 U.S. Navy, Western Task Force, Commander Task Force 122, Action Report on Amphibious Operation in Baie de la Seine, Normandy Invasion, 25 July 1944, Rear Admiral A. G. Kirk, Box 317, File Task Force 122-122.4.4, NHC.

3 H. Kent Hewitt, 'U.S. Naval Operations in the Northwestern African–Mediterranean Theater,' March–July 1943, 20, H. Kent Hewitt Papers, Box 2, NHC.

4 Ibid., 27.

5 Samuel Huntington, *The Soldier and the State: The Theory and Politics of Civil-Military Relations* (Cambridge, Mass.: Belknap Press, 1957), chap. 1.

6 Hewitt, 'U.S. Naval Operations in the Northwestern African–Mediterranean Theater,' 13. See also 'Military Digest: The Army Goes to Sea,' *Marine Corps Gazette* 27, no. 4 (August 1943): 44–48.

7 John Lesslie Hall Jr., 'The Reminiscences of John Lesslie Hall, Jr.', 172, 173, Naval History Project, Oral History Research Office, Columbia University, 1964, NHC.

8 Ibid., 129, 6.

9 Ibid., 176–77.

10 John H. Clagett, 'Skipper of the *Eagle:* Rehearsal for Greatness,' *U.S. Naval Institute Proceedings* 102, no. 4 (April 1976): 58–65.

11 John H. Clagett, 'Admiral H. Kent Hewitt, U.S. Navy: Part II, High Command,' *Naval War College Review* 28, no. 2 (1975): 64.

12 John H. Clagett, 'Admiral H. Kent Hewitt, U.S. Navy: Part I, Preparing for High Command,' *Naval War College Review* 28, no. 1 (1975): 72–86.

13 Samuel Eliot Morison, *Sicily-Salerno-Anzio: January 1943–June 1944* (Boston: Little, Brown, 1954), 14.

14 Clagett, 'Admiral H. Kent Hewitt, U.S. Navy: Part II,' 64.

15 H. Kent Hewitt, 'The Reminiscences of Admiral H. Kent Hewitt,' Naval History Project, Oral History Research Office, Columbia University, 1962, NHC.

16 Ibid., 15-10.

17 Holland M. Smith, *Coral and Brass* (New York: Charles Scribner's Sons, 1949), 84.

18 Admiral Lord Louis Mountbatten, Interview, H. Kent Hewitt Papers, Box 2, NHC.

19 Kent Robert Greenfield, Robert R. Palmer, and Bell I. Wiley, *The Army Ground Forces: The Organization of Ground Combat Troops,* U.S. Army in World War II (Washington, D.C.: Government Printing Office, 1983), 87, 88, 91.

20 U.S. Army Headquarters, 1st Infantry Division, Report of January Amphibious Exercise, January 28, 1942, 3, 9, 10, RG 127, Box 2, NA II.

21   Greenfield, Palmer, and Wiley, *Army Ground Forces,* 91.

22   Smith, *Coral and Brass,* 17, 18: 'I had to fight not only for gunfire but for aviation, ...and against Navy interference. We could not have reached the islands without the Navy, but at that point their duties should have ended. Instead, they tried to continue running the show.'

23   Marshall O. Becker, Captain U.S. Army, *The Amphibious Training Center,* Study no. 22, Historical Section, Army Ground Forces, 1946, D769.1 A423 no. 22, c. 4, 1, MHI; *Amphibious Doctrine and Training,* Study no. 6, Historical Section, Army Ground Forces, n.d., 30, CMH; Greenfield, Palmer, and Wiley, *Army Ground Forces,* 87.

24   Becker, *Amphibious Training Center,* 15; *Amphibious Doctrine and Training,* 37; Greenfield, Palmer, and Wiley, *Army Ground Forces,* 92.

25   Becker, *Amphibious Training Center,* 1.

26   Hewitt, 'Reminiscences,' 10–12.

27   Ibid.

28   William F. Heavey, *Down Ramp: The Story of the Army Amphibian Engineers* (Washington, D.C.: Infantry Journal Press, 1947), 9, 13.

29   'Military Digest,' 44.

30   Admiral H.R. Stark, Letter to Admiral H. Kent Hewitt, 2 September 1943, H. Kent Hewitt Papers, Box 1, Folder 2, NHC.

31   Becker, *Amphibious Training Center,* 48.

32   David J. Coles, '"Hell-by-the-Sea": Florida's Camp Gordon Johnston in World War II,' *Florida Historical Quarterly* 73, no. 1 (July 1994): 1–23; Roland C. Gask, 'Prelude to Invasion: Real Bullets Enforce Lesson at Army Amphibious Training Center,' *Newsweek,* 22 March 1943, 22–23.

33   Omar Bradley and Clay Blair, *A General's Life: An Autobiography by General of the Army Omar N. Bradley* (New York: Simon and Schuster, 1983), 112.

34   Ibid. Bradley wrote: 'It was a new experience for all of us. I had studied amphibious warfare in schools and on my own read a great deal about the British World War I amphibious debacle at Gallipoli in the Turkish Dardanelles, but I had never actually "stormed a beach" in an LCVP' (Omar Bradley, *A Soldier's Story* [New York: Henry Holt, 1951], 12).

35   Admiral Hewitt's assessment that the navy was slow to initiate and develop a comprehensive training center for amphibious operations was emphasized in letters to Admiral Hall written in 1947 and 1948. They exchanged letters in reference to Samuel E. Morison's forthcoming book, *Operations in North African Waters, October 1942–June 1943.* Hewitt wrote: 'At a time when we were making every effort to get yachtsmen and fishermen for our landing craft program, it was very annoying to see large advertisements in New York papers for such people to 'Join the Army's Navy.' It is to be noted that Coast Guard officers were taken away from the hard-pushed amphibious forces to train these Army amphibious engineers at Camp Edwards. Some of these engineers did excellent work in the Mediterranean in boat repair etc., but they should have been in naval uniform, as the Army was always trying to divert them to other duties and it was a constant fight to retain them for the work for which they had been trained. Some of the training, except in actual boat handling, was misdirected because it did not conform to the procedures which had been developed jointly by the Navy and the Army and Marine forces working with the Navy' (Admiral H. Kent Hewitt, Letter to Admiral John Lesslie Hall, 13 March 1947, John Lesslie Hall Papers, 78 H14, Box 21, Folder 2, CWM).
       In response to Hewitt's letter, Morison wrote: 'Army Amphibious Engineers. I agree that it was a mistake to allow the Army to recruit this force, but regard it as partly the Navy's fault that they were allowed to get away with it. The Navy did

not pay sufficient attention before we entered the war, to the need of a greatly expanded small-craft program and obtaining competent personnel to handle them. The Coast Guard Reserve did not amount to much. It was mostly motorboat yachtsmen who knew nothing about seamanship' (Admiral John Lesslie Hall, 'Comments on Dr. Samuel Morison's Book,' 6 February 1948, John Lesslie Hall Papers, 78 H14, Box 21, Folder 2, CWM).

36   Becker, *Amphibious Training Center,* 17.

37   H. Kent Hewitt, Commander Amphibious Force, Atlantic Fleet, Report: Torch Operation, Comments and Recommendations, 22 December 1942, 1, RG 38, Box 530, NA II.

38   George S. Patton, Major General, U.S. Army Commanding, Subject: Lessons from Operation Torch, 30 December 1942, 52, RG 38, Box 1696, NA II.

39   Hewitt, 'Reminiscences,' 10–12, 21–27.

40   U.S. Army, Headquarters Allied Force APO 512, Memorandum, Subject: Corrective Action Based on Recent Amphibious Operations in North Africa, 7 May 1943, James F. Barber, Assistant Adjutant General, 9, RG 407, Files 301-0.3, 301-0.4, NA II.

41   Heavey, *Down Ramp,* 36.

42   Hall, 'Reminiscences,' 128. See also Susan H. Godson, *Viking of Assault: Admiral John Lesslie Hall, Jr., and Amphibious Warfare* (Washington, D.C.: University Press of America, 1982), 61–62. Godson was perhaps a bit unfair to O'Daniel and the army. She wrote: 'The army... often lacked understanding of naval problems of transporting, landing, and supporting troops. Typical of this incomprehension was O'Daniel's plan to send attack forces across the Mediterranean in small rubber boats. Imagine sending thousands of combat troops on a two-hundred-mile sea voyage in tiny rubber boats.' No one in the army considered this an acceptable practice. Hall's oral history states: 'He [O'Daniel] was talking about training his troops to cross the Mediterranean in rubber boats' ('Reminiscences,' 128). What he most likely meant was 'to land in the Mediterranean in rubber boats.'

43   Heavey, *Down Ramp,* 36.

44   U.S. Army, Fifth Army Invasion Training Center, Training Doctrine, 20 May 1943, General John W. O'Daniel, 3, RG 407, Boxes 5661, 5662, File 301-0.3, NA II.

45   U.S. Army, Headquarters Allied Forces APO 512, G-3 Training Section, 'Training Notes from the Sicilian Campaign,' 25 October 1943, 36, RG 407, Box 5665, File 301-0.4, NA II.

46   Hewitt, 'Reminiscences,' 22–27.

47   H. Kent Hewitt, Vice Admiral, Naval Commander, Western Naval Task Force, Action Report Western Naval Task Force, Sicilian Campaign, Operation 'Husky,' July–August 1943, 42–44, Walter Beddell Smith Papers, Boxes 40, 41, Files Op Husky, 1, 2, 3, 4, EL.

48   H. Kent Hewitt, 'The Navy in the European Theater of Operation in World War II,' 4–7 January 1947, 17, H. Kent Hewitt Papers, NWC, and 'U.S. Naval Operations in the Northwestern African–Mediterranean Theater,' 20.

49   Hewitt, 'U.S. Naval Operations in the Northwestern African–Mediterranean Theater,' 26.

50   Eduard Mark, *Aerial Interdiction in Three Wars* (Washington, D.C.: Center of Air Force History, 1994), 76.

51   H. Kent Hewitt, 'The Strategic Employment of the Allied Forces in the Mediterranean in World War II,' 1952, 11, H. Kent Hewitt Papers, NWC.

52   Martin Blumenson, *Salerno to Cassino: The Mediterranean Theater of Operation,* U.S. Army in World War II (Washington, D.C.: U.S. Army Center of Military History, 1969), 79.

53   U.S. Army Center of Military History, *Salerno: American Operation from the Beaches to the Volturno, 9 September–6 October 1943,* Armed Forces in Action Series (Washington, D.C.: U.S. Army Center of Military History, 1990), 28, 29.

54   Ibid., 29.

55   Hewitt, 'Navy in the European Theater of Operation,' 23.

56   H. Kent Hewitt, Vice Admiral U.S. Navy, Commander Western Naval Task Force, Action Report Italian Campaign, Salerno Landings, September–October 1943, 129, 130, H. Kent Hewitt Papers, Box 2, NHC.

57   U.S. Navy, Western Task Force, Commander Task Force 122, Action Report on Amphibious Operation in Baie de la Seine, Normandy Invasion, 25 July 1944, Rear Admiral A. G. Kirk, 7, Box 317, File Task Force 122-122.4.4, NHC.

58   Sir Andrew Cunningham, Royal Navy, 'Avalanche,' Report on Operation, 5 June 1945, 7, RG 38, Box 69, NA II.

59   H. Kent Hewitt, Narrative by Admiral H. Kent Hewitt, USN Mediterranean Area Campaign – North Africa Landing to Southern France, 29 June 1945, 14, 15, RG 28, Box 1728, NA II.

60   Ibid., 15.

61   H. Kent Hewitt, 'Executing Operation Anvil-Dragoon,' *U.S. Naval Institute Proceedings* 78 (August 1954): 899.

62   H. Kent Hewitt, Vice Admiral, U.S. Navy, Report of Naval Commander Western Naval Task Force, Invasion of Southern France, 15 November 1944, 188, 189, RG 38, Box 50, NA II.

63   Robert Frank Futrell, *Ideas, Concepts, Doctrine: A History of Basic Thinking in the United States Air Force, 1907–1964* (Maxwell Air Force Base, Ala.: Air University, 1974), chaps. 3, 4. See also Walt W. Rostow, *Pre-Invasion Bombing Strategy: General Eisenhower's Decision of March 25, 1944* (Austin: University of Texas Press, 1981), and Ronald Schaffer, *Wings of Judgment: American Bombing in World War II* (New York: Oxford University Press, 1985).

64   Hall, 'Reminiscences,' 238–39, 222.

65   Ibid., 240.

66   Hewitt, 'Navy in the European Theater of Operation,' 13.

CHAPTER FOUR

1   Kenneth Edwards, *Operation Neptune* (London: Collins, 1946), 16, 17.

2   Frederick Edgworth Morgan, *Overture to Overlord* (New York: Doubleday, 1959), 65: 'In actuality little original work was needed. COSSAC's first mandate... had been to give "cohesion and impetus" to the planning that had been going on for so long. In fact had not planning and preparation been carried out for many months before the COSSAC organisation was conceived there could have been no possibility whatever of launching the operation in 1944.'

3   Ibid., 17: 'I received a weighty document from General Eisenhower's headquarters which I read and reread and studied until it dawned on me that I did not understand one single word of it.'

4   Edwards, *Operation Neptune,* 36: 'A great difficulty, because it struck at the root of the planning, arose out of the differences between the British and American approaches to a naval plan. The British idea is to have a detailed plan covering every facet of a complicated operation... nothing to chance and no loopholes for error. The American idea of a plan was very different. The Americans were used to being

given broad directives but not detailed plans, and they felt that the latter tied them down too rigidly and left no room for the exercise of their own initiative. This point of view was well expressed to Admiral Ramsay by a senior officer of the United States Navy who said: "When I'm wanted to do something I like to be told what to do, but not how to do it. How I do it is my business."' This view was also expressed by General Bradley: 'With characteristic British thoroughness in military planning, COSSAC had tailored its preparations to fit three possible, if unlikely, contingencies' (Omar Bradley, *A Soldier's Story* [New York: Henry Holt, 1951], 199).

5   John Lesslie Hall Jr., 'The Reminiscences of John Lesslie Hall, Jr.,' 158, Naval History Project, Oral History Research Office, Columbia University, 1964, NHC. See also U.S. Navy, Commander Assault Force 'O' (Commander Eleventh Amphibious Force), Action Report Assault on Colleville-Vierville Sector Coast of Normandy, 27 July 1944, 79–81, Admiral Hall, Box 549, File 11th PHIBFOR, NHC.

6   In his final draft, Admiral Kirk wrote: 'The planning done by the ANCXF was of a very high order but at the same time this operation illustrated once more the great difference in planning methods and concepts of command between the Royal Navy and the U.S. Navy. British plans were issued in great detail from higher to lower echelons. American naval tradition tends to leave details of execution and planning to the officers who are actually charged with doing the job. An operation on the scale of this one, of course, demands a large measure of co-ordination at the highest level, but in fact very much of this can be reduced to a Standing Operating Procedure issued long before security permits the distribution of the Operation Order. What remains, can then be issued in very much shorter and less complicated form' (U.S. Navy, Western Task Force, Commander Task Force 122, Action Report on Amphibious Operation in Baie de la Seine, Normandy Invasion, 25 July 1944, Rear Admiral A. G. Kirk, 6, Box 317, File Task Force 122-122.4.4, NHC).

7   U.S. Navy, Commander Task Force 122, Rough Draft Action Report, 25 July 1944, Planning, 2, Box 317, File Task Force 122-122.4.4, NHC.

8   Hall, 'Reminiscences,' 158. See also Susan H. Godson, *Viking of Assault: Admiral John Lesslie Hall, Jr., and Amphibious Warfare* (Washington, D.C.: University Press of America, 1982), 119. In regard to Admiral Hall's reaction to the orders of the British/Allied naval commander in chief, Godson wrote: 'Distinctly resentful of British operational control of Neptune-Overlord, Hall reacted adversely to Ramsay's memorandum on how to write good orders. American upper echelon orders contained only the barest essentials and left methods of execution to the good sense of subordinate commanders. In contrast, the British overloaded their orders with minute detail, leaving little to the discretion of lower commanders. Ramsay's memorandum, Hall felt, was silly. He paid no attention to it. The memorandum and the ill will it caused was another example of less-than-harmonious relations between Ramsay and American naval offices.'

9   Bradley, *Soldier's Story*, 138.

10   Hall, 'Reminiscences,' 158. See also Bernard Fergusson, *The Watery Maze: The Story of Combined Operations* (New York: Holt, Rinehart and Winston, 1961), 148: 'The British planners gulped when they saw their modest 12 divisions neatly multiplied by four to make 48, and their hundreds of landing-craft translated into thousands; and it took them a little time to raise their sights.'

11   Morgan, *Overture to Overlord*, 127, 137: 'The fact may well be, I think, that in this last war the Americans were having their full-scale experience of dealing in detail with the intricacies of European international relationships. Before this time the interests of the United States in Europe can only have been of a comparatively

superficial nature. Now for the first time they were forced, much against the will of many of them, to concern themselves up to the hilt with matters that they could previously afford to ignore.'

12   Ibid., 127:'For the British it must be said again that they had already been at war for several years. Nor was the experience of 1917–18 to be forgotten. In World War I not only had the British losses been catastrophic, but Anglo-American harmony had not been achieved to any very great extent during or immediately after hostilities. The burden of loss had fallen comparatively lightly on the United States, yet to many British minds the United States had pretty much scooped the pool.'

13   Forrest C. Pogue, *The Supreme Command,* U.S. Army in World War II (Washington, D.C.: Government Printing Office, 1954), 43. Pogue briefly discussed the British command system: 'The British, accustomed to a committee type of joint command in which no service had over-all control, favored a plan [for the invasion of Europe] which gave broad powers to the land, sea and air commander... Under this system the Allied commander in chief became a chairman of a board rather than a true commander.'

14   Morgan, *Overture to Overlord,* 76: 'To the American mind the committee system appeared just exactly what was not needed if we were after positive results and rapid action. For the committee can be described as a negative organisation. It can hardly ever fail to impede progress or to obscure a main issue. On the other hand it provides a form of safety valve and an admirable alibi in the event of misfortune.' See also Arthur W. Tedder, *With Prejudice: The War Memoirs of Marshal of the Royal Air Force Lord Tedder G.C.B.* (Boston: Little, Brown, 1966), 500, 508.

15   Morgan, *Overture to Overlord,* 286.

16   Roger Keyes, *Amphibious Warfare and Combined Operations* (New York: Macmillan, 1943), 77, 79.

17   U.S. Army, Supreme Headquarters Allied Expeditionary Force Files, Notes on the Planning Period of Operation 'Overlord,' British 21st Army Group, May 1945, RG 407, Secretary, General Staff Files, FDM.

18   Morgan, *Overture to Overlord,* 125. See also Fergusson, *Watery Maze,* 129, 140:'At this period [1942] of the war, American amphibious thinking was sadly adrift. Indeed, ...Knox found himself at a high-level American Army meeting, discussing in all seriousness a plan to put the United States Marine Corps ashore in France that autumn, for keeps, using nothing but small, undecked personnel landing craft.' Knox found the U.S. Navy equally naive in its thinking on amphibious operations.

19   R.W. Barker, General U.S. Army, Letter to General Handy, War Department, 17 November 1943, R.W. Barker Papers, Box 1, File October 43–44, EL.

20   Morgan, *Overture to Overlord,* 41.

21   COS (43), 5.

22   F.E. Morgan, Lieutenant General, British Army, Opening Address by Lieutenant General F. E. Morgan, Chief of Staff to the Supreme Commander (Designate), 17 April 1943, R.W. Barker Papers, Box 1, File COSSAC Minutes, EL.

23   Ibid., 2.

24   Ibid., 3.

25   Ibid., 5.

26   Action Report, Kirk, 6.

27   COS (43), 7.

28   Ibid., 8.

29   Morgan, *Overture to Overlord,* 67.

30   The British Combined Operations Headquarters (COHQ) under the leadership of Lord Louis Mountbatten was initially assigned the mission of planning the 're-

invasion' of Europe. The area selected by the COSSAC planners was initially chosen by the COHQ. The studies conducted by the COSSAC planners confirmed the thinking of Mountbatten's planners. See Fergusson, *Watery Maze*, 146.

31   COS (43), 14.
32   Morgan, *Overture to Overlord*, 142.
33   COS (43), 15.
34   Ibid., 106.
35   Ibid., 24.
36   Ibid.
37   Morgan, *Overture to Overlord*, 146.
38   Ibid., 140.
39   COS (43), 9: 'Concentration of the assault force is considered essential if we are to ensure adequate air support and if our limited assault forces are to avoid defeat in detail. An attempt has been made to obtain *tactical surprise* by landing in a lightly defended area' (emphasis added).
40   Morgan, *Overture to Overlord*, 154.
41   Ibid., 140; COS (43), 19.
42   COS (43), 24.
43   Ibid., 28.
44   Morgan, *Overture to Overlord*, 275.
45   U.S. Army, Assault Training Center, 'Conference on Landing Assaults, 24 May–23 June 1943,' Colonel Paul W. Thompson, p. Thompson 1, D756.3.C66 1943, v. 2, c. 3, MHI. See also Colonel Paul W. Thompson, 'Talk at S.A.M.E.,' Washington, D.C., 18 May 1988, 3, transcript, CMH: 'The mission of the Assault Training Center was double-barrelled: First barrel: To train the Combat Teams of Infantry Assault Divisions under sound doctrine and under conditions closely approximating those the troops will encounter in an invasion of the German-held coast of western Europe. Second Barrel:... [T]o develop (the) sound doctrine applicable to assault operations against the German-held coast.'
46   Thompson, 'Talk at S.A.M.E.,' 4.
47   Ibid., 8: 'We put the questions to which we wanted answers to the Board and we got the answers – mostly the answers we wanted and knew we would get.'
48   Gordon Harrison, *Cross-Channel Attack*, U.S. Army in World War II (Washington, D.C.: Government Printing Office, 1951), 164.
49   'Conference on Landing Assaults,' p. Thompson 2.
50   Ibid., p. Chase 2.
51   Hanson Baldwin, a wartime reporter and author, observed: 'More important [in explaining the "carnage"] at Omaha – and in the invasion generally – was the failure of SHAEF and its subordinate echelons to assimilate and properly weigh the many technical lessons learned in the hard-fought amphibious assaults in the Pacific.' See Hanson Baldwin, *Battles Lost and Won: Great Campaigns of World War II* (New York: Harper and Row, 1966), 283, and 'Amphibious Aspects of the Normandy Invasion,' *Marine Corps Gazette,* December 1944, 36. See also Charles H. Corlett, *Cowboy Pete: The Autobiography of Major General Charles H. Corlett* (Santa Fe, N.M.: Sleeping Fox, 1974), 88, 89. General Corlett commanded the XIX Corps in Bradley's FUSA. He had also commanded in the Pacific theater. After frequent contact with European army commanders, he concluded that they were uninterested in developments in the Pacific theater: 'I soon got the feeling that American generals in England considered anything that had happened in the Pacific as strictly "bush league stuff," meriting no consideration.'

52 Hall, 'Reminiscences,' 133, 134. Admiral Hall commanded the amphibious forces that put the 1st ID ashore on D-Day. He wrote: 'When you get engineers and Churchill and Roosevelt all together, you get some very fantastic plans. There's no doubt about that. Of course, I'm probably criticizing my own superiors in my service, and in the Army and Air Force, because they were at this conference [on the artificial harbor]. But I wish they had had some amphibious force commander who had been through the experience. I wish they had had somebody like that there to tear down these engineers. It would have saved a lot of time, a lot of effort, a lot of money, a lot of manpower and a lot of material.'

53 David G. Chandler and James Lawton Collins Jr., eds., *The D-Day Encyclopedia* (New York: Simon and Schuster, 1994), 425.

54 U.S. Navy, DD LCT Unit Commander, Lieutenant Dean L. Rockwell, Memorandum for Commander, Eleventh Amphibious Force, 30 April 1944, RG 407, Box 24377, Files 659, NA II.

55 Chief of Staff to the Supreme Allied Commander (43), 23rd Meeting, Minutes of Chief of Staff to the Supreme Allied Commander Staff Conference, 28 August 1943, Report on Quadrant, 30 August 1943, 2, R. W. Barker Papers, Box 1, File COSSAC Minutes, EL.

56 Ibid.

57 Ibid., 3.

58 R. W. Barker, Major General, Chief of Staff to the Supreme Allied Commander (Designate), Letter to Lieutenant General Morgan, 3 November 1943, R. W. Barker Papers, Box 1, File October 43–44, EL.

59 C. P. Stacey, 'The Raid on Dieppe,' *Military Review,* June 1949, 16. For a complete history of the Dieppe raid, see Terence Robertson, *Dieppe: The Shame and the Glory* (Boston: Little, Brown, 1962), and R. W. Thompson, *At What Cost: The Story of the Dieppe Raid* (New York: Coward McCann, 1956).

60 COS (43), 19. The COSSAC plan addressed the principle of surprise: 'Though it should be possible to effect a considerable measure of *tactical surprise,* it will be impossible to achieve *strategic surprise.* The concentrations of landing craft round the coast of the United Kingdom, far exceeding anything that has previously been seen, *will give the Germans several months warning of our general intention*' (emphasis added). 'Strategic surprise' is not simply a function of knowledge, however; it is also a function of having the wherewithal to influence the situation with strategic forces before the enemy takes decisive action. Hence, knowledge of an operation on a land mass the size of Europe with a western coastline of over 2,000 miles did not preclude the possibility that the Allies might strike 'at a time or place or in a manner' that found the enemy's strategic forces unprepared, that is, in a position or situation where they were unable to influence the invasion during the crucial first four to five days. In the words of General Morgan: 'Our front, so to speak, extended from Spain on the one hand to the Arctic Circle on the other' (*Overture to Overlord,* 132). Strategic surprise was achieved. By the time the Wehrmacht deployed its strategic reserves, Allied forces were of sufficient size and tactical disposition on the Continent to defend themselves.

61 Morgan, *Overture to Overlord,* 146.

62 Ibid., 143.

63 Ibid., 124.

CHAPTER FIVE

1 Dwight D. Eisenhower, *Crusade in Europe* (New York: Doubleday, 1948), 207.

2 The biographies on Eisenhower are numerous and varied. Some biographers loved

and adored him, whereas others believed he was incompetent as a ground force commander. See Stephen E. Ambrose, *Eisenhower: Soldier, General of the Army, President-Elect, 1890–1952* (New York: Simon and Schuster, 1983); David Eisenhower, *Eisenhower at War, 1943* (New York: Random House, 1986); and Charles B. MacDonald, *The Mighty Endeavor* (New York: Oxford University Press, 1969), for Eisenhower's view of World War II in the European theater. See Omar Bradley and Clay Blair, *A General's Life: An Autobiography by General of the Army Omar N. Bradley* (New York: Simon and Schuster, 1983); Arthur Bryant, *The Turn of the Tide, 1939–1943* (New York: Doubleday, 1957); Bernard L. Montgomery, *The Memoirs of Field-Marshal the Viscount Montgomery of Alamein, K.G.* (London: Collins, 1958); and Chester Wilmot, *The Struggle for Europe* (New York: Harper and Brothers, 1952), for those more critical of Eisenhower's leadership. For the best summary of the disagreements between Eisenhower and Montgomery, see G.E. Patrick Murray, *Eisenhower versus Montgomery: The Continuing Debate* (Westport, Conn.: Praeger, 1996).

3   Forrest C. Pogue, *The Supreme Command*, U.S. Army in World War II (Washington, D.C.: Government Printing Office, 1954), 180, 181. See also Walter Bedell Smith, *Eisenhower's Six Great Decisions: Europe, 1944–1945* (New York: Longmans, Green, 1956), 31.

4   Dwight D. Eisenhower, Letter to Leonard T. Gerow, 18 November 1940, Eisenhower Pre-Presidential Papers, Box 13, File 6, EL.

5   Morris Janowitz, *The Professional Soldier* (New York: Macmillan, 1960), 21, 154.

6   Martin Blumenson and James L. Stokesbury, *Masters of the Art of Command* (Boston: Houghton Mifflin, 1975), 303.

7   Ibid., 290. Brooke may have been jealous of Eisenhower since he too aspired to be the supreme commander for the invasion of Europe. And Blumenson and Stokesbury, in *Masters of the Art of Command,* 291, observed that American generals critical of Eisenhower who witnessed his meteoric rise also may have been jealous of his rank and position.

8   Bradley and Blair, *General's Life,* 130. The chapter from which these words are quoted came from the first sections of the book written by Bradley.

9   Gelb, *Ike and Monty,* 187. See also Bradley and Blair, *General's Life,* 151, 162. Later in the war, Marshall came to believe, along with Patton and Bradley, that perhaps the British exerted too great an influence on Eisenhower's decision-making process. See Pogue, *Supreme Command,* 113.

10   Martin Blumenson, *The Patton Papers, 1940–1945* (Boston: Houghton Mifflin, 1974), 164. Blumenson quotes Patton: "'I truly think that the whole set up is the result of clever politics by the British and selfish ambition on our part.... Ike will be a sort of War Department" – detached from the battlefield.'

11   Gelb, *Ike and Monty,* 266. See also Bryant, *Turn of the Tide.*

12   Bradley and Blair, *General's Life,* 161.

13   Gelb, *Ike and Monty,* 183–86.

14   Blumenson, *Patton Papers,* 211, 245.

15   Ibid., 628.

16   Bradley and Blair, *General's Life,* 154.

17   Susan H. Godson, *Viking of Assault: Admiral John Lesslie Hall, Jr., and Amphibious Warfare* (Washington, D.C.: University Press of America, 1982), 122: 'Eisenhower got consistently low marks from Hall. Hall considered the Supreme Allied Commander a mere figurehead, while the British made the important strategic and tactical decisions. Feeding into Hall's evaluation were probably the many occasions in the Mediterranean when he felt Eisenhower or his headquarters had mishandled situations. A fighter, Hall was disdainful of desk-bound generals and admirals.'

18   Merle Miller, *Ike the Soldier: As They Knew Him* (New York: Perigee, 1987), 249. See also Blumenson and Stokesbury, *Masters of the Art of Command,* 294: 'Quick and bright, Eisenhower had a capacity for learning, an ability for assessing complicated situations, a facility for striking to the heart of a problem. He usually came up with just the right solution. In sum his judgment was sound, his balance excellent. Add an ability to get along with people and you have a rare person.'

19   H. A. DeWeerd, ed., *Selected Speeches and Statements of General of the Army George C. Marshall* (Washington, D.C.: Infantry Journal Press, 1945), 249.

20   Kenneth Edwards, *Operation Neptune* (London: Collins, 1946), 68.

21   Gelb, *Ike and Monty,* 122.

22   Dwight D. Eisenhower, Letter to Leonard T. Gerow, 24 February 1943, 1, Leonard T. Gerow Papers, VMI.

23   Eisenhower, *Crusade in Europe,* 210. See also Alfred D. Chandler Jr., ed., *The Papers of Dwight David Eisenhower: The War Years* (Baltimore: Johns Hopkins University Press, 1970), 3:1783.

24   Eisenhower, *Crusade in Europe,* 455, 456: 'All the developments in method, equipment, and destructive power that we were studying seemed minor innovations compared to the revolutionary impact of the atom bomb... [T]he reports that reached us after the first one was used at Hiroshima on August 6 left no doubt in our minds that a new era of warfare had begun... Henceforth, it would seem, the purpose of an aggressor nation would be to stock atom bombs in quantity and to employ them by surprise against industrial fabric and population centers of its intended victim.' This would be Eisenhower's thinking and policy when he became president of the United States.

25   Ibid., 452.

26   Robert Frank Futrell, *Ideas, Concepts, Doctrine: A History of Basic Thinking in the United States Air Force, 1907–1964* (Maxwell Air Force Base, Ala.: Air University, 1974), 90. See also Winston S. Churchill, *The Second World War,* vol. 5, *Closing the Ring* (Boston: Houghton Mifflin, 1951), 528. In a letter to Churchill, Eisenhower wrote: 'We must never forget that one of the fundamental factors leading to the decision for undertaking "Overlord" was the conviction that our overpowering Air Force would make feasible an operation which might otherwise be considered extremely hazardous, if not foolhardy.'

27   Harry C. Butcher, *My Three Years with Eisenhower* (New York: Simon and Schuster, 1946), 530.

28   Jeter A. Isley and Philip A. Crowl, *The U.S. Marines and Amphibious War* (Princeton, N.J.: Princeton University Press, 1951), 6.

29   Pogue, *Supreme Command,* 113; Gordon Harrison, *Cross-Channel Attack,* U.S. Army in World War II (Washington, D.C.: Government Printing Office, 1951), 171.

30   On another matter, Montgomery deferred to Eisenhower for the sake of Allied co-operation. He later regretted his decision: 'I didn't like it... I wish now – as I have often wished – that I hadn't half-heartedly concurred that early August day. But I wanted to show willing to Ike; I had been showing unwilling in other matters, and I sensed then that there were more of these "other matters" to come' (Montgomery, *Memoirs,* 220).

31   U.S. Army, 1st Infantry Division, G-3 Report of Operations, 31 May–30 June 1944, General Huebner, 45, FDM.

32   Forrest C. Pogue wrote: 'From the time that Eisenhower arrived in London in mid-January until the eve of D-Day, he was involved in getting what was needed for victory. In some cases, a long battle was required to convince the U.S. Chiefs of Staff or the American President; other cases involved the acceptance of political decisions displeasing to the British War Cabinet and the Prime Minister; and still

other cases involved attempts to gain the co-operation of General de Gaulle. Only an Allied Commander-in-Chief could have won from various governments what a British or American general could scarcely have asked from his own government. In the major political and military decisions of the period, Eisenhower made his authority felt' ('D-Day – 1944,' in *D-Day: The Normandy Invasion in Retrospect,* ed. Eisenhower Foundation [Lawrence: University Press of Kansas, 1971], 14).

33   Bernard L. Montgomery, *Normandy to the Baltic* (Boston: Houghton Mifflin, 1948), 5.

34   Ibid., 20.

35   Montgomery, *Memoirs,* 210–12. See also Churchill, *The Second World War,* vol. 5, *Closing the Ring,* 436.

36   Supreme Headquarters Allied Expeditionary Force (44), 3rd Meeting, Minutes of Meeting Convened by Supreme Commander Allied Expeditionary Force, 21 January 1944, R. W. Barker Papers, Box 1, File SHAEF, EL.

37   Ibid., 1.

38   Ibid., 2.

39   Chandler, *Papers of Dwight David Eisenhower,* 3:1775.

40   Supreme Headquarters Allied Expeditionary Force (44), 3rd Meeting, 3, 4.

41   Ibid., 4.

42   U.S. Army, Allied Naval Commander Expeditionary Force, Commander in Chief 21st Army Group, and Air Commander in Chief Allied Expeditionary Air Force, 'Neptune' Initial Joint Plan, Omar Bradley Papers, USMA, 18, 19: 'Air Operations (Preliminary Phase). It will be essential that the fighting value of the German Air Forces and its capacity for intensive and sustained operations be reduced as much as possible by the time the decisive air battle is joined. Operation "Point-Blank" is our main means of achieving this and will be maintained to the maximum extent possible.'

43   British Army, Neptune, Initial Joint Plan, Allied Naval Commander Expeditionary Force, Commander in Chief 21st Army Group, Air Commander in Chief Allied Expeditionary Air Force, 1 February 1944, 22, Omar Bradley Papers, USMA. For this operation and its strategic consequences, Montgomery concentrated on the employment of brigades, the U.S. Army equivalent of an RCT, as opposed to divisions and corps. Later in the war, when Bradley's 12th Army Group was composed of three armies and one of those armies contained ten to twenty divisions, the army group commander did not concern himself with brigade-size units. This fact reinforces the notion that small tactical formations have at times been responsible for the success or failure of strategically important missions.

44   Ibid., 23. When this plan was issued on 1 February, the details for the employment of airborne forces had not been completely worked out. The thinking of Bradley and Marshall influenced the final plan for the employment of airborne forces. These matters are addressed below in the discussion of the FUSA's plan for the invasion.

45   For biographies on Montgomery, see L.F. Ellis *et al., Victory in the West,* vol. 1, *The Battle of Normandy* (London: Her Majesty's Stationery Office, 1962); Nigel Hamilton, *Monty: The Battles of Field Marshal Bernard Montgomery* (New York: Random House, 1981); Hamilton's two-volume study *Monty: The Making of a General, 1887–1942* (New York: McGraw-Hill, 1981) and *Master of the Battlefield: Monty's War Years, 1942–1944* (New York: McGraw-Hill, 1983); Alistair Horne with David Montgomery, *Monty: The Lonely Leader, 1944–1945* (New York: Harper Collins, 1994); Richard Lamb, *Montgomery in Europe, 1943–45: Success or Failure* (New York: Franklin Watts, 1984); Ronald Lewin, *Montgomery as Military Commander* (New York: Stein and day, 1971); Alan Moorehead, *Montgomery: A Biography* (New

York: Coward-McGann, 1946); and R.W. Thompson, *The Montgomery Legend* (London: George Allen & Unwin, 1967), and *Montgomery the Field Marshal* (London: George Allen & Unwin, 1969). Montgomery also published a number of articles and books. See '21st (British) Army Group in the Campaign in Northwest Europe, 1944–45,' *Journal Royal United Service Institute,* 1945; *The Path to Leadership* (London, 1961); and *A History of Warfare* (New York: Collins, 1968).

46 Montgomery, *Memoirs,* x: 'National feelings on the subject [the Normandy campaign] have tended to run high and in particular American writers have launched heavy attacks on the British conduct of operations in general and on myself especially... I will try and tell the story truthfully.'

47 Hamilton, *Battles of Field Marshal Bernard Montgomery,* 5.

48 Ibid.

49 Ibid., 6; Gelb, *Ike and Monty,* 39.

50 Hamilton, *Battles of Field Marshal Bernard Montgomery,* 6.

51 H. S. Sewell, 'Montgomery's Tactics,' *Military Review,* August 1945, 128.

52 British Army, 21st Army Group, 'Some Notes on the Conduct of War and the Infantry Division in Battle,' Belgium: 21st Army Group, November 1944, 18–28, and 'Some Notes on the Use of Air Power in Support of Land Operations,' Holland: 21st Army Group, December 1944, Bernard L. Montgomery, Omar Bradley Papers, USMA. The citation on these original autographed documents reads: 'To: Omar Bradley with best wishes and high regard. B.L. Montgomery, Field Marshal,' dated 11 January 1944.

53 Heinz Guderian, *Panzer Leader* (New York: E. P. Dutton, n.d.), 39–46.

54 This statement could also be made of the German defense in the West in 1944, with several exceptions, such as the Pas-de-Calais.

55 J. F. C. Fuller, 'Armor and Counter Armor,' *Infantry Journal,* April 1944, 47.

56 Montgomery, *Memoirs,* 75: 'I was made responsible for the Army side of the planning since I was then commanding the South Eastern Army, from which the troops for the raid were to come.'

57 Ibid., 76.

58 Bernard Fergusson, *The Watery Maze: The Story of Combined Operations* (New York: Holt, Rinehart and Winston, 1961), 171: 'This is one passage in Montgomery's book – there are others – where his memory has played him false. Far from not agreeing with the changes, he was in the chair at the meeting where the decision was taken; and he is not on record in the minutes as having demurred.' Terence Robertson, in *Dieppe: The Shame and the Glory* (Boston: Little, Brown, 1962), 51, also challenged Montgomery's statement on his role in the failed Dieppe raid: 'On Montgomery's orders the military choice was made: a frontal attack. This decision would have a decisive influence on the outcome of the operation and lead directly to such tragedy that the ripple effects would reach almost every corner of Canada.'

59 Gelb, *Ike and Monty,* 180. See also Erwin Rommel, *The Rommel Papers,* ed. Basil H. Liddell-Hart (New York: Da Capo, 1985), 521.

60 'Gen. M'Creery, 69, of British Army,' *New York Times,* 19 October 1967, 42.

61 Bradley and Blair, *General's Life,* 151. See also Blumenson, *Patton Papers,* 608. On 27 December 1944, Patton wrote in his diary: 'Monty is a tired little fart. War requires the taking of risks and he won't take them.'

62 Gelb, *Ike and Monty,* 162.

63 David Fraser, *Knight's Cross: A Life of Field Marshal Erwin Rommel* (New York: Harper Collins, 1993), 458.

64 Paul Carell, *Invasion: They're Coming* (New York: E.P. Dutton, 1963), 15.

65 Fraser, *Knight's Cross,* 460.

66 Ibid., 468.
67 Patrice Boussel, *D-Day Beaches Revisited* (New York: Doubleday, 1966), 12: 'On March 6, there was another four-day tour of inspection [by Rommel] of the coasts of Brittany and Normandy. The 716th Infantry was to hand over to the 352nd the western half of its area; this move was to have momentous consequences for the Americans on D-Day. In February 62,000 mines were laid; in March 100,000 more. Eight kilometers of coast obstacles were ready (slanting poles, antitank obstacles, etc.).'
68 Bernard Montgomery, British Army, Brief Summary of Operation Overlord, 7 April 1944, Eisenhower Pre-Presidential Papers, Box 82, Folder Montgomery, Bernard (S), EL. See also Montgomery, *Normandy to the Baltic,* 29: 'We appreciated that the Germans would be alerted in the Neptune area on the night D-1 as our seaborne forces approached the Normandy coast, and that by the end of D-Day the enemy would himself have appreciated that Overlord was a major operation delivered in strength... In accordance with his policy of defeating us on the beaches, it was to be expected that he would summon initially the nearest available armored and motorised divisions to oppose us, and that in the first stage we should have to meet immediate counter attacks to push us back into the sea.'
69 Edwards, *Operation Neptune,* 128: 'The 14th Minesweeper Flotilla was within sight of the coast by daylight for at least three hours, and 16th Flotilla for about an hour. Before darkness fell the men of the 14th Flotilla could clearly distinguish individual buildings ashore.'
70 For the British assessment of the Montgomery Plan, see Ellis *et al., Victory in the West,* vol. 1, *The Battle of Normandy,* 63, 65: 'There are three essentials to success in any seaborne invasion of a defended coast... Second is the largest obtainable measure of surprise, so that the enemy defense may be handicapped... In order to gain as much as possible of the priceless advantage of surprise and to reduce the danger from coastal batteries, each group of these "landing-ship infantry"... would be stopped several miles from the shore; there the troops on board would embark in the small "landing-craft assault"... and run in with other larger craft loaded with tanks.'
71 Montgomery, *Normandy to the Baltic,* 28.
72 Montgomery and Bradley believed the air force would significantly reduce the flow of enemy reinforcements to the beaches. Bradley commented to his corps and division commanders early in the planning process: 'This figure [G-2 Estimate of Enemy Situation]... looks very bad. They could put nine divisions against your three if there was no interference; and in the new war games *we don't have a chance if you leave out the air. We feel at that time we will have between ten and twelve thousand planes to support this, namely, fighters and bombers and everything else, and, of course, all that bombing is going to delay this movement so it can't possibly reach there.* In addition to that you have your sabotage and dropped troops... We are going to drop troops here for demolition, and so on. So don't let that figure scare you too much. That is as Colonel Dickson [G-2, FUSA] says his optimum' (emphasis added; U.S. Army, First U.S. Army, Overlord Conference, 21 December 1943, 10, RG 407, Box 24309, File 209, NA II).
73 British Army, 21st Army Group, Neptune, Possible Build-up of Enemy Reinforcements in the Neptune Area, Appendix A, RG 407, Box 24373, Files 630–33, NA II.
74 U.S. Army, V Corps, Operation Plan Neptune, Annex 1, G-2 Estimate of Enemy Situation, 1 April 1944, 9, RG 407, Box 3412, Files 205-0.6–0.13, NA II.
75 Ibid., 15 May 1944, 4, Files 205-0.13–1.12.

76   The estimates of alert, assembly, and march times are very conservative and are in
     accordance with British estimates delineated in June 1943. A British intelligence
     officer reported: '[A]vailable armored reserves are... fairly equally spaced some 30
     miles or so behind the coast line; placed so that at least one armored division could
     reach any likely landing area within eight to twelve hours of being ordered to
     move' (U.S. Army, Assault Training Center, 'Conference on Landing Assaults, 24
     May–23 June 1943,' Bell Burton, Lieutenant Colonel British Intelligence, p.
     Burton 16, D756.3.C66 1943, v. 2, c. 3, MHI). A professional infantry division
     anticipating an invasion in a war zone would have been able to get the lead battal-
     ion of the lead regiment on the road in an hour. With a march rate of five miles per
     hour, the lead companies would have arrived at Omaha Beach in five hours.

77   G-2 Estimate of Enemy Situation, 15 May 1944, 18.

78   Fraser, *Knight's Cross,* 488.

79   U.S. Army, First U.S. Army, Report of Operations, 20 October 1943–1 August
     1944, Book 1, 'Enemy Dispositions and Operations,' General Omar Bradley, 48,
     Omar Bradley Papers, USMA. See also Harrison, *Cross-Channel Attack,* 319:
     'Instead of attacking in the sector of one regiment of an overextended static divi-
     sion as expected, General Huebner's troops hit on the front of a full attack infantry
     division, the 352nd, whose presence in the coastal zone had been missed by Allied
     intelligence even though it had been in place for almost three months.' This is the
     historically accepted interpretation.

80   G-2 Estimate of Enemy Situation, 15 May 1944, 13–15.

81   Wesley Frank Craven and James Lea Cate, eds., *The Army Air Forces in World War II,*
     vol. 3, *Europe: Argument to V-E Day, January 1944 to May 1945* (Washington, D.C.:
     Office of Air Force History, 1983), 68, 69. John E. Fagg wrote: 'The mission of the
     air force was to overcome the disadvantages inherent in an overwater attack on a
     well-protected coast. So essential was this function that air considerations fairly
     dictated the choice of the invasion site to some point between Flushing, in the
     Netherlands, and Cherbourg.'

82   Ibid., 143.

83   Sir Arthur Harris, *Bomber Offensive* (London: Creenhill Books, 1990), 205.

84   Montgomery, *Memoirs,* 242.

85   Montgomery, *Normandy to the Baltic,* 38.

86   Robert H. George, in Craven and Cate, *Europe: Argument to V-E Day,* 190.

87   Ibid., 192.

88   Ibid.

89   Arthur B. Ferguson, in ibid., 15, 20.

90   W. Hays Parks, '"Precision" and "Area" Bombing: Who Did Which, and When,' in
     Airpower: Theory and Practice, ed. John Gooch (London: Frank Cass, 1995), 156.

91   Ibid., 162.

92   Ibid., 154.

93   Ibid., 156: 'Of the American attacks against Germany, radar was responsible for 61
     per cent of all bomb tonnage; of the 61 per cent, 81 per cent was delivered using
     H2X.'

94   Bradley and Blair, *General's Life,* 178. This assessment was confirmed by Admiral H.
     Kent Hewitt; see chapter 2.

95   Ibid., 229.

96   Fagg, in Craven and Cate, *Europe: Argument to V-E Day,* 143.

97   Parks, '"Precision" and "Area" Bombing,' 147. Major General Ira C. Eaker, Eighth
     Air Force commander, stated at the Casablanca Conference: 'Day bombing is more
     accurate; small targets like individual targets can be found, seen, and hit... The truth

of the matter is that night bombing is area bombing, good for destruction of cities. Day bombing is point bombing, effective in destroying factories and other key targets.'

98 Ibid.

99 Ibid., 168.

100 British Army, 21st Army Group, Note on Planning Procedures for 'Neptune,' 6 December 1943, A-4, Arthur S. Nevin Papers, MHI. The Neptune operation was divided into four phases: '(a) The assault on, and break through, the coastal defense. (b) The capture and consolidation of a 'Covering position' some 4–5 miles from the beaches. (c) The break-out from the covering position with the object of capturing a bridgehead deep enough for the Rear Maintenance Area and for the construction of airfields. This phase may have to be carried out in several successive stages. (d) Operations for the capture of a port.' Ultimately, phase b was eliminated.

101 British Army, Neptune, Initial Joint Plan, 22: 'The object will be to capture the towns of St Mère-Eglise 3495, Carentan 3984, Isigny 5085, Bayeux 7879 and Caen 0368 by the evening of D-Day.'

102 U.S. Navy, Western Task Force, Commander Task Force 122, Action Report on Amphibious Operation in Baie de la Seine, Normandy Invasion, 25 July 1944, Rear Admiral A. G. Kirk, 7, Box 317, File Task Force 122-122.4.4, NHC.

103 Montgomery, *Normandy to the Baltic*, 32, 33, 38.

104 Fagg, in Craven and Cate, *Europe: Argument to V-E Day*, 143.

105 Montgomery, *Normandy to the Baltic*, 29.

106 Montgomery, *Memoirs*, 220.

107 The original sentence read: 'If you mean by tactical surprise that the enemy will not be ready for you, then I do not think you will not attain it.' Given the context of this statement, the third 'not' was clearly unintended.

108 'Conference on Landing Assaults,' Major General J.C. Haydon, British Combined Operation, p. Haydon 3.

109 Ibid., p. Zeller 2.

110 Haydon, ibid., p. Haydon 3: 'You can consider the means he will use to try and discover what is going on. His PRU reconnaissance will be flown on every possible day and the data checked up by his Intelligence Branch. He will have weather forecasts, just as we will have; he will know the tidal conditions and will sum up those most favourable for landing. Each item will affect his degree of readiness. In 1940, in this country, reconnaissances were flown every day. All enemy activity was checked and noted; all barges and craft carefully counted, so it will be with him. He will endeavor to learn every move of assault shipping wherever it is, on the south or east coast.'

111 U.S. Army, First U.S. Army, Overlord Conference, 21 December 1943, 6, RG 407, Box 24309, File 209, NA II.

112 'Conference on Landing Assaults,' General Norman D. Cota, Assistant Division Commander at Normandy, 29th Infantry Division, p. Cota 7.

113 U.S. Army, V Corps, History of V Corps, 6 June 1944, 51, Government Documents, University of California, Doe Library, Berkeley, Calif.: 'From the Army viewpoint, a landing in darkness was desirable. It was conceded that this would result in greater confusion both in loading craft and in landing, but the additional surprise which could be gained, with resultant lessened effectiveness of enemy defenses, was thought to overcome this. A landing in darkness would bring fewer casualties and losses of material, it was maintained.' The leadership of the 1st ID also preferred a night landing. See G-3 Report of Operations, 45.

CHAPTER SIX

1   Supreme Headquarters Allied Expeditionary Force, Report by the Supreme Commander to the Combined Chiefs of Staff on the Operations in Europe of the Allied Expeditionary Forces, 6 June 1944–8 May 1945, General Dwight D. Eisenhower, 24, Government Documents, University of California, Doe Library, Berkeley, Calif. These vehicles were recognized by Eisenhower as one of the keys to the successful invasion in SHAEF after the action report to the Combined Chiefs of Staff even though they, with the exception of the DD tanks, were not employed on American beaches.

2   Omar Bradley and Clay Blair, *A General's Life: An Autobiography by General of the Army Omar N. Bradley* (New York: Simon and Schuster, 1983), 200.

3   Omar Bradley, *A Soldier's Story* (New York: Henry Holt, 1951), 128, 130.

4   Ibid., 232: 'In urging the Cotentin landing to ensure early capture of Cherbourg, I had emphasized both to Montgomery and Smith the necessity for an airborne drop behind that beach. For while Utah was broad and flat and therefore suitable for seaborne assault, its exits were limited to several narrow causeways traversing a flooded marshland. As long as the enemy held those causeways he could pin us to Utah Beach. "Much as I favor the Cotentin assault," I told COSSAC's planners, "I would sooner see it go by the boards than risk a landing on Utah without airborne help."'

5   There was some disagreement over where the idea for the American airborne operation originated. Both Bradley and the 21st Army Group claimed credit for the idea. See S.L.A. Marshall's 'Commentary,' in The Collected Writings of General Omar N. Bradley, University of Chicago Library, Chicago, Ill., n.d., 6:53: 'I was convinced, on the basis of what we had learned from dealing with all combat units, that the blow dealt by the U.S. airborne behind Utah Beach was the decisive hammerstroke. It was the linchpin of the Neptune Plan of which came success... How General Bradley ramrodded that part of it through, standing fast when there was divided counsel in the camp, is but one episode objectively treated in this chronicle.'

6   U.S. Army, First U.S. Army, Report of Operations, 20 October 1943–1 August 1944, Book 1, 'Enemy Dispositions and Operations,' General Omar Bradley, 39, Omar Bradley Papers, USMA.

7   Ibid.; U.S. Army, First U.S. Army, Overlord Conference, 21 December 1943, 8, RG 407, Box 24309, File 209, NA II.

8   Bradley and Blair, *General's Life,* 252.

9   Bradley, *Soldier's Story,* 272.

10 Martin Blumenson, *The Patton Papers, 1940–1945* (Boston: Houghton Mifflin, 1974), 434. At an Overlord planning conference, Patton wrote in his diary: 'As usual, Bradley said nothing. He does all the getting along and does it to his own advantage.'

11 Bernard L. Montgomery, *Normandy to the Baltic* (Boston: Houghton Mifflin, 1948), 20, 24.

12 Dwight D. Eisenhower, *Crusade in Europe* (New York: Doubleday, 1948), 214, 215. See also Carlo D'Este, *Patton: A Genius for War* (New York: Harper, 1995), 552.

13 Nigel Hamilton, *Master of the Battlefield: Monty's War Years, 1942–1944* (New York: McGraw-Hill, 1983), 658. Montgomery's initial assessment of Bradley was that he was 'dull, conscientious, dependable and loyal' (ibid., 602).

14 Alistair Horne with David Montgomery, *Monty: The Lonely Leader, 1944–1945* (New York: Harper Collins, 1994), 204, 205.

15 Patton's diary, 14 July 1944, in Blumenson, *Patton Papers,* 482. See also D'Este, *Patton,* 617, 420. There was considerable friction between Bradley and Patton.

D'Este wrote that Bradley 'despised' and 'detested' Patton and that '[a]fter World War II, Omar Bradley and some of the original members of the II Corps staff perpetuated the myth that Patton was a mediocre commander, ill served by a poor staff that more often than not failed to do its job – a view, colored by deep prejudices against Patton, that was neither balanced nor accurate.' Patton probably also had prejudices against Bradley, his former subordinate, that influenced his remarks and assessment. See also Martin Blumenson, *Patton: The Man behind the Legend, 1885–1945* (New York: William Morrow, 1985), 228, 230, 232, 236, 306.

16   D'Este, *Patton,* 467, 611. Patton wrote: 'Collins and Bradley are too prone to cut off heads. This will make division commanders lose their confidence. A man should not be damned for an initial failure with a new division. Had I done this with General Eddy of the 9th [ID] in Africa, the army would have lost a potential corps commander' (Patton's diary, 7 July 1944, in Blumenson, *Patton Papers,* 479).

17   Department of the Army, Office, Chief of Information, General Omar Nelson Bradley, Biography, CMH.

18   Bradley, *Soldier's Story,* 14.

19   David Nichols, *Ernie's War: The Best of Ernie Pyle's World War II Dispatches* (New York: Simon and Schuster, 1986), 358. Carlo D'Este disagreed with Pyle's portrayal of Bradley. He quoted S.L.A. Marshall, who wrote: 'The GI's were not impressed with him. They scarcely knew him. He's not a flamboyant figure and he didn't get out much to troops. And the idea that he was idolized by the average soldier is just rot. He didn't make that much of an imprint' (D'Este, *Patton,* 467).

20   Margaret Mead, *And Keep Your Powder Dry* (New York: William Morrow, 1942), chap. 8.

21   Bradley would make this same mistake again during the Korean War when he was chairman of the Joint Chiefs of Staff. General MacArthur did not respond to directives from the Pentagon or the White House, and Bradley failed to act decisively.

22   Chester Wilmot, *The Struggle for Europe* (New York: Harper and Brothers, 1952), 264.

23   Max Hastings, *Overlord: D-Day and the Battle for Normandy* (New York: Simon and Schuster, 1984), 90.

24   Russell F. Weigley, *Eisenhower's Lieutenants* (Bloomington: Indiana University Press, 1981), 89; Wilmot, *Struggle for Europe,* 264.

25   Bradley, *Soldier's Story,* 227–29: 'However, with Crittenberger and Woodruff both cutting their teeth on the same invasion, Eisenhower and I doubted the wisdom of entrusting the entire U.S. assault to an inexperienced trio. Both Crittenberger and Woodruff had come to England with distinguished records: both were long-time friends of Bradley. But neither had as yet experienced combat command in World War II. This was my only prejudice against them.'

26   The Fifteenth Army was not a regular army. Eisenhower created it for administrative purposes and rear area security. Eisenhower wrote: '[T]he Fifteenth, under the command of General Gerow, ...was to have two principal functions. It was to take over matters of military government in rear of advancing troops. It would also provide the necessary Allied strength on the western bank of the Rhine facing the Ruhr to prevent any of the Germans in the region from raiding important points on our supply lines west of the river' (Eisenhower, *Crusade in Europe,* 398).

27   Blumenson, *Patton Papers,* 739, 740.

28   Dwight D. Eisenhower, Letter to Leonard T. Gerow, 16 July 1942, Leonard T. Gerow Papers, VMI. In a letter written to Gerow on 24 February 1943, after Eisenhower was promoted to the rank of four-star general, Eisenhower wrote: 'Of all the congratulations and felicitations that I have received on this latest promo-

tion yours, more than in any other case, I know to be absolutely sincere and disinterested. I especially appreciate your sentiments because I can never get over the feeling, one that I have held ever since I was a Second Lieutenant, that in every respect you have deserved recognition far above myself. If, therefore, I felt that personal fortune and promotion had any slightest importance in this war, I should have to feel almost regretful that such a distinction came to me instead of to you. But you must know, as well as I do, that certain fortuitous circumstances, more than any indication of peculiar merit, were responsible for my advancement' (ibid.). Gerow's letters may have helped sustain Eisenhower's ego during difficult periods when the press, particularly the British press, was not kind to him. Gerow's letters were always supportive. He used glowing terms to compliment Eisenhower on his achievements, and Eisenhower may have responded to Gerow's friendship and loyalty by watching over his career as Patton indicated.

After the Battle of the Bulge, Montgomery sent a letter to Bradley in which he praised American soldiers and leaders, including Gerow. See Harry C. Butcher, *My Three Years with Eisenhower* (New York: Simon and Schuster, 1946), 741: 'He [Montgomery] had found Hodges and Simpson a great pleasure to work with and said that the corps commanders, particularly Gerow, Collins, and Ridgway, had been magnificent.'

29   Alfred D. Chandler Jr., ed., *The Papers of Dwight David Eisenhower: The War Years* (Baltimore: Johns Hopkins University Press, 1970), 1:566.

30   In February 1945, Eisenhower rank-ordered his subordinate commanders based, he wrote, 'primarily upon my conclusions as to value of service each officer has rendered in this war and only secondarily upon my opinion as to his qualifications for future usefulness.' Gerow was ranked eighth behind Bradley, Spaatz, Smith, Patton, Clark, Truscott, and Doolittle and in front of individuals such as Collins, Patch, Hodges, Simpson, Eaker, and Ridgway. Patch, Hodges, and Simpson were army commanders. See ibid., 4:2466.

31   Bradley and Blair, *General's Life,* 223.

32   Bradley, *Soldier's Story,* 227.

33   Ibid., 228. Bradley commented on the VII Corps commander who landed at Utah Beach: 'One of the most outstanding field commanders in Europe, Collins was without doubt also the most aggressive. With a hand picked staff to help him he seasoned an unerring tactical judgment with just enough bravado to make every advance a triumph. To this energy he added boundless self-confidence. Such self-assurance is tolerable only when right, and Collins, happily, almost always was.'

34   Ibid., 227.

35   Gerow's military education included the Infantry School Advanced Course, 1925; U.S. Army Command and General Staff College, 1926 (honorary graduate); U.S. Army War College, 1931; and Chemical Warfare School, Field Officer Course, 1931. His promotion record was second lieutenant, 29 September 1911; first lieutenant, 1 July 1916; captain, 15 May 1917; major, 1 July 1920; lieutenant colonel, 1 August 1935; colonel, 1 September 1940; brigadier general, 1 October 1940; major general, 14 February 1942; and lieutenant general, 1 January 1945. Gerow retired in July 1950 and died on 12 October 1972.

36   Merle Miller, *Ike the Soldier: As They Knew Him* (New York: Perigee, 1987), 138.

37   Ibid.

38   Department of Defense, Office of Public Information Press Branch, Summary of the Career of General Leonard T. Gerow, CMH.

39   Leonard T. Gerow, Letter to Dwight D. Eisenhower, 28 July 1941, Leonard T.

Gerow Papers,VMI.

40 Ed Cray, *General of the Army, George C. Marshall: Soldier and Statesman* (New York:W. W. Norton, 1990), 480, 559.

41 Leonard T. Gerow, Letter to Dwight D. Eisenhower, 19 April 1942, Leonard T. Gerow Papers,VMI.

42 Miller, *Ike the Soldier,* 346. Miller quoted Eisenhower:'When BG Eisenhower took over Gerow's position in the War Department in a letter to retired Major General Van Voorhis he wrote:"Gee and I have really played tag with each other all along the line; but this is the first time I really envy him. My heart is in the field and it is hard to sit at a desk on days such as these.The powers that be have put me in this backbreaking job – so all I can do is hope."'

43 Bradley, *Soldier's Story,* 227, 175: 'Indeed Gerow had been working on a plan for assault since COSSAC published its OVERLORD outline... It's 29th Division had already been scheduled as U.S. vanguard on the invasion.'

44 U.S. Army,V Corps, Report after Action against Enemy, chap. 2, Preparation for the Operation, Planning, November 1944, 4, RG 407, Box 3409, File 205-0.3, NA II: 'Throughout all this period, planning for OVERLORD... was progressing. With the establishment of First United States Army headquarters in the United Kingdom in October 1943 and First U.S. Army Group headquarters [later the 12th Army Group] in London at about the same time, the V Corps' part in the operation was reduced.This Corps became one of the two assault Corps to make the invasion landings rather than the headquarters commanding all field forces as had appeared originally.' Bradley too labored under the false impression that his FUSA would lead the entire invasion. At an Overlord planning conference on 21 December 1943, he stated: 'The actual command of the attack has been given to the First United States Army to command the whole assault, including the American, British and Canadian divisions' (Overlord Conference, 21 December 1943, 1). Montgomery, Churchill, and Eisenhower worked out a relationship that put the British in command of all operational forces.

45 Gerow took command of the 29th ID in the United States in 1942. He deployed with that division to England and trained it for the invasion of Europe. After he was promoted and took command of the V Corps, he retained in that corps the division he had trained, but now with the additional task of planning for the Allied invasion. He had devoted years to this endeavor and no doubt had a well-refined vision of the conduct of the operation. In his mind, he had probably fought the battle for the beaches many times and had worked out solutions to every conceivable eventuality. However, with new leadership and new organizations, a new vision slowly eroded the plan he had formulated.

46 Bradley, *Soldier's Story,* 262.

47 After the war, Bradley became chairman of the Joint Chiefs of Staff and Eisenhower became president of the United States. Gerow remained on active duty and became commandant of the U.S. Army Command and General Staff College (October 1945–January 1948) and then commander of the Second Army in Fort Meade, Maryland, until he retired in July 1950. Although Bradley felt free to criticize Gerow, Gerow may never have felt free to criticize Bradley.

48 Report after Action against Enemy, Planning, 1.

49 Ibid., 2.

50 Ibid.

51 U.S. Army,V Corps, Memorandum to Chiefs of Section, 26 September 1943, RG 407, Box 24309, Files 208–16, NA II.

52 Report after Action against Enemy, Planning, 2.

53   U.S. Army, V Corps, Special Instructions no. 1 to Director, Headquarters, V Corps, Planning Group, 24 September 1943, 1, RG 407, Box 24309, Files 208–16, NA II.

54   Ibid., 2.

55   Ibid.

56   Overlord Conference, 21 December 1943, 1.

57   Ibid., 12.

58   Ibid., 16, 35.

59   Ibid., 17, 18.

60   Ibid., 40.

61   Ibid., 44 (emphasis added).

62   Ibid., 41 (emphasis added).

63   Ibid., 34, 37, 29, 40–42. Bradley told Gerow: 'We will have to rush over as apparently I will have to stay at this setup at Portsmouth with the Navy and Air and we will have to command through you until we can get this advance post set and come over. I don't know whether that is D plus 1 or just when it is' (29).

64   U.S. Army, V Corps, Office of the Corps Commander, Directive (Overlord), 28 January 1944, 1–6, RG 407, Box 24309, File 216, NA II.

65   Ibid.

66   U.S. Army, First U.S. Army, Planning Directive for Overlord, 31 January 1944, 1–2, RG 407, Box 24308, File 200, NA II. The Planning Directive for Overlord from the FUSA to the V and VII Corps described the conduct of the invasion and the specific missions of the two corps. It also specified for the first time which units would be leading the assault: 'The V Corps, initially consisting of 1st, 28th and 29th Infantry Divisions, will assault Beach 46 [Omaha], secure beachhead and advance on to successive phase lines... For the initial assault the 1st Infantry Division (less one CT) with one CT, 29th Infantry Division, attached will be used for the assault. This force will be loaded up in Naval Force "O" with Admiral Hall commanding. The 29th Infantry Division (less one CT) with one CT, 1st Infantry Division attached will constitute the follow-up force and load up in Naval Force "B".' The mission for the VII Corps was stated as follows: 'The VII Corps, initially consisting of the 4th, 3rd and 9th Infantry Divisions and 101st Airborne Division, will assault Beach 49 [Utah], secure beachhead, and advance to successive phase lines... For the initial assault 4th Infantry Division will be used, loading up in Naval Force "U".'

67   Ibid., 2

68   Ibid., 4.

69   U.S. Army, V Corps, Office of the Planning Group, Agenda for Headquarters V Corps, Conference on Planning for Operation 'Overlord,' 4 February 1944, 1, RG 407, Box 24308, File 200, NA II.

70   Ibid., 4 (emphasis added).

71   Ibid.

72   U.S. Army, V Corps, Office of the Planning Group, Note to All Concerned (Minutes), 8 February 1944, 6, 7, RG 407, Box 24308, File 200, NA II.

73   Ibid., 8.

74   U.S. Army, V Corps, Office of the Commanding General, Memorandum for Record, 9 February 1944, RG 407, Box 24309, File 216, NA II.

75   Ibid., 1.

76   Bradley, *Soldier's Story,* 237.

77   Ibid., 236, 272.

78   During this period, Gerow was also conducting training and preparing for inspections. Captain Harry C. Butcher, naval aide to Eisenhower, recorded the following in his diary on Monday, 7 February 1944: 'Leaving from Addison Street Station in the

special train, Ike, Lieutenant General Bradley, Major General J. Lawton Collins... and I arrived at Plymouth Friday morning. Ike and party were met by Major General Gerow, Commanding Officer of the U.S. 29th Division. The day was spent traveling by car to inspect that division and to observe its training activities. How good it will be in battle remains to be seen, as is true of any "unblooded" division' (Butcher, *My Three Years with Eisenhower,* 487). Butcher was mistaken in identifying Gerow as the division commander. Butcher's perspective on 'unblooded' divisions again brings up the question of why the 29th Division was deployed in the initial assault. What was obvious to Butcher must also have been obvious to Bradley and Gerow.

79   U.S. Army, V Corps, Conference Overlord, 7 February 1944, 1, RG 407, Box 24309, File 213, NA II.

80   Ibid.

81   Ibid., 2.

82   U.S. Army, V Corps, Preliminary 'Overlord' Plan, 10 February 1944, RG 407, Box 24309, Files 208–16, NA II.

83   Ibid., 1, 2.

84   U.S. Army, V Corps, Office of the Commanding General, Subject: Landing Force 'B,' Operation 'Neptune,' 14 April 1944, 1, 2, RG 407, Box 24378, File 554, NA II. Gerow's letter to the FUSA stated: 'The present V Corps tactical plan requires the personnel of the 115th Infantry and the 26th Infantry to be put ashore at the earliest possible time on D-day. If Force "B" is not in the transport area when orders are given to land Force "B," the greatest length of time will elapse. Thus, the time of arrival of Naval Force "B" in the transport area is a matter of grave concern to this command.'

85   Preliminary 'Overlord' Plan, 3.

86   Ibid., 2.

87   Overlord Conference, 21 December 1943, 41.

88   Landing Force 'B,' Operation 'Neptune,' 1.

89   First U.S. Army, Report of Operations, Annex 2, Operation Plan 'Neptune,' 97.

90   Ibid., 27: 'The peculiar character of the operation, i.e., assaults on separate beaches, separated by flooded areas in the neighborhood of Carentan, and the fact that First Army Headquarters would in the initial stages not be able to bring much influence to bear upon the operation, placed a great deal of responsibility upon these corps commanders. They were given accordingly a great deal of independence in their planning.'

91   U.S. Army, V Corps, Planning Guide, Operation 'Overlord,' 28 February 1944, RG 407, Box 24373, Files 630–33, NA II.

92   U.S. Army, V Corps, Memorandum for AC of S, G-3, First U.S. Army, Subject: Outline of Operations Plan, V Corps, 21 March 1944, 1, RG 407, Box 24373, Files 630–33, NA II. See also U.S. Army, V Corps, Notes on V Corps Plan 'Neptune,' RG 407, Box 24378, File 670, NA II.

93   Outline of Operations Plan, 2.

94   Ibid., 2, 3.

95   Ibid., 3 (emphasis added).

96   Notes on V Corps Plan 'Neptune,' 4.

CHAPTER SEVEN

1   U.S. Army, First U.S. Army, Intelligence Note no. 16, 24 April 1944, 1, RG 407, Box 24373, Files 630–33, NA II.

2   U.S. Army, Provisional Engineer Group, V Corps, Summary of Activities of the Provisional Engineer Group, 8 July 1944, 1, RG 407, Box 24373, File 205-43.2, NA II.

3   U.S. Army, First U.S. Army, Overlord Conference, 21 December 1943, 44, RG 407,
     Box 24309, File 209, NA II. In both of his books, Bradley was very critical of the
     quantity and quality of direct support the air force typically gave his units. Also,
     heavy bombers had never been deployed in the role that the army was assigning
     them at Normandy. In the Pacific, both naval aviation and the Army Air Force
     took part in the pre-invasion bombardment that was designed to destroy the
     water's edge defense. It was a joint operation. However, air power had not been
     used exclusively to destroy the water's edge defense, which was in essence what it
     was required to do at Normandy since the navy lacked the time and resources to
     perform the mission. It was also known that air power was less precise than naval
     gunfire; thus, in the Pacific, the vast majority of the destruction of the water's edge
     defense was done by the navy. The Army Air Force in the Pacific was probably
     better qualified to perform the close support mission than the air force in Europe
     because it was less enamored of strategic bombing, less orthodox, more innovative,
     and more willing to support the troops on the ground.

4   U.S. Navy, Eleventh Amphibious Force, Message from Commander Task Force
     122, Action COM 11th PHIB, 25 March 1944, RG 407, Box 24373, Files 630–33,
     NA II.

5   U.S. Army, Headquarters Provisional Engineer Special Brigade Group, Message to
     Chief of Staff, First U.S. Army, 30 March 1944, RG 407, Box 24373, Files 630–33,
     NA II (emphasis added).

6   Ibid. (emphasis added): 'In checking the points of C/S, it is shown below that all
     are correct: a. Landing tables do show the loading is not planned for Special
     Brigade Engineers to go in prior to H Hour... c. V Corps plan does require that
     Engr Spec Brig remove mines and obstacles. Work on beach underwater, after
     assault troops have passed through, in order to increase capacity of beaches.'

7   Ibid.

8   U.S. Army, 531st Engineer Shore Regiment, Interim Report: Removal of Beach
     and Underwater Obstacles, 21 May 1943, Colonel R. C. Brown, 3, RG 407, File
     101-20.0, NA II: 'Combat engineer troops integrally included and attached to
     Infantry of Armored Divisions are utilized to perform the required demolition
     using standard engineer cutting and demolition equipment and explosives.'

9   H. Kent Hewitt, 'The Reminiscences of Admiral H. Kent Hewitt,' 15-13, Naval
     History Project, Oral History Research Office, Columbia University, 1962, and
     John Lesslie Hall Jr., 'The Reminiscences of John Lesslie Hall, Jr.,' 128, 129, Naval
     History Project, Oral History Research Office, Columbia University, 1964, NHC.

10   George F. Howe, *The Mediterranean Theater of Operations—Northwest Africa: Seizing
     the Initiative in the West,* U.S. Army in World War II (Washington, D.C.: Government
     Printing Office, 1993), 62.

11   Barry W. Fowle, ed., *Builders and Fighters: U.S. Army Engineers in World War II* (Fort
     Belvoir, Va.: Office of History, U.S. Army Corps of Engineers, 1992).

12   The ESBs were initially army assets. The mission of the ESBs was stated as follows
     in February 1944: 'The Engineer Special Brigade is an organization specially
     trained and equipped for the technical organization of beaches, to regulate and
     facilitate the landing and movement of personnel and equipment on and over the
     beach to assembly areas and vehicle parks, to unload cargo ships, to move and
     receive supplies into beach dumps, to select, organize, and operate beach dumps, to
     establish and maintain communications, and to evacuate casualties and prisoners of
     war over the beach to ships and craft' (U.S. Army, First U.S. Army, Operations
     Memorandum no. 5, 13 February 1944, 3, RG 407, Box 24377, File 659, NA II).

13   Summary of Activities of the Provisional Engineer Group, 1.

14   U.S. Army, 1st Infantry Division, Subject: Operation 'Neptune,' 28 March 1944, 1–3, RG 407, Box 24373, Files 634–36, NA II. See also U.S. Army, V Corps, Letter to Commanding General, First U.S. Army, 29 April 1944, 3, RG 407, Box 24308, File 201, NA II: 'For the accomplishment of the task... the V Corps has allotted the 146th Engineer Combat Battalion (Corps Engineers), and the 299th Engineer Battalion less one company (attached from First U.S. Army), all under command of Lieutenant Colonel O'Neill who has been assigned to command the Provisional Engineer Group.'

15   U.S. Army, 1st Infantry Division, Field Order no. 35, Annex 16, Engineer Plan, 22 May 1944, RG 407, Box 24373, Files 630–33, NA II. See also Summary of Activities of the Provisional Engineer Group, 1.

16   Kenneth P. Lord, Assistant G-3 (Operations), 1st Infantry Division, Personal Narrative, 7, 8, FDM (emphasis added).

17   U.S. Army, First U.S. Army, Report of Operations, 20 October 1943–1 August 1944, Book 1, 'Enemy Dispositions and Operations,' Annex 11, Engineer Special Brigades Plan, General Omar Bradley, 30, Omar Bradley Papers, USMA. It is unfortunate that the U.S. armed forces engaged in such bickering in the midst of a war. Energy, resources, talent, and time wasted away while the armed forces wrangled over such issues as the high-water mark.

18   U.S. Army, V Corps, Memorandum to Commanding General, First U.S. Army, Subject: Breaching Beach Obstacles, 29 April 1944, Major General L.T. Gerow, 2, RG 407, Box 24308, File 201, NA II. One wonders why this had to be written down.

19   U.S. Army, First U.S. Army, APO 230, General Kean, Memorandum to General Bradley, Subject: Underwater Obstacles, 20 April 1944, RG 407, Box 24373, Files 630–33, NA II.

20   Breaching Beach Obstacles, 1.

21   Summary of Activities of the Provisional Engineer Group, 1.

22   Underwater Obstacles, 20 April 1944.

23   Ibid. Kean further noted that the command problem was brought to the attention of Admiral Hall: 'Tubby talked to Admiral Hall's Chief of Staff, concerning the sending of a senior naval officer to take charge of the Navy personnel now at Willicombe. He was told that the best that could be done at this time was to furnish a British Army officer (Major) who has been detailed as LO to Hall. I questioned seriously the wisdom of depending on a British Army officer to make decisions which affect either naval policy or the employment of naval personnel and equipment. Hall's Headquarters did promise to secure someone in the future.'

24   Hoge was also unimpressed with the navy's performance: 'Everything was Navy. And they wouldn't keep their appointments. They were the damnedest people to get along with I'd ever met in my life. They were always alibiing' (Engineer Memoirs, Office of History, U.S. Army Corps of Engineers, 1993; interview, 1974, MHI).

25   Underwater Obstacles, 20 April 1944.

26   U.S. Army, First U.S. Army, Office of AC of S, G-2, Intelligence Note no. 18, Underwater Obstacles, 24 April 1944, 3, 2, RG 407, Box 24373, Files 630–33, NA II. The report described the defenses of Omaha Beach: 'There are approximately 1000 steel hedgehogs in a single broken line on OMAHA beach between 11 feet and 18 feet above BLW stretching for 4500 yards... There are 43 single rows segments, each comprised of 22–29 hedgehogs. The hedgehogs are 10–15 feet apart center to center; segments are staggered approximately 25–50 feet and overlap approximately one hedgehog. They lie from 160 to 400 feet from the back of the beach. Sand has begun collecting around the legs of some of the hedgehogs.'

27 Ibid., 3.

28 Harry C. Butcher, *My Three Years with Eisenhower* (New York: Simon and Schuster, 1946), 529.

29 Ibid., 529, 530.

30 Ibid., 530.

31 U.S. Navy, U.S. Fleet, Headquarters of Commander in Chief, Navy Department, Memorandum, Subject: Distribution of Naval Gunfire Officer, Headquarters V Amphibious Corps, Serial 00671 letter of 7 March 1944, Subject: Naval Gunfire Report on the Marshalls Operation, 22 March 1944, 3, 6–12, RG 407, Files 6-12.060/45, 6-12.0703/44, and U.S. Army, First U.S. Army, Memorandum no. 3, Artillery Information Service, April 1944, RG 407, File 101-160.0ART, NA II. See also Hall, 'Reminiscences,' 131.

32 Butcher, *My Three Years with Eisenhower,* 529.

33 Ibid., 530.

34 Breaching Beach Obstacles, 1.

35 Patrice Boussel, *D-Day Beaches Revisited* (New York: Doubleday, 1966), 12: 'In February 62,000 mines were laid; in March 100,000 more.'

36 Breaching Beach Obstacles, 1.

37 Ibid., 2.

38 Ibid.

39 Ibid., 4, 5 (emphasis added).

40 Hall, 'Reminiscences,' 189.

41 U.S. Navy, Commander Assault Force 'O,' Western Naval Task Force, Action Report, 27 July 1944, 98, Serial 00879, Office of Naval Records, NHC.

42 U.S. Army, 1st Infantry Division, G-3 Report of Operations, 31 May–30 June 1944, General Huebner, 46, FDM. Huebner, commander of the 1st ID, and his troops preferred an early-morning assault. They wanted to attack under the cover of darkness. The 1st ID Report of Operations stated: 'A landing on a defended hostile shore should be made under cover of darkness just before first light.' See also U.S. Army, V Corps, History of V Corps, 6 June 1944, 51, Government Documents, University of California, Doe Library, Berkeley, Calif.: 'From the Army viewpoint, a landing in darkness was desirable. It was conceded that this would result in greater confusion both in loading craft and in landing, but the additional surprise which could be gained, with resultant lessened effectiveness of enemy defenses, was thought to overcome this. A landing in darkness would bring fewer casualties and losses of material, it was maintained.'

43 U.S. Army, Information Section Intelligence Division, OCE Headquarters, ETOUSA, Tidal Illumination Diagrams, 20 June 1944, 4, RG 407, Box 2002, File 101-20.0, NA II.

44 U.S. Army, Headquarters 16th Combat Team, Field Order no. 5, 16 May 1944, Annex 9, 1, RG 407, Box 24374, Files 634–36, NA II.

45 Omar Bradley, *A Soldier's Story* (New York: Henry Holt, 1951), 262, 263.

46 Ibid.

47 U.S. Navy, Western Task Force, Commander Task Force 122, Action Report on Amphibious Operation in Baie de la Seine, Normandy Invasion, 25 July 1944, Rear Admiral A. G. Kirk, 7, Box 317, File Task Force 122-122.4.4, NHC.

48 Hall, 'Reminiscences,' 188, 189.

49 Action Report, Kirk, 7.

50 Overlord Conference, 21 December 1943, 8. Land navigation at night, the need for silence, which limits communication, and the uncertainty that a lack of visibility tends to cause in soldiers are in part the reasons for this disorganization. And no matter how good the commander, friction sets in, and some degree of disorganiza-

tion is inevitable. The longer the movement, the greater the friction. See Carl von Clausewitz, *On War,* ed. and trans. Michael Howard and Peter Paret (Princeton, N.J.: Princeton University Press, 1984), 119–21.

51   Samuel Eliot Morison, *Operations in North African Waters, October 1942–June 1943* (Boston: Little, Brown, 1954), 41, 42.

52   Hall, 'Reminiscences,' 189.

53   Paul W. Thompson, 'D-Day on Omaha Beach,' *Infantry Journal,* June 1945, 44.

54   U.S. Army, V Corps, Outline of V Corps Plan, 17 May 1944, 3, 4, RG 407, Box 24378, File 670, NA II.

CHAPTER EIGHT

1   U.S. Army, First U.S. Army, Report of Operations, 20 October 1943–1 August 1944, Book 1, 'Enemy Dispositions and Operations,' Annex 8, Artillery Section, General Omar Bradley, 166, Omar Bradley Papers, USMA.

2   Ibid., 170: 'On 11 February 1944, the first Joint Fire Plan meeting was held at the request of the Army Artillery Officer. Attending the conference were representatives of the U.S. Army Air Forces and the U.S. Navy. From that date until D-Day, the required co-ordination of the Air and Naval Bombardment for Operation "Neptune" was effected by the Artillery Officer with the knowledge and approval of the Army Commander and the Assistant Chief of Staff, G-3... In addition, assignment of effort was made after consulting the two assaulting corps.'

3   Ibid., 173, 174. Two degrees of damage – the desired effect on the target – are noted in this paragraph: destruction, the highest degree of damage, and neutralization. Destruction could only be achieved by the accurate delivery of bombs from the heavy bombers. The navy alone was incapable of producing this degree of damage with the assets employed and in the time allotted.

4   Alfred D. Chandler Jr., ed., *The Papers of Dwight David Eisenhower: The War Years* (Baltimore: Johns Hopkins University Press, 1970), 3:1773.

5   John Lesslie Hall Jr., 'The Reminiscences of John Lesslie Hall, Jr.,' 131, Naval History Project, Oral History Research Office, Columbia University, 1964, NHC; Samuel Eliot Morison, *The Invasion of France and Germany, 1944–1945* (Boston: Little, Brown, 1957), 56; Susan H. Godson, *Viking of Assault: Admiral John Lesslie Hall, Jr., and Amphibious Warfare* (Washington, D.C.: University Press of America, 1982), 124. Before Hall's death on 6 March 1978, Susan Godson conducted interviews with her uncle while doing research for her Ph.D. dissertation. She concluded that it was Hall's decision to fight for additional warships in the bombardment fleet that precluded defeat at Omaha Beach.

6   Hall, 'Reminiscences,' 131.

7   First U.S. Army, Report of Operations, Annex 12, Prearranged Air and Naval Bombardment Plan, 57.

8   U.S. Army, Assault Training Center, 'Conference on Landing Assaults, 24 May–23 June 1943,' p. Roberts 2, D756.3.C66 1943, v. 2, c. 3, MHI. General Hamilton Roberts stated: 'I consider the 4" shell is not sufficiently heavy for this type of landing and that you want something really big; more in the nature of 12" so that when you hit a target something really happens.'

9   U.S. Army, First U.S. Army, Memorandum no. 3, Artillery Information Service, April 1944, RG 407, File 101-160.0ART, NA II. See also First U.S. Army, Report of Operations, Annex 21, Artillery and Naval Fire Support Plan, Section 6, Employment and Co-ordination of Naval Fire Support, 221.

10 Forrest C. Pogue, *The Supreme Command,* U.S. Army in World War II (Washington, D.C.: Government Printing Office, 1954), 122–26.

11   Chandler, *Papers of Dwight David Eisenhower*, 3:1781.

12   Harry C. Butcher, *My Three Years with Eisenhower* (New York: Simon and Schuster, 1946), 503.

13   Will A. Jacobs, 'The Battle of France,' in *Case Studies in the Development of Close Air Support,* ed. Benjamin Franklin Colling (Washington, D.C.: Office of Air Force History, 1990), 240.

14   Ibid., 241, 242.

15   First U.S. Army, Report of Operations, Annex 13, Air Plan, 68.

16   British Army, Initial Joint Plan, Appendix H, Estimate of the Air Forces Available in the United Kingdom, 1 June 1944, Omar Bradley Papers, USMA.

17   First U.S. Army, Report of Operations, Annex 12, Prearranged Air and Naval Bombardment Plan, 50.

18   Omar Bradley, *A Soldier's Story* (New York: Henry Holt, 1951), 249.

19   U.S. Army, First U.S. Army, Operations Memorandum no. 12, Employment of LCT(SP) and LCT(A) in Support of a Beach Assault, 26 March 1944, Brigadier General W.B. Kean, Chief of Staff, RG 407, File 101-32.3, NA II.

20   First U.S. Army, Report of Operations, Annex 21, Artillery and Naval Fire Support Plan, 220.

21   'Conference on Landing Assaults,' pp. Langley 2, 3; U.S. Navy, U.S. LCT(R) Group, War Diary, Larry W. Carr, USNR Commanding, September 1943–October 1944, Larry W. Carr Papers, in author's possession.

22   Kenneth P. Lord, Assistant G-3 (Operations), 1st Infantry Division, Personal Narrative, FDM. Lord's reasoning that the beaches should not be bombed because soldiers would drown in the craters is questionable. This happened in World War I, but it seemed an unlikely concern in World War II.

23   In his analysis of the Dieppe raid, Bernard Fergusson wrote: 'Somehow the defenders must be drenched with fire and reduced to a state of gibbering with shock at the last moment, when the fire of heavy ships had to be lifted' (*The Watery Maze: The Story of Combined Operations* [New York: Holt, Rinehart and Winston, 1961], 182).

24   William H. Hessler, 'The Battleship Paid Dividends,' *U.S. Naval Institute Proceedings* 72, no. 9 (September 1946): 1146.

25   U.S. Army, Headquarters Allied Forces APO 512, G-3 Training Section, 'Training Notes from the Sicilian Campaign,' 25 October 1943, RG 407, Box 15827, File 301-0.4, NA II.

26   Walter C. Ansel, 'Naval Gunfire in Support of Landings: Lessons from Gallipoli,' *U.S. Naval Institute Proceedings* 58, no. 353 (July 1932): 1001. In July 1945, Ansel petitioned Hall through a mutual friend for duty at sea. The friend wrote: 'He [Ansel] said for me to tell you when I write that he wanted to get out there with you in plenty of time to be in on the final touchdown. He said he would take any job you gave him afloat, if you would get him out of Washington.' At the time, Ansel was serving with the Ship Characteristic Board and was 'rather unhappy about being on the beach.' Given that the war ended a month later, it is not likely that Ansel was present for the 'final touchdown.' See Mays Lewis, Army and Navy Staff College, Letter to Admiral John Lesslie Hall, 3 July 1945, 1–4, John Lesslie Hall Papers, 78 H14, Box 21, Folder 1, CWM.

27   Ansel, 'Naval Gunfire in Support of Landings,' 1005.

28   Ibid., 1008.

29   U.S. Army, *Landing Operations on Hostile Shores,* FM 31-5 (Washington, D.C.: War Department, 1941), 97. The opening pages of the manual stated: 'This manual is based to a large extent on Landing Operations Doctrine, U.S. Navy, 1938' (ii).

30   Memorandum no. 3, Artillery Information Service.

31   Ibid., 8.

32   Bradley, *Soldier's Story,* 272.

33   The *Nevada* (14-inch guns) was a more potent ship with its modern fire control equipment than the *Texas* (14-inch guns) and the *Arkansas* (12-inch guns).

34   Morison, *Invasion of France and Germany,* 334–36, 143–49. See also First U.S. Army, Report of Operations, Annex 12, Prearranged Air and Naval Bombardment Plan, 56.

35   Memorandum no. 3, Artillery Information Service, 8.

36   Hall, 'Reminiscences,' 131.

37   Ibid., 178.

38   Bradley, *Soldier's Story,* 254. If Bradley worked as hard as he indicated to secure additional naval gunfire support, it is an aspect of the Normandy invasion that has gone unrecognized. The controversies over control of strategic air resources and over the use of airborne divisions have been well documented, but this controversy has gone almost unnoticed.

39   Ibid., 271.

40   Ibid., 263.

41   Wesley Frank Craven and James Lea Cate, eds., *The Army Air Forces in World War II,* vol. 3, *Europe: Argument to V-E Day, January 1944 to May 1945* (Washington, D.C.: Office of Air Force History, 1983), 143.

42   Ibid., 15–20. See also Arthur B. Ferguson, 'Winter Bombing,' in ibid., 13–27.

43   Ibid., 143. Fagg wrote: 'Much skepticism prevailed in advance as to the value of this last minute bombardment, and contrary to a common belief it was the air men who held the most conservative views. Ground force commanders tended to overestimate the effects of bomb tonnage on casemated enemy batteries, strongpoints, and the entire hideous apparatus of beach obstacles.'

44   U.S. Navy, U.S. Fleet, Headquarters of Commander in Chief, Navy Department, Memorandum, Subject: Distribution of Naval Gunfire Officer, Headquarters V Amphibious Corps, Serial 00671 letter of 7 March 1944, Subject: Naval Gunfire Report on the Marshalls Operation, 22 March 1944, 3, RG 407, Files 6-12.060/45, 6-12.0703/44, NA II. See also ibid., 6, 7, 12.

45   The *Alabama, North Carolina,* and *South Dakota* were new ships.

46   Distribution of Naval Gunfire Officer, 3–20, and Appendix A, 1–5. The *Indiana, Massachusetts,* and *Washington* were new ships.

47   Bradley, *Soldier's Story,* 253, 254.

48   H. S. Sewell, 'Montgomery's Tactics,' *Military Review,* August 1945, 128. Air power offered Montgomery a way to avoid the carnage he experienced in World War I. His experiences in World War I and faith in air power caused him to overlook established, tested doctrinal practices.

49   Joseph Balkoski, *Beyond the Beachhead: The 29th Infantry Division in Normandy* (Harrisburg, Pa.: Stackpole Books, 1989), 61, 63: 'They [the 116th RCT of the 29th ID] were assured that the Germans on the beach would be blasted with bombs and naval gunfire prior to landing... Bradley emphasized that the 116th was not alone; the navy and Army Air Force, he said, would prepare the way. He concluded with a prediction that men would remember: "You men should consider yourselves lucky. You are going to have ringside seats for the greatest show on earth."' See also Joseph Binkoski and Arthur Plaut, *The 115th Infantry Regiment in World War II* (Washington, D.C.: Infantry Journal Press, 1948), 14: 'It came as quite a shock to many when, just prior to going ashore, the men assembled on the decks of landing craft and heard that they might have to land fighting. Briefing had

stressed the fact that the landing itself would be relatively simple; that the troops would merely walk ashore, make for the high ground, and then walk until the objective was reached.'

50   Hanson Baldwin, 'Amphibious Aspects of the Normandy Invasion,' *Marine Corps Gazette,* December 1944, 36. See also Hanson Baldwin, *Battles Lost and Won: Great Campaigns of World War II* (New York: Harper and Row, 1966), 283, and Charles H. Corlett, *Cowboy Pete: The Autobiography of Major General Charles H. Corlett* (Santa Fe, N.M.: Sleeping Fox, 1974), 88, 89.

51   During Operation Cobra, the breakout at Saint-Lô, the air force again had problems identifying the target area and mistakenly attacked American forces.

52   The U.S. Strategic Bombing Survey (1947) began its studies before the end of the war in Europe. It collected an enormous amount of data on the bombing campaigns in the European and Pacific theaters. Wesley Frank Craven and James Lea Cate's six-volume work *The Army Air Forces in World War II* is one of the most comprehensive studies of air power during the war. The Office of Air Force History and Center for Air Force History in Washington, D.C., have commissioned and published numerous studies, including Kit C. Carter and Robert Mueller, *The Army Air Forces in World War II: Combat Chronology* (1973); Richard H. Kohn and Joseph P. Harahan, eds., *Condensed Analysis of the Ninth Air Force in the European Theater of Operations* (1984) and *Air Superiority in World War II and Korea* (1983); Eduard Mark, *Aerial Interdiction in Three Wars* (1994); Benjamin F. Cooling, *Case Studies in the Development of Close Air Support* (1990); and Richard G. Davis, *Carl A. Spaatz and the Air War in Europe* (1993). The Air University at Maxwell Air Force Base in Alabama has also produced a number of studies on the employment of air power in World War II, for example, Robert Frank Futrell, *Ideas, Concepts, Doctrine: A History of Basic Thinking in the United States Air Force, 1907–1964* (1974). Participants have recorded their thoughts and opinions. See Henry H. Arnold, *Global Mission* (1949); Lewis H. Brereton, *The Brereton Diaries: The War in the Pacific, Middle East, and Europe, 3 October 1941–8 May 1945* (1946); Sir Arthur Harris, *Bomber Offensive* (1947); and Lord Tedder, *With Prejudice: The War Memoirs of Marshal of the Royal Air Force* (1966). Individual scholars have also contributed. See John Gooch, ed., *Airpower: Theory and Practice* (1995); DeWitt S. Copp, *A Few Great Captains: The Men and Events That Shaped the Development of U.S. Air Power* (1980); R. J. Query, *The Air War, 1939–1945* (1980); Lee Kennett, *A History of Strategic Bombing* (1982); Ronald Schaffer, *Wings of Judgment* (1984); John Terraine, *A Time for Courage* (1985); Michael S. Sherry, *The Rise of American Air Power* (1987); Alan J. Levine, *The Strategic Bombing of Germany, 1940–1945* (1992); Conrad C. Crane, *Bombs, Cities, and Civilians* (1993); and Stephen A. Garret, *Ethics and Air Power in World War II* (1993).

53   Wesley Frank Craven and James Lea Cate, eds., *Europe: Torch to Pointblank, August 1942 to December 1943* (Washington, D.C.: Government Printing Office, 1983), 2:224. Arthur B. Ferguson wrote: 'It is difficult to avoid the conclusion that the evaluations, especially in the early days, reflected a natural desire, existing all along the line from the combat crew to AAF Headquarters, to prove the case for daylight bombing. Inflated reports, widely published, sometimes had to be corrected to the embarrassment of the AAF.'

54   James A. Huston, 'Tactical Use of Air Power in World War II: The Army Experience,' *Military Review,* July 1952, 41.

55   Thomas J. Mayock, in Craven and Cate, *Europe: Torch to Pointblank,* 2:205.

56   Futrell, *Ideas, Concepts, Doctrine,* 69. See also Huston, 'Tactical Use of Air Power in World War II,' 34.

57   Futrell, *Ideas, Concepts, Doctrine,* 69. U.S. Army Air Force, *Command and Employment of Air Power,* FM 100-20, Field Service Regulations (Washington, D.C.: War

Department, 21 July 1943), stated: '1. Relationship of Forces. – Land power and air power are co-equal and interdependent forces; neither is an auxiliary of the other.'

58   Futrell, *Ideas, Concepts, Doctrine*, 69; Huston, 'Tactical Use of Air Power in World War II,' 34. Huston wrote: 'Based largely on General Montgomery's Notes on High Command in War, Field Manual 100-20 reflected General Montgomery's statement of principles.'

59   Richard H. Kohn and Joseph P. Harahan, eds., *Air Superiority in World War II and Korea: An Interview with Gen. James Ferguson, Gen. Robert M. Lee, Gen. William Momyer, and Lt. Gen. Elwood R. Quesada* (Washington, D.C.: Office of Air Force History, U.S. Air Force, 1983), 33, 6.

60   British Army, 21st Army Group, 'Some Notes on the Use of Air Power in Support of Land Operations,' Holland: 21st Army Group, December 1944, 5, Bernard L. Montgomery, Omar Bradley Papers, USMA.

61   Futrell, *Ideas, Concepts, Doctrine*, 69; Huston, 'Tactical Use of Air Power in World War II,' 34; Mayock, in Craven and Cate, *Europe: Torch to Pointblank*, 2:205.

62   Ferguson, in Craven and Cate, *Army Air Forces in World War II*, vol. 3, *Europe: Argument to V-E Day*, 5, 26.

63   'Some Notes on the Use of Air Power in Support of Land Operations,' 5.

64   Ibid., 6.

65   Ibid., 13.

66   Futrell, *Ideas, Concepts, Doctrine*, 69.

67   'Some Notes on the Use of Air Power in Support of Land Operations,' 13.

68   Kohn and Harahan, *Condensed Analysis of the Ninth Air Force*, 12.

69   'Some Notes on the Use of Air Power in Support of Land Operations,' 16.

70   Ibid., 29.

71   FM 100-20, 1: '2. Doctrine of Employment. – The gaining of air superiority is the first requirement for the success of any major land operation. Air Forces may be properly and profitably employed against enemy sea power, land power and air power. However, land forces operating without air superiority must take such extensive security measures against hostile air attack that their mobility and ability to defeat the enemy land forces are greatly reduced. Therefore, Air Forces must be employed primarily against the enemy's Air Forces until air superiority is obtained.'

72   Kohn and Harahan, *Air Superiority*, 44. General William Momyer stated: 'You remember that Spaatz and Harris and the rest were hollering: "Don't take us off of the strategic campaign. Give us some more time. If you give us a little bit more time, we are going to be able to wind the war down."'

73   Bradley, *A Soldier's Story*, 249. Quesada's view was a bit different from that of Bradley. He stated: '[A]ll the P-51s were assigned to us [the Ninth Air Force]. Now we had about four months to go before landing in Normandy. To have those people standing by and doing nothing, waiting for the landing, would have been just ridiculous. So everybody, including me, was more than glad to have those planes support the Eighth Air Force' (Kohn and Harahan, *Air Superiority*, 48).

74   Huston, 'Tactical Use of Air Power in World War II,' 37, 32. See also Futrell, *Ideas, Concepts, Doctrine*, 93.

75   Jacobs, 'Battle of France,' 254.

76   U.S. Navy, Gunfire Support Craft, Eleventh Amphibious Force, Action Report, 3 July 1944, Commander L.S. Sabin Jr., 4, Larry W. Carr Papers, in author's possession.

77   Ibid., 5.

78   Ibid., 6.

79   Ibid., 7.

80   Ibid., 32, 33.

81   U.S. Navy, Gunfire Support Craft, LCT(R) Group, Action Report, 2 July 1944, Lieutenant Larry W. Carr, Larry W. Carr Papers, in author's possession.

82   Action Report, Sabin, 15–17.

83   Gunfire Support Craft, LCT(R), 2.

84   Action Report, Sabin, 18.

85   Ibid., 34.

86   Paul W. Thompson, 'D-Day on Omaha Beach,' *Infantry Journal*, June 1945, 41.

87   U.S. Army, 743rd Tank Battalion, Major William D. Dungan, School Commandant, Memorandum for Commander, Eleventh Amphibious Force, 30 April 1944, 3, RG 407, Box 24377, File 659, NA II.

88   J.S. Upham, 'DD Tanks,' *Military Review,* February 1947, 42.

89   A.O. Connor, 'On the Defense: Notes from the Anzio Beachhead,' *Infantry Journal,* July 1949, 35–39.

90   U.S. Army, Colonel S.S. MacLaughlin, Notes on the Assignment of Tank Units to V Corps, 4 February 1944, RG 407, Box 24309, File 210, NA II.

91   Dungan, Memorandum, 1.

92   U.S. Army, Headquarters 116th Combat Team, Force 'O,' Field Order, 11 May 1944, Annex 110.10, Tank Employment Plan, 1, RG 407, Box 24373, Files 630–33, NA II.

93   U.S. Army, Headquarters 16th Combat Team, Field Order no. 5, 16 May 1944, Appendix 4 to Annex 3, 1, RG 407, Box 24373, Files 634–36, NA II.

94   U.S. Navy, DD LCT Unit Commander, Lieutenant Dean L. Rockwell, Memorandum for Commander, Eleventh Amphibious Force, 30 April 1944, 2, RG 407, Box 24377, File 659, NA II.

95   Ibid., 4.

96   Ibid., 2, 3.

97   Ibid., 3.

98   Dungan, Memorandum, 4.

99   Rockwell's and Dungan's reports were probably co-ordinated. They contained much of the same information and similar recommendations. Dungan's report was more thorough and comprehensive.

100 U.S. Army, 16th Infantry Combat Team, S-3 Combat Report, 6 June 1944, 1, FDM.

101 Samuel A. Stouffer *et al., The American Soldier: Combat and Its Aftermath* (Princeton, N.J.: Princeton University Press, 1949), 131.

102 Ronald J. Drez, ed., *Voices of D-Day* (Baton Rouge: Louisiana State University Press, 1994), 234, 235.

103 Chester Wilmot, *The Struggle for Europe* (New York: Harper and Brothers, 1952), 255.

104 U.S. Army, V Corps, Operation Order no. 3-44, Change no. 1, 19 May 1944, 5, RG 407, Box 3411, Files 205-0.6–0.13, NA II: 'Note that DD Tank Discharge Point is shown at 6000 yards and Time Curve of LCT(DD) is correspondingly incorrect. DD Tank Discharge Point is at 5000 yards and curve is changed accordingly to agree with the Enclosures Dog and Easy, Approach Schedules for Red and Green Beach.'

105 Upham, 'DD Tanks,' 45; author's conversation with Dean Rockwell.

106 U.S. Army, First U.S. Army, Overlord Conference, 21 December 1943, 18, RG 407, Box 24309, File 209, NA II.

107 Ibid., 17.

108 Morison, *Invasion of France and Germany,* 134n.

109 U.S. Navy, Commander Assault Force 'O,' Action Report, 27 July 1944, 101, Box 549, File 11th PHIBFOR, 27 July–1 October 1944, NA II.

110 U.S. Army, 1st Infantry Division, Tactical Study of Terrain, 16 May 1944, 8, RG 407, Box 24374, Files 634–36, NA II. The 1st ID's Tactical Study of Terrain discussed the restrictive nature of the terrain: 'Due to the steepness of the slope directly in rear of the beach, tanks accompanying troops in the assault will have to use the corridors as exits from the beach. Since these corridors are narrow and are provided with concrete road blocks, enemy tank defense in this sector is greatly facilitated.'

111 Department of the Army, U.S. Total Army Personnel Command, Mortuary Affairs Branch, Alexandria, Va.

CHAPTER NINE

1   U.S. Army, 1st Infantry Division, G-3 Report of Operations, 31 May–30 June 1944, General Huebner, 45, FDM.

2   U.S. Army, Headquarters 7th Field Artillery Battalion, Comments and Criticisms of Operation 'Neptune,' Lieutenant Colonel George W. Gibbs, Commanding, 1 July 1944, 1, FDM.

3   G-3 Report of Operations, 46, FDM.

4   Paul W. Thompson, 'D-Day on Omaha Beach,' *Infantry Journal*, June 1945, 44.

5   H. R. Knickerbocker *et al.*, *Danger Forward: The Story of the First Division in World War II* (Washington, D.C.: Society of the First Division, 1947), 205.

6   Martin Blumenson and James L. Stokesbury, 'Huebner,' in *Masters of the Art of Command* (Boston: Houghton Mifflin, 1975), 164–72.

7   John F. Votaw, 'Huebner, Clarence R.,' in *The D-Day Encyclopedia*, ed. David G. Chandler and James Lawton Collins Jr. (New York: Simon and Schuster, 1994), 302, 303. Votaw listed three sources: Blumenson and Stokesbury, *Masters of the Art of Command;* Omar Bradley and Clay Blair, *A General's Life: An Autobiography by General of the Army Omar N. Bradley* (New York: Simon and Schuster, 1983); and Arthur L. Chaitt, 'Clarence R. Huebner: Lieutenant General, U.S.A. (Retired), 1888–1972,' *Bridgehead Sentinel*, Spring 1973, 1–23.

8   Ronald Joe Rogers, Major U.S. Army, 'A Study of Leadership in the First Infantry Division during World War II: Terry De La Mesa Allen and Clarence Ralph Huebner' (master's of military art and science thesis abstract, U.S. Army Command and General Staff College, Fort Leavenworth, Kans., 1965), MHI. Retired Colonel Rogers stated in a telephone conversation on 22 July 1997 that he no longer had possession of his letters from Huebner or his interview notes. He recalled that he had left them at the Combined Arms Research Library at Fort Leavenworth, which he said held the master's theses of graduates; however, the library staff said the library did not hold the research papers of graduates or the letters of Huebner or the papers of Rogers.

9   Blumenson and Stokesbury, 'Huebner,' 164.

10 Rogers, 'Study in Leadership,' 53. Rogers's footnote read: 'Letter from Lt. Gen. Clarence R. Huebner, Ret., March 8, 1964. Unless otherwise noted, all background information concerning Gen. Huebner is from this reference.'

11 Blumenson and Stokesbury, 'Huebner,' 166.

12 Department of Defense, Office of Public Information Press Branch, Summary of the Career of Lieutenant General Clarence Ralph Huebner, 3, CMH. See also Chaitt, 'Clarence R. Huebner,' 3.

13 Summary of the Career of Lieutenant General Clarence Ralph Huebner, 3.

14 Ibid.

15 Blumenson and Stokesbury, 'Huebner,' 166: 'Entering real combat as the war became mobile again, the Americans would have a far different experience from

that of their exhausted allies. A generation later, when the defensive-minded French were collapsing, Huebner would be training units once more for mobile warfare.'

16   Nigel Hamilton, *Monty: The Battles of Field Marshal Bernard Montgomery* (New York: Random House, 1981), 5.

17   John Shy, 'The American Military Experience: History and Learning,' in *A People Numerous and Armed* (Ann Arbor: University of Michigan Press, 1990), 265–94; Maurice Matloff, 'The American Approach to War, 1919–1945,' in *The Theory and Practice of War*, ed. Michael Howard (New York: Frederick A. Praeger, 1965), 211–43; Russell F. Weigley, *The American Way of War* (Bloomington: Indiana University Press, 1977).

18   Huebner letter, in Rogers, 'Study in Leadership,' 55.

19   Ibid.

20   Ibid. The date that Rogers gives for Huebner's promotion differs from that in the Summary of the Career of Lieutenant General Clarence Ralph Huebner, which states that he was promoted to the 'temporary' rank of brigadier general on 16 February 1942.

21   Morris Janowitz, *The Professional Soldier* (New York: Macmillan, 1960), 162.

22   Harry C. Butcher, *My Three Years with Eisenhower* (New York: Simon and Schuster, 1946), 692. In his diary on 29 October 1944, Butcher wrote: 'When I had spoken to General Huebner about General Marshall's desire to have the U.S. Army Band play a concert in the first big German city captured by the Americans, he said he wished this could be done, but the concert would have to be on an occasion such as a ceremony to include General Hodges. He felt it unwise to permit the band to play within 3000 yards of the front line. If the Germans heard the music, there would be a refrain of artillery, and not only members of the band, but General Hodges might be killed. Consequently, he had disapproved the idea. So General Marshall has been defeated.'

23   Bradley and Blair, *General's Life*, 195: 'Clarence R. Huebner, a flinty disciplinarian who had just been fired as an "American adviser" to Alexander for being too outspoken, replaced Allen as division commander.'

24   Blumenson and Stokesbury, 'Huebner,' 168.

25   Huebner letter, in Rogers, 'Study in Leadership,' 56.

26   Omar Bradley, *A Soldier's Story* (New York: Henry Holt, 1951), 156, 157; Bradley and Blair, *General's Life*, 195. Bradley did not like Allen's leadership style. Bradley and Allen were very different men with very different command philosophies. Allen's brash, cocky, informal, ad hoc, 'do it my way' leadership style clashed with Bradley's more rigid, conformist style. Bradley did not want rebels. He wanted 'judicious, reasonable and likable' commanders like himself (Carlo D'Este, *Patton: A Genius for War* [New York: Harper, 1995], 617). The men of the 1st ID had come to identify with their commander and his ways. They had adopted his attitude and tended not to go by the book.

27   Bradley, *A Soldier's Story*, 156: 'Responsibility for the relief of Terry Allen was mine and mine alone.' See also Bradley and Blair, *General's Life*, 195: 'In the initial assault on Tronia, Allen flubbed badly. He miscalculated the enemy's strength and verve and was thrown back with heavy losses. Throughout the seven days of heavy fighting that ensued, he attempted to operate much as he had in the past, as an undisciplined, independent army, unresponsive to my wishes – or in some cases, orders. Without meaning any disrespect to the individual soldiers – who fought with great valor – the whole division had assumed Allen's cavalier attitude.' Although Bradley accepted responsibility for relieving Allen, there was also friction between

Patton and Allen. See D'Este, *Patton,* 465, 466. See also Stanhope Brasfield Mason, Major General U.S. Army, retired, 'Reminiscences and Anecdotes of World War II,' Birmingham, Ala., 1988, 151, FDM: 'I have never been able to understand how General Allen managed to control his own, sometimes fiery, temper as well as he did, when confronted with a Patton diatribe which so offensively denigrated both the 1st Division and its commander.'

28 Mason, 'Reminiscences,' 186.

29 Blumenson and Stokesbury, 'Huebner,' 170. Chaitt wrote: 'Few men have ever assumed command under so difficult conditions. Major General Terry Allen was known and loved by all of the men of the Division. So was his Assistant Division Commander, Brigadier General Teddy Roosevelt. Any one who replaced the Allen-Roosevelt team was sure to incur the wrath and disdain of the entire division' ('Clarence R. Huebner,' 4).

30 Bradley, *A Soldier's Story,* 154.

31 Ibid., 157.

32 Ibid., 155, 154.

33 Bradley and Blair, *General's Life,* 195.

34 Rogers, 'Study in Leadership,' 56, 57. See also John W. Baumgartner *et al., The 16th Infantry, 1798–1946* (Bamburg, Germany, 1946), 65: 'Later in the afternoon, General Allen appeared at the regimental CP to introduce to the officers and non-coms of the regiment, the new First Division Commanding General Clarence Huebner. In a little introductory speech, General Allen referred to the 16th's combat of the preceding several days... "[T]he battle of Troina was by far the toughest battle we've had – far tougher than any in Africa. I'm proud of the tenacity of the 16th... the indomitable defiance displayed by all of you... the spirit each man has shown and is still showing. You are to be congratulated for a truly great performance."'

35 Rogers, 'Study in Leadership,' 57.

36 Mason, 'Reminiscences,' 198. Mason paraphrased Huebner: '"Allen had never paid attention to details and was not a disciplinarian. Ted Roosevelt's attitude had fostered a reputation for cockiness in the Division. Ike, Patton, and Bradley were thoroughly dissatisfied and had moved him in for a house cleaning." In spite of that, Huebner added, the Division had performed well and he had no intention of firing anybody until he was absolutely certain it should be done.'

37 Bradley, *Soldier's Story,* 156, 157.

38 Mason letter, in Rogers, 'Study in Leadership,' 60.

39 Bowen letter, in ibid. Bowen retired a lieutenant general. He commanded the 3rd Battalion, 26th Infantry, and later the 26th Infantry Regiment.

40 Huebner interview, in ibid., 61.

41 Ibid.

42 Ibid., 63.

43 Ibid.

44 Ibid., 64, 65.

45 Andrus letters, in ibid.

46 Knickerbocker *et al., Danger Forward,* 205, 206.

47 Diary, 29 October 1944, in Butcher, *My Three Years with Eisenhower,* 691, 692: 'The 1st Division's capture of Aachen, General Huebner said, was methodical, and relatively inexpensive in lives. A great deal of artillery was used and the city was 'cleaned up' house by house and block by block. He said his division had lost only 150 men killed and 1200 wounded in taking the city.'

48 Huebner interview, in Rogers, 'Study in Leadership,' 69.

49   Summary of the Career of Lieutenant General Clarence Ralph Huebner, 3.

50   Martin Blumenson, *Patton: The Man behind the Legend, 1885–1945* (New York: William Morrow, 1985), 268.

51   U.S. Army, First U.S. Army, Engineer Headquarters, Beach Study Overlord, 17 February 1944, 1, RG 407, Box 24308, NA II. The mission was stated as follows: 'To seize and secure Beach No. 46 [Omaha] and 49 [Utah] and develop initial communication facilities within the American Sector. This mission includes the landing of assault echelons on the beaches, the seizure of the beaches and the initial beachheads, preparations for supply over beaches, and the development and maintenance of beach exits and initial road net in the beach-heads.' The report described the tides along the Normandy coast: 'The off-shore approach to the objective is through the Baie de la Seine east to the Cotentin (Cherbourg) Peninsula. There are two tidal rises daily. The Spring rise varies from 22 to 26 feet above Admiralty Chart Datum... The neap tide varies between a mean low water of 7 to 9 feet and a mean high water of 19 to 21 feet, chart datum. The high tides hold for a period of 75 to 105 minutes with a stage variation of less than one foot... As might be expected from the tidal range, the tidal currents are strong, varying from one and one-half to three knots per hour just offshore.'

52   U.S. Army, 1st Infantry Division, Tactical Study of Terrain, 25 March 1944, RG 407, Box 24374, Files 634–36, NA II.

53   Ibid., 13: 'The enemy will have difficulty in covering the winding corridors and narrow draws leading from the beach with effective flat trajectory fire. Unless all of these are effectively covered, attacking forces will be able to find protection in them from flat trajectory weapons and to infiltrate through them to the rear of pillboxes on the beach.' Of course it was logical to think that enemy forces were smart enough to draw these same conclusions and take the necessary actions to prevent the use of these corridors to gain access to the rear of their pillboxes.

54   Ibid., 8, 13, 14.

55   Ibid., 14.

56   U.S. Army, V Corps, Conference Overlord, 7 February 1944, 4, RG 407, Box 24309, File 213, NA II.

57   Tactical Study of Terrain, 14.

58   Ibid., 8, 9.

59   Conference Overlord, 44.

60   Bernard L. Montgomery, *Normandy to the Baltic* (Boston: Houghton Mifflin, 1948), 11: 'While accepting the suitability of the Baie de la Seine for the assault, I considered that the operation required to be mounted in greater strength and on a wider front. It was vital to secure an adequate bridgehead at the outset, so that operations could be developed from a firm and sufficiently spacious base... Moreover the relatively narrow front of assault proposed in the Cossac plan appeared to me to give the enemy the opportunity of 'roping off' our forces quickly in a shallow covering position... An increased frontage would make it more difficult for the enemy to discover the extent of our operation and delay him in deciding the direction of our main axes of advance inland; at the same time we should have greater opportunity for finding and exploiting soft spots.'

61   Gordon Harrison, *Cross-Channel Attack* (Washington, D.C.: Government Printing Office, 1951), 319n.

62   Ralph Bennett, *Ultra in the West: The Normandy Campaign of 1944–45* (London: Hutchinson, 1979), 54.

63   Charles Fenyvesi, 'Japan's Unwitting D-Day Spy: Berlin Envoy's Intercepted Cables Provided Crucial Intelligence,' *Washington Post,* 26 May 1998, A10.

64   U.S. Army, V Corps, Operation Plan Neptune, Annex 1, G-2 Estimate of Enemy Situation, 1 April 1944, 7, 8, RG 407, Box 3412, Files 205-0.6–0.13, NA II (emphasis added).

65   Ibid., 15 May 1944, 13–15 (emphasis added).

66   Ibid., 13.

67   Ibid., 15.

68   U.S. Army, *Operations*, FM 100-5 (Washington, D.C.: Headquarters Department of the Army, 1993), 7–11.

69   Thompson, 'D-Day on Omaha Beach,' 37.

70   Walter C. Ansel, 'Naval Gunfire in Support of Landings: Lessons from Gallipoli,' *U.S. Naval Institute Proceedings* 58, no. 353 (July 1932): 1004.

71   Thompson landed on Omaha Beach with soldiers from his 6th ESB and the 116th Infantry at H+45 minutes. Before the beach obstacles were breached, he was shot twice, once in the right shoulder and once through the jaw.

72   FM 100-5, 103.

73   An infantry battalion with three rifle companies and a weapons company can defend every inch of a 1,000-meter front. Each rifle company can cover 300 to 400 meters, and the defense can be extended with mines and obstacles. There were nine battalions in the 352nd Division. The area on Omaha Beach on which an amphibious assault could take place was roughly seven kilometers.

74   A memorandum from V Corps to the 1st ID set the following timetable: '1. It is established that by H+1 hr equipment and personnel can start work opening up beach exits for movement of vehicles. 2. It is established that tracked vehicles and some wheel vehicles of good cross-country ability can begin moving through beach exits at H+2 hrs. 3. It is established that wheel vehicles can begin moving in a continuous stream out of all four beach exits by H+3. 4. It is estimated that the tactical situation at H+3 will be such as to permit the dispersal into transit areas of the continuous flow of vehicles referred to in par. 3 above. 5. The time phasing of vehicles will conform to the above estimates.' This timetable indicates that the tactical commanders were very optimistic and accepted the vision of the operational commanders. See U.S. Army, V Corps, Memorandum to General, 1st Infantry Division, Subject: Decision Made at 0900 Hours, 22 March 1944, RG 407, Box 24375, File 640, NA II.

75   G-3 Report of Operations, 2.

76   Ibid., 4.

EPILOGUE

1   William Shanahan, 'H-Hour to Be Announced,' *Military Review,* October 1951, 4, 5.

2   H. Kent Hewitt, 'The Reminiscences of Admiral H. Kent Hewitt,' 22–27, Naval History Project, Oral History Research Office, Columbia University, 1962.

3   Raymond S. McLain, 'Intangible Factors in Combat,' *Military Review,* March 1947, 11. When this article was published, Gerow was the commandant of the U.S. Army Command and Staff College, where the *Military Review* was edited and published.

4   Samuel Eliot Morison, *The Invasion of France and Germany, 1944–1945* (Boston: Little, Brown, 1957), 152.

5   John W. Baumgartner *et al.*, *The 16th Infantry, 1798–1946* (Bamburg, Germany, 1946), 83.

6   H.R. Knickerbocker *et al.*, *Danger Forward: The Story of the First Division in World War II* (Washington, D.C.: Society of the First Division, 1947); Joseph Balkoski, *Beyond the Beachhead: The 29th Infantry Division in Normandy* (Harrisburg, Pa.: Stackpole Books, 1989), 61, 63 (emphasis added).

7   Joseph Binkoski and Arthur Plaut, *The 115th Infantry Regiment in World War II* (Washington, D.C.: Infantry Journal Press, 1948), 14 (emphasis added).

8   Max Hastings, *Overlord: D-Day and the Battle for Normandy* (New York: Simon and Schuster, 1984), 51.

9   U.S. Army, Headquarters Allied Forces APO 512, G-3 Training Section, 'Training Notes from the Sicilian Campaign,' 25 October 1943, RG 407, Box 15827, File 301-0.4, NA II.

10   James M. Gavin, *On to Berlin* (New York: Viking Press, 1978), 51.

11   John Lesslie Hall Jr., 'The Reminiscences of John Lesslie Hall, Jr.,' 205, 208, Naval History Project, Oral History Research Office, Columbia University, 1964 (emphasis added).

12   U.S. Army, V Corps, Conference Overlord, 7 February 1944, RG 407, Box 24309, File 213, NA II.

13   U.S. Army, V Corps, 'Officers and Men of the V Corps,' 15 May 1944, General Gerow, RG 407, Box 24373, Files 630–33, NA II.

14   U.S. Army, ETOUSA, *Army Talk,* 13 May 1944, General Bernard L. Montgomery, 7, RG 407, Box 24378, File 669, NA II.

15   S. L. A. Marshall, *The Soldier's Load and the Mobility of a Nation* (Quantico, Va.: Marine Corps Association, 1980), 38.

16   Joseph H. Ewing, *29th Let's Go!: A History of the 29th Division in World War II* (Washington, D.C.: Infantry Journal Press, 1948), 49.

17   The personal narratives of Eldon Wiehe, 16th Infantry, and others in his unit on 6 June 1944 at Omaha Beach are available at the FDM. Portions of these narratives were also published in Ronald J. Drez, ed., *Voices of D-Day* (Baton Rouge: Louisiana State University Press, 1994).

18   Lord Moran, *The Anatomy of Courage: The Classic Study of the Soldier's Struggle against Fear* (New York: Avery, 1987), 38: 'In the presence of danger man often finds salvation in action. To dull emotion he must do something; to remain immobile, to stagnate in mind or body, is to surrender without terms. Whereas movement, work of any kind, helps to deliver him from those feelings which are traitors to his better nature.'

19   Adolf von Schell, *Battle Leadership* (1933; reprint, Quantico, Va.: Marine Corps Association, 1982), 13, 14, 17. Schell, an infantry leader in World War I, wrote: 'When a soldier lies under hostile fire and waits, he feels unable to protect himself, he has time; he thinks; he only waits for the shot that will hit him. He feels a certain inferiority to the enemy. He feels that he is alone and deserted.' S.L.A. Marshall made similar observations in *Men against Fire: The Problem of Battle Command in Future War* (Gloucester, Mass.: Peter Smith, 1978), 129. The effects on the human mind noted by Schell were multiplied by the severity of the situation at Omaha Beach and the nature of amphibious operations.

20   John Kelly, 'Shoot, Soldier, Shoot,' *Infantry Journal,* January 1946, 47.

21   This analysis is based on discussions with Professor Robin Fisher at the University of California at Los Angeles, Department of Neuroscience, 20–23 April 1995.

22   U.S. Army, 1st Infantry Division, 16th Infantry Regiment, Citation for War Department Distinguished Unit Citation, FDM.

23   Martin van Creveld, *Fighting Power: German and U.S. Army Performance, 1939–1945* (Westport, Conn.: Greenwood Press, 1982), 95.

24   Dwight D. Eisenhower, *Crusade in Europe* (New York: Doubleday, 1948), 455.

25   Drez, *Voices of D-Day,* 211.

26   Ewing, *29th Let's Go!,* 41.

27   H.J. Matchett, 'Let's Teach Battlefield Training,' *Infantry Journal,* January 1946, 49.

28 Omar Bradley, *A Soldier's Story* (New York: Henry Holt, 1951), 272. Ibid., 236.

30 Supreme Headquarters Allied Expeditionary Force, *History of COSSAC*, 38, Historical Sub-Section, Office of Secretary, General Staff, John Votaw's Files, May 1944, FDM.

31 Ibid., 39.

32 See John Dollard, 'Twelve Rules for Meeting Battle Fear,' *Infantry Journal*, May 1944, 36–38; 'Meeting Battle Fear,' *Infantry Journal*, June 1944, 40–41; Donald R. Roberts and Edmund H. Torkelson, 'Preparing the Mind for Battle,' *Infantry Journal*, April 1945; 'Fear,' *Marine Corps Gazette*, September 1943, 26–29; Phillips D. Carleton, 'Causes and Conquest of Fear,' *Marine Corps Gazette*, March 1944; Charles Edmundson, 'Why Warriors Fight,' *Marine Corps Gazette*, September 1944; and Percy A. Webb, 'Conquering Fear,' *Marine Corps Gazette*, March 1944, 27.

33 Omar Bradley and Clay Blair, *A General's Life: An Autobiography by General of the Army Omar N. Bradley* (New York: Simon and Schuster, 1983), 159.

34 Eisenhower, *Crusade in Europe*, 453.

35 Hastings, *Overlord*, 46.

36 Bernard L. Montgomery, *The Memoirs of Field-Marshal the Viscount Montgomery of Alamein, K.G.* (London: Collins, 1958), 217.

37 Bradley, *Soldier's Story*, 227.

38 Leo Meyer, 'The Decision to Invade North Africa (Torch),' and Richard M. Leighton, 'Overlord versus the Mediterranean at the Cairo-Tehran Conference,' in *Command Decisions*, ed. Kent Robert Greenfield (Washington, D.C.: U.S. Army Center of Military History, 1987), 173–98, 258–86.

39 Arthur Bryant, *The Turn of the Tide, 1939–1943* (New York: Doubleday, 1957), 491–93. See also Thomas E. Griess, ed., *The Second World War: Europe and the Mediterranean* (Wayne, N.J.: Avery, 1984), 190.

40 Stephen E. Ambrose, *D-Day, June 6, 1944: The Climactic Battle of World War II* (New York: Simon and Schuster, 1994), 49.

41 Moran, *Anatomy of Courage*, 3.

42 Balkoski, *Beyond the Beachhead*, 87.

43 Theo G. Aufort, 16th Infantry, Personal Narrative, FDM.

44 16th Infantry Regiment, Citation for War Department Distinguished Unit Citation, FDM.

Select Bibliography

PRIMARY SOURCES

COLLEGE OF WILLIAM AND MARY, MANUSCRIPT AND RARE BOOKS DEPARTMENT, SWEM LIBRARY, WILLIAMSBURG, VA.

Admiral John Lesslie Hall, 'Comments on Dr. Samuel Morison's Book,' 6 February 1948, John Lesslie Hall Papers, 78 H14, Box 21, Folder 2.

Admiral John Lesslie Hall, Operation Plan Neptune, Western Naval Task Force, Assault Force 'O' (Task Force One Two Four), USS *Ancon,* Flagship, Annex E, Gunfire Support Plan, 20 May 1944, John Lesslie Hall Papers, 78 H14, Box 13, Folder 4.

Admiral H. Kent Hewitt, Letter to Admiral John Lesslie Hall, 13 March 1947, John Lesslie Hall Papers, 78 H14, Box 21, Folder 2.

Mays Lewis, Army and Navy Staff College, Letter to Admiral John Lesslie Hall, 3 July 1945, John Lesslie Hall Papers, 78 H14, Box 21, Folder 1.

EISENHOWER LIBRARY, ABILENE, KANS.

R.W. Barker, General U.S. Army, Letter to General Handy, War Department, 17 November 1943, R.W. Barker Papers, Box 1, File October 43–44.

R.W. Barker, Major General, Chief of Staff to the Supreme Allied Commander (Designate), Letter to Lieutenant General Morgan, 3 November 1943, R.W. Barker Papers, Box 1, File October 43–44.

Chief of Staff to the Supreme Allied Commander (43), 23rd Meeting, Minutes of Chief of Staff to the Supreme Allied Commander Staff Conference, 28 August 1943, Report on Quadrant, 30 August 1943, R.W. Barker Papers, Box 1, File COSSAC Minutes.

Dwight D. Eisenhower, Letter to Leonard T. Gerow, 18 November 1940, Eisenhower Pre-Presidential Papers, Box 13, File 6.

H. Kent Hewitt, Vice Admiral, Naval Commander, Western Naval Task Force, Action Report Western Naval Task Force, Sicilian Campaign, Operation 'Husky,' July–August 1943, Walter Beddell Smith Papers, Boxes 40, 41, Files Op Husky.

Bernard Montgomery, British Army, Brief Summary of Operation Overlord, 7 April 1944, Eisenhower Pre-Presidential Papers, Box 82, Folder Montgomery, Bernard (S).

F.E. Morgan, Lieutenant General, British Army, Opening Address by Lieutenant General F.E. Morgan, Chief of Staff to the Supreme Commander (Designate), 17 April 1943, R. W. Barker Papers, Box 1, File COSSAC Minutes.

Albert H. Smith, 'Lecture Transcript: Operation Overlord and D-Day, 6 June 1944,' presented to Armor School, Fort Knox, Ky., 16 August 1984.

Supreme Headquarters Allied Expeditionary Force (44), 3rd Meeting, Minutes of Meeting Convened by Supreme Commander Allied Expeditionary Force, 21 January 1944, R. W. Barker Papers, Box 1, File SHAEF.

U.S. Army, Headquarters 29th Infantry Division, Lieutenant Shea, Letter to Colonel Mason, 16 June 1944, Norman Cota Papers, Box 1, File 201.

U.S. Army, Historical Service, Personal Recollections of General Norman Cota, Norman Cota Papers, Box 2, File Lieutenant Jack Shea.

FIRST DIVISION MUSEUM, WHEATON, ILL.

Kenneth P. Lord, Assistant G-3 (Operations), 1st Infantry Division, Personal Narrative.

Stanhope Brasfield Mason, Major General U.S. Army, retired, 'Reminiscences and Anecdotes of World War II,' Birmingham, Ala., 1988.

Supreme Headquarters Allied Expeditionary Force, *History of COSSAC,* Historical Sub-Section, Office of Secretary, General Staff, John Votaw's Files, May 1944.

U.S. Army, 1st Infantry Division, G-3 Report of Operations, 31 May–30 June 1944.

U.S. Army, 1st Infantry Division, 16th Infantry Regiment, Citation for War Department Distinguished Unit Citation.

U.S. Army, Headquarters 7th Field Artillery Battalion, Comments and Criticisms of Operation 'Neptune,' Lieutenant Colonel George W. Gibbs, Commanding, 1 July 1944.

U.S. Army, 16th Infantry Combat Team, S-3 Combat Report, 6 June 1944.

U.S. Army, Supreme Headquarters Allied Expeditionary Force Files, Notes on the Planning Period of Operation 'Overlord,' British 21st Army Group, May 1945, RG 407, Secretary, General Staff Files.

MARINE CORPS UNIVERSITY ARCHIVES, QUANTICO, VA.

Headquarters U.S. Marine Corps, Division of Operations and Training, 'Memorandum for the Major General Commandant,' 23 July 1921.

NATIONAL ARCHIVES, ARCHIVE II, COLLEGE PARK, MD.

British Army, 21st Army Group, Neptune, Possible Build-up of Enemy Reinforcements in the Neptune Area, Appendix A, RG 407, Box 24373, Files 630–33.

Combined Operations Headquarters, Combined Report on the Dieppe Raid, 1942, RG 38, Box 1708.

Sir Andrew Cunningham, Royal Navy, 'Avalanche,' Report on Operation, 5 June 1945, RG 38, Box 69.

H. Kent Hewitt, Commander Amphibious Force, Atlantic Fleet, Report: Torch Operation, Comments and Recommendations, 22 December 1942, RG 38, Box 530.

H. Kent Hewitt, Narrative by Admiral H. Kent Hewitt, USN Mediterranean Area Campaign: North Africa Landing to Southern France, 29 June 1945, RG 28, Box 1728.

H. Kent Hewitt, Vice Admiral, U.S. Navy, Report of Naval Commander Western Naval Task Force, Invasion of Southern France, 15 November 1944, RG 38, Box 50.

H.B. Knowles, Captain, Commander Task Force 53.1, Transportation Group, Action Report on Tarawa Operation, 1 December 1943, RG 38, Box 545.

George S. Patton, Major General, U.S. Army Commanding, Subject: Lessons from Operation Torch, 30 December 1942, RG 38, Box 1696.

U.S. Army, ETOUSA, *Army Talk,* 13 May 1944, General Bernard L. Montgomery, RG 407, Box 24378, File 669.

U.S. Army, Fifth Army Invasion Training Center, Training Doctrine, 20 May 1943, General John W. O'Daniel, RG 407, Boxes 5661, 5662, File 301-0.3.

U.S. Army, V Corps, Conference Overlord, 7 February 1944, RG 407, Box 24309, File 213.

U.S. Army, V Corps, Memorandum for AC of S, G-3, First U.S. Army, Subject: Outline of Operations Plan, V Corps, 21 March 1944, RG 407, Box 24373, Files 630–33.

U.S. Army, V Corps, Memorandum to Chiefs of Section, 26 September 1943, RG 407, Box 24309, Files 208–16.

U.S. Army, V Corps, Memorandum to Commanding General, First U.S. Army, Subject: Breaching Beach Obstacles, 29 April 1944, Major General L.T. Gerow, RG 407, Box 24308, File 201.

U.S. Army, V Corps, Memorandum to General, 1st Infantry Division, Subject: Decision Made at 0900 Hours, 22 March 1944, RG 407, Box 24375, File 640.

U.S. Army, V Corps, Notes on V Corps Plan 'Neptune,' RG 407, Box 24378, File 670.

U.S. Army, V Corps, Office of the Commanding General, Memorandum for Record, 9 February 1944, RG 407, Box 24309, File 216.

U.S. Army, V Corps, Office of the Commanding General, Subject: Landing Force 'B,' Operation 'Neptune,' 14 April 1944, RG 407, Box 24378, File 554.

U.S. Army, V Corps, Office of the Corps Commander, Directive (Overlord), 28 January 1944, RG 407, Box 24309, File 216.

U.S. Army, V Corps, Office of the Planning Group, Agenda for Headquarters V Corps, Conference on Planning for Operation 'Overlord,' 4 February 1944, RG 407, Box 24308, File 200.

U.S. Army, V Corps, 'Officers and Men of the V Corps,' 15 May 1944, General Gerow, RG 407, Box 24373, Files 630–33.

U.S. Army, V Corps, Operation Order no. 3-44, Change no. 1, 19 May 1944, RG 407, Box 3411, Files 205-0.6–0.13.

U.S. Army, V Corps, Operation Plan Neptune, Annex 1, G-2 Estimate of Enemy Situation, 1 April, 15 May 1944, RG 407, Box 3412, Files 205-0.6–0.13.

U.S. Army, V Corps, Outline of V Corps Plan, 17 May 1944, RG 407, Box 24378, File 670.

U.S. Army, V Corps, Planning Guide, Operation 'Overlord,' 28 February 1944, RG 407, Box 24373, Files 630–33.

U.S. Army, V Corps, Preliminary 'Overlord' Plan, 10 February 1944, RG 407, Box 24309, Files 208–16.

U.S. Army, V Corps, Report after Action against Enemy, November 1944, RG 407, Box 3409, File 205-0.3.

U.S. Army, V Corps, Special Instructions no. 1 to Director, Headquarters, V Corps, Planning Group, 24 September 1943, RG 407, Box 24309, Files 208–16.

U.S. Army, 1st Infantry Division, Field Order no. 35, Annex 16, Engineer Plan, 22 May 1944, RG 407, Box 24373, Files 630–33.

U.S. Army, 1st Infantry Division, Subject: Operation 'Neptune,' 28 March 1944, RG 407, Box 24373, Files 634–36; V Corps, Letter to Commanding General, First U.S. Army, 29 April 1944, RG 407, Box 24308, File 201.

U.S. Army, 1st Infantry Division, Tactical Study of Terrain, 25 March 1944, RG 407, Box 24374, Files 634–36.

U.S. Army, First U.S. Army, APO 230, General Kean, Memorandum to General Bradley, Subject: Underwater Obstacles, 20 April 1944, RG 407, Box 24373, Files 630–33.

U.S. Army, First U.S. Army, Engineer Headquarters, Beach Study Overlord, 17 February 1944, RG 407, Box 24308.

U.S. Army, First U.S. Army, Intelligence Note no. 16, 24 April 1944, RG 407, Box 24373, Files 630–33.

U.S. Army, First U.S. Army, Memorandum no. 3, Artillery Information Service, April 1944, RG 407, File 101-160.0ART.

U.S. Army, First U.S. Army, Office of AC of S, G-2, Intelligence Note no. 18, Underwater Obstacles, 24 April 1944, RG 407, Box 24373, Files 630–33.

U.S. Army, First U.S. Army, Operations Memorandum no. 5, 13 February 1944, RG 407, Box 24377, File 659.

U.S. Army, First U.S. Army, Operations Memorandum no. 12, Employment of LCT(SP) and LCT(A) in Support of a Beach Assault, 26 March 1944, Brigadier General W.B. Kean, Chief of Staff, RG 407, File 101-32.3.

U.S. Army, First U.S. Army, Overlord Conference, 21 December 1943, RG 407, Box 24309, File 209.

U.S. Army, First U.S. Army, Planning Directive for Overlord, 31 January 1944, RG 407, Box 24308, File 200.

U.S. Army, 531st Engineer Shore Regiment, Interim Report: Removal of Beach and Underwater Obstacles, 21 May 1943, Colonel R. C. Brown, RG 407, File 101-20.0.

U.S. Army, Headquarters Allied Forces APO 512, G-3 Training Section, 'Training Notes from the Sicilian Campaign,' 25 October 1943, RG 407, Box 5665, File 301-0.4.

U.S. Army, Headquarters Allied Force APO 512, Memorandum, Subject: Corrective Action Based on Recent Amphibious Operations in North Africa, 7 May 1943, James F. Barber, Assistant Adjutant General, RG 407, Files 301-0.3, 301-0.4.

U.S. Army, Headquarters 116th Combat Team, Force 'O,' Field Order, 11 May 1944, Annex 110.10, Tank Employment Plan, RG 407, Box 24373, Files 630–33.

U.S. Army, Headquarters Provisional Engineer Special Brigade Group, Message to Chief of Staff, First U.S. Army, 30 March 1944, RG 407, Box 24373, Files 630–33.

U.S. Army, Headquarters 16th Combat Team, Field Order no. 5, 16 May 1944, RG 407, Box 24374, Files 634–36.

U.S. Army, Information Section Intelligence Division, OCE Headquarters, ETOUSA, Tidal Illumination Diagrams, 20 June 1944, RG 407, Box 2002, File 101-20.0.

U.S. Army, Colonel S.S. MacLaughlin, Notes on the Assignment of Tank Units to V Corps, 4 February 1944, RG 407, Box 24309, File 210.

U.S. Army, Provisional Engineer Group, V Corps, Summary of Activities of the Provisional Engineer Group, 8 July 1944, RG 407, Box 24373, File 205-43.2.

U.S. Army, 743rd Tank Battalion, Major William D. Dungan, School Commandant, Memorandum for Commander, Eleventh Amphibious Force, 30 April 1944, RG 407, Box 24377, File 659.

U.S. Navy, Commander Assault Force 'O,' Action Report, 27 July 1944, Box 549, File 11th PHIBFOR, 27 July–1 October 1944.

U.S. Navy, DD LCT Unit Commander, Lieutenant Dean L. Rockwell, Memorandum for Commander, Eleventh Amphibious Force, 30 April 1944, RG 407, Box 24377, File 659.

U.S. Navy, Eleventh Amphibious Force, Message from Commander Task Force 122, Action COM 11th PHIB, 25 March 1944, RG 407, Box 24373, Files 630–33.

U.S. Navy, U.S. Fleet, Headquarters of Commander in Chief, Navy Department, Memorandum, Subject: Distribution of Naval Gunfire Officer, Headquarters V

Amphibious Corps, Serial 00671 letter of 7 March 1944, Subject: Naval Gunfire Report on the Marshalls Operation, 22 March 1944, RG 407, Files 6-12.060/45, 6-12.0703/44.

NAVAL HISTORICAL CENTER, WASHINGTON, D.C.

John Lesslie Hall Jr., 'The Reminiscences of John Lesslie Hall, Jr.,' Naval History Project, Oral History Research Office, Columbia University, 1964.

H. Kent Hewitt, 'The Reminiscences of Admiral H. Kent Hewitt,' Naval History Project, Oral History Research Office, Columbia University, 1962.

H. Kent Hewitt, 'U.S. Naval Operations in the Northwestern African–Mediterranean Theater,' March–July 1943, H. Kent Hewitt Papers, Box 2.

H. Kent Hewitt, Vice Admiral U.S. Navy, Commander Western Naval Task Force, Action Report Italian Campaign, Salerno Landings, September–October 1943, H. Kent Hewitt Papers, Box 2.

Admiral Lord Louis Mountbatten, Interview, H. Kent Hewitt Papers, Box 2.

Admiral H. R. Stark, Letter to Admiral H. Kent Hewitt, 2 September 1943, H. Kent Hewitt Papers, Box 1, Folder 2.

U.S. Navy, Commander Assault Force 'O' (Commander Eleventh Amphibious Force), Action Report Assault on Colleville–Vierville Sector Coast of Normandy, 27 July 1944, Admiral Hall, Box 549, File 11th PHIBFOR.

U.S. Navy, Commander Assault Force 'O,' Western Naval Task Force, Action Report, 27 July 1944, Serial 00879, Office of Naval Records.

U.S. Navy, Commander Task Force 122, Rough Draft Action Report, 25 July 1944, Planning, Box 317, File Task Force 122–122.4.4.

U.S. Navy, Western Task Force, Commander Task Force 122, Action Report on Amphibious Operation in Baie de la Seine, Normandy Invasion, 25 July 1944, Rear Admiral A. G. Kirk, Box 317, File Task Force 122-122.4.4.

NAVAL WAR COLLEGE, NEWPORT, R.I.

H. Kent Hewitt, 'The Navy in the European Theater of Operation in World War II,' 4–7 January 1947, H. Kent Hewitt Papers.

H. Kent Hewitt, 'The Strategic Employment of the Allied Forces in the Mediterranean in World War II,' 1952, H. Kent Hewitt Papers.

UNIVERSITY OF CALIFORNIA, DOE LIBRARY, BERKELEY, CALIF.

Supreme Headquarters Allied Expeditionary Force, Report by the Supreme Commander to the Combined Chiefs of Staff on the Operations in Europe of the Allied Expeditionary Forces, 6 June 1944–8 May 1945, General Dwight D. Eisenhower, Government Documents.

U.S. Army, V Corps, History of V Corps, 6 June 1944, Government Documents.

U.S. ARMY CENTER OF MILITARY HISTORY, WASHINGTON, D.C.

Amphibious Doctrine and Training, Study no. 6, Historical Section, Army Ground Forces.

Department of Defense, Office of Public Information Press Branch, Summary of the Career of General Leonard T. Gerow.

Department of Defense, Office of Public Information Press Branch, Summary of the Career of Lieutenant General Clarence Ralph Huebner.

Department of the Army, Office, Chief of Information, General Omar Nelson Bradley, Biography.

Colonel Paul W. Thompson, 'Talk at S.A.M.E.,' Washington, D.C., 18 May 1988, transcript.

U.S. ARMY MILITARY HISTORY INSTITUTE, CARLISLE BARRACKS, PA.

Marshall O. Becker, Captain U.S. Army, *The Amphibious Training Center,* Study no. 22, Historical Section, Army Ground Forces, 1946, D769.1 A423 no. 22, c. 4.

British Army, 21st Army Group, Note on Planning Procedures for 'Neptune,' 6 December 1943, Arthur S. Nevin Papers.

Derrill M. Daniel, Lieutenant Colonel U.S. Army, Infantry, Commander 2nd Battalion, 26th Infantry, 1st Infantry Division, 'Landings at Oran, Gela, and Omaha Beach: An Infantry Battalion Commander's Observations,' 9 November 1950, Accession no. 16759.2.

General William M. Hoge, Engineer Memoirs, Office of History, U.S. Army Corps of Engineers, 1993; interview, 1974.

Ronald Joe Rogers, Major U.S. Army, 'A Study of Leadership in the First Infantry Division during World War II: Terry De La Mesa Allen and Clarence Ralph Huebner,' master of military art and science thesis abstract, U.S. Army Command and General Staff College, Fort Leavenworth, Kans., 1965.

U.S. Army, Assault Training Center, 'Conference on Landing Assaults, 24 May– 23 June 1943,' D756.3.C66 1943, v. 2, c. 3.

U.S. MILITARY ACADEMY, MAIN LIBRARY, WEST POINT, N.Y.

British Army, Neptune, Initial Joint Plan, Allied Naval Commander Expeditionary Force, Commander in Chief 21st Army Group, Air Commander in Chief Allied Expeditionary Air Force, 1 February 1944, Omar Bradley Papers.

British Army, Office of the War Cabinet, Chiefs of Staff Committee, Operation 'Overlord' Report and Appreciation, COS (43) 416 (0), 30 July 1943, Omar Bradley Papers.

British Army, 21st Army Group, 'Some Notes on the Conduct of War and the Infantry Division in Battle,' Belgium: 21st Army Group, November 1944, Bernard L. Montgomery, Omar Bradley Papers.

British Army, 21st Army Group, 'Some Notes on the Use of Air Power in Support of Land Operations,' Holland: 21st Army Group, December 1944, Bernard L. Montgomery, Omar Bradley Papers.

U.S. Army, Allied Naval Commander Expeditionary Force, Commander in Chief 21st Army Group, and Air Commander in Chief Allied Expeditionary Air Force, 'Neptune' Initial Joint Plan, Omar Bradley Papers.

U.S. Army, First U.S. Army, Report of Operations, 20 October 1943–1 August 1944, Book 1, 'Enemy Dispositions and Operations,' General Omar Bradley, Omar Bradley Papers.

VIRGINIA MILITARY INSTITUTE, PRESTON LIBRARY, LEXINGTON, VA.

Dwight D. Eisenhower, Letters to Leonard T. Gerow, 16 July 1942, 24 February 1943, Leonard T. Gerow Papers.

Leonard T. Gerow, Letters to Dwight D. Eisenhower, 28 July 1941, 19 April 1942, Leonard T. Gerow Papers.

SECONDARY SOURCES

Ambrose, Stephen E. *Eisenhower: Soldier, General of the Army, President-Elect, 1890–1952.* New York: Simon and Schuster, 1983.

Ansel, Walter C. 'Naval Gunfire in Support of Landings: Lessons from Gallipoli.' *U.S. Naval Institute Proceedings* 58, no. 353 (July 1932): 1001–10.

Baldwin, Hanson. 'Amphibious Aspects of the Normandy Invasion.' *Marine Corps Gazette,* December 1944, 36.

—. *Battles Lost and Won: Great Campaigns of World War II.* New York: Harper and Row, 1966.

Balkoski, Joseph. *Beyond the Beachhead: The 29th Infantry Division in Normandy.* Harrisburg, Pa.: Stackpole Books, 1989.

Ballandorf, Dirk A., and Merrill L. Bartlett. *Pete Ellis: An Amphibious Warfare Prophet, 1880–1923.* Annapolis, Md.: Naval Institute Press, 1997.

Baumgartner, John W., *et al. The 16th Infantry, 1798–1946.* Bamburg, Germany, 1946.

Beaumont, Roger A. *Joint Military Operations: A Short History.* Westport, Conn.: Greenwood Press, 1993.

Binkoski, Joseph, and Arthur Plaut. *The 115th Infantry Regiment in World War II.* Washington, D.C.: Infantry Journal Press, 1948.

Blumenson, Martin. *Patton: The Man behind the Legend, 1885–1945.* New York: William Morrow, 1985.

—. *The Patton Papers, 1940–1945.* Boston: Houghton Mifflin, 1974.

—. *Salerno to Cassino: The Mediterranean Theater of Operation.* U.S. Army in World War II. Washington, D.C.: U.S. Army Center of Military History, 1969.

Blumenson, Martin, and James L. Stokesbury. *Masters of the Art of Command.* Boston: Houghton Mifflin, 1975.

Boussel, Patrice. *D-Day Beaches Revisited.* New York: Doubleday, 1966.

Bradley, Omar. *A Soldier's Story.* New York: Henry Holt, 1951.

Bradley, Omar, and Clay Blair. *A General's Life: An Autobiography by General of the Army Omar N. Bradley.* New York: Simon and Schuster, 1983.

Bryant, Arthur. *The Turn of the Tide, 1939–1943.* New York: Doubleday, 1957.

Butcher, Harry C. *My Three Years with Eisenhower.* New York: Simon and Schuster, 1946.

Callwell, C.E. *Military Operations and Maritime Preponderance: Their Relations and Interdependence.* Edinburgh: William Blackwood and Sons, 1905.

Carell, Paul. *Invasion: They're Coming.* New York: E.P. Dutton, 1963.

Chandler, Alfred D., Jr., ed. *The Papers of Dwight David Eisenhower: The War Years.* 5 vols. Baltimore: Johns Hopkins University Press, 1970.

Chandler, David G., and James Lawton Collins, Jr., eds. *The D-Day Encyclopedia.* New York: Simon and Schuster, 1994.

Churchill, Winston S. *The Second World War.* Vol. 2, *Their Finest Hour.* Boston: Houghton Mifflin, 1949. Vol. 3, *The Grand Alliance.* Boston: Houghton Mifflin, 1950. Vol. 5, *Closing the Ring.* Boston: Houghton Mifflin, 1951.

Clagett, John H. 'Admiral H. Kent Hewitt, U.S. Navy: Part I, Preparing for High Command.' *Naval War College Review* 28, no. 1 (1975): 72–86.

—. 'Admiral H. Kent Hewitt, U.S. Navy: Part II, High Command.' *Naval War College Review* 28, no. 2 (1975): 64.

—. 'Skipper of the *Eagle:* Rehearsal for Greatness,' *U.S. Naval Institute Proceedings* 102, no. 4 (April 1976): 58–65.

Clausewitz, Carl von. *On War.* Ed. and trans. Michael Howard and Peter Paret. Princeton, N.J.: Princeton University Press, 1984.

Clifford, Kenneth J. *Amphibious Warfare Development in Britain and America from 1920–1940.* New York: Edgewood, 1983.

—. *Progress and Purpose: A Developmental History of the U.S. Marine Corps, 1900– 1970.* Washington, D.C.: U.S. Marine Corps, 1973.

Coles, David J. '"Hell-by-the-Sea": Florida's Camp Gordon Johnston in World War II.' *Florida Historical Quarterly* 73, no. 1 (July 1994): 1–23.

Connor, A.O. 'On the Defense: Notes from the Anzio Beachhead.' *Infantry Journal,* July 1949, 35–39.

Corlett, Charles H. *Cowboy Pete: The Autobiography of Major General Charles H. Corlett.* Santa Fe, N.M.: Sleeping Fox, 1974.

Craven, Wesley Frank, and James Lea Cate, eds. *The Army Air Forces in World War II.* 6 vols. 1948. Reprint, Washington, D.C.: Office of Air Force History, 1983.

Cray, Ed. *General of the Army, George C. Marshall: Soldier and Statesman.* New York: W.W. Norton, 1990.

D'Este, Carlo. *Decision in Normandy.* London: Collins, 1983.

—. *Patton: A Genius for War.* New York: Harper, 1995.

DeWeerd, H.A., ed. *Selected Speeches and Statements of General of the Army George C. Marshall.* Washington, D.C.: Infantry Journal Press, 1945.

Drez, Ronald J., ed. *Voices of D-Day.* Baton Rouge: Louisiana State University Press, 1994.

Dupuy, Ernest, and Trevor N. Dupuy. *The Encyclopedia of Military History: From 3500 B.C. to the Present.* 2nd ed. New York: Harper and Row, 1986.

Edwards, Kenneth. *Operation Neptune.* London: Collins, 1946.

Eisenhower, Dwight D. *Crusade in Europe.* New York: Doubleday, 1948.

Ellis, L.F., *et al. Victory in the West.* Vol. 1, *The Battle of Normandy.* London: HMSO, 1962.

Ewing, Joseph H. *29th Let's Go!: A History of the 29th Division in World War II.* Washington, D.C.: Infantry Journal Press, 1948.

Fergusson, Bernard. *The Watery Maze: The Story of Combined Operations.* New York: Holt, Rinehart and Winston, 1961.

Fowle, Barry W., ed. *Builders and Fighters: U.S. Army Engineers in World War II.* Fort Belvoir, Va.: Office of History, U.S. Army Corps of Engineers, 1992.

Fraser, David. *Knight's Cross: A Life of Field Marshal Erwin Rommel.* New York: Harper Collins, 1993.

Fuller, J.F.C. 'Armor and Counter Armor.' *Infantry Journal,* April 1944, 47.

Futrell, Robert Frank. *Ideas, Concepts, Doctrine: A History of Basic Thinking in the United States Air Force, 1907–1964.* Maxwell Air Force Base, Ala.: Air University, 1974.

Gask, Roland C. 'Prelude to Invasion: Real Bullets Enforce Lesson at Army Amphibious Training Center.' *Newsweek,* 22 March 1943, 22–23.

Gavin, James M. *On to Berlin.* New York: Viking Press, 1978.

Gelb, Norman. *Ike and Monty: Generals at War.* New York: William Morrow, 1994.

Godson, Susan H. *Viking of Assault: Admiral John Lesslie Hall, Jr., and Amphibious Warfare.* Washington, D.C.: University Press of America, 1982.

Greenfield, Kent Robert, ed. *Command Decisions.* Washington, D.C.: U.S. Army Center of Military History, 1987.

Greenfield, Kent Robert, Robert R. Palmer, and Bell I. Wiley. *The Army Ground Forces: The Organization of Ground Combat Troops.* U.S. Army in World War II. Washington, D.C.: Government Printing Office, 1983.

Guderian, Heinz. *Panzer Leader.* New York: E. P. Dutton, n.d.

Hamilton, Nigel. *Master of the Battlefield: Monty's War Years, 1942–1944.* New York: McGraw-Hill, 1983.

—. *Monty: The Battles of Field Marshal Bernard Montgomery.* New York: Random House, 1981.

—. *Monty: The Making of a General, 1887–1942.* New York: McGraw-Hill, 1981.

Harrison, Gordon. *Cross-Channel Attack.* U.S. Army in World War II. Washington, D.C.: Government Printing Office, 1951.

Harvey, George M. 'Iwo Jima and Amphibious Operations in the Central Pacific.' *Military Review,* September 1945, 24.

Hastings, Max. *Overlord: D-Day and the Battle for Normandy.* New York: Simon and Schuster, 1984.

Heavey, William F. *Down Ramp: The Story of the Army Amphibian Engineers.* Washington, D.C.: Infantry Journal Press, 1947.

Heinl, Robert D., Jr. 'Naval Gunfire Support.' *Military Review,* December 1946, 19–21.

—. 'Naval Gunfire Support in Landings.' *Marine Corps Gazette,* September 1945, 40.

Hessler, William H. 'The Battleship Paid Dividends.' *U.S. Naval Institute Proceedings* 72, no. 9 (September 1946): 1146.

Hewitt, H. Kent. 'Executing Operation Anvil-Dragoon.' *U.S. Naval Institute Proceedings* 78 (August 1954): 899.

Horne, Alistair, with David Montgomery. *Monty: The Lonely Leader, 1944–1945.* New York: Harper Collins, 1994.

Hough, Frank O., Verle E. Ludwig, and Henry I. Shaw. *History of the U.S. Marine Corps Operations in World War II: Pearl Harbor to Guadalcanal.* Vol. 1, FMFRP 12-34-I. Washington, D.C.: Historical Branch, G-3 Division, Headquarters, U.S. Marine Corps, 1989.

Howe, George F. *The Mediterranean Theater of Operations – Northwest Africa: Seizing the Initiative in the West.* U.S. Army in World War II. Washington, D.C.: Government Printing Office, 1993.

Huntington, Samuel. *The Soldier and the State: The Theory and Politics of Civil-Military Relations.* Cambridge, Mass.: Belknap Press, 1957.

Huston, James A. 'Tactical Use of Air Power in World War II: The Army Experience.' *Military Review,* July 1952, 41.

Isley, Jeter A., and Philip A. Crowl. *The U.S. Marines and Amphibious War.* Princeton, N.J.: Princeton University Press, 1951.

Jacobs, Will A. 'The Battle of France.' In *Case Studies in the Development of Close Air Support,* ed. Benjamin Franklin Cooling, 237–93. Washington, D.C.: Office of Air Force History, 1990.

Janowitz, Morris. *The Professional Soldier.* New York: Macmillan, 1960.

Keegan, John. *Six Armies in Normandy: From D-Day to the Liberation of Paris.* New York: Penguin, 1983.

Kelly, John. 'Shoot, Soldier, Shoot.' *Infantry Journal,* January 1946, 47.

Keyes, Roger. *Amphibious Warfare and Combined Operations.* New York: Macmillan, 1943.

Knickerbocker, H.R., *et al. Danger Forward: The Story of the First Division in World War II.* Washington, D.C.: Society of the First Division, 1947.

Kohn, Richard H., and Joseph P. Harahan, eds. *Air Superiority in World War II and Korea: An Interview with Gen. James Ferguson, Gen. Robert M. Lee, Gen. William Momyer, and Lt. Gen. Elwood R. Quesada.* Washington, D.C.: Office of Air Force History, U.S. Air Force, 1983.

—. *Condensed Analysis of the Ninth Air Force in the European Theater of Operations.* Washington, D.C.: Office of Air Force History, U.S. Air Force, 1984.

Lamb, Richard. *Montgomery in Europe, 1943–45: Success or Failure.* New York: Franklin Watts, 1984.

Lewin, Ronald. *Montgomery as Military Commander.* New York: Stein and day, 1971.

Lewis, Adrian R. 'The Failure of Allied Planning and Doctrine for Operation Overlord: The Case of Minefield and Obstacle Clearance.' *Journal of Military History* 62, no. 4 (October 1998): 787–807.

—. 'The Navy Falls Short at Normandy.' *Naval History* 12, no. 6 (December 1998): 34–39.

Liddell-Hart, Basil H. *When Britain Goes to War: Adaptability and Mobility.* London: Faber and Faber, 1932.

MacDonald, Charles B. *The Mighty Endeavor.* New York: Oxford University Press, 1969.

Mahan, Alfred Thayer. *The Influence of Sea Power upon History.* New York: Hill and Wang, 1957.

Mark, Eduard. *Aerial Interdiction in Three Wars.* Washington, D.C.: Center of Air Force

History, 1994.

Marshall, S.L.A. 'Commentary.' In *The Collected Writings of General Omar N. Bradley,* 6:53. Chicago: University of Chicago Library, n.d.

—. *Men against Fire: The Problem of Battle Command in Future War.* Gloucester, Mass.: Peter Smith, 1978.

—. *The Soldier's Load and the Mobility of a Nation.* Quantico, Va.: Marine Corps Association, 1980.

Matloff, Maurice. 'The American Approach to War, 1919–1945.' In *The Theory and Practice of War,* ed. Michael Howard, 213–43. New York: Frederich A. Praeger, 1965.

Mead, Margaret. *And Keep Your Powder Dry.* New York: William Morrow, 1942.

'Military Digest: The Army Goes to Sea.' *Marine Corps Gazette* 27, no. 4 (August 1943): 44–48.

Miller, Edward S. *War Plan ORANGE: The U.S. Strategy to Defeat Japan, 1897–1945.* Annapolis, Md.: Naval Institute Press, 1991.

Miller, Merle. *Ike the Soldier: As They Knew Him.* New York: Perigee, 1987.

Millett, Allan. *Semper Fidelis: The History of the United States Marine Corps.* Rev. ed. New York: Free Press, 1991.

Millett, Allan, and Williamson Murray, eds. *Military Effectiveness.* 3 vols. Boston: Allen and Unwin, 1988.

Montgomery, Bernard L. *A History of Warfare.* New York: Collins, 1968.

—. *The Memoirs of Field-Marshal the Viscount Montgomery of Alamein, K.G.* London: Collins, 1958.

—. *Normandy to the Baltic.* Boston: Houghton Mifflin, 1948.

—. '21st (British) Army Group in the Campaign in Northwest Europe, 1944–45.' *Journal Royal United Service Institute,* November 1945.

Moorehead, Alan. *Montgomery: A Biography.* New York: Coward-McGann, 1946.

Moran, Lord. *The Anatomy of Courage: The Classic Study of the Soldier's Struggle against Fear.* New York: Avery, 1987.

Morehouse, Clifford P. 'New Landing Craft: Vast Building Program Has Made New Invasions Possible.' *Marine Corps Gazette,* December 1943, 7–12.

Morgan, Frederick Edgworth. *Overture to Overlord.* New York: Doubleday, 1959.

Morison, Samuel Eliot. *The Invasion of France and Germany, 1944–1945.* Boston: Little, Brown, 1957.

—. *Operations in North African Waters, October 1942–June 1943.* Boston: Little, Brown, 1954.

—. *Sicily-Salerno-Anzio: January 1943–June 1944.* Boston: Little, Brown, 1954.

Nichols, David. *Ernie's War: The Best of Ernie Pyle's World War II Dispatches.* New York: Simon and Schuster, 1986.

Overy, Richard. *Why the Allies Won.* New York: W.W. Norton, 1995.

Parks, W. Hays. '"Precision" and "Area" Bombing: Who Did Which, and When.' In *Airpower: Theory and Practice,* ed. John Gooch, 145–74. London: Frank Cass, 1995.

Pogue, Forrest C. 'D-Day—1944.' In *D-Day: The Normandy Invasion in Retrospect,* ed. Eisenhower Foundation, 3–41. Lawrence: University Press of Kansas, 1971.

—. *The Supreme Command.* U.S. Army in World War II. Washington, D.C.: Government Printing Office, 1954.

Potter, E.B. *The United States and World Sea Power.* Englewood Cliffs, N.J.: Prentice Hall, 1955.

Richmond, Herbert. *Amphibious Warfare in British History.* Historical Association Pamphlet no. 119. Cambridge, Eng., 1941.

Robertson, Terence. *Dieppe: The Shame and the Glory.* Boston: Little, Brown, 1962.

Rommel, Erwin. *The Rommel Papers.* Ed. Basil H. Liddell-Hart. New York: Da Capo, 1985.

Rostow, Walt W. *Pre-Invasion Bombing Strategy: General Eisenhower's Decision of March 25, 1944.* Austin: University of Texas Press, 1981.

Schaffer, Ronald. *Wings of Judgment: American Bombing in World War II.* New York: Oxford University Press, 1985.

Schell, Adolf von. *Battle Leadership.* 1933. Reprint, Quantico, Va.: Marine Corps Association, 1982.

Sewell, H. S. 'Montgomery's Tactics.' *Military Review,* August 1945, 128.

Shanahan, William. 'H-Hour to Be Announced.' *Military Review,* October 1951, 4, 5.

Shulimson, Jack. *The Marine Corps Search for a Mission, 1880–1898.* Lawrence: University Press of Kansas, 1993.

Shy, John. 'The American Military Experience: History and Learning.' In *A People Numerous and Armed,* 265–94. Ann Arbor: University of Michigan Press, 1990.

Smith, Holland M. *Coral and Brass.* New York: Charles Scribner's Sons, 1949.

Smith, Walter Bedell. *Eisenhower's Six Great Decisions: Europe, 1944–1945.* New York: Longmans, Green, 1956.

Stacey, C.P. 'The Raid on Dieppe.' *Military Review,* June 1949, 16.

Stouffer, Samuel A., *et al. The American Soldier: Combat and Its Aftermath.* Princeton, N.J.: Princeton University Press, 1949.

Tedder, Arthur W. *With Prejudice: The War Memoirs of Marshal of the Royal Air Force Lord Tedder G.C.B.* Boston: Little, Brown, 1966.

Thompson, Paul W. 'D-Day on Omaha Beach.' *Infantry Journal,* June 1945, 41–44.

Thompson, R.W. *At What Cost: The Story of the Dieppe Raid.* New York: Coward McCann, 1956.

Upham, J.S. 'DD Tanks.' *Military Review,* February 1947, 42.

U.S. Army. *Landing Operations on Hostile Shores.* FM 31-5. Washington, D.C.: War Department, 1941.

—. *Operations.* FM 100-5. Washington, D.C.: Headquarters Department of the Army, 1993.

U.S. Army Air Force. *Command and Employment of Air Power.* FM 100-20. Field Service Regulations. Washington, D.C.: War Department, 21 July 1943.

—. *The Development of the Heavy Bomber, 1918–1944.* Historical Study no. 6. Maxwell Air Force Base, Ala.: U.S. Air Force, 1951.

U.S. Army Center of Military History. *Salerno: American Operation from the Beaches to the Volturno, 9 September–6 October 1943.* Armed Forces in Action Series. Washington, D.C.: U.S. Army Center of Military History, 1990.

van Creveld, Martin. *Fighting Power: German and U.S. Army Performance, 1939–1945.* Westport, Conn.: Greenwood Press, 1982.

Weigley, Russell F. *The American Way of War.* Bloomington: Indiana University Press, 1977.

—. *Eisenhower's Lieutenants.* Bloomington: Indiana University Press, 1981.

Weinberg, Gerhard L. *A World at Arms: A Global History of World War II.* New York: Cambridge University Press, 1994.

Weller, Donald M. 'The Development of Naval Gunfire Support in World War II.' In *Assault from the Sea: Essays on the History of Amphibious Warfare,* ed. Merrill L. Bartlett, 261–81. Annapolis, Md.: Naval Institute Press, 1983.

Wilmot, Chester. *The Struggle for Europe.* New York: Harper and Brothers, 1952.

Index